# THE UNITED STATES MARINES

# THE UNITED STATES
# MARINES
## A HISTORY

*Third Edition*

Edwin Howard Simmons

NAVAL INSTITUTE PRESS
*Annapolis, Maryland*

Library of Congress Cataloging-in-Publication Data
Simmons, Edwin H., 1921–
    The United States Marines : a history / Edwin Howard Simmons.
    —3rd ed
        p.  cm.
    Includes bibliographical references and index.
    ISBN 1-55750-840-2
    1. United States. Marine Corps—History.  I. Title.
VE23.S55  1998
359.9'6'0973—dc21                                    98-29987

Printed in the United States of America on acid-free paper ♾
05 04 03 02 01 00 99 98   9 8 7 6 5 4 3 2
First printing

Unless otherwise noted, all photographs are from the U.S. Marine Corps.
Maps by Charles Waterhouse from sketches by the author.

To all the Marines I have known

# Contents

# *Foreword*

Ed Simmons is one of the foremost authorities on the United States Marine Corps. In this, his latest contribution to the documentation of our legacy, he has done the Corps and the American people whom we serve, a great service. Within the pages that follow, is an up-to-date and complete history of the evolution, performance, and dedication of the world's premier expeditionary fighting force. And, to the extent that it might ever be possible to put into words the almost mystical meaning of being a Marine, he has chronicled much of the honor, courage, and commitment, which are tattooed on the souls of all who bear the title "United States Marine."

Here, Ed Simmons heralds the Corps' preparations as we lean into the twenty-first century, when the challenges our nation will face will be very different from the ones we are accustomed to. The battlefields of tomorrow will be dominated by the world's littoral urban landscapes. Crises will be caused, not so much by nation-states, but by non-state actors. Fomenters of chaos will see the asymmetric attack as the only viable option with which to challenge America's overwhelmingly superior military might. It is into this environment that our Corps must be prepared to deploy, be first to fight, and to win.

As we ready ourselves for tomorrow's chaotic battlefields, it is important that we not forget—never forget—the lessons written across our storied past—lessons bought with the blood of fallen comrades. That is why this book is so important to Marines everywhere. It is more than a documentation. It is a collection of hard-earned lessons.

Ed Simmons is a decorated hero and a veteran of three wars. For thirty years he served proudly as a leader of Marines. But his contributions to country and Corps did not end when he reached his thirty year mark. Immediately upon retirement, he was recalled to active duty, and then to civil service, that he might continue his work as the Corps historian. And, since the ending of his formal duties in 1996, he has continued to serve as Director

Emeritus of Marine Corps History and Museums. For over half a century Ed Simmons has been an influential contributor to our beloved institution.

This volume is an important part of his continuing contribution. On its pages, the Marines, battles, and actions from two and a quarter centuries of hard fought history come to life. They are there that we might remember from whence we came . . . we will never forget.

C. C. Krulak
General, U.S. Marine Corps

# THE UNITED STATES MARINES

# 1

# *1775-1785*
## To Serve to Advantage by Sea

### Congress Passes a Resolution

In the fall of 1775 the Second Continental Congress, then sitting in Philadelphia, blew hot and cold on the debated proposition to create a Continental navy. On 30 October the Congress named a Naval Committee (also called, in those confused and imprecise times, the Marine Committee) with John Adams of Massachusetts as one of its seven members. Tradition has it that the committee met in Peg Mullan's Beef-Steak House. The tavern, at the corner of King Street and Tun Alley, once the best in the city, was now of declining reputation but it was conveniently close to the State House.

If there were to be a Continental navy, then there would have to be Continental marines. In those days no one argued against the shipboard uses of marines. They were as much a part of a man-of-war's furniture as its spars, or sails, or guns. Marines preserved internal order and discipline. Marines gave national character to the ship. Marines were uniformed, sailors were not. Marines were usually berthed between the officers and the remainder of the ship's company, a large percentage of which was often foreign born and not always reliable. In sea battles some marines took their muskets and grenades into the fighting tops while others stood by on the gun decks to see to it that the sometimes dubious ship's crew stayed at its guns.

Marines, being half soldier, half sailor, were useful in amphibious expeditions. Britain's colonial wars had given ample evidence of their usefulness, not only of English marines (who were now annoyingly present at Boston) but also of the several regiments of American marines which in earlier wars had been raised to help fight England's New World battles.

So must have gone the committee's discussion in Peg Mullan's second-floor rooms. Gen. George Washington, the Virginian who commanded the

Continental army then besieging Boston (and whose half brother Lawrence had served as a captain in Gooch's Regiment of Marines at Cartagena in 1740, and who had later named his plantation after the English admiral, Edward ("Old Grog") Vernon, had already raised a small navy of his own, complete with marines. Besides Washington's navy—armed fishing schooners manned for the most part by Marblehead fishermen—eleven of the colonies had organized navies and most of these had marines; so did many of the privateers and letters of marque. Accordingly, the committee put together a resolution and on 10 November 1775 it was passed by the Congress:

> *Resolved,* that two Battalions of Marines be raised consisting of one Colonel, two lieutenant Colonels, two Majors & Officers as usual in other regiments, that they consist of an equal number of privates with other battalions; that particular care be taken that no person be appointed to office or inlisted into said Battalions, but such as are good seamen, or so acquainted with maritime affairs as to be able to serve to advantage by sea, when required. That they be inlisted and commissioned for and during the present war between Great Britain and the colonies, unless dismissed by order of Congress. That they be distinguished by the names of the first & second battalions of American Marines, and that they be considered a part of the number, which the continental Army before Boston is ordered to consist of.

A petition had been received a week earlier from the citizens of Passamaquoddy, Nova Scotia, asking for admission into, as they called it, "the association of the North Americans." Congress appointed a committee to consider the matter. The work of the Nova Scotia Committee overlapped that of the Naval Committee. John Adams, a member of both committees, saw a chance not only to bring the blessings of liberty to the Nova Scotians, but also to secure sorely needed military and naval supplies from the depots in Halifax.

The original scheme was that the two Marine battalions would be drawn from Washington's army, then outside Boston. The marines would march from there to ports in Massachusetts or New Hampshire, embark for Nova Scotia, land, and march on Halifax. Washington was not enthusiastic about the plan, objecting particularly to stripping two battalions from his forces. He got out from under the requirement by suggesting that the marines be raised in New York or Philadelphia, where, said Washington, "there must be number of Sailors unemployed."

John Hancock, president of the Congress, on 28 November 1775 signed a captain's commission (with the same bold signature that on 4 July 1776 would appear on a better-known document—the Declaration of Independence) for thirty-one-year-old Samuel Nicholas, better known for his fishing and fox-hunting skills than for his maritime prowess. Fifers and drummers were sent out to gather up recruits for the new corps. The drums, as Benjamin Franklin noticed, were painted with a coiled rattlesnake and the motto "Don't Tread on Me."

According to legend, the recruiting rendezvous was Tun Tavern, but it is more likely that it was the Conestoga Waggon, a tavern owned by the Nicholas family on Market Street, between Fourth and Fifth Streets. Five companies, or a total of about three hundred Continental marines, were raised by early December. Pennsylvania's resourceful Committee on Public Safety provided them with muskets and necessary accouterments, but there was hardly time for uniforms.

They would not go to Nova Scotia, however, but to the Caribbean. While Nicholas was assembling his marines, the Continental navy was putting together its first squadron. During November a number of merchant ships had been purchased for conversion. At a Philadelphia wharf, under the critical eye of a demanding young Scot named John Paul Jones, the 450-ton *Black Prince* had her sides pierced for twenty guns and became the flagship *Alfred*. Profane old Commo. Esek Hopkins, forty years a sailor and a privateer in the French and Indian Wars, came hell-roaring down from Rhode Island and on 3 December took command of the squadron on the deck of the *Alfred* while Marine fifers and drummers whistled and banged away. Three weeks later Dudley Saltonstall of Connecticut arrived to be captain of the *Alfred*. John Paul Jones, reverting to first lieutenant, disliked the new flag captain on sight, calling him the "sleepy gentleman."

## THE NEW PROVIDENCE RAID

Commodore Hopkins took his makeshift squadron down the Delaware into the Bay on 7 January 1776. Here he waited for a month, hampered by ice and a fractious crew, until he had collected eight ships, all conversions, ranging from the 20-gun *Alfred* to the 6-gun *Fly*. The squadron put to sea on 17 February. Altogether there were about fifteen hundred men in the eight ships, including the three hundred Continental marines. Captain Nicholas was in the *Alfred* as senior Marine officer.

The sailing orders given Hopkins were hopelessly ambitious. He was to clear the British navy from the Chesapeake, make himself master of the North and South Carolina coasts, and then "attack, take, and destroy all the Enemy's Naval force you may find" in Rhode Island. However, in the event of bad winds, stormy weather, or any other unforeseen accident or disaster, he was permitted "to follow such Courses as your best Judgement shall suggest."

"The Wind after we came out came on to blow hard," as Hopkins reported later to the Congress, giving him an excuse to pursue his own more modest plan, a raid into the Bahamas to get gunpowder for Washington's army. Nassau Town, a sunburnt little colonial port set down on the flat and scrubby island of New Providence, was protected by two stone forts, Nassau and Montagu, both fairly formidable, but the garrison of British regulars had been taken off and the sloop-of-war, HMS *Savage,* usually on station, was also gone. The defense of the island rested in the hands of some half-pay officers and two hundred of what Hopkins called the "Inhabitants."

His original plan was to put two hundred marines under Captain Nicholas, along with fifty seamen, into two captured sloops and try for a surprise attack against the town. But they were seen, there was no surprise, and Fort Nassau warned them off with a couple of cannon shots. The two sloops now proceeded to the eastern end of the island, and on 3 March 1776, covered by the 12-gun *Providence,* the landing party went ashore, was unopposed, and marched against Fort Montagu.

The British governor, Montford Browne, sent out an emissary who cautiously inquired of their intentions. Nicholas replied that he was to take "possession of all warlike stores belonging to the crown, but had no desire of touching the property of any of the inhabitants." The defenders of the fort let fly with three rounds of twelve-pound shot. That was the only resistance; then, honor served, they spiked their cannon and withdrew. Nicholas ran up the Grand Union flag (not yet the Stars and Stripes) and spent an undisturbed night in the fort. Then, as he reports it:

> The next morning by daylight we marched forward to take possession of the Governor's house . . . and demanded the keys to the fort, which were given to me immediately and then took possession of Fort Nassau. In it were 40 cannon mounted and well loaded for our reception with round, langridge, and canister shot. All this was accomplished without firing a single shot from our side. We found in this fort a great quantity of shot and shells, with 15 brass mortars, but the grand article, powder, the Governor sent off the night before, viz. 150 casks.

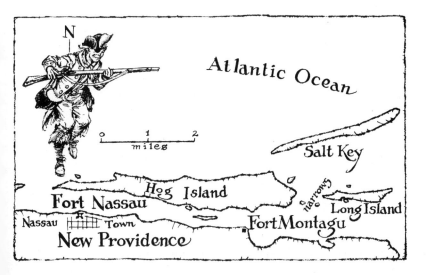

Governor Browne had used the night well. The powder had gone out in a merchant vessel through the unguarded eastern channel. Hopkins's squadron now came into the harbor and the next two weeks were spent in loading the spoils. The squadron headed for home on 17 March; Rhode Island was the destination.

On 4 and 5 April, south of Block Island, they took four small prizes. At one in the morning on the sixth, with a full moon and a north wind, *Glasgow*, a 20-gun English corvette, crossed the squadron's bows. Not recognizing the squadron as hostile, *Glasgow* came alongside *Cabot*, 14, to hail and in answer got a hand grenade on her deck from a marine in the maintop. *Cabot* then touched off a broadside and got back two in return, which put her out of action. A cannon ball carried away the *Alfred*'s wheel block and tiller lines. *Andrew Doria*, 16, closed on *Glasgow*'s port quarters, but her guns were too light and too few. *Columbus*, 28, came up next. *Glasgow*, much cut up and expecting to be boarded, broke off and ran for Newport. At dawn, Hopkins collected his scattered squadron and his prizes, and on 8 April took them into New London, Connecticut. Marine Lt. John Fitzpatrick was dead. So were six other marines, with four more wounded.

At first there were congratulations. Then there were second thoughts. The showing against the *Glasgow* had been poor and, if Hopkins were to be excused for taking liberties with his orders, where was the powder? There were investigations in Philadelphia. Hopkins, who deserved better, was censured and eventually dismissed from the service. Nicholas emerged not only with his reputation intact but on 25 June was promoted to major, with pay increased to thirty-two dollars a month and orders to raise four companies of marines, one each for the four new frigates—*Randolph,* 32; *Washington,* 32; *Effingham,* 28; and *Delaware,* 24—then being built either in Philadelphia or close by. Peg's son, Robert Mullan, got one of the new captain's commissions and probably used Tun Tavern (another name for the Beef-Steak House) as his recruiting rendezvous.

On 5 September the Naval Committee came out with uniform regulations for the Continental marines: green coats with white facings, a round hat with the left brim pushed up and pinned to the crown with a cockade. Marine drill instructors have been telling Marine recruits for a hundred years that the color green was chosen because it was the traditional color of riflemen. But the Continental marines were armed with muskets, not rifles—English Tower muskets in the beginning of the war, French Charleville muskets later on. Even if rifles had been available in quantity, which they were not, they would not have been a good weapon for marines. They were too slow to load. A good musketeer could get off five rounds while a rifleman was getting off one, and a rifle had no place to put a bayonet.

Green seems to have been chosen simply because green cloth was plentiful in Philadelphia. A group of militia, called the "Associators," wore a similar uniform. Also prescribed was a leather stock, borrowed from the British, regarded by some as a vestigial bit of body armor to protect a man's throat from a cutlass slash and by others as simply a device to keep a man's head erect. Whatever its use, the stock, praised by the officers and damned by the men, would persist until after the Civil War, its memory still preserved by the best known of Marine nicknames: "Leatherneck."

As the fall of 1776 deepened into winter, only one of the frigates, the *Randolph,* was ready to go to sea. Marine Capt. Samuel Shaw, with two lieutenants, took one of Nicholas's four companies on board her in November. The situation for the newly-declared-independent United States was increasingly precarious. Howe's move to New York had dislodged Washington, who withdrew across New Jersey, his small army fraying away with desertions and the expirations of short-term enlistments.

## PRINCETON

In December 1776, "the Enemy having overrun the Jerseys, & our Army being greatly reduced," Nicholas was ordered to join Washington's army at Trenton. On the night of 2 December 1776, he loaded his remaining three companies into flat-bottomed galleys and rowed upriver to Trenton. Washington, with a great number of things on his mind, was not immediately certain what to do with the marines. The next day, 3 December, a brigade of three battalions of Philadelphia militia (including the Associators in their green uniforms) was organized under command of Col. John Cadwalader. Perhaps because of their green uniforms, Washington added Nicholas's "battalion" to Cadwalader's brigade. Washington then withdrew his army to the Pennsylvania side of the Delaware and, on 8 December, the British occupied Trenton.

Cadwalader's brigade was posted at Bristol to watch for any British move to cross the river. Nicholas billeted his marines in the town's Quaker meeting hall. Capts. Benjamin Dean, Andrew Porter, and Robert Mullan commanded his three companies. Strength returns for 20 December show Dean as having fifty-five officers and men present and fit for duty, Porter forty-two, and Mullan forty-four, giving Nicholas an effective strength of 141. The same returns show an additional thirty-six marines on the sick list. Mullan's company had two men, Isaac and Orange, listed as "Negroes." They may well have been the first two black marines.

On Christmas night Washington made his famous crossing of the Delaware, going over himself at McKonkey's Ferry, nine miles north of Trenton, with his strongest division, and capturing the Hessian garrison. Cadwalader, freshly promoted to brigadier general and commanding a division (his own Philadelphia brigade and a brigade of Rhode Island Continentals), was to cross at Bristol but let bad weather and ice in the river stop him.

Lord Cornwallis, after the capture of the Hessians, hurried across New Jersey with eight thousand men. Washington crossed into Trenton a second time. Cadwalader got across farther downriver. The addition of Cadwalader's division would bring Washington's strength up to about six thousand. By sunrise on 2 January 1777, Nicholas's marines, as part of the Philadelphia brigade, had marched over muddy roads to Trenton and moved into positions on the south bank of Assunpink Creek. Brig. Gen. Hugh Mercer's brigade was on their left, Maj. Gen. Arthur St. Clair's brigade on their right. Hessian grenadiers and British light infantry tried to cross a bridge to get at them. Cadwalader's light troops, Nicholas's marines among them, managed to hold the bridge. By nightfall on 2 January the two armies were lined up on opposite banks of the creek.

Cornwallis's staff urged a night attack, but the English lord said that he would "bag the old fox" in the morning. Leaving his campfires burning, Washington made a night march on that dark and cold night around Cornwallis's flank. At sunrise Washington divided his army into two columns. One column under Maj. Gen. Nathaniel Greene, with Mercer's and Cadwalader's brigades, was to cut the main road from Trenton to Princeton.

On the British side, at dawn, Lt. Col. Charles Mawhood with three regiments, the 17th, 55th, and 40th Foot, began his march from Princeton to Trenton. Mawhood bumped into Mercer's brigade near Stony Brook bridge. General Mercer was mortally wounded and his brigade fell back in confusion. Cadwalader heard the firing and double-quicked his brigade to the scene. He got to within fifty yards of the British, but was faltering when Washington rode up in a temper and rallied his brigade. Arrival of reinforcements from Maj. Gen. John Sullivan's division tipped the scales firmly in favor of the Americans. It was now Mawhood's turn to run.

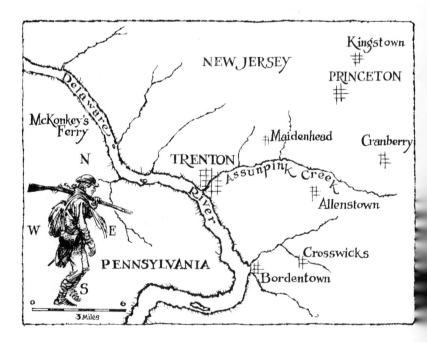

Cornwallis, awakened to learn that the Americans had escaped, rushed from Trenton to Princeton. Washington eluded Cornwallis's pursuit and on 6 January reached his winter quarters, defenses already prepared, at Morristown, New Jersey. The Marines were detached from Cadwalader's brigade and billeted with the artillery under Brig. Gen. Henry Knox on the presumption that they were familiar with ship's guns. Nicholas's strength was down to eighty men, of whom two were sick.

On 20 February Captain Mullan's company marched back to Philadelphia as escorts for a party of British prisoners. In March, Captain Porter left the Marines to accept a commission in the Continental artillery. Captain Dean's company returned to Philadelphia about the first of April and went on board the frigate *Washington*.

The barracks for Nicholas's last two companies was a house on Second Street between Arch and Race Streets. They must have been a dirty lot, because the barracks master gave them a bad inspection report. That summer and fall the few who were left found employment in the defense of the Delaware and the fighting preceding the British capture of Philadelphia.

## BILLINGSPORT

Three major forts guarded the Delaware River approach to Philadelphia: Forts Mifflin and Mercer facing each other just south of the city and, farther south on the Jersey side, Billingsport, which French engineers considered most important of all. On the night of 28 September 1777, the British 10th Regiment of Foot—once the hated garrison at Boston—and the 42d Foot—the infamous Black Watch, now much romanticized—marched out of Germantown, south to Chester, where they crossed the Delaware at about the site of the present day's Commodore Barry Bridge.

Two skirmishes were fought against the New Jersey militia under Brig. Gen. Silas Newcomb. Then the two British regiments, under command of Lt. Col. Thomas Stirling, came down the line of the Mantua Creek to move against the fort at Billingsport from the rear.

Washington had no Continentals to spare for the defense of Billingsport. Newcomb considered it a trap and refused to garrison it with New Jersey militia. The defense of the fort, therefore, was left to Col. William Bradford and about 112 Pennsylvania militiamen. Obviously, Colonel Bradford could not hold against two regiments of British regulars.

The Continental brig *Andrew Doria* came across the river to evacuate the garrison. Landing parties under Marine lieutenants Dennis Leary and William Barney went ashore in guard boats. They lifted off the garrison and most of the ammunition, set the fort's buildings on fire, spiked its five cannon, and exchanged a few rounds of musket fire with the Black Watch, which was coming across the field toward them, before jumping into their boats and rowing safely back to the *Andrew Doria.*

## WILLING ON THE MISSISSIPPI

In the summer of 1777, before Howe's occupation of Philadelphia, James Willing, the twenty-six-year-old black sheep member of a prominent Philadelphia merchant family, returned home from a wild life at Natchez with a scheme to take a party of raiders down the Mississippi. He would open up the river by routing out the scattered British and Tory settlers on the east bank and then join up with the Spanish in New Orleans. It was a dubious plan, but the Commerce Committee of the Continental Congress (which quite probably did not have the authority to do so) gave him a commission as a captain in the navy for the purpose.

His jumping-off point was Fort Pitt (now Pittsburgh), where the Allegheny and the Monongahela join to form the Ohio. He arrived there on 12 December 1777 and boldly presented the commander with a list of his requirements: a detachment of marines and a boat to put them in, along with weapons and stores.

Willing successfully recruited a first and second lieutenant and thirty-four marines, most of them volunteers from the 13th Virginia Regiment. He was given an open boat, well-named *Rattletrap,* which had a mast and a some-time-sail and twelve or fourteen oars to propel it, along with the current, which fortunately was going in the right direction. The expedition got underway on the night of 10 January 1778.

Near where the Wabash enters the Ohio, Willing relieved a party of French traders of their accumulated fur pelts and their trading stock of brandy. On his reaching the Mississippi, two canoes and ten Americans, who were most probably river pirates, joined him. A short distance above Natchez, on 19 February, he and his band raided the plantation of a Loyalist, Anthony Hutchins. The next day he pushed on to Natchez, the inhabitants of which thought it better to capitulate than to resist. Some joined him; others accepted his guarantee of protection in exchange for a pledge of neutrality.

From Natchez south, Willing burned and pillaged the homes and farms of suspect planters, carrying off their slaves and other portable valuables. With his growing force, he captured the British armed sloop *Rebecca,* 16, and the brig *Neptune.*

The Spanish officials in New Orleans, still officially neutral but leaning toward the United States and against their old enemy England, did not know quite what to make of Willing. The American agent, Oliver Pollock, who had considerable influence with the Spanish governor, Bernardo de Gálvez, tipped the scales in Willing's favor. Barracks space was provided for his men and permission granted for him to auction off his plunder, chiefly slaves. A profit of about $60,000 was realized—not much considering the destruction that had been wrought.

The British protested, as well they might, and sent the sloop *Sylph* up the Mississippi to press their point. Gálvez decided that much of the captured property should be restored to its British owners. The *Neptune* had to be returned, but Pollock purchased the *Rebecca.* Refitted, it became the Continental sloop *Morris,* 24, complete with Marine guard, and would give good service until lost in a hurricane the following year.

Willing sent a detachment under Lt. Richard Harrison upriver to enforce the oath of neutrality on the British planters who had broken their parole, including Anthony Hutchins, who suddenly seems to have become a colonel. There was fighting and Harrison had to withdraw with five men killed. Willing's line of communication back to Fort Pitt was effectively cut and he had to accept the reality that his force was too small to enforce his control of the river.

Both Gálvez and Pollock continued to find it difficult to do business with Willing. Pollock was anxious to get him out of New Orleans. Willing wanted to go north through Spanish territory and under Spanish protection (essentially the Spanish controlled the west bank of the Mississippi and the British, intermittently, the east bank). Two of his lieutenants swore an oath to Gálvez that they would not bother the English; they were allowed to depart with the original party of marines, eventually to join George Rogers Clark at Kaskaskia in present-day Illinois.

Willing himself did not leave New Orleans until mid-November. Then he was allowed to go as a carrier of dispatches for Congress from Gálvez and Pollock. The sloop that took him was captured off the Delaware Capes by a

British privateer. He was taken as a prisoner to New York, eventually to be exchanged late in 1779.

## CRUISE OF THE *RANDOLPH*

Of all the thirteen frigates built by the Continental Congress, the 32-gun *Randolph,* commanded by Capt. Nicholas Biddle and with Shaw's company of Marines on board her, would be the first to go to sea. She would have the most glorious, if finally fatal, time of it of any of the frigates. In December 1776 she was still at her Philadelphia pier, undermanned and bottled up in the Delaware by British ships patrolling the bay. With a crew rounded out with captured British seamen released from Philadelphia's jail, she finally slipped down the ice-choked river and put to sea at the end of January 1777. Her orders were to cruise off the Virginia Capes and perhaps find the British frigate *Milford,* which had been annoying American shipping. A gale struck in March and broke two of her masts. As *Randolph* limped toward Charleston for repairs, fever broke out and some of the crew died. The English members of the crew mutinied, which provided work for Shaw's marines. Once safe in Charleston, it was early June before she was ready to sail again. Incredibly, lightning split her main mast twice again before the summer was out.

The repaired *Randolph* put to sea on the first of September, her masts now protected by Benjamin Franklin's new invention, the lightning rod. Sailing south, she took the British privateer *True Briton,* 20, out of Jamaica with a cargo of rum intended for the British troops in New York. Three lesser merchantmen, loaded with rum, sugar, salt, ginger, and logwood, were also taken before *Randolph* ran with her prizes back to Charleston. The frigate was proving to be a slow sailor, so Biddle careened her to scrape her fouled bottom.

By early December she was re-rigged and ready to go. Captain Shaw had lost both his lieutenants, one cashiered, the other resigned. South Carolina authorities hoped that *Randolph,* with four smaller ships of the South Carolina navy, could break the British blockade that had closed the port. After considerable wrangling, the little squadron set sail and cleared the Charleston Harbor bar on 12 January 1778. They found no British frigates and sailed south for the Barbados. Near sunset on 7 March they came up against the 64-gun ship-of-the-line *Yarmouth.* Biddle audaciously attacked. The Britisher was an old ship and something of a relic, but with sixty-four guns that threw several times the weight of shot of *Randolph*'s broadsides. Early in the fight Biddle was seriously wounded in the thigh. Propped up in a chair, he continued to direct the fight. *Randolph* was giving better than she was receiving when her powder magazine exploded—no one really knows why—and blew her apart, killing all but four of the 305 souls on board. Both Biddle and Shaw were among the dead.

## With John Paul Jones

John Paul Jones had gone to Portsmouth, New Hampshire, in July 1777 to take command of the new sloop-of-war *Ranger*. *Ranger* was rated at twenty guns (although Jones prudently reduced his ordnance to eighteen 9-pounders). This meant, by rule-of-thumb—one marine for every gun or a little more—a Marine guard of twenty-two or twenty-four. Jones chose a friend, Capt. Matthew Parke, to be his senior marine. Samuel Wallingford of Portsmouth was named lieutenant. Captain Parke was told to take "a Drum, Fife, and Colours" and go recruit his marines. The *Ranger*'s maiden voyage would carry to Dr. Benjamin Franklin in Paris the first dispatches reporting the surrender of Burgoyne at Saratoga.

*Ranger* put to sea on 1 November and reached France in thirty-one days. The crew and officers were mostly Portsmouth men. They did not like Captain Parke, so Jones removed him from command of the marines and put Wallingford in his place. After some tentative cruising off the French coast in February and March, Jones sailed on 10 April 1778 from Brest for the Irish Sea. In the next ten days the *Ranger* took two merchant ships, brushed against a revenue cutter, and sank a Scots schooner loaded with oats and barley. On 20 April they spoke with a fishing boat who told them that HMS *Drake*, 20, was in Belfast Lough.

Jones then mounted a raid on Whitehaven in Solway Firth. He had sailed from there as a thirteen-year-old boy. His Portsmouth crew wanted no part of the venture; there was almost a mutiny, stopped by Jones's putting a pistol to a recalcitrant's head. A landing party of two boats' crews was made up, about twenty men in each, Jones commanding one, Wallingford the other. At midnight on 22 April the boats pulled away from the *Ranger*, three hours of hard rowing to the harbor. Jones went up the wall of the south battery, found the gunners asleep, took them prisoner, and spiked the guns. He repeated the performance at the north battery. Then an Irishman broke away from his crew and raced down the street, banging on doors and shouting that Yankee pirates had come to burn their homes and ships. It was now five in the morning and broad daylight. With the town thoroughly roused, the two boat crews reassembled and pulled safely back to the *Ranger.*

Jones next crossed Solway Firth to St. Mary's Isle with the idea of carrying off the earl of Selkirk as a hostage who could be traded for American prisoners. Midmorning on the twenty-third he put a cutter in the water, taking with him the sailing master, David Cullam, Wallingford, and a dozen hands. Posing as a press gang, they learned from the head gardener that the earl was away, benefiting from the waters at Buxton. Jones gave Cullam and Wallingford permission to carry off the family silver so as not to go back to the *Ranger* empty-handed. The countess of Selkirk afterward wrote that the sailing master "had a vile blackguard look," but the other officer "was a civil young man in a green uniform, an anchor on his buttons which were white." With the *Ranger* safely back in Brest on 8 May, Jones wrote to the countess telling her of his intentions of buying the plate when it was sold and restoring it to her. He also told her of his encounter with the *Drake* the day following the visit to St. Mary's. The English ship had struck her colors after an engagement lasting sixty-five minutes, her captain killed by a Marine musket ball through the head. Among the American dead, as Jones could have told the countess, was the civil young man in the green uniform.

## PENOBSCOT BAY

Leave Jones there, cross the Atlantic once again, and move forward a year: It is now June 1779. Brig. Gen. Francis McLean has come down from Halifax to Penobscot Bay in Maine to set up Fort George near present-day Castine. He has with him 640 troops—440 from the 75th Foot (the Argyle Highlanders) and two hundred from the 82d Foot (the Hamilton regiment of lowland Scots). He also has three sloops-of-war: the *Albany,* 14; *North,* 14; and *Nautilus,* 16.

Maine is a province of Massachusetts and the move causes consternation in Boston. The State Board of War plans an expedition to be prosecuted with or without the help of the Continental Congress in distant Philadelphia. There are three ships of the Continental navy in Boston harbor. Captain Saltonstall, late of the *Alfred,* has the fine new frigate, *Warren,* 32, along with the 12-gun sloop *Providence* and the 12-gun brig *Diligent,* and is named commodore. To his force are added four Massachusetts navy brigs, a 20-gun ship from New Hampshire, and twelve privateers. There are also twenty merchantmen, mostly sloops and schooners, to serve as transports and stores ships.

The landing force is to be under Brig. Gen. Solomon Lovell of the Massachusetts militia. The call goes out for fifteen hundred militiamen. Only 873 respond, but 227 Continental and Massachusetts marines are also embarked, so that there are about eleven hundred troops. His chief of artillery is the Boston silversmith, Lt. Col. Paul Revere. This formidable force gets under way on 19 July 1779, and by the twenty-fourth is in the mouth of Penobscot Bay. That night a Marine scouting party goes ashore and learns that the British are well along in the construction of Fort George, a dirt-and-log breastworks pierced here and there for cannon, on a fishhook-shaped promontory sticking out into the bay.

Next day, 25 July, the militia make a hesitant effort to land, lose an Indian scout, and come back to their transports. On Monday, 26 July, Commodore Saltonstall takes his ships past the fort and the English sloops pop away at

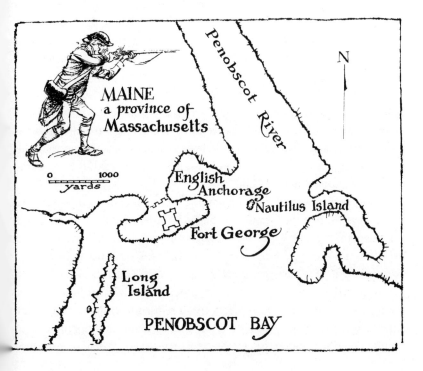

them for an indecisive two hours. At dusk a party of marines and militia land on Nautilus (or Banks) Island out in the bay, half a mile east of Fort George, to secure the island as a site for Revere's artillery. They drive off twenty British marines and capture four light field pieces. A spruce tree is trimmed to serve as a flag pole and the Stars and Stripes goes to the top.

Assault of the fort is to come at dawn on 28 July. The Continental and State marines are combined into a "landing division" under Marine Capt. John Welsh of the *Warren*. The landing from flat-bottomed boats is to be west of the fort in three columns, the Marine column under Captain Welsh on the right. The marines get ashore, the militia lagging somewhere to the left rear. The beach is badly chosen. The marines have to go up a heavily wooded 45-degree slope, a typical bit of Maine rock-bound coast.

Marine Sgt. Thomas Philbrook of the *Providence,* who thought that Lovell would be better placed on a deacon's bench than at the head of an army, wryly observed that "Our brave General did not lead in the van in the ascent, neither did he bring up the rear. Probably he and the Commodore were walking the *Warren's* quarter-deck with their spyglasses to see the fun."

At the top of the slope, hidden by the thick evergreen woods, the Hamilton regiment is waiting for the marines. The lowland Scots fight stubbornly and well, their rear guard commanded by an eighteen-year-old lieutenant named John Moore. Moore will live to become one of Britain's greatest soldiers; he will die in Spain in 1809 fighting Napoleon.

On the American side, Captain Welsh, who had come from Ireland to fight the English, is among the dead, as are thirteen more marines, who also count twenty wounded. The English retire to their fort and the militia comes ashore. The fort, as Paul Revere saw it, was "as high as a man's chin and built of square logs." A militiaman disdainfully remarked he could "jump over the walls with a musket in each hand."

The attack is resumed the next day, the Marine line in the advance. Five hundred yards from the fort they are halted by order of General Lovell. In the fort, General McLean waited wonderingly: "I was in no situation to defend myself; I meant only to give them one or two guns, so as not to be called a coward, and then to have struck my colours."

But Lovell would not assault until Saltonstall brought his ships in close enough to join the barrage and Saltonstall refused to close because of the three British sloops-of-war. ("I am not going to risk my shipping in that damned hole.") The impasse persisted for sixteen days. Then, on the afternoon of 13 August, the privateer *Active* came flying in through the fog with the news that a British squadron was entering the bay. It was the 64-gun *Raisonable,* four frigates, and three sloops-of-war. Saltonstall spent an apprehensive night. Next morning at first light he flew the signal, "All ships fend for yourself." Setting the example, he took the *Warren* upstream, drove her into the bank, and set her afire. The Americans lost nineteen ships, two of them surrendered to the British, the rest abandoned and burned. Marines, militiamen, and seamen floundered through the Maine wilderness. Most found their way back to Boston. There was, of course, a board of inquiry. Findings were such that the "narrow-minded" Saltonstall was brought before a court-martial and cashiered.

## A FEW GOOD MEN

William Jones, captain of Marines in the *Providence* (the 28-gun frigate, not the 12-gun sloop) then at Boston, advertised in the 20 March 1779 *Providence* (R.I.) *Gazette* the need for "a few good Men" to engage in "a short Cruize" and gave the Marine Corps a recruiting slogan it would be using two hundred years later. The frigate went out in June in company with two smaller ships, sailed eastward, intercepted a large convoy from Jamaica, and took eleven prizes, three of which got away. The *Providence* did not sail again until late in November, arriving in Charleston, South Carolina, just before Christmas. Jones and his detachment were taken off the ship to man shore batteries. The British took him prisoner in May 1780. He was paroled, but never exchanged, and finished out the war in his family's hardware store in Providence.

## *BONHOMME RICHARD V. SERAPIS*

In France, John Paul Jones had gotten a new ship, *Bonhomme Richard,* formerly an East Indiaman, built in 1766, and now somewhat tired. John Adams dined with Jones in L'Orient on 13 May 1779. That night he entered in his diary, "After Dinner walked out, with Captains Jones & Landais to see Jones's Marines—dressed in the English Uniforms, red & white."

Marines in red coats instead of green? Adams disapproved but Adams was in error; the marines were French, not American, and they were in the proper uniform of the Walsh Regiment of the Irish Brigade of the French Army: red coats with yellow and blue facings, white waistcoats, and white breeches.

In her conversion to a man-of-war the *Bonhomme Richard* received a mixed battery of forty-four guns, so, by the usual rule-of-thumb, her Marine guard should have numbered forty-five or fifty. But there were 137 French marines assigned to the ship, because Jones originally envisioned the *Bonhomme Richard* as a kind of amphibious command ship for a raid against Liverpool to be led by Lafayette. In the conversion he put in extra berthing for the landing force and its commander. The raid did not come off, but Jones thought an extra complement of marines would be useful and he was right.

These Irish soldiers from the French Army were under the nominal command of two lieutenant colonels on leave from the French Army, Paul de Chamillard and Antoine-Felix Wuibert. Real control, however, fell to three lieutenants with the un-French names of Edward Stack, Eugene MacCarthy, and James O'Kelly. All three were given Continental marine commissions. (Benjamin Franklin in Paris had an ample supply of commissions signed in blank by John Hancock.)

On 14 August 1779 the *Bonhomme Richard,* in company with the new American-built frigate *Alliance,* 36, and the *Pallas,* 26, sailed from L'Orient, embarked on the great clockwise cruise around the British Isles. The final, climactic battle took place off Yorkshire's Flamborough Head on 23 September. At three in the afternoon, Jones sighted the *Serapis,* new, copper-bottomed, rated a "forty-four" but carrying fifty guns, and the *Countess of Scarborough,* 20. Two hours later Jones's French-Irish Marine drummers beat the roll to General Quarters. At about seven in the evening the battle began with an exchange of broadsides between *Bonhomme Richard* and *Serapis.* Outgunned and against a better ship, Jones's one chance was to hold tight to the Englishman and depend, as much as anything, upon the marksmanship of his French marines. It was a seaman, not a marine as sometimes reported, who dropped a hand grenade from the yard of the *Richard* into an open hatch of the *Serapis* and exploded a magazine. British Capt. Richard Pearson, his ship on fire and his mainmast giving way, at ten-thirty tore down the Red Ensign from where it had been nailed to its staff.

All three of the Irish-born Marine lieutenants had done well. Stack did good work from the main top with fifteen marines and four seamen. MacCarthy, stationed in the powder magazine, was wounded when three of Jones's 18-pounders on the deck above him exploded. O'Kelly, on the forecastle deck with twenty Marines, was mortally wounded when the erratic Capt. Pierre Landais in the *Alliance* raked the *Bonhomme Richard* with a broadside.

LAST DAYS

In September 1781, while Cornwallis pondered surrender at Yorktown, Robert Morris, the finance minister and Rothschild of the American Revolution, had a secret mission in Philadelphia, one last adventure for his friend Maj. Samuel Nicholas and his few remaining marines. There were a million silver crowns (a loan from Louis XVI) waiting at Boston. Nicholas brought them down by ox cart, 350 miles, much of the way through Tory country, arriving safely on 6 November. Two months later, on 7 January 1782, Morris opened the Bank of North America, its assets secured by the French silver.

In 1783 Great Britain recognized the United States as a sovereign and independent power and the war was over. By then the Continental navy had been swept from the seas. The *Alfred*, the *Bonhomme Richard*, the *Ranger*, the *Providence*, the *Andrew Doria*, and the rest—some brave, some not so brave—were all gone and with them their Marine guards. On 3 June 1785, Congress authorized the selling of the decommissioned *Alliance*, the last vessel of the Continental navy. The Continental marines had already disappeared.

The original resolution of Congress had the sound idea of a corps of Marines from which battalions could be formed for expeditionary service and from which detachments could be spun off for service afloat. The idea got lost due to: insufficient resources, distances that were too great, communications that were too slow. After Penobscot, there was no major effort at an amphibious operation. Records show that 131 officers held Continental Marine commissions. Major Nicholas is held by the U.S. Marines to be their first commandant. He never was actually so designated, but he was the only field-grade officer and the duties as "Muster Master" give some legitimacy to the tradition. The number of Continental marines enlisted is not exactly known, but probably did not exceed two thousand. In all, counting states' navies and privateers, perhaps twelve thousand had some claim to the title "Marines of the Revolution."

# 2

## *1785-1811*

## To Be Called the Marine Corps

### Congress Passes a Resolution

Troubles with Algerian corsairs began before the ink was dry on the Peace of Paris. But there was no Navy and not much of an Army, nothing more than a few quartermasters and a sergeant's guard or two. As for the Marines, only the slenderest thread of continuity can be claimed by virtue of "marines" serving in the Revenue Cutter Service. Nothing was done until the Naval Act of 27 March 1794 authorized the building of six frigates, and before they could be completed an ignominious treaty with Algiers was reached in September 1795 at a cost of $1 million in ransoms and bribes.

The next vexation was Revolutionary France, piqued because the United States would not join her against Great Britain. From July 1796 until the end of 1797, French raiders took 316 merchant ships flying the American flag. American attitudes stiffened. There was a new slogan: "Millions for defense, but not one cent for tribute." Work on three of the frigates, *United States, Constitution,* and *Constellation,* was resumed and other ships were authorized for building or conversion. There were to be Marine quotas for the new ships— "quotas," not "detachments," because there was no corps from which they could be detached. Samuel Sewall, chairman of the House Naval Committee, arguing that all marines should be in one corps for better discipline, order, and economy, offered the following resolution:

> *Resolved,* That, in addition to the present Military Establishment, there shall be raised a battalion, to be called the Marine Corps, to consist of a Major, and suitable commissioned and non-commissioned officers, five hundred privates, and the necessary musicians, including the marines now in service; and the marines which shall be employed in the armed vessels and galleys of the United States shall be detachments from this corps.

Sewall's bill quickly passed the House, moved to the Senate (where there were amendments), and on 11 July 1798, the true birthday of the Corps, President John Adams approved "An act for establishing and organizing a Marine Corps" and it became law. (Unfortunately, the Senate amendments had taken out the provision for battalion organization and had perpetuated the Revolutionary War practice, copied from the English custom, that Marines were to be governed by the Articles of War when ashore and Naval Regulations while afloat.) Next day the President appointed William Ward Burrows of Philadelphia major of the new Corps. On 23 August 1798, Burrows opened his headquarters in Philadelphia, at that time still the nation's capital. An economical administration gave the new Marine Corps a stock of uniforms left over from "Mad Anthony" Wayne's Legion, blue with red facings, and this was the beginning of the U.S. Marines' familiar "dress blues." A round hat, edged in yellow, with the brim turned up over the left ear, went with the uniform. It gave trouble at sea, was difficult to store, and easily blown over the side.

In May 1799 another Philadelphian, Daniel Carmick, was ordered to the frigate *Constitution*. After viewing his fifty-man Marine detachment he wrote to the major commandant, "I think it is not possible to produce such another shabby set of animals in this world."

Most of the French raiders, mixed up with Spanish privateers and some regular French navy ships, were in the Caribbean. *Constitution*, 44, commanded by Capt. Silas Talbot, took station there with orders to cooperate with Toussaint-L'Overture, the black Haitian general who had expelled the French and Spanish from almost all of Santo Domingo. Talbot learned that the 14-gun French privateer *Sandwich* (that un-French name because she was a captured English packet) was loading coffee and sugar at Puerto Plata, a north coast Dominican port still in Spanish hands. Talbot commandeered the American merchant sloop *Sally* and put his first lieutenant, Isaac Hull, and Carmick into it with ninety marines and sailors. At high noon, 12 May 1800, they sailed into the harbor and lay alongside the *Sandwich*. They caught the crew below decks at mess, one or two rounds went off by accident, but there was no resistance. Carmick now loaded his marines into the *Sandwich*'s boat and pulled for Fortaleza San Felipe on the eastern arm of the harbor. Here again there was no opposition, although the French and Spanish were supposed to have five hundred men in and around Puerto Plata. Guns of the fort spiked, the Americans hurriedly rerigged the *Sandwich* and sailed her out of the harbor. Thus went the first of many U.S. Marine landings to be made on the beautiful, unhappy island of Hispaniola.

In June 1800 the national capital was moved from Philadelphia to the new Federal city of Washington. Major Burrows brought his marines down from Philadelphia and set them up in a temporary camp (not far from today's Lincoln Memorial). In France, Bonaparte was now First Consul. No great friend of the Americans but a realist who did not want a continuing enemy in the New World, he caused the war which was never declared to end. The Peace Establishment Act drastically cut away at the Navy. The Marines were reduced from a strength of about eleven hundred to seven hundred.

Even so, Burrows was giving permanent shape to the Corps. The 1798 law included provision for a "drum major, a fife major and thirty-two drums and fifes." Burrows was determined to have a proper Marine Band. He assessed his officers ten dollars each to buy additional instruments.

The Marine Band gave its first open-air concert on 21 August 1800, and made its debut at the President's House on New Year's Day, 1801. Thomas Jefferson had defeated John Adams in the election of 1800, and the band played at his inauguration in March 1801 (as it has played for every inauguration since, becoming the "President's Own").

On 31 March Burrows rode out with the new president to look "for a proper place to fix the Marine Barracks on." They chose a square in Southeast Washington, bounded by Eighth, Ninth, G, and I Streets, because "it lay near the Navy Yard" and was within easy marching distance of the Capitol. The quadrangle was to be laid out in typical nineteenth-century barracks style. On the north side, on G Street, would be the Commandant's House.

Burrows, whose title had become lieutenant colonel commandant, could also sternly instruct a junior officer, struck by a Navy lieutenant, to "wipe away this Insult," citing approvingly that "On board the Ganges, about 12 mos. ago, Lt. Gale, was struck by an Officer of the Navy, the Capt. took no notice of the Business and Gale got no satisfaction on the Cruise; the moment he arrived he call'd the Lieut. out and shot him; afterwards Politeness was restor'd."

## BARBARY WARS (1801–1815)

With the war with France behind them, there was work for the Navy in the Mediterranean against the Barbary pirates. Yusef Karamanli had made himself Bey of Tripoli by murdering one older brother and chasing a second brother out of the country. Looking at the favors given Algiers and Tunis and greedy for his share of the same, in May 1801 he cut down the flagstaff in front of the American Consulate and declared war on the United States.

President Jefferson dispatched a squadron to the Mediterranean, the forerunner in an almost unbroken line to the Sixth Fleet of today, but not much was done with it until, in September 1804, Commo. Samuel Barron came out with fresh ships and took command of the squadron. He brought with him Mr. William Eaton, Arabic scholar, eccentric, and one-time captain in the U. S. Army. Eaton had just been appointed naval agent for the Barbary States and he had a secret plan approved by Jefferson. He proceeded in the brig *Argus* (commanded by Isaac Hull, Carmick's companion in the cutting-out at Puerto Plata) to Egypt, found Hamet Karamanli, Yusef's deposed brother, living several hundred miles up the Nile with the Mamelukes, and persuaded him to join in an expedition against the Bey.

A polyglot "army" was put together in Alexandria, most of it made up of Arabs, but also some European soldiers-of-fortune, thirty-eight Greek mercenaries, and Marine Lt. Presley N. O'Bannon with a sergeant and six privates from *Argus*. Counting camel drivers and camp followers, the column numbered perhaps four or five hundred. There was a lurid march of six hundred miles across the Libyan desert, punctuated with demands for more money, murders, mutinies, and fights between the two factions: Christians and Muslims. On 27 April 1805 *Argus*, 18, *Hornet*, 10, and *Nautilus*, 12, bombarded the walled city of Derna while Eaton launched his attack from the desert. Hamet and his Arabs came in from the southwest, while O'Bannon and his "Christians" attacked from the southeast. O'Bannon charged through the town, seized the harbor fort, and turned the guns on the governor's palace. In two hours the palace was taken and Hamet's Arabs were pursuing the defeated defenders across the desert. The Christians had lost thirteen men, including two marines killed and one wounded. On 3 June a peace treaty was concluded at Tripoli with Yusef. Hamet, who had expected to become the Bey, was mollified by the promise of a U.S. pension. O'Bannon came away with a Mameluke sword, reputedly a present from Hamet. (The regulation Marine officer's sword was patterned after O'Bannon's Mameluke scimitar in 1826 and the design has persisted except for one brief interlude. In 1859 the Mameluke pattern was abandoned for the heavier, more businesslike U.S. Army infantry officer's saber. In 1875 the Mameluke sword was restored, the saber being continued for noncommissioned officers. In World War II, Marine officers were officially encouraged to turn in their swords for scrap metal. There is no record of any officer being so foolish as to do so, and after the war the sword was quickly restored as a required item for regular officers.)

In Washington, ill health forced the resignation of Lieutenant Colonel Commandant Burrows on 7 February 1804 (he would be dead within the year). His successor was Franklin Wharton, another Philadelphian. At the Marine Barracks, Wharton pushed the construction of the Commandant's House. The design was Georgian-Federal: two stories and an attic with dormer windows and a hipped roof. The soft salmon-color bricks were baked on the site from clay dug in a pit halfway between the barracks and the Navy Yard.

In March 1804 new uniform regulations came out. The colors were still blue for the coat, white for the pantaloons, and scarlet for the facings, but the cut was along the latest European lines, with a high collar, black calf-length gaiters, and, most impressive of all, a tall shako with a red plush plume and a large octagonal brass plate on the front embossed with an eagle and bearing the word "Marines" and the motto *Fortitudine* ("with Fortitude").

Early in 1804 Capt. Daniel Carmick was sent with about one hundred marines to garrison New Orleans, which had just become American by way of the Louisiana Purchase. In the next several years he put down bits and pieces of revolt and insurrection, and was promoted to major in 1809. Larger employment for him and his marines was in the offing.

# 3

## *1812-1815*

### SHALL I BOARD HER, SIR?

Impressment was the device by which Britain's Royal Navy was kept manned. Distinctions between American and Briton were slight. The language was the same and appearance not much different. (Although officers in charge of press gangs were advised that "the typical American has a degenerate, hang-dog air quite different from that of our noble British tars.")

The new president, James Madison, was a scholarly, mild-mannered man who did not want war, but by 1812 the number of impressed American seamen had grown to six thousand and it was claimed there were more Americans in the Royal Navy than in the U.S. Navy. Madison, forced to choose between war and further degradation, asked Congress for a declaration of war and he got it on 18 June 1812.

The Marine Corps was at about half strength; the muster rolls for 30 June 1812 show only ten officers and 483 enlisted men. Of these, more than half were on board ship or serving in the near-useless gunboats built by the inventive Jefferson for coast defense. An East Florida expeditionary force was campaigning variously against Spaniards, Indians, and pirates. The few other marines were strung out in small detachments from Boston to New Orleans.

The war started with the great frigate duels. On 19 August the *Constitution,* cruising off Newfoundland, met the *Guerrière,* 38. After an hour of maneuver and bombardment the two frigates came together. Marine Lt. William S. Bush went up on the rail, called to Capt. Isaac Hull, "Shall I board her, sir?" and was shot dead by a Royal Marine. The *Guerrière's* own decks were swept clear by musket fire from the *Constitution's* decks and tops. Hull-shot, sinking, and allowed no chance to board, the *Guerrière* surrendered. Too damaged to bring into port, she was burned.

Next honors went to the *Wasp*, an 18-gun sloop under the command of Master-Commandant Jacob Jones. She intercepted *Frolic*, a 20-gun brig-of-war convoying fourteen merchantmen, southwest of Bermuda on 18 October 1812. In a rough-weather battle of less than an hour, in which 1st Lt. John Brooks Jr., son of a Revolutionary War general, and his sixteen marines did their share, the *Frolic* was taken. But before battle damage could be repaired and the *Wasp* could get away with her prize, the 74-gun *Poictiers* came bearing down and captured them both.

A week later the *United States*, captained by Stephen Decatur, met the *Macedonian*, 38, a strong new frigate, in the mid-Atlantic. The *Macedonian* was forced to strike and was brought safely into port.

Meanwhile, the *Constitution* was at sea again. The more senior William Bainbridge had replaced Isaac Hull in command. On 29 December 1812, off the coast of Brazil, the *Constitution* encountered the frigate *Java*, 38. In a particularly bloody two-and-a-half-hour fight, the Englishman was battered into surrender.

Three British frigates lost in four months? Nothing like that had happened in fourteen years of naval war with France. The London *Times*, which at the war's beginning had sneered at the American navy as a "Handful of fir-built frigates with bits of striped bunting at their mast-heads, manned by bastards and outlaws," now cried, "Good God! Can such things be?"

## Cruise of the *Essex*

At the end of October 1812, with 318 souls on board, the 32-gun frigate *Essex* under Capt. David Porter cleared Delaware Bay with orders to rendezvous in the South Atlantic with the *Constitution*. Porter's Marine officer was Lt. John Marshall Gamble. On 12 December 1812, the *Essex* took His Majesty's packet *Nocton*, 10, and found $55,000 in gold in her strongbox. Porter then zigzagged across the South Atlantic but could not find the *Constitution* (which was on her way home for repairs), so he decided to take the *Essex* into the Pacific to go after the British whaling trade.

After a hard passage around the Horn, the *Essex* reached the whaling grounds in and around the Galapagos Islands. Prizes, in the shape of British whalers and privateers, came thick and fast. Porter kept six ships and eighty guns and made himself commodore of a squadron. Running out of Navy officers to command the prizes, he gave the 10-gun letter-of-marque *Green-*

*wich* to Gamble, who with it captured the biggest prize of all, the 14-gun raider *Seringapatam.*

His Majesty's frigate *Phoebe,* 36, and two 24-gun sloops, *Raccoon* and *Cherub,* were now in the Pacific with orders to find the *Essex.* Porter decided he had done a good year's work and retired discreetly to the Marquesas. He went in at Nukuhiva Island, impressed the natives with a parade of his marines, and possessed it in the name of the United States. One tribe remained rebellious. Porter launched an amphibious landing. Slung stones and spears proved tougher opposition than he anticipated and for a time the expedition was down to Porter, Gamble, and the ship's doctor firing from behind one small tree. The next day Porter went back with two hundred Americans, burned ten villages in as many skirmishes, and peace settled on the island. Six weeks later, after refitting, Porter sailed off with the *Essex* and most of his force, leaving Gamble behind with three ships and twenty-two men. The *Essex* was scarcely over the horizon before there was a native rebellion. Gamble put it down but his own men were becoming mutinous.

Gamble hung on grimly in the Marquesas, but on 7 May 1814 the mutineers gained the upper hand, set sail in the *Seringapatam* (flying the Union Jack), and held Gamble, a musket ball in his heel, prisoner. The mutineers put Gamble in an open boat with a few loyal hands. He managed to get back to Nukuhiva and after more hostilities sailed in the *Sir Andrew Hammond* with seven men for the Hawaiian Islands, where they were taken prisoner by the *Cherub.* They learned that on 28 March 1814 the *Essex* had been caught in Valparaiso harbor by the *Phoebe* and *Cherub.* The English ships stood off, using their long guns. The *Essex* caught fire; there was an explosion below decks and she was finished. Eventually, Gamble and his survivors were put ashore under parole at Rio de Janeiro and at the war's end made their way back to New York.


## ON THE GREAT LAKES

While these events were taking place at sea, the U.S. Army's ambitious land campaign against the Canadian border had failed disastrously. One of the causes was continued British control of the Great Lakes. The first step taken to challenge this control was to establish a U.S. naval base at Sacketts Harbor on the eastern end of Lake Ontario. By April 1813 there was a flotilla of fourteen more-or-less effective Lake ships and a Marine force mustering three officers and 121 men. Because of the Niagara Falls, it was not possible to transit ships to the equally vital Lake Erie; hence, a separate squadron had to be established there. A fortunate choice as commander was Commodore Oliver Hazard Perry. He set up his base at Erie and began construction of his fleet.

Perry's friend, James Lawrence, commanding the *Hornet*, the 18-gun sister to the *Wasp*, had on 24 February 1813 sunk the brig *Peacock*, also eighteen guns, in a fourteen-minute battle. Lawrence was promoted, given command of the *Chesapeake*—that unlucky 36-gun frigate which had been humiliated by HMS *Leopard* in 1807—and ordered to put to sea at once from Boston. He did so reluctantly. The *Chesapeake* was not ready. On 1 June 1813 she was met off Boston by the frigate *Shannon*, 38, Capt. Philip B. V. Broke, RN. There was an exchange of broadsides. Lawrence was struck in the hip, then hit again. Mortally wounded, he was carried below. "Don't give up the ship," he pleaded. "Sink her. Blow her up." Ten minutes after the action began, *Shannon*'s nine-pounders had cleared the American marines from the fighting tops and Captain Broke was leading a boarding party onto the *Chesapeake*. Fifteen marines were killed, including Lt. James Broom, and twenty more were wounded.

On Lake Erie, Perry, with ten vessels and a total of fifty-four guns, on 12 August 1813 met the British squadron of six ships and sixty-one guns. Perry's flagship was the new 20-gun brig *Lawrence*, named for his friend, and from her masthead flew a blue battle flag crudely lettered "Don't Give Up the Ship." The English commodore, Robert H. Barclay, was in the *Detroit*, a 20-gun corvette and a fair match to the *Lawrence*. Lt. John Brooks had the Marine detachment in the *Lawrence*. Exchanged since his capture by the *Poictiers*, he had been sent west in April with twelve marines and orders to recruit more along the way. He had no success with his recruiting and the dozen marines had to be augmented with Army volunteers, some of them Kentucky riflemen. In the fight between the squadrons, Brooks had his hip shattered by a round shot and bled to death. When it was all over, and the British squadron had surrendered, Perry in his report would coin another American naval slogan: "We have met the enemy and they are ours."

## BRITAIN'S STRATEGY

After Napoleon was exiled to Elba in May 1814, England could give larger attention to the troubles in America. Her strategy had three parts: invasion of New York by way of Lake Champlain (reminiscent of Burgoyne's vain venture), a tightened blockade against the Atlantic seaboard with forays against the principal cities, and an expedition against New Orleans to detach the Mississippi Valley from the Union.

Sir George Prevost marched down from Canada with eleven thousand troops and halted outside the American works at Plattsburg to await the arrival of the British lake fleet. Commo. George Downie had contrived a first-class 38-gun frigate, the *Confiance,* in addition to a brig, two sloops, and twelve row-galleys. On the American side, Navy Lt. Thomas Macdonough had the 24-gun *Saratoga,* a brig, a schooner, and ten gunboats. He had asked for marines and had gotten none, so soldiers had to serve as such. The squadrons came together on 11 September 1814 off Valcour Island. Commodore Downie was killed early in the action and at the end there was not a mast left in either squadron sound enough to bear sail, but the Americans had won. General Prevost was watching from shore, and next day began his march back to Canada.

On the Atlantic coast, early in 1813, Rear Adm. George Cockburn had raided the Chesapeake and burned Havre de Grace, Maryland. He then began operations around Norfolk, Virginia. The *Constellation* and twenty of Jefferson's gunboats were bottled up in Hampton Roads. The British landed twenty-five hundred infantry and marines against Craney Island on 22 June 1813. The American garrison of 750 (including the *Constellation's* fifty marines under Lt. Henry B. Breckinridge) held them off. The British did take Hampton, defended by a few hundred militia stiffened by a handful of marines.

On 27 June 1814 an expedition of some four thousand British troops sortied from the Gironde under the command of Maj. Gen. Robert Ross, a distinguished veteran of the Spanish Peninsular campaign against Bonaparte. Point of attack was to be decided by Vice Adm. Alexander Cochrane. The admiral and the general rendezvoused in Bermuda and on 3 August sailed for the Chesapeake. Ross landed his troops at Benedict, Maryland. Impeded by nothing more than the blazing August sun, he marched to Marlboro, arriving there on 23 August and meeting with Cockburn's force, which included two battalions of Royal Marines.

## Bladensburg

On the American side, the defense of Washington had been entrusted to the uncertain hands of Brig. Gen. Henry Winder, USA. There were no prepared

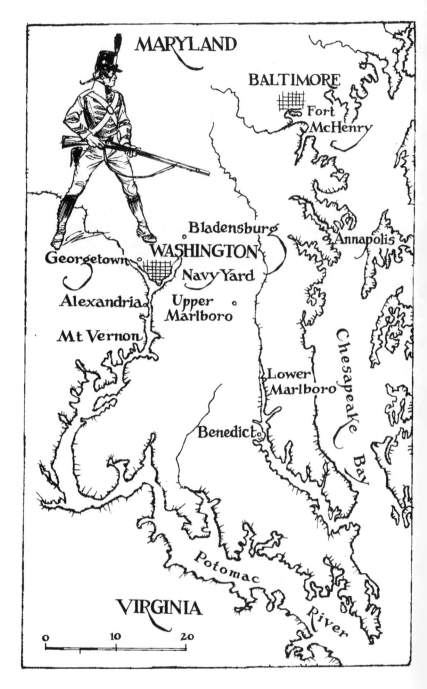

defenses, but on paper he had about ten thousand troops available, mostly militia. Commo. Joshua Barney, who had earlier burned his flotilla of useless gunboats, had about four hundred seamen and five guns with which to cover the bridge over the Eastern Branch (now called the Anacostia River), which led to the Navy Yard. He was joined there by Capt. Samuel Miller, Marine Corps adjutant, and 103 marines from the Washington Barracks.

On 24 August the British committed themselves to the easier crossing at Bladensburg, farther up the Eastern Branch, and some five miles from the Capitol. On the west side of the river, Winder, with six or seven thousand men, of whom not more than three hundred were regulars, had thrown a line. Barney, not under Army orders and with no intention of putting himself under Winder's immediate command, moved to a position on a commanding piece of ground astride the road to Washington and about a mile behind the American line.

The British advance, led by the Light Brigade, came across the river—some by the bridge, some wading—behind a barrage of Congreve rockets. Winder's militia scattered and the British assumed the road to Washington to be open, but Barney's force handed them a rude and unexpected shock. The five guns, served man-of-war style, cleared the advance from the road with grape and canister. After a third charge failed to budge the sailors and marines, the English began to work around both flanks. Barney was shot through the thigh and Miller was also wounded. Almost encircled, they ordered their troops to retire. Both were then captured.

The Marines had lost eight killed and fourteen wounded. British casualties were sixty-four killed, 185 wounded. Meanwhile, Madison's government was fleeing Washington. Lieutenant Colonel Commandant Wharton, having sent Miller off to battle with every available man, now loaded the Marine pay chest into a commandeered wagon and headed, in company with the paymaster, for Frederick, Maryland.

By nightfall, the British were in the capital. As Ross and Cockburn rode into Capitol Square they received some rounds of small-arms fire from the Gallatin House. Ross's horse was killed and he ordered the house burned and the occupants put to the sword. The Capitol building was then set afire. Ross and Cockburn, with two hundred men, marched on to the White House and personally put it to the torch. Elsewhere in the city, Commo. Thomas Tingey, superintendent of the Navy Yard, ordered it burned to keep its works and ships from falling into British hands. Next morning, while Ross went about the business of destroying public buildings, Cockburn amused himself by sacking the offices of the newspaper *National Intelligencer.* "Be sure all the C's are destroyed," he ordered, "so that the rascals cannot any longer abuse my name."

The Commandant's House and the Marine Barracks were left untouched. There are several legends to explain the omission. One is that Cockburn and Ross left the house and barracks unmolested as a mark of their esteem for the stand the marines had made at Bladensburg. Another suggests that, as professional officers, they would not burn married officers' quarters. However, there is no evidence to support any of these explanations, and perhaps the barracks and house went unburned simply because they escaped the incendiaries' attention.

The British marched out that night, leaving their dead unburied at Bladensburg and their wounded in American hands, retiring swiftly and in good order to the Chesapeake. Reembarked, they moved next against Baltimore. Aghast at the fate of Washington, the Americans undertook the defenses of Baltimore with more determination. Among the defenders was a naval brigade which included the Marine survivors of Bladensburg. Ross landed fourteen miles from the city, his advance was checked, and he himself killed. There was then some effort at a night attack on 13 September. The British fleet bombarded the defensive works, primarily Fort McHenry, all day and on up until midnight, but when dawn came, as a young American, Francis Scott Key, held by the British, saw it, ". . . our Flag was still there."

## New Orleans

On 19 September Admiral Cochrane sailed for Halifax, and there were no more raiding expeditions in the Chesapeake. The British landing force, after Baltimore, went to Jamaica, where they were joined in November by Lt. Gen. Sir Edward Pakenham, Wellington's brother-in-law, sent out to take Ross's place.

At New Orleans, Maj. Daniel Carmick's marines, now up to about three hundred in strength, had been fighting Creole pirates under Jean Lafitte. On 16 September 1814 Carmick put the pirate stronghold at Barataria to the torch. Admiral Cochrane is supposed to have offered Lafitte thirty thousand pounds sterling and a commission in the Royal Navy to join the British.

Lafitte refused, volunteering himself and his men for the defense of New Orleans in exchange for an American pardon. Maj. Gen. Andrew Jackson, now on the scene as the American commander, accepted.

The British plan was to move against New Orleans through Lake Borgne. For once, Jefferson's gunboats gave good service. Navy Lt. Thomas ap Catesby Jones's lake force of five gunboats and 182 men, including thirty-five marines, was attacked on 14 December by nearly a thousand English embarked in forty-seven barges. One by one the gunboats were captured, but the attack cost the British three hundred killed and wounded.

When Jackson took up his famous defensive line behind the Rodriguez Canal, one flank on the Mississippi, the other secured by a cypress swamp, Carmick's marines were in the center and Lafitte's buccaneers were manning much of the artillery. Pakenham ordered an attack on 28 December, but after feeling out the strength of Jackson's defense, broke it off. Carmick, leading a countercharge, fell with wounds that would eventually cost him his life. Pakenham's main attack came on 8 January 1815. He sent 1,200 troops across the river while the main body, 5,300 strong, advanced in a frontal assault. Waiting behind the breastworks were some 3,500 Americans with another thousand in reserve. In twenty minutes, the British had lost 2,036 killed and wounded. Pakenham, hit three times, was dead. American casualties, by some accounts, were as few as eight killed, thirteen wounded. Jackson let the British bury their dead, about seven hundred of them, and go back to their ships unmolested. Pakenham's body went home to Ireland in a cask of rum.

Ironically, the war was officially over before the battle was fought; the Treaty of Ghent had been signed on Christmas Eve, 1814. Even so, New Orleans was not the last engagement of the war. Ships at sea could not be informed of the peace, and isolated actions continued for another six months. On 20 February 1815 the *Constitution*, already known as "Old Ironsides," with Capt. Archibald Henderson on board as senior Marine, engaged and captured the miniature frigate *Cyane,* 34, and the sloop-of-war *Levant,* 20, in a four-hour battle.

So ended the second war with Britain. The muster rolls of the Corps for 30 June 1814, at the peak of hostilities, show only eleven officers and 579 enlisted men, although actual strength may have been somewhat higher. First priority had been to provide detachments to the ships of the blue-water Navy. There were never enough marines to do even this, let alone provide marines for the equally critical Lake squadrons. Company-sized units under Miller and Carmick had fought heroically at Bladensburg and New Orleans but apparently no thought was given to forming an expeditionary force or even a permanent battalion structure. Nor indeed did the nature of the war offer any particularly inviting amphibious targets. As the nation turned from war to peace, the future of the Marine Corps was ambiguous.

# 4

## *1816-1844*
### Insult to the Flag Reveng'd

<br>

### Courts-Martial for Commandants

Archibald Henderson (brevetted a major for gallant service in the *Constitution*) and others thought Wharton's failure to take the field at Bladensburg disgraceful. Henderson, born in 1783 at Colchester, Virginia, almost within the boundaries of the present-day base at Quantico, charged the commandant with neglect of duty and conduct unbecoming an officer and gentleman. There was an Army general court-martial (ashore, remember, the Marine Corps was subject to the Articles of War and Army jurisdiction) in September 1817, but to Henderson's intense disgust Wharton was acquitted. The new president, James Monroe, urged Wharton to resign, but he doggedly continued in office until his death the following year, 1 September 1818.

By the workings of the iron rules of seniority, Irish-born Anthony Gale, duelist of the *Ganges,* was appointed lieutenant colonel commandant on 3 March 1819. Gale's hot temper and dubious personal habits soon put him at cross-purposes with the secretary of the Navy. Again there was an Army general court-martial. Among the charges was one of "being intoxicated in common dram shops and other places of low repute in the City of Washington." Gale pleaded not guilty by reason of temporary insanity, but the court found him guilty as charged. President Monroe approved the sentence, which was dismissal from the service, and it was put into execution on 16 October 1820.

Henderson, who was commanding at Carmick's old post in New Orleans, was now named commandant. The Peace Establishment Act of 1817 had put the authorized strength of the Corps at fifty officers and 942 enlisted marines. The Act had also created the posts of adjutant and inspector, quartermaster, and paymaster, a staff structure which would continue until World

War II. Actually on board on 30 June 1820, according to official returns, were nineteen officers and 552 enlisted men. Henderson decreed that all newly commissioned officers would come to duty at Headquarters for training, the beginning of what is now called The Basic School. Also at Headquarters a skeleton battalion was to be maintained both for training and expeditionary uses.

In the Caribbean and along the Gulf of Mexico, there was a plethora of revolutionary governments all issuing letters of marque, and the line between privateering and outright piracy was indistinguishable. In 1822 a West India Squadron was created, and a year later, Commo. David Porter, the Marines' old friend, was given command. He built a base at mosquito-infested Key West, got the shallow-draft boats he needed for in-shore work and some three hundred marines for expeditionary use. Constrained by orders from the secretary of the Navy which urged harmony with local Spanish officials and cautioned against overzealousness, Porter found it advantageous to operate in concert with the British navy. American courts showed a tendency to release prisoners for lack of evidence. British captains were less squeamish and inclined to hang pirates without judicial ceremony. With sometimes the cooperation, sometimes the opposition of the Spanish governors, Porter's squadron swept the coasts of Santo Domingo, Cuba, and parts of Yucatán. Then, on 14 November 1824, he landed two hundred sailors and marines at Fajardo, Puerto Rico. This went beyond his orders and was an embarrassment to Washington. Porter was recalled and court-martialed. Given six months' suspension, he resigned from the United States' service and went off to be commander in chief of the Mexican navy.

In these years there were other expeditions and actions in more faraway places, against pirates, slavers, and sundry unenlightened heathen. They were of the kind where the after-action report almost invariably concluded with the words "insult to the Flag reveng'd." Some examples follow:

In April 1820, marines on board the *Cyane,* now under the American flag and refitted as a 24-gun sloop, helped in the taking of seven slaving schooners off the coast of West Africa. In the summer and fall of 1827, marines in the sloop *Warren,* 18, and schooner *Porpoise,* 12, searched out pirates in the Greek archipelago. A landing party from the *Lexington,* 18, went ashore in the Falkland Islands on 1 January 1832, impressed the Argentines with a fanfaronade of musketry, and shook loose three impounded American schooners. On the other side of the world, pirates had seized the merchantman *Friendship,* loading pepper in the harbor of Kuala Batu, Sumatra, and had killed several members of the crew. The *Potomac*, 44, put 250 marines and sailors ashore on 7 February 1832, and in two bloody days they killed the local sultan, captured four pirate forts, and burned the town.

At home there were troubles of a different kind. Andrew Jackson was now president. Like many other Army generals and several presidents since, he saw no reason for a separate corps of Marines and, in December 1829, recommended to the Congress "that the Marine Corps be merged in the artillery or infantry, as the best mode of curing the many defects in its organization. . . . Details for Marine service could well be made from the artillery or infantry, there being no peculiar training required for it."

There was serious confusion as to the legal and administrative status of the Corps stemming from the ambiguous nature of the 1798 Act. Was the Corps part of the Army or Navy, or was it something of a unique nature? Hearings were held by both houses of Congress. In 1831 Secretary of the Navy John Branch recommended the "discontinuance of the Marine Corps or its transfer entirely" to either the Army or Navy. There were supporters of the Corps, though, among the public and in the Congress and on 30 June 1834, "An Act for the Better Organization of the Marine Corps" was passed. It established that, afloat or ashore, the Marine Corps was part of the Department of the Navy, a separate service, sister to but not part of the U.S. Navy, but that the president could direct the Marines to perform such duties as his judgment dictated, including service with the Army. (The distinctions made were exceedingly fine and successive Army and Navy generations have not always completely understood them so that they have required constant reassertion.) The Act of 1834 additionally raised the rank of the commandant to colonel and the authorized strength of the Corps to sixty-three officers and 1,224 enlisted (actual strength was a third less). Also in 1834, President Jackson took the marines out of their blue uniforms and put them into a grass-green coat with buff facings and gray trousers.

## SEMINOLE WAR (1836–1842)

Next year there was trouble in Florida. The government had decided to relocate the Seminoles to what is now Arkansas and sent troops to Florida to enforce the move. The Seminoles under their principal chief Osceola, who was half English, half Creek, withdrew to the almost inaccessible depths of the Everglades, and by the spring of 1836, with a thousand soldiers trying to round up three thousand Indians, the Army was in difficulty. The Creek Indians, parent nation to the Seminoles, now elected to go on the warpath in southern Georgia and Alabama. Colonel Henderson volunteered a regiment of Marines and on 21 May 1836 Andrew Jackson, using the authority of the Act of 1834, ordered all available marines to service with the Army.

By stripping down all shore stations, Henderson was able to field half the strength of the Corps in a two-battalion regiment commanded by himself. He left Sergeant Major Triguet behind at Headquarters to do the administration ("He is a respectable old man, and has no other failing than that which too often attends an old soldier"), and the Marine Band to flesh out the guard at the Marine Barracks and Navy Yard.

Lt. Col. Samuel Miller, late of Bladensburg, assembled the 1st Battalion at Fortress Monroe, Virginia, where Henderson joined them, and on 2 June they left in the chartered steamer *Columbus* for Charleston, South Carolina, and then went by "steam car" to Augusta, Georgia. From there it was a thirty-four-day foot march to Columbus, Georgia, where Henderson reported to Maj. Gen. Winfield Scott. The 2d Battalion, formed at New York, arrived a few days later. Scott was planning a careful, deliberate campaign. Jackson, who disliked Scott in any case, grew impatient and replaced him with Maj. Gen. Thomas S. Jesup.

Some of the marines were armed with Samuel Colt's new revolving cylinder rifles, but these proved to have the distressing habit of going off on their own accord, so the marines went back to their muskets. By the end of the summer, the Creeks were on their way to the Oklahoma Territory and attention could be returned to the Seminoles in Florida. Jesup divided his forces into two brigades. Henderson was given command of the 2d Brigade and it included, in addition to his Marine regiment, a battalion of friendly Creeks officered by marines, the 4th Infantry Regiment, an artillery regiment, and some Georgia volunteers. Henderson's brigade pushed the Seminoles back to the Hatchee-Lustee River northeast of Tampa. On 27 January 1837, in a long day's confused fight, the Americans crossed the river. Only one dead Indian and two dead Negroes were counted, but it was a victory, and four days later a Seminole chief, Abraham, offered to parley. The chiefs agreed to move their people to a reservation and a peace treaty was signed on 6 March 1837.

On 22 May, Henderson, thinking the war was over, started back for Washington, leaving behind a two-company battalion of 189 officers and men under the command of Samuel Miller. On 2 June, seven hundred Seminoles waiting at Tampa for transportation were spirited away by a war party headed by Osceola himself, and the war was on again. In September, Osceola asked for a meeting with Jesup. Jesup ignored the truce, arrested Osceola, and had him carried off to Fort Moultrie in South Carolina, where he died in January 1838. By the summer of 1842 the war had worn itself out and the Marine battalion returned north. In addition, some 130 marines had served in the "Mosquito Fleet," a shallow-draft division of the West India Squadron that patrolled the coast and probed the watery reaches of the Everglades. Sixty-one marines had died in six long years. Archibald Henderson was brevetted a brigadier general, the first marine to hold that rank, for his victory at Hatchee-Lustee. As for the Seminoles, there never was a formal treaty, and while some four thousand were moved to Oklahoma, many slipped away and, as every tourist in Florida knows, they are still in the Everglades.

Jackson's grass-green uniform did not outlast the war. The green faded badly in field service; a return to the blue uniform was authorized in 1839, and executed in 1841. The new uniform had a dark blue coat and light blue trousers (with a scarlet stripe down the seam for the officers and NCOs). For dress, there was still a tall leather shako. For undress use, there was a dark blue cloth cap with a patent leather visor. The cap device was a fouled anchor encircled by a wreath done in gold embroidery.

# 5

# *1845–1859*

## To the Halls of the Montezumas

### Filibustering in California

At eight in the evening of 30 October 1845, 1st Lt. Archibald H. Gillespie met secretly with President James K. Polk. Before seeing the president, the thirty-three-year-old Gillespie had been questioned by the secretary of the Navy as to his proficiency in Spanish and told that he was to carry dispatches to California, going by way of Mexico and observing conditions there. He was also to deliver a packet of personal letters to Capt. John C. Frémont, then on his third exploration of the West.

Gillespie, thinly disguised as a Scotch-whisky salesman, sailed to Veracruz, proceeded overland to Mexico City, found the country torn by revolution but anti-Yankee, and formed a low opinion of its soldiery. It was February before he emerged on the West Coast at Mazatlán and reported to the elderly Commo. John D. Sloat, commander of the Pacific Squadron, who sent him on to Honolulu in the 18-gun sloop *Cyane* (namesake of the War of 1812 capture), ostensibly as a merchant bound for China. *Cyane* then doubled back to Monterey, California. Here, on 17 April 1846, Gillespie delivered his memorized dispatches to the American consul. California was already in a state of insurrection, but it appeared the Californians would accept a British protectorate rather than ask for annexation by the United States. The British Pacific Fleet, including the flagship *Collingwood,* was off the California coast and out-gunned the American Pacific Squadron several times over.

First leg in Gillespie's search for Frémont was to go up the Sacramento to Sutter's Fort. There, Gillespie recruited a couple of local Americans as guides and with a total party of five men started north through Indian country. Frémont, who had left St. Louis in June 1845 with sixty mountain men, including the already-legendary Kit Carson, had broken a trail across the Salt

Desert, made a winter crossing of the High Sierras, and since December had been oscillating between Oregon and California, fighting Indians when the need arose and brushing with the Californian authorities.

Gillespie and Frémont met on the banks of the Klamath the night of 9 May 1846. There were, Frémont estimated, about eight hundred Americans in northern California, all good citizens, armed and equipped for service. That night, an Indian raiding party caught them in their blankets and Frémont lost three men before the raiders were beaten off. The next morning, Frémont marched to the nearest Indian village, burned it, killed fourteen or fifteen warriors and perhaps a woman or two, and then headed for the California settlements.

## MEXICAN WAR (1846–1848)

On the very day that Frémont and Gillespie met in Oregon, the battle of Resaca de la Palma had been fought in Texas and a state of war existed between the United States and Mexico. In California, oblivious to these events, Gillespie had been sent ahead by Frémont to Yerba Buena (present-day San Francisco) to get supplies. By the time he got back up to the Sacramento, in mid-June, the Bear Flag had been run up at Sonoma and California declared a republic. A California Battalion was formed, four companies, totaling 224 rifles, with Frémont as commander and Gillespie as his adjutant.

On the coast dispatches as to the official state of war reached Commodore Sloat and on 7 July 1846 the U.S. flag was raised over Monterey. Frémont's assortment of mountain men, traders, horse thieves, Indians, and sailors had by this time assumed the approximate status of a battalion of irregular mounted naval infantry. He reached Monterey on 19 July, where Commo. Robert F. Stockton had replaced the lethargic Sloat. The California Battalion was crowded on board the *Cyane,* sailed for San Diego, and took it without a fight on 29 July. A week later Stockton landed 350 Marines and seamen and marched on Ciudad de los Angeles. Frémont joined him from San Diego and together they chased Gen. José Castro and his army out of town. Stockton then issued a proclamation naming Gillespie Military Commandant of the South and left him with about fifty men to hold the City of the Angels. Gillespie's position was almost immediately invested by an enemy force he generously estimated at six hundred. He elected to march out with full military honors rather than fight, and at the end of September was picked up at San Pedro by the 18-gun sloop-of-war *Vandalia*.

Stockton now made a couple of tries at recapturing Los Angeles with the help of a landing force of some three hundred sailors and marines. These operations were interrupted by news that Brig. Gen. Stephen W. Kearny, USA, with an advance party of his Army of the West, was just east of San Diego. Stockton dispatched Gillespie with a detachment of the California Battalion to find Kearny. He did, and found that Kearny, who had already been met by Kit Carson, had no army with him, but only about a hundred dragoons on worn-out horses.

A fairly good-sized force of Mexicans was at Rancho Santa Margarita (site of present-day Camp Pendleton), and on 6 December 1846 the Battle of San Pascual was fought, American dragoons and riflemen against Californian lancers. Although the Mexicans left the field to the Americans, Kearny had suffered nineteen killed and thirty wounded (including Gillespie and himself) out of a total of 153 Americans. His force too weakened to move, Kearny took up a hilltop position near San Bernardo which was quickly surrounded by the Californians. Kit Carson slipped through the Mexican lines and on 11 December brought back a relief column that included Lt. Jacob Zeilin, who had the Marine detachment in the frigate *Congress*.

When they all got together at San Diego, the combined American strength was about six hundred. With the dual American commanders, Stockton and Kearny, eyeing each other suspiciously, the column started north on 29 December. There was a last fight on 8 January 1847 at the crossing of the San Gabriel, and two days later Stockton reoccupied Los Angeles.

## WITH SCOTT AT VERACRUZ

While these heady events were taking place in California, more conventional operations were being pursued along the rim of the Gulf of Mexico. Having fought and won the battles of Palo Alto and Resaca de la Palma on 8 and 9 May 1846 against the gorgeously uniformed but poorly armed Mexican army, Brig. Gen. Zachary Taylor crossed the Rio Grande into Mexico on 18 May, a historic moment somewhat marred by a Marine landing party's having gone ashore at Burrita on the Mexican side of the river some hours earlier.

The problem facing Commo. David Conner's Gulf Squadron was twofold: the blockade of the Mexican Gulf ports and the support of Taylor's army as it

moved south into Mexico. By combining all the Marine detachments in the squadron, a two-hundred-man provisional battalion was formed under Capt. Alvin Edson. There were raids against Frontera and Tampico in October; Tampico was secured in November; and two unsuccessful attempts were made at taking Alvarado.

By then it had been recognized that no matter what success Taylor might continue to have, it was a long, perhaps impossible, march from the Rio Grande to Mexico City. Accordingly, half his army was detached for service with Maj. Gen. Winfield Scott, who was to land at Veracruz.

Scott landed on 9 March 1847, putting twelve thousand men ashore on an undefended beach some three miles south of the city. Edson's battalion, numbering some 180 marines, went ashore with Maj. Gen. William J. Worth's division. Scott, in coordination with Conner, brought Veracruz under siege. On 21 March Commo. Matthew C. Perry, who had been the naval second in command and acting as what we would now call the amphibious force commander, succeeded Conner in command of the Gulf Squadron. There was a strenuous bombardment of the city, the walls were breached, and Veracruz capitulated on 29 March 1847.

Perry, the younger brother of Oliver Hazard Perry, had had landing force experience before coming to the Gulf when he commanded the Africa Squadron. Under the Webster-Ashburton Treaty the United States had been cooperating with the British in the suppression of the slave trade. In November 1843 Perry had landed with a party of marines and sailors in Liberia to investigate the reported murder of some Americans. Perry got into a scuffle with the native chief, one King Ben Crack-O. A Marine sergeant shot Crack-O. Some other marines pinned the chief to the ground with their bayonets until he could be tied up and carted off. In the general melee that followed, Crack-O's village and several others were burned.

With Veracruz captured, Commodore Perry went back to the neutralization of the remaining Gulf ports. More aggressive and imaginative than Conner, he formed a landing force brigade, about fifteen hundred strong, with Edson's battalion serving as a nucleus. Alvarado was captured on 1 April and Tuxpan on 18 April. This left Frontera, at the mouth of the Tabasco River, the one port of consequence still to be won. Perry put his landing force ashore at Frontera on 15 May 1847. He then sent a column of shallow-draft steamers, gunboats, and barges up the river toward San Juan Bautista. On 14 June, there was a final fight for the town; four hundred Mexican defenders were chased away and twelve guns and six hundred muskets were captured. Perry elected to hold the town until 22 July, when the approach of the yellow fever season made it wise to withdraw.

## ON TO MEXICO CITY

In Washington, Archibald Henderson was set upon repeating his performance in the Seminole wars. On 3 March he had gotten approval from President Polk to form a Marine regiment for service with Scott. The regimental headquarters and 1st Battalion were formed at Fort Hamilton, New York, under command of Lt. Col. Samuel E. Watson, and arrived at Veracruz on 1 July 1847. Captain Edson's marines were supposed to form the 2d Battalion, but Commodore Perry, busy with his Tabasco expedition, was not about to release them, so the regiment had to be reorganized into a single battalion.

Scott had moved out of Veracruz on 8 April. In front of him were three hundred miles, all uphill, to the Mexican capital. Dictator Antonio López de Santa Ana, after being defeated at Buena Vista in February by "Old Rough

and Ready" Taylor, had hurried south and was in good position to stop Scott, all advantages as to terrain, numbers, and logistics being in the defenders' favor. But Scott beat him in a series of battles beginning with Cerro Gordo, and the American army had now paused at Puebla to bring up supplies and reinforcements for the final drive against Mexico City. The Marine battalion arrived at Puebla on 6 August and was brigaded with Brig. Gen. John A. Quitman's division. Lieutenant Colonel Watson, who had served under Scott in the War of 1812, was given command of the 2d Brigade and Maj. Levi Twiggs, also an elderly veteran of the War of 1812, moved up to command of the Marine battalion. Two days later, Scott, with eleven thousand men, cut his lines of communications and marched out of Puebla.

The Mexican army in front of him now numbered thirty-two thousand. A month's hard fighting, in which the Marine battalion did little except protect the baggage trains, brought Scott within assaulting distance of Mexico City. Key to the city was Chapultepec Castle, protecting the two causeways which led to San Cosme and Belen gates. Scott planned to attack the castle with Pillow's division coming against the west face and Quitman's division against the southern face. Major Twiggs was to lead the assault in Quitman's attack, with Capt. John G. Reynolds heading the "pioneer storming party" made up of forty volunteer soldiers and marines. At eight o'clock in the morning, 13 September, following two hours of bombardment, the attack began. Major Twiggs, wearing an India rubber coat and carrying a favorite double-barreled fowling piece, stepped out in front. Immediately behind came Captain Reynolds, his pioneers carrying scaling ladders, pickaxes, and wrecking bars. Unexpected fire from five Mexican guns to their right rear caused them to take cover in a ditch. Quitman told them to hold at that point. Twiggs got tired of waiting, climbed out into the open, and was shot dead by a volley from the castle. Reynolds now urged Watson to get things moving but the old man was waiting for orders from Quitman. Capt. George C. Terrett went off on his own with his company and captured the troublesome battery. Terrett then started across the causeway with sixty-seven men and two sections of Army light artillery. A troop of Mexican lancers clattered out but failed to stop Terrett. He was now providentially joined by 2d Lt. Ulysses S. Grant and twenty-six soldiers from the 4th Infantry. Together they carried the San Cosme Gate.

To their rear both Pillow's and Quitman's divisions had gotten over the walls and into Chapultepec. By nightfall Quitman had taken the Belen Gate.

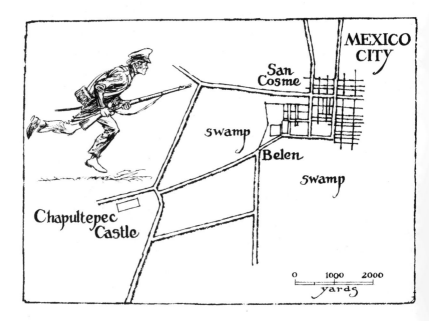

During the night the Mexican army, except for some irregulars, evacuated the city. Quitman marched in the next morning. The marines were given the job of clearing the Palacio Nacional. A Marine lieutenant cut down the Mexican colors and ran up the Stars and Stripes. General Scott ("Old Fuss and Feathers" to distinguish him from "Old Rough and Ready" Taylor), a man of immense girth, heavily climbed the stairs of the "Halls of Montezuma" to write his victory dispatch.

In the West, the conquest of California completed, the Pacific Squadron turned its attention to Mexico's West Coast ports. Mazatlán, Guaymas, Muleje, San Blas, and San José were quickly, and, for the most part, uneventfully, taken. The landing at Mazatlán was on 10 November 1847, the Corps' seventy-second birthday. A force of 730 sailors and marines went ashore, covered by the frigates *Congress* and *Independence* and the ubiquitous *Cyane*. Jacob Zeilin, now a captain, was ensconced in the Presidio as military governor, where he remained until 17 June 1848.

By that time, the Marine battalion from Scott's army had returned to the capital. The citizens of Washington gave the commandant a new set of colors emblazoned with a new motto: "From Tripoli to the Halls of the Montezumas."

## PANAMA, JAPAN, CHINA, AND ELSEWHERE

Gold was discovered near Sutter's Fort in January 1848. There were three routes to California: across the plains, around Cape Horn, or, quickest of all, across the Isthmus of Panama. In 1846 the United States had concluded a treaty with New Grenada (now Colombia) giving the United States "the right of way or transit across the Isthmus of Panama upon any modes of communication that now exist or that may be hereafter constructed."

In 1855, after seven years' work and a high death rate from fever, the American-owned Panama Railroad was opened across the narrow neck. To protect it, Marines made landings at Panama City in 1856 and again in 1860. In neighboring Nicaragua there had been three landings in the years 1852 to 1854, the last on 12 July 1854 when Greytown was bombarded and burned.

Much farther south, landings were made at Montevideo, Uruguay, in November 1855 and January 1858, the second landing being in company with the British, John Reynolds, now a brevet major, leading the U.S. Marines. That same year, three hundred marines, the combined detachments of the Brazil Squadron, went up the Paraná River to Asunción, Paraguay, in a show of force.

In July 1853 Commo. Matthew Perry took the East India Squadron on its historic visit to Japan, stopping en route at Okinawa and in the Bonins. In the squadron, now-major Jacob Zeilin had six officers and two hundred enlisted marines. You can see them in contemporary Japanese woodprints: blue jackets, white trousers and crossbelts, and tall black shakos. There was a second, even more elaborate, visit in February 1854. On 31 March the first treaty between Japan and the United States was concluded; two ports, Shimoda and Hakodate, were opened to trade. The modernization of Japan had begun.

China was in the grip of the Taiping Rebellion. The East India Squadron was based at Hong Kong. On 4 April 1854 the sloop *Plymouth* put her sergeant's guard ashore in company with Royal Marines to protect foreign concessions at Shanghai. The performance was repeated by the steam frigate *Powhattan* on 19 May 1855, and on 4 August marines from the *Powhattan* again joined the British, this time in an action against a pirate base near Hong Kong.

Canton was a treaty port and in the fall of 1856 there was trouble. The main contestants were the British and French against the Cantonese, but a small Marine guard had been put into the city to look after U.S. interests (consuls, missionaries, and traders). About the time that Capt. Andrew H. Foote, commanding the sloop *Portsmouth,* accepted the Cantonese governor's assurances of protection and agreed to withdraw the landing party, his boats were fired upon by the so-called "Barrier Forts." There were four of these forts in the Pearl River, European-engineered and armed with a profusion of heavy guns behind seven-foot breastworks faced with granite. On 16 November 1856 the East India, or Asiatic, Squadron, moved against the offending forts with the steam frigate *San Jacinto* and the two sloops *Portsmouth* and *Levant.* On the twentieth, Captain Foote went ashore at the head of 287 sailors and marines (the marines being under command of Capt. John D. Simms, who had been among those present at Chapultepec). The first fort was taken from the rear, the remaining three systematically reduced. Some 170 cannon were captured—up to 8- and 10-inch caliber—and either spiked or rolled into the river. Of the five thousand (by U.S. estimate) Chinese defenders, at least 250 and perhaps five hundred were dead. American losses were seven killed and twenty wounded.

In these years the Home Squadron cruised from Newfoundland to the mouth of the Amazon, with special attention given the Caribbean. Cuba was in revolt and part of the Squadron's mission was enforcing U.S. neutrality.

The Mediterranean Squadron had had a quiet time since the affairs with the Barbary pirates. The Africa Squadron continued its anti-slave trade patrols. The remaining squadron, the Pacific Squadron, usually based at Valparaiso, had a wide expanse of water to cruise. There were punitive landings in the Fiji Islands in 1855 and 1858. The sloop-of-war *Decatur* was kept on station at the village of Seattle in the Oregon Territory to keep the Puget Indians in check, and one sharp action occurred there on 26 January 1856. Duties afloat had not changed much since the days of the Continental navy. There were still landing parties, still sharpshooters in the fighting tops, still practice at repelling boarders, but internal discipline was easier. There were new uniform regulations in 1859. The dress uniform had a French-style shako with a pompom which was not popular; but the rakish fatigue cap, copied after the French képi, would stay in style for fifty years.

Archibald Henderson died in office on 6 January 1859 at age seventy-six, having been commandant for thirty-nine years. The next senior officer, Lt. Col. John Harris, was named colonel commandant. In his forty-five years of service Harris had seen three wars and he was already sixty-six years old.

# 6

## 1859-1865
### This Negro Question

On a Sunday night, 16 October 1859, a man with a long gray beard and a fierce eye who called himself Isaac Smith came into Harpers Ferry, where the Shenandoah joins the Potomac, with some eighteen armed men, white and black. They took possession of the U.S. Arsenal—no soldiers were in garrison there—and rounded up a number of hostages. By now "Smith" had been recognized as the abolitionist John Brown, last heard from in Bloody Kansas. The local militia came gingerly onto the scene, there was some shooting, and Brown took his men and hostages into a brick building on the arsenal grounds where the fire engines were kept.

In Washington, after the first confused reports came clacking in by telegraph, the secretary of War ordered Lt. Col. Robert E. Lee, who was at Arlington (home on leave from Texas), to put down the insurrection. A cavalry lieutenant, J.E.B. (Jeb) Stuart by name, volunteered to go along as his aide. They left that afternoon for Harpers Ferry on the five o'clock train.

There were no Federal soldiers immediately available, but a detachment of eighty-six marines from the Washington Barracks had already gone forward under Lt. Israel Greene, their officer of the day, who had orders to report to the senior Army officer present. By ten o'clock Lee and Stuart had joined up with them. They marched together onto the Arsenal grounds and relieved the militia, who showed no disposition to close with the fanatic in the firehouse. At daybreak, Lee told Greene to form two storming parties and have them ready. Stuart was sent forward with a note demanding surrender. There was to be no parley. If the answer from Brown was no, Stuart was to wave his hat and get out of the way, and Greene and his men would go forward.

That's the way it worked out. Jeb Stuart waved his plumed hat, of a kind that would later become famous, and the marines went forward in two squads of twelve men each: blue frockcoats, sky-blue trousers, and white crossbelts. They hammered at the double doors of the engine house with sledges, made no impression; they found a ladder and used it as a battering ram. Greene led the way through the opened door. The second and third marines behind him were hit. Greene saw a bearded man down on one knee reloading his carbine. Greene slashed down on him with his sword, cut him deep in the neck, then bent his sword double in a thrust that caught on a leather strap. The wounded Brown was hauled out on the grass and put on a mattress, his men all dead or captured, and the hostages freed.

Next day Brown talked to his captors: "You may dispose of me very easily. I am very nearly disposed of now; but this question is still to be settled—this Negro question, I mean. The end is not yet."

## THE UNION DIVIDES

Lincoln was elected president on 6 November 1860. On 20 December, the South Carolina legislature voted unanimously to take South Carolina out of the Union. Outgoing President James Buchanan took some hesitant, fumbling steps to preserve the Union. On 5 January, forty marines were sent down the Potomac to man the moldering ruins of Fort Washington, across from Mount Vernon. Another thirty were dispatched to Baltimore to garrison Fort McHenry. In Florida, several hundred Alabama militia marched against the Pensacola Navy Yard. It fell without opposition on 16 January, the Marine detachment accepting a parole.

On 1 January 1861 the strength of the Marine Corps had stood at 1,892 officers and men. Half the captains in the Corps and two-thirds of the lieutenants resigned to take commissions under the Confederacy. Among those who went South were some of the best, including Terrett of Mexico City, Simms of the Barrier Forts, and Greene of Harpers Ferry. John Harris himself wavered—to the extent of giving a letter of recommendation to an officer going South. All the field-grade officers stood firm (or perhaps, considering their age, infirm), except Maj. Henry B. Tyler, the adjutant and inspector, who, with his second lieutenant son, joined the Rebellion. Lincoln, inaugurated 4 March, put an abrupt end to the resignations. Officers so requesting found their names stricken from the list and themselves summarily dismissed.

Enlisted marines did not enjoy the privilege of resigning to go South. Most had been recruited in the larger seaports of the Northeast, and many were Irish or German immigrants. It is not likely that any significant number were Southern sympathizers. Some few may have deserted to join the Confederacy.

When Maj. Gen. Irving McDowell's 35,000-man half-trained army of volunteers moved out of Washington on 16 July 1861, there was in the line of march a hastily-put-together Marine battalion of thirteen officers and 336 men, mostly recruits. Hard-fighting, sometimes hard-drinking Maj. John Reynolds was in command. Maj. Jacob Zeilin had a company.

On 21 July, the Union right wing, in the opening moves of the First Battle of Manassas, crossed Bull Run at Sudley Springs and turned left against the Confederate flank. Reynolds's battalion was ordered to support Capt. Charles

Griffin's West Point Battery, a Regular Army unit. Griffin lost one gun but got five to the top of Henry House Hill, where he was joined by another battery of six guns. On the right of the two Union batteries, a blue-clad regiment emerged from the woods. The blue line was almost onto the guns before the regiment was recognized as the 33d Virginia. About this time, Jeb Stuart, now a colonel of the Virginia cavalry, came riding out of the woods. The guns were lost, then recaptured. Three times the Marine battalion threatened to break, with Reynolds holding them together. Then the whole Union line began to waver. At first the disengagement was handled in good order, then it gained momentum. There was a disorganized retreat back to Washington. A grim-faced Reynolds posted himself at the Long Bridge leading over the Potomac, sorted out his marines from the formless blue column, and marched them back to the barracks. The Marine battalion had taken forty-four casualties. Among the seriously wounded was Jacob Zeilin. Colonel Commandant Harris reported sadly to Secretary of the Navy Gideon Welles that this was "the first instance in Marine history where any portion of its members turned their backs to the enemy."

## WITH THE BLOCKADERS

After that, things got better. On 28 August 1861, 250 marines and soldiers, landing in surfboats, took Fort Clark on the eastern side of Hatteras Inlet and three days later took Fort Hatteras on the other side of the inlet. These forts were held by the Union for the remainder of the war and gave a foothold for further operations against the Carolina coastline.

Flag Officer Samuel F. DuPont, who had the South Atlantic Blockading Squadron, saw the need for a special landing force separate from the ships' Marine detachments. Major Reynolds joined him with a three-hundred-man battalion. It was to spearhead the landing of thirteen thousand Army troops at Port Royal, South Carolina. Unfortunately, for transport, the Marines were given the *Governor,* a fragile, side-wheeler river steamer. In the rough weather off Hatteras the *Governor* began to break up. Before she went down on 3 November 1861, there was a successful transfer of the battalion to the steam frigate *Sabine;* only seven marines were lost, but the delay made the battalion miss the assault.

Reynolds's battalion continued to serve with DuPont's squadron, pecking around at the Carolinas and Georgia in a minor way, until it was landed against Saint Augustine, Florida, in March 1862. There was no fight, Saint Augustine had been abandoned, and DuPont reluctantly decided there was no further mission for Reynolds's battalion and returned it to Washington.

The restive Reynolds, now a lieutenant colonel, managed to get into trouble with the lethargic Harris. Gideon Welles confided to his diary that "almost all the elder officers of the Marine Corps are at loggerheads and should be retired." In May 1862 Harris brought Reynolds up before a court-martial on charges of drunkenness and contempt for a superior officer. The court acquitted Reynolds, who immediately retaliated by preferring charges against Harris. Gideon Welles cut short the business of charge and counter-charge by issuing a letter of reproof to both Harris and Reynolds.

Flag Officer David G. Farragut, with the Western Gulf Blockading Squadron, had meanwhile forced the mouth of the Mississippi and had proceeded against New Orleans. The three hundred marines in the squadron were formed into a four-company battalion under command of Capt. John L. Broome. On 29 April 1862 they went ashore at New Orleans, ran up the Union flag over the customhouse and city hall, and held the city until the Army arrived two days later.

The sea gates to Charleston, South Carolina, were defended by nine major works, including Fort Sumter. There was a joint attack in July 1863, the naval forces under Rear Adm. John A. Dahlgren, the gun expert. This failed. In August, Major Zeilin was sent down with a fresh battalion of three hundred marines. It was inflated into a regiment and training in landing operations began. Zeilin was dissatisfied with what he had to work with, and he was sick besides. He was replaced by Reynolds, who reduced the regiment back to a battalion and turned it over to Capt. Charles G. McCawley. Fort Wagner, pounded to rubble by naval gunfire, was taken by the Army on 7 September 1863. This was to be followed next day by a Marine assault against Fort Sumter. It was to be a night landing to be made from strings of small boats towed inshore by tugs. Control was bad and the boats went off in every direction. Only 150 marines and sailors landed on the proper beach and these were beaten back by Rebel rifle fire, the Marines taking forty-four casualties. After this fiasco, the Marine battalion went into camp on Folly Island where they endured much sickness. They continued under these unhappy circumstances until early 1864, when the battalion was finally broken up and its pieces parceled out to other duties.

## WITH LINCOLN AT GETTYSBURG

Gideon Welles was asked if the Marine Band could play at the dedication of the new National Cemetery at Gettysburg on 19 November 1863. Welles passed the request to Harris, who issued the necessary orders to the Marine Barracks commander. Second Lt. Henry Clay Cochrane was detailed to go along. The band would be going on the same train as the president. Young Lieutenant Cochrane, barely twenty-one, found himself seated face-to-face with Lincoln. He offered the president the New York *Herald* to read. The news that morning was not particularly good, being about Burnside at Knoxville, Sherman at Chattanooga, and Meade on the Rapidan, but Lincoln found something in the paper that made him laugh heartily. When they changed trains at Baltimore, the president went out on the platform, scooping up two or three babies and kissing them in best politician fashion. The Marine Band, twenty-seven pieces, emerged and played a number of rousing selections.

Lunch was served from a baggage car that had been joined to the train at Baltimore. Lincoln swapped stories with a circle of politicians and high-ranking officers for about an hour and then Cochrane heard him say: "Gentlemen, this is all very pleasant, but the people will expect me to say something to them tomorrow, and I must give the matter some thought."

Next morning, in the procession to the cemetery, Mr. Lincoln rode a beautiful chestnut bay. Cochrane, following in the second rank, had trouble keeping his brute of a horse from nibbling at the tail of the president's mount. Cochrane was surprised, and a little subdued, to see how much evidence of the great battle fought there in July still remained: "Rifle pits, cut and scarred trees, broken fences, pieces of artillery wagons and harness, scraps of blue and gray clothing, bent canteens, abandoned knapsacks, belts, cartridge boxes, shoes, and caps, were still to be seen on nearly every side."

The Marine Band played "Old Hundred," a favorite hymn of the time. When it was Lincoln's turn to speak, he fished a piece or two of paper out of his pocket (some say out of his hat), put on his steel-bowed glasses, and stood up. Cochrane's recollection was that "He began in a slow, solemn and deliberate manner, emphasizing nearly every word, and in two minutes sat down."

## A New Commandant

On 12 May 1864, Col. Cmdt. John Harris died, old and worn-out by wartime demands that exceeded his capabilities. Gideon Welles attended Harris's funeral, then confided to his diary: "His death gives embarrassment as to a successor." A month passed while Welles wrestled with the problem; then on 9 June, he pithily observed in his diary: "Concluded to retire the Marine officers who are past legal age, and to bring in Zeilin as Commandant of the Corps. There seems no alternative." Major Zeilin was then serving, remote from the war, as commanding officer of the Marine Barracks at Portsmouth, New Hampshire. Next day, President Lincoln named him the seventh commandant of the Marine Corps.

## Confederate Marines

On the other side of the lines, the Confederacy's seagoing navy was limited by geography and resources to blockade runners and raiders. There was no great role to be played by the Confederate States Marine Corps. The Confederate Congress on 20 May 1861 had authorized a marine corps of ten companies. The colonel commandant was Lloyd J. Beall. He did his best with a near-impossible situation. One of his last reports is dated 30 October 1864:

> By this return it will be seen that the aggregate strength of the Corps amounts to 539. Of this number, 2 captains, 3 lieutenants, and 62 enlisted men are prisoners of war in the hands of the enemy.
>
> Not included in this return are 32 recruits received at the naval station, Charleston, from the conscript camp near Raleigh, N.C.
>
> The Marine Corps is distributed at the following naval stations: Mobile, Savannah, Charleston, Wilmington, and on Drewry's Bluff; also on board the three ironclad steamers in the James River, and as guards at the Richmond Navy Yards. Marine Guards have been assigned to the armed steamers *Tallahassee* and *Chickamauga*, destined to operate against the enemy's commerce at sea.
>
> Since my last report the Marines have been under the enemy's fire at Drewry's Bluff near Richmond and on the James River; also in the naval and land engagements near Mobile on the 5th and 6th of August last. A Marine guard under Lt. Crenshaw was attached to the Confederate steamship *Tallahassee* during the late cruise, when much damage was inflicted upon the enemy's shipping at sea.

Upon all occasions when the Marines have been called upon for active service they have displayed the promptness and efficiency of well-disciplined soldiers.

There had been a long-standing order in England for parchment commissions, suitably engraved. These finally arrived by blockade runner in November 1864. By that time engraved commissions were the least of the Confederacy's needs.

## FORT FISHER

By the end of 1864, the only Atlantic port remaining reasonably open to Confederate blockade runners was Wilmington, North Carolina, defended at Cape Fear by the formidable Fort Fisher. The assault of Fort Fisher turned into a curious affair, fought twice because the Federals tried once, failed, and then tried again. Landing force commander for the first attack was the Massachusetts politician Maj. Gen. Benjamin F. Butler, who had an amateur's notion that if an explosive-filled ship were moved close inshore and then blown up, the earthen walls of the fort would tumble down. This was tried on 24 December 1864. It didn't work and next day, Christmas, while Rear Adm. David Dixon Porter's big guns pounded the fort, Butler with three thousand men went ashore north of the main work, made a hesitant approach, observed a mine field with alarm, and after two days' fumbling, gave up and went back aboard ship.

Command of the expedition now passed to the more resolute Maj. Gen. Alfred H. Terry. Porter promised him two days' bombardment with a total weight of six hundred guns, followed by an attack against the seaward face of the fort. Meantime, Terry, his force now up to a strength of eighty-five hundred, was to come in from the land side.

The assault was executed on 15 January 1865. The marines of Porter's squadron, about four hundred of them, organized into a provisional battalion, were to land, dig in, and then cover with rifle fire the sixteen hundred sailors who were to "board" Fort Fisher with cutlass and pistol. This harebrained plan of attack went all wrong. The sailors were shot to pieces before the marines could get into position, but, even badly executed, the diversion served its purpose. Terry's soldiers got through the mine field and over the breastworks and the fort was taken before the day was done.

The Navy was quick to blame the failure of its assault on the Marines. If the time spent in charges and countercharges had been used instead for careful analysis, Fort Fisher might have yielded all the lessons, negative and positive, required as a basis for a modern amphibious doctrine. The requirement for a single, not divided, command; the folly of last-minute "provisional" landing-force organizations; the need for adequate ship-to-shore communications; and the value of naval gunfire, properly applied, were all demonstrated, if the quarreling participants had only taken time to look at them.

Within months of Fort Fisher, the United States' worst war was over. The Corps had expanded modestly to a peak strength of 4,167 officers and men, and had lost 148 killed and 312 dead of other causes. Seventeen marines had received the Medal of Honor. All of them were enlisted because at that time officers were not eligible for the medal. Officers still received brevet promotions, sometimes very generous, for gallantry in action. The first marine to receive the Medal of Honor was Cpl. John F. Mackie of New York City and that was for actions on board the ironclad *Galena* in the Battle of Drewry's Bluff (there were some Confederate marines on the bluff) eight miles below Richmond on the James River on 15 May 1862. A 10-inch Confederate shell swept away the Navy gun crew from the *Galena*'s after battery. Corporal Mackie with twelve marines cleared away the casualties and wreckage and put the guns back in action. About half of the marines who received the Medal of Honor during the Civil War were foreign born and that was probably about the percentage of foreign born serving in the Corps.

During the war there had been grave moments and the glimmerings of proper amphibious usage, but overall the Corps had gained little in the way of reputation. In 1864, there was a Congressional resolution introduced to transfer the Marine Corps to the Army. After debate, the resolution was tabled, but the thought did not go away.

# 7

## 1865-1898

### As a Separate Corps Be Preserved

#### The Gilded Age

The next thirty years, from the close of the Civil War until the Spanish-American War, was a time of shrinking strength, an aging officer corps, and a questioning of the Corps' status and future useful purpose. The Navy was in a slow, sometimes reluctant, transition from sail to steam. The traditional duties of seagoing marines seemed questionable in the new iron ships. The need for the seizure and defense of advance bases was only dimly foreseen. The state of the amphibious art stayed at the level of ships' landing parties and provisional battalions. These improvisations were good enough for the landings that had to be made "to protect American lives and property": China (1866, 1894, 1895), Formosa (1867), Japan (1867, 1868), Nicaragua (1867, 1894, 1896, 1898), Uruguay (1868), Mexico (1870, 1876), Korea (1871, 1888, 1894), Panama (1873, 1885), Hawaii (1874, 1889, 1893), Egypt (1882), Haiti (1888, 1891), Samoa (1888), Argentina (1890), Chile (1891), and Colombia (1895).

Sometime during this period, the archetypal war correspondent Richard Harding Davis coined the much-used phrase: "The Marines have landed and have the situation well in hand." Internally the marines also had their uses in the sometimes strident political and labor unrest in the cities. They were called out on occasion for riots and affrays in Baltimore, Boston, Philadelphia, and New York.

The new commandant, Jacob Zeilin, was another Philadelphian, born there in 1806, and with his square-cut beard and clean upper lip he looked like a Pennsylvania Dutch farmer. On 18 June 1866, with the Civil War over only a year, the House of Representatives directed its Committee on Naval Affairs to consider abolishing the Marine Corps and transferring its functions to the Army. The committee listened to a long line of witnesses and on 21 February 1867 reported:

> . . . no good reason appears either for abolishing it, the Marine Corps, or transferring it to the Army; on the contrary, the Committee recommends that its organization as a separate Corps be preserved and strengthened.

For good measure, Zeilin was promoted to brigadier general. He now set about quietly to strengthen the fabric and institutions of the Corps. In 1867 he adopted the Army's new system of infantry tactics, developed by Maj. Gen. Emory Upton, USA, and approved for the Army by a board headed by Ulysses S. Grant. All that a lieutenant or brigadier general needed to know about infantry tactics, even the startling effects of the new breech-loading rifles, had been reduced to a little blue-bound book that could be carried in a tunic pocket.

It was about this time that "The Marines' Hymn" was first being heard. Curiously, not much is known about its origins. Apparently not able to rhyme "Montezuma," the unknown poet inverted his chronology and came out with the familiar, "From the Halls of Montezuma to the Shores of Tripoli." The verse has an easy meter and can be fitted to many tunes. The melody which was used, and which has become world-famous, is unmistakably the same as a marching song in Offenbach's operetta *Geneviève de Brabant.*

On 19 November 1868, the Marine Corps emblem in essentially its present form was adopted. There was borrowing from the Royal Marines in that the globe (Western hemisphere, to be sure) was used as the center of the device. A fouled anchor was put behind it and an American bald eagle perched on top. Next year, 1869, the Corps adopted a blue-black shell jacket and trousers, both liberally encrusted with gold braid, as officers' evening dress. The uniform survives today, almost unchanged, except for slightly less ornamentation.

## KOREA (1871)

On 30 May 1871, Rear Adm. John Rodgers with five ships of the Asiatic Squadron was attempting to convey the American minister to Seoul when the defenders of the Hermit Kingdom had the bad manners to fire upon him from the forts guarding the Han River approaches. Rodgers put a landing force ashore on 10 June 1871. A two-company Marine "battalion" under Capt.

McLane Tilton was out in front. Tilton had been on the board that in 1869 had adopted the Remington .50-caliber "rolling-block" breech-loader for Navy use, and he was unhappy about going ashore with "muzzle fuzzels" as he called the .58-caliber muzzle-loading rifled muskets which were the standard Civil War arm. Muzzle fuzzels or not, the marines got ashore, four officers and 105 men, and across the mud. An improvised brigade of bluejackets followed the marines, the forts were carried, and when the day was done 481 cannon (numerous but antique) had been captured, along with forty or fifty impressively large battle standards. The landing force had only eleven casualties, two of them marines, and counted 243 Korean dead. Six marines received Medals of Honor. In those days this was the only medal for gallantry in action and it was rather freely given to enlisted men. Officers' valor was still recognized by brevet promotions.

## CAPTAIN FORNEY'S YEAR IN EUROPE

As part of the reexamination of the Marine Corps, Secretary of the Navy George M. Robeson sent Bvt. Lt. Col. James Forney (actual rank captain) to Europe in 1872 to do a survey of foreign marine corps. Gone for a year, Forney came back with a 421-page report, written in careful copperplate script, plus attachments. Among the attachments were photographs and water colors of the uniforms he had seen. Forney, in particular, found much to admire in Britain's Royal Marines. They had a depot at Deal where all new recruits were trained and drilled. Headquarters was at Eastney. Six thousand Royal marines were afloat, eight thousand ashore. Those ashore included both light infantry and artillery. Their uniforms, red for the infantry and blue for the artillery, were handsome.

He made a point that Royal Marine officers got paid in their brevet rank. Forney was sensitive on the subject. He had received three brevet promotions: one for serving in the screw sloop *Brooklyn* in the capture of New Orleans in 1862, another for taking a landing party ashore in Formosa in 1867 in a punitive raid against pirates, and the third, retroactively in 1870, for bringing down a battalion from Philadelphia in 1864 to help repel Jubal Early's raid against Washington. No pay came with it and little privilege other than being addressed informally by brevet rank.

The new imperial German marine corps came in next to the British in

Forney's estimation. He noted the German marines were "armed with the needle gun" and wore a uniform "of dark blue, greatly resembling ours." And he thought the three thousand U.S. marines should be organized into a three-regiment brigade, much like the Germans, with the companies and regiments being given permanent numbers.

He was less impressed by the marines or naval infantry of France, Spain, Portugal, Turkey, and Italy. In all the services visited he noted that great attention was paid to musketry "and continual exercise at target practice." U.S. marines, he wrote, "seldom understand the weapon they carry, and are consequently nervous in using it at even simple funeral services."

Officers for the U.S. Marine Corps, Forney suggested, "should be instructed at West Point" and appointments should no longer be made from civil life. While he still had pen in hand, he recommended that the "old Corps sword with the steel scabbard, be restored to the officers, as a distinctive badge of the Marine Corps." He was referring, of course, to the sword patterned on the Mameluke saber adopted in 1826 and then dropped in 1859 in favor of the heavier, more businesslike U.S. Army's infantry officer's saber.

Forney would retire in 1904 in the grade of brigadier general and would live until 1921, time enough for him to see most of his "suggestions" woven into the warp and woof of the Marine Corps. As was said before, the Mameluke sword came back in 1875 for officers, with the Army foot officer's saber continuing as the Marine NCO sword. A new set of uniform regulations came out that same year. The French influence continued strong despite the disastrous Franco-Prussian War, but there were British and German touches, coming, no doubt, from Forney's report. The undress uniform got a shorter jacket and the képi-style forage cap was a little flatter. The full-dress shako was shortened. For a time, company grade officers were supposed to wear an English model "pillbox" or "round cap" for fatigue duty but it was never popular. The leather stocks which had been on the uniform list for a hundred years now disappeared forever.

## ZEILIN RETIRES, McCAWLEY COMES IN

In 1874 there was another Congressional crisis as to the future of the Corps. Once again the Corps survived, although the new act did require that the rank of the commandant be reduced to colonel on Zeilin's retirement. As the next senior marine, Charles Grymes McCawley was his obvious successor, and Zeilin in 1871 had brought him to Washington for duty with that in mind. McCawley, the son of a Marine captain, was another Philadelphian, born there in 1827. He had been commissioned in 1847, barely in time to join Watson's regiment as it sailed for Veracruz, and was brevetted a first lieutenant for Chapultepec and a major for the aborted assault on Fort Sumter.

Having provided for his orderly succession, Brig. Gen. Jacob Zeilin, age seventy and with forty-five years' service, retired voluntarily on 1 November 1876. Colonel McCawley, white-haired, mustached, and of impressive girth, was a methodical man. Before assuming office he had prepared a series of careful memoranda on his objectives and intentions. Most of these centered on higher enlistment standards, better training, better officer selection and instruction, enforcement of uniform regulations, standard tables of organization, and regularizing of staff and command procedures. It was under McCawley that the ubiquitous typewriter entered the service.

Until now Marine officers had been drawn by direct appointment from civilian life. In 1882 McCawley succeeded in getting a quota of graduates from the Naval Academy assigned to the Marine Corps. This would be the sole source of Marine officers until the Spanish-American War. (An exception was the direct appointment, in a bit of posthumous nepotism, of his son, Charles L. McCawley, in 1897 as a captain and assistant quartermaster.) Fifty officers came in from the Academy during those years, including five future commandants—Barnett, Lejeune, Neville, Fuller, and Russell—and thirteen other generals.

Colonel McCawley succeeded in getting a clothing factory for Marine uniforms started in Philadelphia. It would survive until gobbled up in the McNamara consolidations of the 1960s. McCawley did not tinker much with the uniform regulations themselves, except to authorize in 1880 a cork sun helmet, covered with white duck and complete with a detachable Prussian-style spike and brass chin strap. Two years later a less fortunate winter service version in black was adopted. Never popular, it was poor on board ship for the same reasons that the tar-bucket shakos of the first half of the nineteenth century had been awkward and disliked.

## MUSIC AND MOTTOES

On 9 June 1868, John Philip Sousa was enlisted in the Marine Corps as a music boy. His enlistment contract shows him to be "13 years 6 months 3 days of age" and the term of enlistment was for "7 years 5 months 27 days." His father, Antonio Sousa, worked at the Marine Barracks, Washington, as a carpenter and sometime member of the Marine Band. The boy, who was musical, had shown an inclination to run off and join a circus, so his father had marched him over to the barracks and signed him up.

At twenty-one, having served out his enlistment, John Philip Sousa left the Corps for the civilian world of music. By 1880 the Marine Band was in the doldrums. The leader was dismissed as "unfit for the Service," and Sousa, with a little prodding of the commandant by his father, was appointed band leader with a stipend of ninety-four dollars a month. The prolific and inventive Sousa then proceeded to turn out marches, change instrumentation, recruit musicians, and perform with increasing aplomb and virtuosity that commanded first national and then international attention.

Of Sousa's many marches, none is more stirring than "Semper Fidelis," the only march officially authorized for a service by the Congress and habitually used by the Marines for the march-past in parades and reviews. *Semper Fidelis* had been adopted as the Corps motto in 1883, succeeding the various other tentative mottoes, including *Fortitudine,* used in the early 1800s, and a most blatant borrowing from the Royal Marines in 1876 of *Per Mare, Per Terram,* sometimes used in its English form, "By Sea and by Land." The new motto (not completely unique, it is shared with the Devonshire Regiment) was put on a ribbon placed in the beak of the eagle on the Marine Corps emblem and thus, firmly fixed, it has endured.

There is a tradition that the Marine Band may not leave the capital without presidential permission. In 1891 Sousa asked President Benjamin Harrison if he could take the band on tour. Permission was granted and the tour was a great success; so much so that Sousa could not resist the blandishments of the commercial theater and he left the Marine Corps on 30 July 1892 to go on to become the international March King.

## AT ALEXANDRIA, PANAMA, AND THE BERING SEA

In 1882 the combined British and French protectorate of the Khedive in Egypt was threatened by the nationalist Arabi Pasha. The British Mediterranean Fleet converged on Alexandria in June, and the microscopic U.S. European Squadron, three ships with the flag in the screw sloop *Lancaster,* went along. On 11 July the British bombarded the city. The Americans put a landing party ashore on the fourteenth under command of Marine Capt. Henry Clay Cochrane, who, it will be remembered, had attached himself to Lincoln at Gettysburg. Cochrane announced that his landing party would "stick by the British and take their chances." The risk was not all that great. By that time the British had four thousand troops, including 450 Royal Marines, ashore. Among the American marines was a new second lieutenant, a Virginian named, somewhat redundantly, Littleton Waller Tazewell Waller, who would bear watching.

In 1884 the Marines got a new rifle, the celebrated Springfield .45-70 single-shot breech-loader (a few were still extant in 1942 and used for bayonet training at Quantico), and a year later in Panama there was an opportunity to try it out. French efforts to build a canal across the Isthmus had collapsed. The Colombian government had withdrawn its troops to combat revolution elsewhere. USS *Alliance*, a rebuilt wooden gunboat, arrived on the Atlantic side on 18 January 1885 and put its Marine detachment ashore to guard the property of the American-owned Panama Railroad. By March a loose coalition of rebels controlled the railroad right-of-way and the cities of Panama and Colón. Another gunboat, the *Galena*, took station off Colón, a good portion of which was burning, and landed its marines under 2d Lt. Charles A. Doyen to guard the U.S. consulate.

On the first of April, Colonel McCawley telegraphed Lt. Col. Charles Heywood at Brooklyn Navy Yard to have 250 marines ready for service in Panama in twenty-four hours. Heywood, a native of Maine, had been commissioned in the Corps in 1858 and in the Civil War had made his reputation at the captures of Forts Clark and Hatteras and at sea with Farragut. He sailed for Panama with a battalion on 3 April. Four days later, a second battalion of marines and one of bluejackets left New York.

Meanwhile, the Gulf Squadron had converged on Panama and its marines landed in a provisional battalion. Heywood arrived on 11 April, crossed the Isthmus with his brigade, securing the railroad as he went, and established himself at Panama City on the Pacific side. By the thirtieth, Colombian troops were back and policing the city. The Marines began to thin out their forces and on 25 May the last of the brigade embarked for home. The success established the pattern for interventions in the Caribbean and Central America for the next half century.

## HEYWOOD REPLACES MCCAWLEY

Colonel McCawley retired on 29 January 1891 and Charles Heywood became the colonel commandant the next day. Despite McCawley's best efforts, the Marine Corps was stagnant. Promotions were glacially slow. The Military Retirement Act of 1885 had nudged only a few of the officers of Civil War vintage into retirement. Heywood instituted fitness reports and promotion examinations.

In 1889 Capt. Daniel Pratt Mannix, having just come off sea duty, arrived at Marine Corps headquarters and was assigned as commanding officer, Marine Barracks, Washington. Mannix sat, as the Marine Corps representative and not always well received, on the Greer Board, named for Commo. James A. Greer, which was examining organization and tactics, including landing operations, for the new steel Navy. Not all Navy officers thought marines on board ship served much purpose.

Mannix had come into the Marine Corps at the end of the Civil War, had graduated from the Navy's torpedo school and the Army's artillery school, and had been an instructor with the Chinese navy from 1881 to 1885. To bring the Marine Corps up to speed in the new technology, such as manning the secondary batteries, Mannix recommended first to McCawley and later to Heywood that the Marines organize a school of application for both officers and men. He envisioned a two-hundred-man school battalion that could also double as expeditionary troops.

In May 1891 Heywood received the secretary of the Navy's approval to create a School of Application at headquarters. Mannix, in addition to command of the barracks, was to command the school and be its director of instruction. There were to be two divisions: officer and enlisted. Heywood encouraged his major Marine shore commanders to set up similar schools.

The first class of the officer division formed on 1 September 1891 with seven new second lieutenants, freshly graduated from the Naval Academy. (One of them was Ben Fuller, a future commandant.) The second officer class (with Wendell Neville, another future commandant) and the first enlisted class (with sixty marines) convened a year later. The classes had a new machine gun and a new Hotchkiss revolving 37-mm gun to practice with. The standard text was still Upton's *Tactics*. The Corps' older officers, who regarded themselves as "practical" men, were skeptical of these academic affectations.

The Marines had provided some gun crews to the ironclads and wooden ships of the Civil War; Heywood argued that the Marines should man the secondary batteries of the new steel battleships and cruisers. A considerable segment of young Navy officers, headed by Lt. (later Rear Adm.) William F. Fullam, thought that the day for shipboard duties for Marines had passed, although Fullam did see a use for Marines as expeditionary troops. The Marines saw Fullam as an enemy, but what Fullam saw was the future.

The first half of the decade was very quiet. Some slight titillation was caused by a foray into the Bering Sea in 1891. For some years there had been a wholesale killing of fur seals at their breeding grounds by poachers, mostly British. England and the United States agreed to police the area jointly. Great Britain sent three ships. The United States sent four Navy ships and two revenue cutters, and chartered a small steamer to be used as a prison ship. The marines involved were under Henry Clay Cochrane, still a captain. The breeding grounds were patrolled, suspicious ships were boarded and searched, and seal poaching was suppressed, but as an expedition it didn't amount to much. As cold weather set in, the exercise was closed out and in October the little fleet sailed for home.

The next year, 1892, there were some exceedingly practical changes to the field uniforms—apparently inspired by the dress habits of the Indian-fighting Regular Army. A broad-brimmed "campaign" or "field" hat, creased "fore and aft" with a large Marine Corps emblem on the left side, was adopted, along with high canvas leggings. The leggings would last, growing increasingly shorter, until the middle of the Korean War. Also, sensibly, a blue flannel shirt usually was substituted for a coat in the field.

Revolution in Cuba, always endemic, broke out afresh in 1895. Spain sent 120,000 soldiers under Capt. Gen. Valeriano ("the Butcher") Weyler to put it down. He had some interesting techniques for population control, such as "reconcentration camps." Congress passed resolutions recognizing the Cubans as belligerents. President Grover Cleveland held back on putting the resolutions into effect, choosing to recognize the Cuban revolutionaries as insurgents rather than belligerents—thus creating a new status in international law which would have interesting applications in subsequent twentieth-century happenings. President Cleveland was succeeded by William McKinley. The Marine Band played at the inauguration on 4 March 1897. During the drive from the Capitol to the White House, Cleveland remarked to McKinley, "I am deeply sorry, Mr. President, to pass on to you a war with Spain. It will come within two years. Nothing can stop it."

# 8

## 1898-1902
### CIVILIZE 'EM WITH A KRAG

THE SPANISH-AMERICAN WAR

There was a sharp report and then a heavier explosion deep in the bowels of the armored cruiser *Maine* as she rode at anchor in Havana's harbor on the night of 15 February 1898. Capt. Charles Sigsbee, interrupted in the writing of a letter to his wife, left his cabin, went out into the smoke-filled passageway, and stumbled into his Marine orderly.

"Sir," said Pvt. William Anthony, drawing himself up to attention and saluting, "I beg to report that the Captain's ship is sinking."

The *Maine* had come into the harbor on 25 January. Spanish reception had been cool but correct. Now 232 seamen and twenty-eight marines were dead. First Lt. Albertus W. Catlin, the senior marine, was unharmed. Like his captain, he had been in his stateroom writing a letter home when the explosion occurred. Although no definitive evidence, then or now, connected the Spanish with the sinking, the cry went up, "Remember the *Maine*!" On 19 April, Congress passed a resolution of intervention. Three days later, President McKinley informed the neutral nations that a state of war existed between the United States and Spain.

On 27 April Col. Cmdt. Heywood ordered a Marine battalion formed, and five days later it sailed from Brooklyn for Key West aboard the ex-banana boat USS *Panther*. The five rifle companies had the new Lee rifle, a bolt-action .236-caliber weapon using smokeless powder. There was also an artillery company equipped with a battery of four 3-inch landing guns. The commanding officer was Lt. Col. Robert W. Huntington, who had been with Reynolds as a lieutenant at First Manassas and in the Carolinas.

In the Pacific, Commo. George Dewey, commanding the Asiatic Squadron, caught Adm. Patricio Montojo's elegant but antique squadron at anchor off Sangley Point, the southwestern lip of Manila Bay, as dawn broke on 1 May. He gave his famous order to the captain of his flagship *Olympia:* "You may fire when you are ready, Gridley."

Battle stations for the marines in Dewey's five cruisers were the rapid-fire guns of the secondary batteries. For two hours the Americans blazed away, retired for breakfast, then came back and finished the job. Seven Spanish ships were destroyed and three land batteries silenced; 381 Spanish sailors were dead and many wounded. Dewey had two officers and six men, none of them marines, who were slightly hurt.

Two days later, on 3 May, the Marine detachment from the protected cruiser *Baltimore,* under 1st Lt. Dion Williams, landed and raised the flag over Cavite naval station. But there were still thirteen thousand Spanish troops in Manila itself and a kind of uneasy standoff was maintained until sufficient Army troops could arrive to take the city.

In Washington, on 4 May, the Naval Appropriation Act raised the commandant's rank once again to brigadier general, and brought the Marine Corps up to a permanent authorized strength of 3,073 men, plus a wartime augmentation of forty-three lieutenants and 1,580 men. One of the new lieutenants, commissioned on 20 May, was a Pennsylvania Quaker named Smedley D. Butler, age eighteen (or maybe sixteen—there is a suspicion that he added two years to his age). He had an inside track to the new commissions. His father was a member, and later chairman, of the House Naval Affairs Committee.

## Guantánamo

In the Caribbean, by the end of May, Rear Adm. William T. Sampson had bottled up the Spanish fleet under Adm. Pascual Cervera in Santiago de Cuba, but he needed an advance base close by from which to coal his blockaders. "Can you not take possession of Guantánamo, occupy as a coaling station?" asked the secretary of the Navy. "Yes," said Sampson. "Send me Huntington's Marine battalion."

On 7 June the *Panther* chugged out of Key West with Huntington's battalion on board. Meanwhile, the protected cruiser *Marblehead* was shelling Guantánamo, defended by a single decrepit gunboat and a reported seven to nine thousand Spaniards. Some of Sampson's fleet marines had gone ashore to reconnoiter. On 10 June, Huntington's battalion landed inside Guantá-

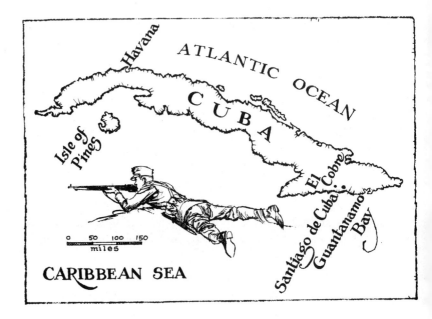

namo Bay, forty miles from Santiago. There was no opposition at the beach. First Spanish reaction came at midnight and for the next three days Huntington was sniped at and harassed, losing his men by ones and twos. The crux of the matter seemed to be Cuzco Well, the Spanish water supply (water supply at semiarid Guantánamo has always been a consideration).

On 14 June, Huntington sent out two companies of marines, along with sixty to seventy Cuban guerrillas, to take the well. The dispatch boat *Dolphin* was to provide naval gunfire support. Sun and heat caused more casualties than Spanish bullets and command eventually devolved upon Capt. George F. Elliott. The *Dolphin*'s shells began dropping on the marines' position. Lean, cadaverous Sgt. John H. Quick went up on a ridge line to wigwag an adjustment. The estimated five hundred Spanish defenders were routed. The marines counted up and found their own casualties to be six killed, sixteen wounded.

There was no further fighting of consequence at Guantánamo. On 3 July, Admiral Cervera elected to come out of Santiago. The victory was even more lopsided than Manila Bay. Cervera's four armored cruisers and three destroyers were no match for Commo. Winfield Scott Schley's five battleships and armored cruiser. Every Spanish ship was sunk or surrendered.

In the Pacific, on 21 June, the protected cruiser *Charleston* had approached Guam and fired twelve rounds with its 3-pounders at old (and abandoned) Fort Santa Cruz. A Spanish officer came out in a small boat with apologies; he had no powder with which to return the "salute," and had to be informed that a state of war existed between Spain and the United States. First Lt. John Twiggs ("Handsome Jack") Myers took the *Charleston's* marines ashore and the amenities of surrender were observed.

Hostilities ceased on 12 August. On 13 August (the apparent extra day was the consequence of a cut cable and the international date line) the American army came out of the trenches it had thrown around Manila and entered the city. Years later, in testifying before the House Naval Affairs Committee, Admiral Dewey said that if he had had five thousand marines embarked with his squadron at Manila Bay he could have taken Manila on 1 May and the Philippine Insurrection might have been avoided.

## In the Philippines

There had been a revolt against the Spaniards, led by twenty-seven-year-old Emilio Aguinaldo, in 1896. Directly after the Battle of Manila Bay, Dewey brought the half-Tagalog, half-Chinese Aguinaldo back by gunboat from exile in Hong Kong. On 12 June 1898 Aguinaldo had declared an independent Philippine Republic with himself as president and commander in chief. He cooperated with the Americans in the languid siege of Manila and on 13 August entered the city with the U.S. Army, fully expecting the government to be turned over to him. Instead, he was told to march himself and his "army" out of the city. On 4 February 1899 actual hostilities began with an abortive attack against Manila.

"Civilize 'em with a Krag!" was the American battle cry for the nasty little war that followed. (In 1900, the Marine Corps, which was beginning to learn that its weapons had to be the same as the U.S. Army's, would abandon its straight-pull Lee rifle in favor of the Army's .30-caliber Krag-Jorgensen. The Marine Corps had also gotten its first machine gun, the high-wheeled Colt-Browning "potato digger.")

On 9 March 1899 Dewey cabled for a Marine battalion to reinforce the naval station at Cavite. The "First Battalion of Marines," fifteen officers and 260 enlisted men, under command of Col. Percival C. Pope, arrived on 23 May. This was not considered enough and a 2d Battalion, under George

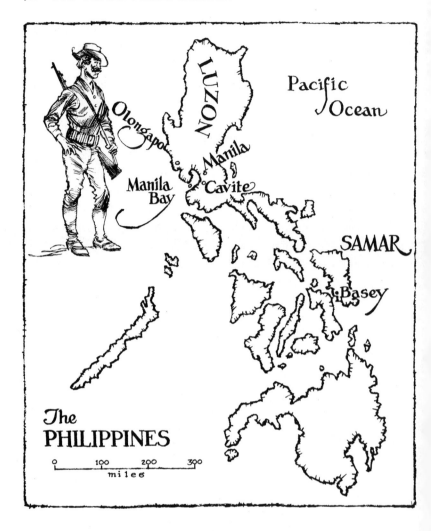

Olongapo

LUZON

Pacific
Ocean

Manila

Manila
Cavite

Manila
Bay

SAMAR

Basey

The
PHILIPPINES

0        100        200        300
miles

Elliott (last heard from at Cuzco Well and now a major), came out on 21 September and had almost immediate employment.

In concert with larger U.S. Army operations, Elliott (about this time elevated to lieutenant colonel) made a frontal assault on 8 October against the fortified town of Novaleta, southwest of Cavite. The attack, divided into two columns, sloshed through swamp and rice paddy, and with the help of a little naval gunfire from the gunboat *Petrel* drove the insurgents from the town at a cost of one marine killed, ten wounded.

A 3d Battalion, under the pugnacious Maj. Littleton W. T. ("Tony") Waller, a thick-legged little man with a large mustache and a larger ego, arrived on 15 December 1899. A reinforced company under Capt. Henry L. Draper was sent to Subic Bay, above the northern edge of Manila Bay, to begin the pacification of the area around Olongapo. Draper set himself energetically to the task (including the burning of the town of Benectian on 16 February 1900). Operations in the Philippines were then interrupted by events in China.

## THE BOXER REBELLION

Secretly supported by the Dowager Empress, the "Righteous Fists of Harmony" (the Europeans called them the "Boxers") were raging across North China determined to expunge the "foreign devils." The legations in Peking, dubious of the protection of the imperial Chinese government, had sent out a call for help.

On 24 May 1900, Capt. John Myers landed at Taku from the USS *Oregon* with twenty-eight marines and five seamen and orders to get to Peking and establish a legation guard. (After his adventure at Guam, Myers, on 23 September 1899, had landed at Olongapo with a detachment from the USS *Baltimore* and captured a threatening rifled gun from the Philippine insurgents.) On 29 May "Handsome Jack" was joined by Capt. Newt H. Hall with twenty-six more marines from the USS *Newark*. Under command of the more senior Myers, the combined detachments commandeered a tug to haul them forty miles upstream to Tientsin. On 31 May, two trains were made up (after a threat to hang the station master) and loaded with an unlikely mélange of American, French, Russian, German, Austrian, Italian, and Japanese sailors and marines. The trains got to Peking that night. The American marines marched off to the U.S. Legation through a dense-packed, muttering mass of Chinese, the five sailors dragging behind them their high-wheeled Colt machine gun (which would prove invaluable in days to come).

On 6 June the rail line to Tientsin was cut by the Boxers—the track torn up, bridges blown, stations burned. Boxers in full ceremonial regalia were now circulating through Peking working up the Chinese into a xenophobic fury. Demonstrations began in earnest on 13 June. Captain Hall went out from the Legation compound and cleared the street at bayonet point. Chinese Christians, many of them horribly burned or wounded, began coming into the Legation Quarter.

Meanwhile, an eight-nation, twenty-five-hundred-man relief column had been organized in Tientsin under Vice Adm. Sir Edward Seymour, RN. The U.S. contingent were mostly bluejackets, stiffened by a couple of squads of marines under a first sergeant, all commanded by Capt. Bowman H. McCalla, USN, of the *Newark*. McCalla was no stranger to expeditionary service. He had commanded the naval forces ashore at Panama in 1885 and had been senior officer present at the Guantánamo landing. On the morning of 10 June, the whole force moved out, repairing the railroad as they went, and harried by both the Boxers and Imperial troops. After a week they had gotten as far as An Ping, sixty-five miles up the line (where the U.S. Marines would have another "incident" in 1946), and still twenty-five miles short of Peking. At An Ping on 18 June, Seymour's column was stopped cold by the Chinese and began a retreat back to Tientsin.

More help was on the way. The navies of Europe and Japan were converging on Taku. At Cavite, on 14 June, Major Waller mounted out a bobtailed battalion, seven officers (including 1st Lt. Smedley Butler as one of his company commanders) and 131 men. They landed at Taku on 19 June, coaxed an old locomotive and a string of flat cars into life, and started for Tientsin. En route they joined forces with a battalion of 440 white-bloused Russian infantry, continuing along the railroad until stopped by a blown bridge twelve miles short of Tientsin. The Russian colonel argued for an attack beyond the bridgehead, first thing in the morning. Waller, no shrinking violet when it came to combat, agreed. The Russians and Americans moved out in the last hours of darkness and in the bright light of morning found that they had moved into a sleeve, with Imperial troops on their front and right, Boxers on their left, perhaps fifteen hundred or more in all. The Russians withdrew, leaving the marines alone, with three dead and nine wounded. They carried out their wounded, got back to the bridgehead, found an Allied force building up there, and attached themselves to the six-hundred-man British naval contingent under Cdr. Christopher Cradock, RN.

This was on the twenty-first of June. By the next day, Seymour's column had worked its way back to the Hsi-ku arsenal six miles north of Tientsin. Seymour's Royal Marines, supported by the Germans and the Americans, captured the arsenal and Seymour led his weary column inside its walls to await help. Of McCalla's 112 sailors and marines, thirty-two had been killed or wounded.

Two days later, on the twenty-fourth, the international force which had built up south of Tientsin drove into the foreign quarter against light resistance, and the next day the force reached Seymour at Hsi-ku arsenal. McCalla, himself three times wounded, turned over the residue of his command to Waller.

In Peking there had been heavy fighting. The Legation Quarter was roughly a square, cut from east to west by Legation Street and from north to south by a canal. At the southwest corner was the American Legation backed up against the Tartar Wall, sixty feet high and forty feet wide. The U.S. Marines threw a barricade across the wall facing west toward Chien Men gate. The Germans had a comparable position facing east toward Hata Men gate. The British Legation, where the foreign women and children had been concentrated, was at the northwest corner of the quarter. The British minister, Claude MacDonald, was chosen to be commander in chief of the mixed defense force.

On 23 June the Chinese set fire to Hanlin Yuan Academy, just outside the British compound. In an effort to save it, Royal and U.S. Marines sallied forth to drive off the Boxers. On the next night the Chinese attacked the British compound itself. On the twenty-seventh the Chinese made a daylight attack against Myers's position. His Colt machine gun cut them down. On 1 July the Germans gave way after receiving heavy shelling and the American rear was left exposed. The U.S. Marines momentarily fell back, then, with the help of the British marines, counterattacked and regained their position on the wall.

Next day, 2 July, the Chinese pushed a fifteen-foot tower into place on the wall overlooking Myers's strongpoint. That night, in a blinding rainstorm, he got off a raid with thirty American marines, twenty-six British marines, and fifteen Russian sailors. The signal was "Go!" and they moved out at 1:30 A.M. They overran the Boxer barricade, killed thirty-six, and took two flags. Myers tripped over a Chinese spear and got the head of it through his calf. Two American marines were killed, and a British marine and a Russian sailor were wounded.

"Captain Myers's post on the wall," wrote MacDonald, "is the peg which holds the whole thing together."

After the night attack the Chinese showed more caution. Fighting slowed to desultory sniping by both sides. Myers's leg became badly infected (later, he would get typhoid) and command devolved on Captain Hall. There was a flare-up on 15 July. Pvt. Daniel Daly held an advanced post on the wall alone until Hall could bring up reinforcements. Next day, the sixteenth, a kind of truce was agreed upon.

The event which caused the Imperial government to desist in its support of the attacks against the Legation Quarter was the fall of Tientsin's native city. There were now close to six thousand foreign troops in Tientsin. The headquarters of the 1st Marine Regiment, along with its commander, Civil War veteran Col. Robert L. Meade, and another battalion had arrived at Taku from Cavite on 10 July. Two battalions of the U.S. 9th Infantry had come in four days earlier and these were brigaded with the marines under Meade's command, about a thousand Americans altogether.

With these forces in place, the attack against Tientsin's native quarter began 13 July. The Russians and the French were acting independently. The British, Americans, and Japanese were loosely grouped under Brig. Gen. A.R.F. Dorward, British Army. For the attack the U.S. Marines had the left flank of Dorward's group. The 2d Battalion, Royal Welch Fusiliers, were on their right. (And since then, on Saint David's Day, 1 March, and the Marine Corps Birthday, 10 November, the commandant of the Marine Corps and the colonel of the Royal Welch exchange the watchword, "and Saint David.")

The native city had two walls around it. The outer wall was pounded earth. Dorward's attack went over the outer wall at seven in the morning and then through the muck of flooded rice paddies to the second wall, which was of stone. A Marine artillery company that had arrived with Meade banged away with its battery of 3-inch landing guns. The battery commander was Capt. Ben H. Fuller, a future commandant. Lieutenant Butler went down with a bullet through his thigh. There was no getting over the wall and at nightfall the attack pulled back. Next morning, before dawn, the Japanese blew in the south gate and by daylight the Allies were in the city en mass. There was much burning and looting, all of which the marines virtuously ascribed to someone else.

Fresh foreign troops were arriving in a steady stream. On 30 July Maj. Gen. Adna R. Chaffee, USA, arrived to take command of all U.S. forces, which now numbered about three thousand. On 3 August a new Marine battalion, designated the 4th, came into Tientsin under Maj. William P. Biddle. Colonel Meade at this point was invalided home and Biddle, who was senior to Waller, moved up to command of the 1st Marine Regiment. The international force now numbered 18,600. One Marine battalion was left behind in Tientsin. The regiment with two battalions and its artillery company, 482 marines, was to make the march to Peking. Butler, who had just reached nineteen, argued his way out of the hospital and rejoined his company as it prepared to move out.

By 13 August the outskirts of Peking had been reached, the heat and dust of the march proving more of an affliction than the Chinese. The Allies had agreed to a day of rest but on the fourteenth the Russians went charging into the city, and this brought along everyone else. Waller's 1st Battalion was assigned to cover a battery of the 5th Artillery in breaching the Chien Men gate. Butler got his second wound entering the Chinese City, a bullet excising "South America" from a Marine emblem tattooed on his chest. There was some slimy work going through the Water Gate from the Chinese City into the Legation Quarter but resistance was not great. By late afternoon the foreign legations were reached. They found that of the Legation Quarter's defenders, totaling something less than five hundred, sixty-five had been killed and 135 wounded. Of the fifty-six U.S. marines and sailors, seventeen were casualties.

## BACK TO THE PHILIPPINES

On 28 September the secretary of the Navy ordered the 1st Marine Regiment returned to Cavite. The regiment marched out of Peking on 3 October and on 10 October sailed from Taku for the Philippines. Once back in the Philippines, the marines were able to reorganize into a proper brigade, two regiments of two battalions each, aggregate strength 1,678. The 1st Regiment went to Olongapo; Brigade headquarters and the 2d Regiment stayed at Cavite. The insurrection on the main island of Luzon had been fairly well put down. But while the Christian Tagalogs had come to accept American rule, the Muslim Moros of the southern islands were not yet mollified. The island of Samar was most troublesome. On 28 September 1901, Company C, 9th Infantry, was caught at evening mess at Balangiga and massacred. Waller was sent with his battalion, fourteen officers and three hundred men, including Gy. Sgt. John Quick, to help. On 24 October he landed with two companies at Basey. His other two companies went in at Balangiga.

Brig. Gen. Jacob M. ("Hell-Roaring Jake") Smith, USA, reportedly told Waller, "I want no prisoners. I wish you to burn and kill. The more you burn and kill, the better it will please me."

Operating against some three thousand Moros, Waller's two columns "burned and killed" through the first two weeks of November. The hard-core Moros withdrew to a jungle stronghold in the cliffs above the Sojoton River, an area never penetrated by the Spaniards. Waller went after them on 15 November, three columns converging in a hair-raising night attack that finished off organized Moro resistance, or so it seemed.

General Smith now ordered Waller to reconnoiter a telegraph route from the east coast of Samar to Basey. Waller decided to start from Lanang, work up the Lanang River as far as he could go, find a trail to the Sojoton River, and then down the Sojoton to Basey. The maps were no good but it looked to be about fifty-two miles. They started off three days after Christmas 1901, five Marine officers, fifty marines, two Philippine guides, and thirty-three native bearers. The trails they followed made no sense. Rations ran short. Waller began suspecting the loyalty of the guides. Fever was weakening his men. He decided to push on to Basey with the strongest men and leave the rest to follow at a more leisurely pace. He arrived at Basey on 6 January, picked up help and supplies, and started back the next morning. For nine days he searched without luck, getting back to Basey, sick and exhausted, on 17 January.

Capt. David D. Porter, namesake of the Civil War admiral, left behind with the main body, had decided to go back to Lanang, going off with seven marines (including Gunnery Sergeant Quick) and six natives. The remainder were to follow along as best they could. In all, ten marines were lost.

Convinced that the disaster had been caused by treachery, Waller held a drumhead court-martial on 20 January 1902 in the plaza of Basey and shot eleven of the natives. His battalion then embarked for Cavite, where, to Waller's surprise, he was brought up before an Army general court-martial on 17 March on charge of murder. He was acquitted and eventually the whole proceedings were thrown out on a technicality, but the shadow of the incident hung on and may well have kept Waller from becoming commandant.

# 9

## *1899-1916*

## A Pacific Effect upon the Oriental Mind

### Panama and the Canal

On 1 April 1899, marines from the protected cruiser *Philadelphia* went ashore in Samoa, in a combined landing party with Royal marines from two British ships, to intercede in an argument between two chiefs as to the succession to the Samoan throne. They burned a village, managed to get themselves ambushed, and withdrew ignominiously. Samoa was eventually partitioned among Great Britain, Germany, and the United States. A naval station was set up at Tutuila in American Samoa in 1904 and the Fita-Fita guard, trained and commanded by Marine NCOs, was established. There were also landings in Nicaragua (1899), Panama (1901, 1902, 1903), Honduras (1903), the Dominican Republic (1903), Beirut, Syria (1903), Tangier (1904), and a minor expedition to Abyssinia (1903).

The commandant, Charles Heywood, was promoted to major general, the first in the Corps' history, in July 1902 (but with the proviso that his successor be a brigadier general). He retired on 3 October 1903 at age sixty-four, and in his final report noted that the Corps' strength was 278 officers and 7,532 men, an all-time high. The new commandant was Alabama-born George F. Elliott, already fifty-seven years old.

The Spanish-American War had revived American interest in a canal across the Isthmus of Panama. The rights and property of the moribund French Panama Company had been acquired for $40 million. Colombia, proprietor of the Isthmus, was offered $10 million in gold and $250,000 a year in exchange for absolute U.S. sovereignty over a ten-mile-wide strip. Colombia asked for $25 million. President Theodore Roosevelt said not one dollar more, and the Colombian Congress adjourned on 31 October 1903 without taking action. Three days later, in a bloodless coup, revolutionaries seized control of

Panama City. Numbers of U.S. marines were conveniently close. A landing party from the gunboat *Nashville* went ashore at Colón (on the Atlantic side) with orders to keep the Colombian garrison from crossing the Isthmus to Panama City. A battalion of marines under Maj. John A. Lejeune, embarked in the transport *Dixie,* was ordered forward from Jamaica. It came into Colón on 5 November and Lejeune promptly landed two companies. The Colombian garrison was persuaded to depart on board a Royal Mail steamer for Cartagena, and next day President Roosevelt recognized the independence of the new Republic of Panama. On 9 November a second Marine battalion put out from Philadelphia for Panama on board the auxiliary cruiser *Prairie.* Then, on 3 January 1904, Brigadier General Elliott himself arrived in the *Dixie* with two more battalions, one of them commanded by Lt. Col. Tony Waller.

That same day the Marine detachment from the light cruiser *Detroit* was landing at Puerto Plata in the Dominican Republic. Two days later, three officers and a hundred marines would arrive in Seoul from the Philippines to protect American lives and property endangered by the Russo-Japanese War. In Africa, Capt. George C. Thorpe and nineteen marines were wending their way back to Djibouti, after having escorted a diplomatic mission to the court of Emperor Menelik in mysterious Addis Ababa.

In Panama, Elliott collected his battalions into a provisional brigade of two regiments and stayed on until 16 February, by which time the new regime was firmly in place. On 4 January, President Roosevelt had explained the occupation to the Congress in a special message: "No one connected with this government had any part in preparing, inciting or encouraging the late revolution of the Isthmus of Panama." Digging on the canal got started in May. At least one Marine battalion would remain in Panama until 1914.

A detachment of a hundred marines from the Philippines under Capt. Harry Lee relieved a company of the 9th Infantry on 12 September 1905 as Legation Guard in Peking, beginning a long spell of "China duty" which would continue until interrupted by World War II. In December of the same year, marines were also assigned to guard the U.S. embassy in troubled Saint Petersburg.

## CUBAN PACIFICATION (1906–1909)

The Spanish-American War had left the United States with the problem of what to do with Cuba. The Cubans were encouraged to hold a constitutional convention, and the result was almost a carbon copy of the U.S. constitution and government with one interesting exception, the so-called "Platt Amendment," which gave the United States "the right to intervene for the preservation of Cuban independence, the maintenance of a government adequate for the protection of life, property and individual liberty, and for discharging the obligations with respect to Cuba imposed by the Treaty of Paris." Such intervention by U.S. marines would be required eight times between 1906 and 1917.

In August 1906 the Liberal party, defeated in a somewhat fuzzy election, went into open revolt and President Tomás Estrada Palma, head of the incumbent Moderate party, asked for U.S. help. On 13 September an improvised battalion of 130 marines and sailors from the light cruiser *Denver* went ashore at Havana and camped in front of the president's palace. Another battalion under Maj. Albertus Catlin came into the harbor in the much-used *Dixie* on 16 September.

Ships' detachments were landing along the north coast to protect American-owned sugar plantations and railroad property. A special commission under William H. Taft, then secretary of War, arrived on 19 September to help and advise. An anguished President Palma resigned, effective 28 September; virtually his last official act was to ask for a guard on the Cuban treasury (which was provided by a platoon of thirty marines). Roosevelt told Taft to form a provisional government with himself as governor. Two more Marine battalions had arrived in Havana harbor from Norfolk and Philadelphia. These were combined with Catlin's battalion into the 1st Regiment under Lt. Col. George Barnett.

A 2d Marine Regiment was formed under Lt. Col. Franklin J. Moses, a veteran of the march to Peking, two of its battalions being shaken out of the Atlantic Fleet. The ubiquitous Tony Waller, promoted to colonel the previous year, arrived on 1 October to take command of the two regiments combined into a brigade. By then Barnett was ashore and had occupied Cienfuegos.

The U.S. Army of Cuban Occupation began arriving 10 October. The Marine brigade was disbanded (after reaching a peak strength of ninety-seven officers and 2,795 men) and Waller left for Norfolk on 1 November. But the 1st Marine Regiment stayed on under Army command. There was no fighting for them to do but a good deal of guard duty—and that sine qua non of pacification, collection of illicit weapons. The last Marine elements sailed for home on 23 January 1909.

## THE GREAT WHITE FLEET

All was not in complete harmony in Washington. A clique in the Navy was urging the president to take the Marines off the Navy's capital ships. The Army had revived the old proposition that the Corps, or at least its functions, be transferred to the Army. While these interesting proposals were being argued, sixteen battleships, painted white and as beautiful as gigantic yachts, put out from Hampton Roads, Virginia, on 16 December 1907. The cruise of the Great White Fleet was under way. The Russo-Japanese War was over, thanks to the mediation of President Roosevelt, but the Japanese were restive. So the fleet was to go to Japan on a friendly visit, the president, in the words of naval historian Commo. Dudley W. Knox, "correctly believing that a display of overpowering force would have a pacific effect upon the Oriental mind."

In Washington, Elliott continued to battle for the status of the Corps. Twice he was offered personal advancement to major general, but he held out for the rank to go to the office, not the man. This was finally done. Congress created the permanent grade of major general commandant and Elliott was promoted in May 1908. On 12 November of that year President Roosevelt was persuaded to sign Executive Order 969, which spelled out the duties of the U.S. Marines:

(1) To garrison the different navy yards and naval stations, both within and beyond the continental limits of the United States.

(2) To furnish the first line of the mobile defense of naval bases and naval stations beyond the continental limits of the United States.

(3) To man such naval defenses, and to aid in manning, if necessary, such other defenses, as may be erected for the defense of naval bases and naval stations beyond the continental limits of the United States.

(4) To garrison the Isthmian Canal Zone, Panama.

(5) To furnish such garrisons and expeditionary forces for duties beyond the seas as may be necessary in time of peace.

No mention of duties afloat! Withdrawal of marines from combatant ships had already begun in October. Elliott, Waller, and others sought help in Congress. There was a strong friend in the person of Congressman Thomas Butler, father of Smedley Butler, and now chairman of the House Naval Affairs Committee. On 22 February 1909, Washington's Birthday, the Great White

Fleet steamed back into Hampton Roads, the forty-thousand-mile cruise a fitting climax to Roosevelt's spectacular administration, having been received enthusiastically everywhere and nowhere more so than in Japan. On 3 March, as Roosevelt's protégé, William Taft, was about to begin his presidency, a rider was tacked on to the Naval Appropriations Bill:

> Provided, that no part of the appropriations herein made for the Marine Corps shall be expended for the purposes for which said appropriations are made unless officers and men shall serve as heretofore on board all battleships and armored cruisers and also on such other vessels of the Navy as the President may direct.

So the marines stayed on the battleships and those who had come off prematurely were put back on with a few extra added.

## Advance Base Studies

In 1901 a detachment of four officers and forty enlisted marines under Maj. Henry C. Haines at Newport, Rhode Island, had been directed to begin a study of advance-base operations, building on Spanish-American War experience. They tested their findings with small-scale exercises at Newport and Nantucket, and the following year there was a regimental-size landing problem at Culebra, a small island east of Puerto Rico.

The Marines began to think about the uses of keeping a battalion or regiment afloat in transports. Such a force in the Caribbean, for example, would be conveniently at hand to half-a-dozen potential trouble spots. In these years a number of small liners brought into the Navy during the Spanish-American War as auxiliary cruisers were increasingly used as transports. Closest to an assault transport was the 6,100-ton *Dixie*, which carried ten 6-inch guns and could make 16 knots flank speed. There were also the larger but slower *Prairie* and *Buffalo*—6,900 tons and 14.5 knots. Pondering these matters, General Elliott in 1908 recommended "transports for the sole and exclusive use of the Marine Corps."

That it was a time of change was apparent even in the uniforms. Khaki had come into use for tropical field service during the Spanish-American War. (Heywood had sent "campaign suits of brown linen" to Huntington at Guantánamo; Huntington had replied that the "lightweight underclothes would be much better if they were lighter in weight.") A mustard-colored flannel shirt replaced the blue shirt of the Philippine Insurrection and Boxer Relief. In 1901 the Marine Corps emblem moved from the side to the front of the field hat. In 1903, a standing-collar khaki blouse was added. Next year the spiked helmet disappeared without lament and a bell-crowned visored cap came in. In 1912 a new model field hat was introduced, stiffer, with a narrower brim, and a four-dent "Montana peak" to replace the fore-and-aft crease. In the same year it was decided to adopt a forest-green winter service uniform, with dull bronze ornaments and buttons.

General Heywood had been dismayed at Marine marksmanship in the 1890s and had gotten the Corps into competition shooting. At the Sea Girt matches in 1901, the Marine Corps team managed only sixth place, but a new second lieutenant from Delaware, Thomas Holcomb, won a gold medal for highest individual score and by the next year he was world's champion. In 1906, the Mauser-type bolt-action Springfield M1903 began replacing the Krag-Jorgensen. In the same year Congress authorized monthly pay of one dollar for marksman, two dollars for sharpshooter, and three dollars for expert. With "beer money" to shoot for, Marine marksmanship improved dramatically and a forty-year love affair with the "Oh-Three" began.

Congress was also quite liberal with construction money. The Marine Barracks at Eighth and I Streets, Washington, was overcrowded and worn out with use. Various Victorian excrescences had gone onto the Commandant's House in the 1840s, along with a bathroom. In the 1890s a mansard roof was added. In 1903 the enlisted and bachelor quarters were condemned by a Navy medical board and pulled down. By 1910 the quadrangle had been rebuilt, essentially in its present form, with hard-burnt brick.

## NICARAGUA (1909–1913)

In November 1909 Maj. Smedley Butler was sent down to the Isthmus to take command of the Panama battalion. A month later he and his battalion were off to Corinto on the west coast of Nicaragua. Dictator José Santos Zelaya, an anticlerical "Liberal," had a bad reputation for stirring up trouble. Besides, he was heavily in debt—both to the United States and Europe. The staunchly Catholic "Conservatives" under Juan J. Estrada made a revolution against him. The United States, deciding that the Conservatives more nearly represented the Nicaraguan people, broke diplomatic relations with Zelaya's government. A provisional regiment of 750 marines under Col. James E. Mahoney came down from Philadelphia. Most of the force stayed in Corinto, but Butler reconnoitered the full length of the railroad to Granada and came to certain conclusions as to what he would do if he had to fight along that line. In March, Mahoney went home to Philadelphia and Butler returned to Panama.

But on the east coast, by late spring, the Conservatives were pushed back into Bluefields. So, on 19 May 1910, the *Paducah,* a new 1,000-ton gunboat, put its landing force ashore, and on 30 May Major Butler arrived with fifteen officers and 450 men. General Estrada, much encouraged, now moved west and triumphantly marched into the capital at Managua. By September, Butler and his battalion were out of the country and back in Panama.

Major General Commandant Elliott retired on 30 November 1910 at the age of sixty-four, and for a while there was no commandant (and there were pressures from some segments of the Army and Navy to keep it that way). Acting commandant was rotund William P. Biddle, who had come up from Panama the previous April. The Corps thought that Tony Waller would be the new commandant, but there was the matter of his smudged record in the Philippines. The Pennsylvania Republicans closed in on President Taft and persuaded him that Biddle of the Philadelphia Biddles should be named. Accordingly, on 3 February 1911, Biddle became the eleventh commandant of the Marine Corps.

Slavery had ended in Cuba in 1886, but race problems had continued and in 1912 the blacks erupted in the Negro Rebellion. On 22 May the 1st Provisional Marine Regiment came together with practiced ease at Philadelphia, this time commanded by Col. Lincoln Karmany, and next day was on its way to Guantánamo on board the *Prairie.* A 2d Regiment was assembled at Key West under Colonel Mahoney. Its 1st Battalion was sent to Guantánamo; its 2d Battalion went into Havana. Both regiments were combined into the 1st Provisional Marine Brigade under Karmany. Of great concern were the American-owned sugar plantations and mines near El Cobre and Siboney. The marines fanned out into Oriente Province, put companies or platoons into twenty-six towns, and rode all the trains. The Cuban government got things under control. The marines pulled back into Guantánamo and in late July came home.

While those events were taking place in Cuba, things were going badly for the incumbent Conservative government in Nicaragua. Cries for help came out of the U.S. Legation at Managua. Butler's battalion was again summoned and arrived at Corinto, 354 officers and men, on 14 August. Butler worked his way up the ninety miles of railway to Managua, half by bluff, half by force, finding bits and pieces of U.S. landing parties along the way. While Butler was setting things to rights in Managua, Col. Joseph H. ("Uncle Joe") Pendleton arrived at Corinto on 4 September with the 1st Provisional Marine Regiment, 780 men in the *Buffalo*. Pendleton, who had come into the Marine Corps from the Naval Academy in 1884, was then fifty-two years old, a portly, pleasant man with a loose mustache and steel-rimmed glasses.

Butler was told to open the rail line from Managua southeast to Granada on the edge of Lake Nicaragua. About halfway, near Masaya, his train had to run the gauntlet of shelling from two hilltop forts, called Coyotepe and Barranca. He marked their position for further attention and shot his way through. The last fifteen miles to Granada took five days. Butler was running hot from fever and temper and his men began to call him "Old Gimlet Eye."

There were still the two bypassed forts outside of Masaya to be attended to. Butler backtracked to meet with Pendleton, who was coming up the railroad with the main body. The rebel position stretched from hill to hill and they seemed to have about a thousand men up there. Pendleton began banging away with three field pieces on 2 October. Before daylight on 4 October, 850 marines and sailors moved out, holding hands so as to keep contact in the darkness. At 5:15 A.M., the assault began and in forty minutes it was all over. Twenty-seven rebels were dead (they shot their general) and nine captured. Government cavalry went off in pursuit of the rest. There had been eighteen Marine casualties. In November Pendleton left with most of his regiment and Butler again returned to Panama. By January 1913 all marines were out except for a hundred left behind at Managua as a legation guard.

General Biddle was tiring of the job as commandant. In Washington, there was always the chronic hostility of the Army and some parts of the Navy to combat and the chilly Wilson was even less friendly to the Corps than Roosevelt or Taft had been. There was also a residual coolness between Biddle and the pro-Waller faction of his own officer corps. He retired voluntarily on 24 February 1914. Under Biddle the Corps had grown to a strength of ten thousand. He had worked hard on training and organization, insisting on three months of recruit training, and dividing each Marine post and station into a barracks detachment of nondeployables and one or more numbered companies, each with two officers and a hundred men, ready for instant expeditionary service. Recruit depots were set up at Philadelphia, Port Royal, Mare Island, and Puget Sound. In 1912 he argued prophetically for "one large post on each coast, eventually to be capable of housing a brigade of two regiments at war strength." Perhaps most important of all, on 23 December 1913, he activated the Marine Advance Base Force under command of Col. George Barnett. It was to be a small brigade of two regiments. The 1st Regiment, also called the "Fixed Defense Regiment," was the forerunner of the defense battalions of World War II. The 2d Regiment, organized along infantry lines with four rifle companies, a machine-gun company, and a battery of landing guns, was the prototype of the battalion landing teams of World War II and later. (Somewhat confusingly, the regiments later exchanged numbers so that the 1st Regiment was in fact the ancestor of today's 2d Marines and the 2d Regiment the ancestor of the 1st Marines.) The Advance Base Brigade also had an aviation detachment, activated on 27 December 1913, with two officers, seven enlisted men, and two Navy flying boats.

The Marine Corps was just getting into the "aeroplane" business. In 1911, 1st Lt. Alfred A. Cunningham, while stationed at Marine Barracks, Philadelphia, had rented a pusher-type contraption for twenty-five dollars a month from a Philadelphia inventor and thrashed around the half-mile field inside the Navy Yard. He never succeeded in getting "Noisy Nan" off the ground, but his enthusiasm was rewarded with orders in May 1912 to the new aviation camp at Annapolis. From here he was sent off to Marblehead, Massachusetts, where, on 1 August 1912, after two hours and forty minutes of instruction, he soloed in a Curtiss seaplane, and became the first Marine pilot (and the fifth naval aviator). Next to qualify was 1st Lt. Bernard L. Smith and it was Smith who was given command of the new Aviation Detachment in the Advance Base Force.

## VERACRUZ (1914)

On Biddle's retirement, Colonel Barnett was ordered to Washington, and on 25 February 1914 he was named major general commandant for a four-year term, this fixed tenure with the possibility of a four-year extension having been legislated the year before by Congress. Barnett was the first graduate of the Naval Academy (class of 1881) to become commandant.

Almost immediately his Marine Advance Base Force got its first expeditionary testing. In Mexico, Francisco Madero had been assassinated. Gen. Victoriano Huerta had made himself dictator-president. On 9 April 1914 the paymaster and boat crew from the dispatch boat *Dolphin* went ashore at Tampico to buy gasoline and were thrown in jail. General Huerta, as soon as he was informed, ordered their release and sent a note of apology and regret, but Rear Adm. Henry T. Mayo was not satisfied. He asked for a twenty-one-gun salute to the American flag, and this Huerta refused. The Navy then moved into a kind of loose blockade of Mexico's Gulf ports.

The Marine Advance Base Force was poised at New Orleans and Pensacola, with leathery John Archer Lejeune, now a colonel, in momentary command. A "Cajun" from Pointe Coupee Parish in southern Louisiana, Lejeune had been born on his family's cotton plantation in 1867, had graduated from the Naval Academy in 1888, and had been the Marine officer in the cruiser *Cincinnati* during the Spanish-American War. His brigade was now called forward to Veracruz.

On 20 April, President Wilson received word that a German merchant ship was coming into Veracruz with a cargo of arms for Huerta. A message was sent crackling to the Fleet: "Take Veracruz at once." The 2d Marine Regiment, led by Lt. Col. Wendell C. "Buck" Neville, was first ashore next morning, 21 April. They landed against no resistance, took the cable station and power plant, and by noon developed a hot fire fight in the railroad yards. In support Neville had a provisional 3d Regiment scoffed up from the fleet and placed under Albertus Catlin, also now a lieutenant colonel. On the marines' left were several Navy battalions in coffee-dyed whites. At nightfall Neville was joined by Butler, who had come charging onto the scene with his Panama battalion in the scout cruiser *Chester*. Next morning Neville resumed the attack and it turned out to be a house-to-house proposition, going over the roofs and through the walls.

Lejeune was now in the harbor with the rest of the Marine Brigade. He came ashore midmorning on the twenty-second (falling overboard between ship's boat and sea wall in the process) and that afternoon the 1st Marine Regiment under Lt. Col. Charles G. Long began to land. The Naval Brigade was also building up so that the landing force, under overall command of Rear Adm. Frank F. Fletcher, had a total of about seven thousand men ashore. By 24 April Veracruz was pacified; American casualties had been about 135. On 29 April Brig. Gen. Frederick Funston, USA, arrived with an Army brigade and assumed command of operations ashore. Two days later Col. Tony Waller came in and relieved Lejeune of the Marine Brigade—no reflection on Lejeune, but Waller was senior. The brigade strength stood at about 3,100. Huerta was persuaded to leave Mexico on 15 July and the Carranza government took over. Some marines stayed on at Veracruz until 23 November 1914.

## HAITI (1915)

In 1902, Germany, Britain, and Italy, in pursuing claims against Venezuela for damages sustained during a revolution as well as a bond default, had blockaded that hapless republic, captured its fleet, and bombarded the coast in three places. After a year of this, Roosevelt advised Kaiser Wilhelm (whom he mistook for the ringleader) that if the three powers did not submit their claims to The Hague for arbitration, he would send down Admiral Dewey with the Atlantic Fleet to break the blockade. Roosevelt told the Congress that the United States would not go to war to prevent a European nation from collecting its just debts providing the European action did "not take the form of acquisition of territory." However, in what would come to be called the Roosevelt Corollary, he went on to say that in case of "chronic wrongdoing or impotence" on the part of a Latin American state, the United States was bound by the Monroe Doctrine "however reluctantly" to intervene and to "exercise an international police power."

This was the case with the Dominican Republic. By 1904, debts owed European banks had reached $32 million and the interested powers, in light of the Venezuelan incident, were asking Roosevelt what he intended to do about it. His solution was to indemnify the debt, appoint a financial receiver for the bankrupt government, and take over the customhouses, import duties being the one sure form of taxation.

Haiti's finances collapsed. The foreign banks were anxious to get their money. Germany, France, Great Britain, and the United States all found reason to put marines ashore. The United States offered the Haitian government an indemnification and financial receivership similar to the Dominican formula, but this was refused. In December 1914 the Marine detachment from the gunboat *Machias* landed at Port-au-Prince and carted off for safekeeping the last $500,000 in Haiti's treasury.

In March 1915 a revolution put Vilbrun Guillaume Sam into the presidency. On 27 July, there was a bloody uprising in Port-au-Prince. Losing control, President Sam gave orders for the slaughter of 167 political prisoners and then took refuge in the French Legation. The crowd sought him out, pulled him apart, and ate his heart. Next day, Rear Adm. William B. Caperton, with his flag in the armored cruiser *Washington,* landed an improvised "regiment" under his senior marine, Capt. George Van Orden: one battalion of bluejackets and two companies of fleet marines. They went into Port-au-Prince against sniper fire and restored order. The 2d Marine Regiment, under Col. Eli K. Cole, came down from Philadelphia in the battleship *Connecticut,* arriving 4 August. The 1st Marine Regiment and Headquarters, 1st Marine Brigade, under Colonel Waller came in on 15 August on board the armored cruiser *Tennessee.* Waller, with two thousand marines to work with, took over ten customhouses and garrisoned the more important towns. He himself went north to Cap Haitien, where most of the problem seemed to be, taking the 1st Battalion, 1st Marine Regiment, and Major Butler as a kind of roving battalion commander and executive officer.

The insurgents in the north called themselves "Cacos," after a red-plumed bird of prey, and they managed to wear something red on their ragged clothing as a badge. "General" Rameau and his particular band of Cacos had been harassing the Marine detachment at Gonaïves. Butler came storming over the mountains, caught up with Rameau on 18 September, literally yanked him off his horse, and sent him into Port-au-Prince as a prisoner. In this exercise he was helped by a young lieutenant from Virginia named Alexander A. Vandegrift.

Butler next volunteered to reconnoiter Fort Capois, reputedly the Caco mountain stronghold. For his patrol he took twenty-six marines mounted on local ponies. They got themselves ambushed at a stream crossing after dark on 24 October. The animal carrying the patrol's only machine gun was killed in midstream and the rest of the pack train was scattered. Gy. Sgt. Dan Daly volunteered to go back and get the machine gun, which he did, adding a second Medal of Honor to the one he had earned on the Wall at Peking. There was an all-night fight that cost the Cacos seventy-five dead, by Butler's count, to one marine wounded. Waller then gave Butler five companies of marines and two of sailors to clean out Fort Capois, which he did on 5 November.

The Cacos' last fixed bastion, which they thought impregnable, was the ruins of an eighteenth-century French fort eight miles south of Grande Rivière and on top of 4,000-foot Montagne Noire. Butler was given three companies of marines and one company of sailors in Marine uniforms to do the job. They began the climb the night of 17 November 1915, Butler moving at the front of the 13th Company. Butler got to the wall with two lieutenants and twenty-four marines, found the sally port bricked up, and located an open drain with Caco bullets whanging through it.

"Oh, hell," said a sergeant. "I'm going through." He went, followed by Butler and his orderly, with the rest of the 13th Company close behind. There was a wild hand-to-hand fight, Marine bayonets against Caco swords and clubs, called *cocomacaques*. The Cacos who didn't die went over the wall into the bush. "General" Josefette's body was found in its frock coat, with a large brass chain adorning his chest, and his top hat lying near by.

Major Butler was given a second Medal of Honor for Fort Rivière to add to one he had tried to refuse for Veracruz. (Medals of Honor were now authorized for officers of the naval service and he thought them much too freely handed out for the Mexican intervention.) In Port-au-Prince there was a new government friendly to the United States which agreed to the creation of a Haitian constabulary officered by Americans. First commandant of the Gendarmerie d'Haiti was Butler, promoted to lieutenant colonel and grandly fleeted up to major general in the Haitian service. With the field grades being filled with Marine officers and the company grades with Marine NCOs, the Gendarmerie went up to 120 Americans and 2,500 Haitians. The gendarmes were clothed in surplus Marine uniforms, armed with Krags, and drilled in English. With occasional Marine help, they maintained the government, kept law and order, and outdid themselves in what another generation would call "civic action." They built roads, overhauled the telegraph system, put in a postal system, improved the water supply and general sanitation, took an interest in the schools, refurbished the lighthouses and navigational aids, and provided fire-fighting services to the principal towns.

## SANTO DOMINGO (1916)

Across the border separating the third of Hispaniola that is black and French-speaking from the two-thirds that is predominantly mulatto and Spanish-speaking, there was new trouble. Marine landing parties had been bobbing in and out of the Dominican Republic since the turn of the century, but the civil war of 1916 would require a more prolonged stay.

By April things were out of control and, on 5 May 1916, Capt. Frederic M. "Dopey" Wise came over from Port-au-Prince in the *Prairie* with the 6th and 9th Companies. He moved into Fort Geronimo outside Santo Domingo. By the fifteenth, a hefty battalion of 375 marines and 225 bluejackets had been lined up under command of Maj. Newt Hall (second-in-command at Peking) for an assault against the ancient walls of the oldest city in the New World. Wise remarked later that it was like Veracruz, but without the fighting; not a shot was fired, not a weapon found. On 26 May, Wise went around the island in the old *Panther* to the northwest corner of the Republic, landed at Monte Cristi (important then for cowhides, tallow, and logwood), ran into 150 ragged rebels, and chopped them down with his single machine gun. On 1 June, fleet marines came ashore against stiff rifle fire at Puerto Plata, the north coast's most important port and very European, and pushed the rebels up into the hills.

Something more substantial in the way of a Marine force was required, and on 4 June the 4th Marine Regiment, commanded by "Uncle Joe" Pendleton, was moved by rail from San Diego (where it formed the West Coast Expeditionary Force) to New Orleans whence it outloaded for the Dominican Republic. Pendleton landed at Monte Cristi on 18 June. He was nominally in command of the 2d Marine Brigade (all the marines in the Republic, nose count forty-seven officers and 1,728 enlisted men), but at Monte Cristi he had only a few more than a thousand. Leaving 235 marines to garrison the place, he started down the road with 833 officers and men toward Santiago de los Caballeros, some 100 kilometers away. That part of Hispaniola is semi-arid, rough *bosque* with cactus and thorn bushes and not much grass. Thirty kilometers down the road was Las Trencheras, a ridgeline crossing the road at right angles, where the Dominicans had beaten the Spanish in 1864. Pendleton pummeled the ridge with his artillery, got his machine guns into an enfilade position, and on 27 June the marines made a stand-up bayonet attack that cleared the ridge. The Dominicans counterattacked the night of the twenty-eighth under the mistaken notion that Pendleton's machine guns wouldn't function at night. The final fight on the road to Santiago was at Guayacanas, another ridgeline position. On 3 July, the artillery and machine guns again did their work. Meanwhile, a battalion had landed at Puerto Plata under Maj. H. I. ("Hiking Hiram") Bearss. The two columns met at Navarrete on 4 July and marched into Santiago two days later without further resistance.

On 29 November 1916, Capt. (soon to be Rear Adm.) Harry S. Knapp became military governor in a combination of the Cuban and Haitian pacification formulae. Ten towns were garrisoned and the 2d Marine Brigade settled down to an eight-year stay. The Guardia Nacional Dominicana, patterned on the Gendarmerie d'Haiti, was activated on 7 April 1917. It was authorized a strength of 1,234 officers and men and its first commandant was Lt. Col. George Thorpe, the same Thorpe who made the march to Addis Ababa. The officer ranks were open to Dominicans but not many members of the better families cared to join. One of the brightest and best was a young sugar plantation policeman named Rafael Leónidas Trujillo.

## BACK IN WASHINGTON

Barnett was proving to be exactly the right commandant for the Corps of that time, fully qualified for the home-guard wars of Washington. Deftly, unobtrusively, but firmly, he set about improving relationships with the Navy. The old Naval Station at Port Royal, South Carolina, was now called Paris (not yet spelled "Parris") Island and receiving all recruits from east of the Mississippi. Recruits from west of the Mississippi were sent to Mare Island in California. San Diego, home of the West Coast Expeditionary Force, was developing into a major base. An embryonic Marine Corps Reserve was started. The National Defense Act of August 1916 entitled the Marine Corps to seven brigadier generals. Three went to the staff: the adjutant and inspector, the quartermaster general, and the paymaster general. There were four promotions in the line: Waller, Lejeune, Pendleton, and Cole.

Ex-President Theodore Roosevelt, mellowed by the years or perhaps just pleased by the workings of the Roosevelt Corollary, remarked that the three most efficient military-constabulary organizations in the world were the French Foreign Legion, the Royal Canadian Mounted Police, and the U.S. Marines, each supreme in its own sphere of operations.

# 10

## 1917-1918
### The Whole Nation Has Reason to Be Proud

OVER THERE

War against Germany and the Central Powers was declared on 6 April 1917. Spurred by the slogan "First to Fight" there was a rush of recruits into the Marine Corps. The newborn Marine Corps Reserve, mobilized on 16 April, contributed three officers and thirty-three enlisted men. The recruit depots at Parris Island and Mare Island were soon swamped, and temporary recruiting centers had to be opened at Philadelphia, Brooklyn, and Norfolk Navy Yards. On 14 May, six thousand acres were leased at Quantico, south of Washington, as the beginnings of a major new base.

Maj. Gen. Cmdt. George Barnett was determined that a Marine expeditionary force would be on board the first convoy to sail for France. On 29 May, President Wilson approved the sending of a Marine regiment equipped as infantry. The stipulation was that the Marine regiment be organized and equipped according to the new wartime tables of organization developed by the Army. Marine regiments, such as they were, were small affairs of about eight hundred to a thousand men, a collection of numbered rifle companies of about 100 men each, with regiments and companies scattered all over the world. The companies would have to be brought up to a strength of about 250 men and organized into battalions and then into regiments, with such things as machine-gun companies added. Barnett pulled in companies from such places as Pensacola, Norfolk, Cuba, Haiti, and the Dominican Republic, filled out the companies to war strength with recruits, and formed them up into the 5th Regiment of Marines, with battalions at Philadelphia Navy Yard and the tent camp at the new base at Quantico.

Commanded by Charles Doyen, now a colonel, the regiment sailed on 14 June, much of it in the new Navy transport *Henderson,* and arrived at Saint-

Nazaire on 27 June 1917. Pershing parceled out the regiment as line-of-communication troops, mostly as military police. The 6th Marines under Albertus Catlin, now also a colonel, and the 6th Machine Gun Battalion came over in late 1917. The marines were brought together in early 1918 as the 4th Brigade, 2d U.S. Division, commanded by Doyen, promoted to brigadier general. It was a big brigade, 280 officers and 9,164 enlisted marines, as big as most of the understrength French and British divisions of the time. There was some winter training under the Chasseurs Alpins, whose disdain for the rifle except as a place to put the bayonet was in sharp conflict with Marine traditions.

The marines had worn their "khakis" and "greens" to France, but in January 1918 Pershing ordered them into Army olive drab to simplify the problems of supply and, also, it was said, to make unit identification by the enemy more difficult. Doyen had acceded to the order reluctantly. Except in rear areas, the beloved field hat also had to be given up and the soft "overseas" cap substituted. In the line the flat British-style trench helmet would be worn, sometimes dressed up with the addition of a Marine Corps emblem.

On Saint Patrick's Day, the brigade went into a quiet bit of trenches southeast of Verdun. Four days later the Germans began their Amiens offensive. Foch, reconstituting his reserve, pulled out the French division and left the Marine brigade with a division front. Here they learned the realities of trench warfare: cooties, rats, wire parties, raids, and gas.

The brigade was relieved on 9 May and along with the rest of the 2d Division moved to an assembly area northwest of Paris. Rumor was that they would follow the 1st U.S. Division into the attack at Cantigny. Pershing was mercilessly thinning the ranks of senior officers he considered too old or infirm for field command. Brigadier General Doyen was one of the casualties. He was invalided home and replaced by a Pershing favorite, Army Brig. Gen. James Harbord. Harbord had been Pershing's chief of staff and he had gone from major to brigadier general in a year. Col. Buck Neville, now the commander of the 5th Marines and far senior to Harbord at the war's beginning, had every reason to think he should have been given command of the brigade. On Harbord's arrival, when Neville handed him a pair of Marine Corps emblems, it was half a greeting, half a challenge. Harbord promptly put them on his collar.

In addition to the Marine brigade, the division, commanded by Maj. Gen. Omar Bundy, had the 3d Brigade of Infantry, three artillery regiments, an engineer regiment, and a field signal battalion, altogether some twenty-eight thousand men. This was a Regular Army division. Pershing's AEF—the American Expeditionary Forces—was made of three kinds of divisions: Regular Army, National Guard, and National Army. Generally speaking, the level of training and experience was highest in the Regular Army divisions, less so in the National Guard divisions, and least so in the National Army divisions.

The Marines enjoyed an important advantage over their Army counterparts. Some 20 percent of the 5th Marines and 10 percent of the 6th Marines were "old-timers" (defined as someone with more than one year's service). The 9th Infantry and 23d Infantry regiments, their opposite numbers in the 3d Brigade of Infantry, had only about 5 percent.

More significantly, the officer corps of the pre-war Regular Army of some 130,000 men was spread very thin in a new American army that was expanding explosively to one million, two million, three million, four million men. The expansion of the Marine Corps was proportionately much less: from fifteen thousand to seventy-six thousand. From the grade of captain on up, the Marine Corps had a reservoir of experienced officers who had seen battle of a sort in such places as China, Panama, Nicaragua, Cuba, Haiti, and Santo Domingo. The same was true of the senior Marine NCOs.

On 31 May, the 75th Company, 1st Battalion, 6th Marines, was billeted at a French farm with a stone barn so vast that it could sleep the entire war-strength company of 250 marines. Sgt. Gerald C. Thomas and several buddies had gone to regimental headquarters about five kilometers away for Memorial Day services. A company runner found them and told them to get back to the company area; they were moving out. The company got into heavy marching order and out onto the road. French *camions* came along and they were on their way, not to Cantigny, but to the Paris-Meaux sector, up near a place called Château-Thierry.

## Château-Thierry and Belleau Wood

On 27 May 1918, Ludendorff, with forty-odd divisions, had launched his Chemin des Dames offensive, the northern front had been sliced in two, and the Germans were coming through a four-kilometer gap left by the wreckage of the French 43d Division. The weather was intolerably hot. The beaten French were streaming to the rear. A French major, attempting to acquaint the Americans with the realities of the situation and not trusting his spoken English, scribbled out a note to Capt. Lloyd Williams, commanding the 51st Company, 2d Battalion, 5th Marines. It read: "Retreat, the Germans are coming." Williams, one of the "old-timers," looked at the Frenchman coldly and said, "Retreat, hell. We just got here."

A half-dozen others, Marine and Army, subsequently claimed the "Retreat, hell" quotation, but best evidence is that it was said by Captain Williams. Whoever said it, it reflected the mood of the U.S. 2d Division. On 1 June 1918 they formed a line astride the Paris-Metz road, 23d Infantry on the left flank, 6th and 5th Marines in the center, 9th Infantry on the right. At dawn on 2 June, the German 28th Division, a good one much admired by the Kaiser's wife, attacked along the axis of the road, destination Paris, and hit the Marine center. The German veterans got a lesson in rifle fire that began to kill at eight hundred yards. A French aviator thought he saw the American line falling back and so reported to his corps commander. An inquiry came down through channels; Harbord in turn asked Maj. Thomas Holcomb, commander of the 2d Battalion, 6th Marines. "When I do my running," said Holcomb flatly, "It will be in the opposite direction."

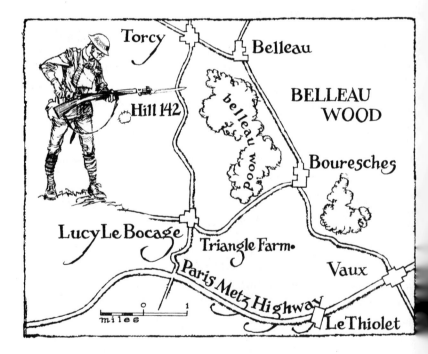

Lemuel C. Shepherd had graduated from Virginia Military Institute the year before. Now he was a twenty-two-year-old first lieutenant and a platoon leader in the 55th Company, 5th Marines. On 3 June the 55th Company was holding at Les Mares Farm. Shepherd, with a dozen marines, was out in front of the company in an outpost. The Germans probed the position. A machine-gun bullet cut into Shepherd's throat a quarter inch from his jugular vein, but he refused to be evacuated. The next day, 4 June, the 55th Company held their positions against an afternoon attack coming at them through a field of waist-high wheat. This was as close as the Germans got to Paris.

The Germans attacked again on the fifth of June, then sullenly took up defensive positions. Belleau Wood, in front of the Marines, was a natural fortress, a square mile of woods and tumbled boulders. Behind it were the villages of Torcy, Belleau, and Bouresches. In the woods were two battalions of the 461st Imperial German Infantry, short on riflemen but liberally augmented with Maxim machine guns.

The French general, Jean Degoutte, ordered an attack by the Americans. It began on the morning of 6 June, the 1st Battalion, 5th Marines, going forward in four waves, lines neatly dressed—tactics preached by the French but not practiced by them since 1915. Across the wheat fields, dotted with blood-red poppies, the German machine gunners let the marines get close before opening fire. By noon the 1st Battalion, 5th Marines, had taken Hill 142 west of the wood. Now came the second phase of the attack. The 2d Battalion, 5th Marines, and the 2d and 3d Battalions, 6th Marines, went into the wood itself. The marines were working with Springfield rifles and bayonets, Chauchat automatic rifles, and Hotchkiss machine guns. They had no trench mortars, no signal flares or Very pistols, and there was a shortage of grenades. The marines had to either shoot the German machine gunners or crawl up and bayonet them. War correspondent Floyd Gibbons, before he himself was wounded, heard 1st Sgt. Daniel Daly (of Peking and Haiti) yell to a platoon that had lost its leader, "Come on, you sons of bitches. Do you want to live forever?"

Colonel Catlin of the 6th Marines went down, shot through the right lung. Two platoons of the 6th Marines, one of them under a young Tennessee law graduate, 1st Lt. Clifton B. Cates, got into the village of Bouresches and held it against repeated counterattacks. Sgt. Maj. John Quick (he of Guantánamo and Samar) brought up the ammunition to Cates in a Ford truck and earned the Army's Distinguished Service Cross. The Marines took two-thirds of the woods that first day but the price was high: 1,087 Marine casualties, dead and wounded.

Next day, the captain of the 55th Company was killed and for a few hours Lt. Lem Shepherd was the company commander. Then he too was hit. His second wound was a bullet through the leg. He had a little dog named Kiki who followed the stretcher bearers to the aid station. When an orderly tried to separate him from Kiki, Shepherd said, "Either take my dog or leave me here." The dog went with him.

The brigade consolidated on the seventh, digging a line of shallow rifle pits. Someone called them "foxholes" and the name stuck. The Germans tried a counterattack on the eighth. The marines went forward again next day and by the night of 12 June had all the northern tip of the woods. The attack was costly and among the Marine dead was Captain Williams of the 51st Company, he who had best claim to "Retreat, hell." The Germans counterattacked in strength on 13 June behind a cloud of mustard gas. The marines held their ground, but by the fifteenth Harbord was demanding that his brigade be relieved. The 7th U.S. Infantry, half-trained, came up on the night of 16 June, and filed into the random line of foxholes. The Marine brigade, some of its battalions down to one-third strength, went into division reserve. The 7th Infantry lasted three days before it was used up. The marines went back in the attack on 23 June, and on the twenty-sixth Harbord could send the signal: "Woods now U.S. Marine Corps entirely." General Degoutte, commanding the French Sixth Army, on 30 June decreed, "Henceforth in all official papers, Belleau Wood shall bear the name, 'Bois de la Brigade de Marine.'"

The Germans made their own sober assessment and begrudgingly allowed that the marines, with more experience, might be considered to be of storm-trooper quality. The marines earnestly told each other that the Heinies were calling them "Teufelhunden," or "Devildogs," but there is no evidence of this in German records.

On the fourth of July the French held a big parade in Paris to honor the American Expeditionary Forces. Each American regiment sent a platoon to take part. Cates commanded the platoon from the 6th Marines. Shepherd, on crutches and with his little dog Kiki, stood on the curb at Place de Concorde to watch the parade go by. Suddenly he saw his old platoon from the 55th Company in the line of march. He joined them on his crutches.

The Marines got what the Army considered to be an inordinate amount of publicity for Belleau Wood. On 6 June, Floyd Gibbons had filed a story that began, "I am up front and entering Belleau Wood with the U.S. Marines." He was then badly wounded, including the loss of his left eye. Under the heavy-handed press censorship the names of units and their locations were not ordinarily allowed in press dispatches. However, the censors, thinking that Gibbons was dying and had filed his last dispatch, allowed his story to go through uncensored. An American public, hungry for war news, seized on the story that the Marines had saved Paris. This did not go down well with the Army, which chafed at the lack of mention of what the Army components of the 2d Division had done, to say nothing of the considerable contributions of the 3d Division at Château-Thierry. Worse, some newspapers gave the Marines credit for Château-Thierry itself. It was something that would rankle the Army for many years to come.

Meanwhile, Brigadier General Lejeune had arrived in France with Barnett's offer of another Marine brigade for the American Expeditionary Forces and the personal expectation of becoming the Marine division commander. Pershing tartly reported to the secretary of War that "While Marines are splendid troops, their use as a separate division is inadvisable." He was, however, willing to take another Marine infantry brigade. An offer of a Marine artillery regiment, the 10th Marines, was turned down—although individual Marine artillery officers would be acceptable as replacement officers. Lejeune was ordered to the command of a National Guard brigade.

## SOISSONS

On Bastille Day, 14 July, Harbord, a jaunty hybrid in his *poilu*'s helmet and Marine emblems, moved up to command of the 2d Division, replacing General Bundy, who went quietly elsewhere. Buck Neville took over the Marine brigade and would soon be promoted to brigadier general.

Next day, 15 July, Ludendorff launched the last German offensive of the war. The 2d Division went forward in a counterattack southeast of Soissons. The Marine brigade on the night of 17 July moved through mud and rain into attack positions in the Forest of Retz. Next morning, at dawn, the 5th Marines jumped off and by nightfall had taken the village of Vierzy. Next day, the 6th Marines passed through the 5th Marines and advanced a mile and a half before running headlong into a corps-size German counterattack.

Cliff Cates, now the commander of the 96th Company, found himself in an abandoned trench and sent back a scribbled message: "I have only two men left out of my company and 20 out of other companies. . . . I have no one on my left, and only a few on my right. I will hold."

That night a fresh division came up and relieved the brigade which in two days' fighting had lost 1,972 Marines, dead and wounded. Veterans of both battles said that it was worse than Belleau Wood.

## NANCY AND MARBACHE

On 23 July the 2d Division received orders to march to a rest area near Nanteuil-le-Haudoin. Lejeune arrived there two days later and took command of the 4th Brigade. On 29 July, Harbord was detached to take over the AEF's troubled Service of Supply, and Lejeune, in an Army concession to Marine sensibilities, moved up to command of the 2d Division. Neville, soon to be promoted to brigadier general, resumed command of the brigade. Meanwhile, the division was on the move to the vicinity of Nancy to refit, train, and absorb replacements.

The young assistant secretary of the Navy, Franklin D. Roosevelt, on a tour of the Western Front, inspected the Marine brigade on 5 August. Roosevelt had just visited Belleau Wood. On the spot he authorized the enlisted marines to wear Marine Corps emblems on the collars of their Army issue uniforms (until then an officer's privilege) "in recognition of the splendid work of the Marine Brigade."

Next morning the 2d Division was again on the march, this time to the Marbache sector, a quiet twelve-kilometer front on the south face of the Saint-Mihiel salient. The 5th Marines went in on the east bank of the Moselle, the 6th Marines on the left bank, the regimental boundary conveniently marked by the bridge at Pont-à-Mousson. This time the now battlewise marines allowed a quiet sector to remain quiet. The ten-day stay at Marbache was almost idyllic.

## SAINT-MIHIEL

Coming up next was the first big all-American push, two U.S. corps to pinch out the Saint-Mihiel salient. Stout Col. Harry Lee now had the 6th Marines and Col. Logan Feland the 5th Marines. The 3d Infantry Brigade led off at dawn on 12 September, following behind a four-hour artillery preparation. As always, there was mud and rain. The marines passed through next day and by nightfall on the fifteenth both regiments had their objectives. It was an easy fight compared to Belleau and Soissons but nevertheless there were 706 fresh Marine casualties to be added to the bill.

Brig. Gen. Eli Cole brought over the 5th Marine Brigade in September. The War Department told Pershing to use it as he saw fit. Command was passed from Cole to Smedley Butler, a brigadier general at thirty-seven, youngest in Corps history. To "Old Gimlet Eye" Butler's intense disgust, because of Pershing's unwillingness to combine it with the 4th Brigade into a Marine division, the brigade was assigned to guard duty with the Service of Supply with headquarters at Brest. In fairness to Pershing, the two Marine brigades could not have been combined into a division along with a brigade of artillery and a regiment of engineers and other supporting troops with any hope of the division being combat-ready before the spring of 1919. But no one expected the war to end until 1919, and all of Pershing's plans pointed toward a great American army being fully ready by then. There were even some very secret plans being discussed at U.S. Navy headquarters in London of an amphibious landing that would put a Marine division ashore in the Adriatic against the flank of Austro-Hungary.

## IN THE AIR

On the day war was declared there were six officers, headed by Capt. Alfred Cunningham, one warrant officer, and forty-three enlisted men in the Marine Aeronautical Section at Naval Aeronautic Station, Pensacola. Soon afterward the detachment was transferred to the Navy Yard at Philadelphia. There, a hangar was built on the river with openings at both ends—one for seaplanes, and the other for land planes. Total flying inventory consisted of "two land aeroplanes, two sea aeroplanes, one school land aeroplane, and two kite balloons."

In October 1917 the detachment was split into the 1st Marine Aviation Squadron (land planes)—which was moved to Mineola, Long Island—and the 1st Marine Aeronautic Company (seaplanes). The latter company, under command of Maj. Francis T. ("Cocky") Evans (first pilot to loop a seaplane), sailed from Philadelphia on 9 January 1918 with ten Curtiss R-6 seaplanes and two Curtiss N-9s for Ponta Delgada in the Azores. From then until the

Armistice they assiduously would fly antisubmarine patrols without ever sighting a U-boat.

In early 1918 the 1st Marine Aviation Squadron had moved from Mineola to Gerstner Field in Louisiana. About this time, Cunningham returned from France, where he had been exploring opportunities for employment. His recommendation was that four Marine squadrons be sent to form the day wing of a proposed Navy Northern Bombing Group to be based near Calais. Accordingly, the 1st Marine Aviation Squadron was transferred from Louisiana to Curtiss Field (redesignated "Marine Flying Field") in Miami in April 1918 and expanded into the 1st Marine Aviation Force, with four squadrons—A, B, C, and D. Senior squadron commander was thirty-three-year-old Capt. Roy S. Geiger. Captain Cunningham, as commander, 1st Marine Aviation Force, arrived at Brest on 30 July with Squadrons A, B, and C (Squadron D would not arrive until October). Room was found for them on fields near Calais. Redesignated as Squadrons 7, 8, and 9, they were to receive the first seventy-two American-built De Havilland–4 bombers to arrive in France, but the DH-4s when they arrived were so badly put together that they had to be rebuilt. Meanwhile, the Marine pilots were assigned to RAF Squadrons 217 and 218, which had the British De Havilland, and a lucky few to RAF Squadron 213, which had the Sopwith Camel.

## BLANC MONT

On the ground, the 2d Division had moved over to Gen. Henri Gouraud's Fourth Army for the Meuse-Argonne offensive. The Allies were now up against the Hindenburg Line. By the end of September the French had been stopped near Somme-Py in the Champagne Sector. Key terrain was Blanc Mont—the "White Mountain"—held by the Germans since 1914. Lejeune told Gouraud the 2d Division could take Blanc Mont. The marines would attack frontally against the ridge. The 3d Infantry Brigade would come in from the right. The French would advance on the left against a projection called the Essen Hook.

On 3 October 1918 the 6th Marines jumped off at 0555 hours on the heels of a thunderous five-minute preparation by two hundred guns and had its objective before noon. Meanwhile, the French were lagging two miles behind, stopped by the Essen Hook. The 5th Marines took it for them in a right angle attack ("Remarkable," said Gouraud's operations summary).

Next day, the 5th Marines changed direction once again, passed through the 6th Marines on the ridge, and drove to Saint-Étienne, three miles away. The Germans counterattacked in regimental strength but failed to halt the advance. On 6 October, the marines entered Saint-Étienne and their part of the battle was over. It had cost them 2,538 casualties and brought a third citation in French Army orders. This entitled the two regiments to the streamer of the Croix de Guerre and to this day the 5th and 6th Marines wear the red-and-green *fourragère*.

## MEUSE-ARGONNE

After Blanc Mont the 2d Division moved back to the American First Army and was assigned to Maj. Gen. Charles P. Summerall's V Corps for the final drive of the war. The division was assigned a narrow, two-kilometer front in the center of the First Army line and given the mission of driving a wedge into what the Americans called "the Hindenburg Line." Facing the marines was the German 61st Division, in process of being relieved by the 52d Division, supported by the Bavarian 15th Division, which the Leathernecks had previously met on Blanc Mont. Supported by three hundred guns and a company of fifteen light tanks, the 2d Division jumped off on 1 November with the Marine brigade in the assault. The battalions leap-frogged forward, and by nightfall the marines had advanced nine kilometers and taken seventeen hundred prisoners. The Germans withdrew behind the Meuse. Elsewhere along the Western Front the German Army was in general retreat but against the American First Army they showed a streak of stubbornness.

On the night of 4 November the division fought its way forward to the Meuse River. At daylight patrols were pushed up and down the near bank to search for crossing sites. On the evening of 7 November, Summerall issued orders for the division to be prepared to cross the river and seize the heights on the east bank. The 2d Division crossed the Meuse the night of 10 November, the one hundred and forty-third birthday of the Corps. Nagging at Lejeune was the realization that his marines and doughboys knew that an armistice was about to be signed. The crossing was a bloody night's work, but by 11 o'clock the next morning, 11 November, the time of the armistice, two battalions of the 5th Marines, with the 1st Battalion, 9th Infantry, had linked up with elements of the 89th Division which had also crossed.

To the troops it seemed a senseless attack and there was much bitterness in the brigade. The marines and doughboys put the blame on Summerall, the corps commander, but Summerall had gotten his orders from First Army and First Army had gotten its orders from Pershing who had gotten his orders from Marshal Foch in a telegram dated 9 November to "expedite" movement against the retreating enemy. Pershing was able to report: "The Fifth Corps in the First Army forced a crossing of the Meuse east of Beaumont, and gained the commanding heights within the reentrant of the river, thus completing our control of the Meuse River line."

In the air, Major Cunningham (he had been promoted in August) had not been able to get his squadrons into action in their own equipment until October and then only by some shrewd trading of new Liberty engines for British fuselages. By this time the original targets of the Northern Bombing Group, the submarine pens at Ostend, Zeebrugge, and Bruges, had been abandoned by the Germans. Pershing assigned the group to support the British and it was given the general mission of attacking any rear-area targets which might hinder the retreat of the German Army. When it was over on 11 November, 1st Marine Aviation Force in its brief period of action had lost four dead, shot down twelve Germans, and flown fifty-seven bombing missions. In the nineteen months the United States was in the war, Marine aviation had expanded to 280 officers, 2,200 men, and 340 aircraft.

The 4th Brigade of Marines marched on foot into Germany. A few days after the fighting was over they received new Browning machine guns and automatic rifles to replace their cranky Chauchats and clumsy Hotchkiss guns. Lejeune received a reprimand for the shabby appearance of his division from spit-and-polish inspectors who came down from GHQ.

After an uneventful tour of duty along the Rhine in the Army of Occupation, the Marine brigade came home to Quantico in the summer of 1919. On 12 August there was a march past the White House and the next day at Quantico the brigade was demobilized and most of its members went home, taking with them their tin hats and gas masks as authorized souvenirs. Some thirty-two thousand marines had served in France. There had been 11,366 casualties of whom 2,459 were killed or were forever missing in action. Only twenty-five marines were taken prisoner. ("Surrendering wasn't popular," said Colonel Catlin.)

After that last review, President Woodrow Wilson wrote Major General Commandant Barnett a brief note which said: "The whole nation has reason to be proud of them."

# 11

## *1917-1941*
## IF ATTACKED, SHOOT AND SHOOT TO KILL

### WEST INDIES AND SIBERIA (1917–1920)

There had been an excursion to Siberia, beginning on 29 June 1918, when the veteran USS *Brooklyn* put her marines ashore in Vladivostok. The Japanese, British, and French were also there and the marines were given the old Imperial Navy Yard to patrol.

In the Caribbean, while larger events were taking place in Europe, revolt had flamed up again in Cuba. The Platt Amendment was invoked and marines from the Atlantic Fleet were landed in eastern Cuba in February 1917. They came out in May—the declaration of war with Germany causing higher priorities for their employment. Then in August 1917 the new 7th Marines were landed. (Sugar was a strategic material and this was the Sugar Intervention.) The 9th Marines followed in December, along with the 3d Marine Brigade headquarters. In July 1918 the brigade headquarters and the 9th Marines went to Texas to join the 8th Marines, who were already there, watching the border in the belief that German agents were somehow fomenting a Mexican reconquest of the Southwest. In December the 1st Marines came down from Philadelphia to join the 7th Marines in Cuba and both the regiments were put under 6th Brigade command. By the end of August 1919 all marines were gone from Cuba except for one battalion which remained in Camagüey, near Guantánamo, until 1922.

Across the Windward Passage, a new Caco chieftain had emerged in Haiti, one Charlemagne Masséna Peralte. In March 1919 the commandant of the Gendarmerie asked for the help of the 1st Marine Brigade, which had been standing on the sidelines. The brigade was essentially the lightweight 2d Marine Regiment, less than a thousand men, but reinforcements began to arrive, including Squadron E with seven Curtiss HS-2 flying boats and six Curtiss "Jennies."

From April to September the marines and gendarmes fought 131 actions against the Cacos. By then the old campaigner, Col. Frederic Wise, had come down to take command of the Gendarmerie and on 2 October Col. John H. Russell took over the brigade. Four days later Charlemagne sent three hundred men on a raid into Port-au-Prince. Thirty Cacos were killed but it was now obvious that the rebellion would not be put down until Charlemagne himself had been dealt with.

On the night of 30 October 1919, Capt. Herman H. Hanneken (permanent rank, sergeant, USMC) started out with 1st Lt. (corporal, USMC) William R. Button (faces blackened), led by Private François, a gendarme "deserter," to get Charlemagne personally. The bait was a Browning automatic rifle Button was carrying, ostensibly captured from the *blancs*. This plus François's persuasiveness got them past the challenges of six Caco outposts and into Charlemagne's camp in the hills above Grande Rivière. François pointed out the Caco chief in the firelight. Hanneken put two .45-caliber slugs into Charlemagne while Button chopped away at his bodyguard with the BAR. Charlemagne's body was lashed across a mule and packed down to Cap Haitien where, after a proper Christian service, it was buried in a block of concrete so the Cacos wouldn't dig it up and perhaps resurrect Charlemagne as a zombie.

Another Caco leader, Benoît Batraville, rose to take Charlemagne's place. Colonel Russell, reinforced by the 8th Marines, who arrived in December 1919, worked out a plan to comb the bandit-infested country with relays of fresh patrols, never letting up the pressure. First move, though, came from Batraville. On the night of 14 January 1920 he infiltrated three hundred men into Port-au-Prince. Marine and gendarme patrols searched them out during the early morning hours on the fifteenth and there was a good deal of shooting. By daylight, sixty-six Cacos were dead and twice that number wounded.

Some thirty-two hundred real or professed Cacos surrendered during January and February. But Batraville himself fought on. Marine fliers had been experimenting with bombs dropped out of mail sacks tied to the landing gear spreaders of their Jennies and DH-4s. Then some proper bomb racks arrived from the States and they found that if they dived at a target at a 45-degree angle they got good accuracy. In March, two Marine aircraft caught Batraville on a hilltop near his native Mirebalais and drove him into the rifle and machine-gun fire of converging Marine patrols. In the slaughter that followed, Batraville lost two hundred more Cacos killed and wounded.

On 4 April 1920 Batraville ambushed a small patrol and ritualistically ate the roasted heart and liver of the Marine lieutenant, but the magic did him little good. On 19 May another Marine patrol found him, a Marine sergeant knocked him down with a burst from his BAR, and a second sergeant finished him with a bullet through the head. There would now be a long period of peace in Haiti under the firm hand of newly promoted Brigadier General Russell, U.S. High Commissioner.

## SANTO DOMINGO

Across the frontier (marked in the north by the well-named Rio Massacre) the neighboring Dominicans were not all submitting meekly to Rear Admiral Knapp's military government, a government in which "Uncle Joe" Pendleton held the portfolios of War and Navy, Interior, and Police. On 29 November 1916, 1st Lt. Ernest C. ("Bolo") Williams had shot his way into the *fortaleza* at San Francisco de Macorís. Governor Pérez took umbrage at Williams's action and went off into the bush with two hundred followers. Converging Marine columns from La Vega and Sánchez drove Pérez south and his band was gradually worn away. After Pérez there were other smaller *grupos* to be hunted down. One of the stiffest actions of 1917 was that fought against a bandit called "Chacha" at Consuelo sugar plantation near San Pedro de Macorís by another old campaigner, Lt. Col. "Hiking Hiram" Bearss. That was in January. There was also Vincentico Evangelista who was holding out farther north near El Seibo. "Chacha" gave himself up and Evangelista was eventually killed.

A system of provost courts was set up. In 1917 and the first half of 1918, some fifty-three thousand firearms were collected. More than a hundred skirmishes were fought in 1918. The most difficult operation of the year was the 250-mile pursuit of one Dios Olivorio into the western mountains. Brig. Gen. Ben Fuller relieved "Uncle Joe" Pendleton on 21 October 1918 as commander of the 2d Brigade, which now had the 3d Marines as well as the 4th Marines. In February 1919 Fuller got another regiment, the 15th Marines, added to his brigade and Squadron D arrived with six DH-4s. There were two hundred fire fights that year.

In December 1920 President Wilson announced that the marines were going to be withdrawn. Strength of the brigade, now under Brig. Gen. Logan Feland, stood at about 120 officers and two thousand men. A systematic series of cordons-and-searches in the eastern provinces ensured that virtually every male Dominican was picked up for screening. By the spring of 1922 banditry was almost at a halt. Command of the brigade next rotated to Brig. Gen. Harry Lee, and in December he also became the military governor. During the year the 3d and 15th Regiments were disbanded and their assets absorbed by the 4th Marines and the reactivated 1st Marines.

The Guardia, never popular with the Dominicans, had gotten up to twelve hundred in 1918 then had sagged as low as 350 in 1921. It was now renamed the Policia Nacional Dominicana, built back up to twelve hundred, and began taking over the garrisoning of the *fortalezas* and *puestos*. By 1923 the shrinking brigade was acting mainly as a reserve for the National Police. A new constitutional government was sworn in on 12 July 1924. In August the 4th Marines started back to San Diego from whence they had come eight years earlier, and on 16 September 1924 the last Marine company left Santo Domingo. Said General Lee in his final report: "We left a state enjoying peace, and with a loyal and well-developed military force, with fine roads, many schools, a fine military hospital, and, in short, with every promise for a future of stable government under Dominican rule."

## Lejeune Becomes Commandant

On 12 February 1918 General Barnett had been appointed to a second term as commandant, but in the years following the end of the war he had trouble with the secretary of the Navy, abstemious Josephus Daniels. On 18 June 1920 he received a sealed letter from the secretary demanding that he retire immediately or accept a reduction to brigadier general and reassignment. Barnett bit the bullet and was sent to the Department of the Pacific in San Francisco, a newly created kind of West Coast Marine Corps headquarters. The new commandant, as of 30 June 1920, was the leathery Cajun and 2d Division commander, John Lejeune.

In 1921 Lejeune published a birthday message to the Corps. It makes passing mention of the Argonne and maybe he was thinking of the last night of the war when he had it published. It begins: "On November 10, 1775, a Corps of Marines was created by a resolution of Continental Congress. Since that date many thousand men have borne the name 'Marine.'" It is still read to all hands on every Marine Corps Birthday.

Lejeune understood that readiness was the hallmark of the Marine Corps and specifically, although it had been obscured by the events of World War I, amphibious readiness. In 1921, the Marine Corps Schools at Quantico were consolidated. Three courses were offered: the Basic Course (in 1924 it moved to Philadelphia, where it would remain until World War II), the Company Officers Course, and the Field Officers Course.

The Advance Base Force headquarters (which during the war years had been under tough old Tony Waller) was also moved to Quantico. In 1922 Lejeune recommended to the Navy General Board that the term "Advance Base Force" be discontinued. His argument was that the primary war mission of the Marine Corps was to supply a mobile force to accompany the fleet for operations ashore. The Advance Base Force accordingly became the East Coast Expeditionary Force, matching the West Coast Expeditionary Force, formed in 1916 at San Diego.

One of Lejeune's planners was Lt. Col. Earl H. ("Pete") Ellis, who had been adjutant of the 4th Marine Brigade in France. In 1923 Ellis took a year's leave to tour Micronesia and died in the Japanese-held Palau Islands under circumstances still not fully explained. But before that, in 1921, he had developed the 50,000-word Operation Plan 712, "Advanced Base Operations in Micronesia" in which, predicting that Japan would strike first, he had written: "It will be necessary for us to project our fleet and landing forces across the Pacific and wage war in Japanese waters. To effect this requires that we have sufficient bases to support the fleet, both during its projection and afterwards."

In the early 1920s the marines from Quantico under Smedley Butler (their dress uniforms were a convenient blue for the Union, while cadets from Virginia military schools wore the Confederate gray) amused themselves and official Washington with reenactments of some of the Civil War battles: Wilderness, Gettysburg, New Market, and Antietam. There was also strenuous athletic competition—boxing, football, and baseball.

On Broadway, *What Price Glory?*, coauthored by Maxwell Anderson and Lawrence T. Stallings, was a great hit (and banned in Boston for its shocking language). As a new lieutenant, Stallings had joined the 3d Battalion, 5th Marines, at Belleau Wood and commanded a platoon at Bouresches. Going against a machine-gun nest on 25 June 1918 got him wounds that eventually cost him a leg and caused his retirement as a captain in 1920. There was also his friend Capt. John W. Thomason Jr., of the 49th Company, 1st Battalion, 5th Marines, whose book *Fix Bayonets!* came out in 1926 and was followed by a long series of articles and stories in *The Saturday Evening Post*. Thomason's florid Kiplingesque prose was illustrated with his own lean, pungent, pen-and-ink sketches. The tough, wise-cracking, hard-as-nails, heart-of-gold Marine sergeant, as played by Edmund Lowe, Victor McLaglen, and Wallace Beery, began to appear on the American movie screen. The public image of the United States marine was taking shape: lean, sunburnt, in faded khaki and rakish field hat, rattling through some jungled banana republic on board a narrow-gauge railroad, an '03 rifle in one hand and a bottle in the other, or in olive drab with a tin helmet and heavy marching order, shouldering arms and starting down a shell-rutted road for the Western Front murky with gray-green fog, turning to grin and wave good-by to Mademoiselle, the innkeeper's gallant if naughty daughter.

Meanwhile, less colorful marines were analyzing the mistakes of Gallipoli and identifying the bare bones of a viable amphibious doctrine. In 1922 and 1923, there were exploratory, battalion-size landing exercises at Guantá-namo, Panama, and Cape Cod. In 1924, there was a brigade-size maneuver that established an advance base at Culebra Island off Puerto Rico in con-cert with an assault against the Panama Canal. The next year, there was a joint Army-Navy problem at Oahu with fifteen hundred marines simulating a 42,000-man landing force. There would be no more exercises for the next seven years but the lessons learned began to get down on paper. The crux of the matter was getting from ship to shore with the necessary men and materiel. A good deal of attention was focused on landing craft and the pos-sibility of amphibian vehicles.

In 1921, there was a rash of mail robberies. On 11 November, Secretary of the Navy Edwin Denby (himself a World War I marine) put marines to watch-ing post offices and riding the mail trains and postal trucks with orders "if attacked, shoot and shoot to kill." The mail robberies came to a sudden halt. (In October 1926 the robberies began again. Twenty-five hundred marines were detailed to guard the mails and once more the robberies stopped abruptly.)

## SECOND NICARAGUAN CAMPAIGN (1926–1933)

In Nicaragua the seesaw between the Conservatives and Liberals had contin-ued. The presence of a company-size Marine Legation Guard in Managua cooled off a Liberal revolt in 1922. A partially U.S.-supervised and almost-honest election in 1924 chose a coalition government: Conservative Carlos Solarzano as president, Liberal Juan Sacasa as vice president. The Legation Guard packed up and left on 4 August 1925.

With the Marines gone, a coalition government was more than Conservative general Emiliano Chamorro Vargas could stomach. Open revolt began in October, Solarzano and Sacasa fled the country, and in January 1926 Chamorro made himself president. In May, the protected cruiser *Cleveland* briefly put a landing party ashore at Bluefields. By August, a Liberal army under José María Moncado had pushed the Conservatives back into Bluefields, and the marines and seamen came ashore once again (this time from the cruiser *Galveston*), declaring Bluefields and its environs a neutral zone. The Liberals and Conservatives were persuaded to accept a truce and promised to attend a peace conference at Corinto on the opposite coast. A landing party was put ashore from the *Denver* at Corinto (which was also declared a neutral zone). Chamorro viewed the whole proceedings with growing suspicion and on 30 October resigned as president and withdrew. Adolfo Díaz, who had been a pliant president during the intervention of 1912, was elected chief executive by the rump conference. His government was promptly recognized by the United States, and he equally promptly asked for help in protecting American lives and property. Meanwhile, Mexico was insisting that Sacasa, somewhere in Guatemala, was the legitimate president. Also, General Moncado was still in the field in eastern Nicaragua and proving resistant to Díaz's offers of honors and money. With Mexican help, Sacasa came back into the country in early December 1926 and joined up with Moncado. Together they came storming down the Mosquito Coast, helping themselves to American-owned supplies and equipment as needed. An American was killed at Puerto Cabeza and marines went ashore from the Special Services Squadron to establish neutral zones there and also at Prinzapolca and Río Grande. On 10 January 1927 the 2d Battalion, 5th Marines, under Lt. Col. James J. Meade, arrived from Guantánamo and landed at Bluefields.

Blocked by the Americans, Moncado marched west toward Managua. Meade, leaving one company in position on the Escondido River west of Bluefields, reembarked the rest of his battalion, took them through the Canal, and landed them at Corinto. He then took his bobtailed battalion up the old familiar ninety miles of railroad to Managua, relieved the Legation Guard, and assumed responsibility for the defense of the capital from a completely willing President Díaz.

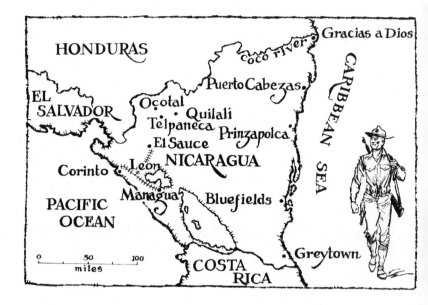

Marine Observation Squadron One under Maj. Ross E. ("Rusty") Rowell arrived on 26 February with six vintage De Havillands. The transport *Henderson* came down from Quantico with the rest of the 5th Marines. President Coolidge had also hurriedly authorized the sale of three thousand Krag rifles, two hundred Browning machine guns, and three million rounds of ammunition to the Díaz government. On 26 March the 2d Marine Brigade was reactivated under command of Logan Feland. The Conservatives and Liberals were now facing each other at Matagalpa, up in the hills north of Managua. The marines slid in between them and established another "neutral zone" on 17 April.

About this time Henry L. Stimson arrived on the scene to arbitrate. The Stimson-Díaz plan offered general amnesty with a restoration of property and both sides turning in their weapons. There was a thirty-minute conference on the banks of the Tipitapa River the afternoon of 4 May and a deal was struck whereby the Conservatives were to stay in office until 1928, when there were to be U.S.-supervised elections. Meanwhile, the Marine brigade would guarantee law and order, disarm both sides, and create a Guardia Nacional.

Disarmament was sweetened by a U.S. offer of ten dollars for every firearm relinquished. One Liberal not acceding to the order to stack arms was

Augusto César Sandino, who took off with 150 men up into the mountains of Nuevo Segovia, near the Honduran border. A Marine detachment was sent after him. The new Guardia, patterned on the Haitian and Dominican models, was supposed to have sixty officers (thirty-five of them marines) and a thousand men, but it was having trouble getting started. One of the new Guardia companies with forty-eight men joined the thirty-eight-man Marine detachment at Ocotal on 5 July. Sandino slipped into Ocotal the night of 15 July. The fire fight began about one o'clock in the morning and went on until eight o'clock, when Sandino sent in a demand for surrender under a flag of truce. The marines refused and the battle started again. Two DH-4s came over on morning patrol, saw something was wrong, and, while one strafed the attackers, the other landed outside the town to interrogate some of the locals. "Rusty" Rowell came on station at two-thirty with four De Havillands, each armed to the teeth with four 25-pound bombs and all the machine-gun ammunition it could carry. He led a dive-bombing attack which would later interest certain German students of air warfare. Fifty-six Sandinistas were killed and about twice that number wounded. Altogether the marines claimed, perhaps with a degree of enlargement, to have killed nearly three hundred bandits. Their own losses were one dead and five wounded.

Sandino's stronghold was reported to be a place called El Chipote, but no one was quite sure where that was. Some 225 marines and *guardias* were sent into Nuevo Segovia to look for it. On 19 September, a fair-sized battle was fought at Telpaneca, ten miles from Ocotal. Then, on 8 October, a Marine plane was shot down on razor-backed Sapotillal ridge, a few miles north of Telpaneca. A patrol sent out to rescue the pilot and observer walked into an ambush but fought its way clear. Two larger patrols then converged on the ridge, fighting an estimated 250 Sandinistas and killing or wounding sixty, but the downed plane was not reached until 30 October and then it was too late. Sandino had already captured and hanged the two fliers.

On 23 November Rowell's observers finally pinpointed El Chipote northeast of Sapotillal ridge. In early December, two columns of marines and *guardias,* about two hundred men altogether, were sent forward to set up a base at Quilali before moving against El Chipote. And on 30 December, there was a hard fight on the banks of the Jicaro River outside Quilali. The marines pushed through, were hit again, then pushed through a second time. The second column was intercepted at Sapotillal, lost both its officers, but managed to hold a piece of high ground until the first column could reach it. Once joined, they beat their way back to Quilali, where they were promptly besieged by Sandino.

Tied down by thirty wounded, there appeared to be no way to break out. The town's main street was turned into an improvised airstrip, and on 6 January, 1st Lt. Christian F. Schilt came in with an 02U-1 biplane, the original Vought Corsair. The plane had no brakes and the marines had to halt it as it went careening down the street by grabbing at its wings, but in three days Schilt made ten round trips, brought in fourteen hundred pounds of supplies, and took out eighteen of the more critically wounded.

Reinforcements arrived on 10 January 1928 and the marines started north again from Quilali. On 14 January, Major Rowell worked over El Chipote with a four-plane flight. The patrols cautiously probed toward the crest, got there on the twenty-sixth of January, and found it deserted. Sandino had ducked across the Honduran border. He came back into the high coffee country with six hundred men and on 27 February, near a place called Bromaderos, attacked a pack train escorted by a platoon of marines. The mules were driven off but the marines got to a ridgeline where they held out until a company could come to their rescue.

The Coco River, which begins at Cabo Gracias a Dios on the Mosquito Coast, forms two-thirds of Nicaragua's border with Honduras and reaches as far west as Quilali and Ocotal. The marines working along the east coast were mostly from the ships of the Atlantic Fleet. Capt. Merritt A. Edson, a remote cousin of Alvin Edson of the Mexican War, had the detachment from the *Denver*. Edson, red-haired, wiry, pale-skinned, and with ice-blue eyes, had left the University of Vermont at the beginning of World War I to go into the Marine Corps and had served variously as aviator, ordnance officer, and match shot. In April 1928 he moved up the Coco with a strong patrol but missed Sandino. He went out on a second patrol on 26 July. The Coco, never pleasant in its upper reaches, turned wild under torrential rains. Battling the elements and malaria and resupplied by air drop, Edson made his first contact with the bandits on 4 August. There was a second fight on 6 August, a third skirmish on 14 August, and three days later he reached his destination at Poteca, some four hundred miles upstream from Cabo Gracias a Dios. But Sandino himself once again eluded the marines.

Elections were held, as promised, on 4 November 1928, with some nine hundred marines and sailors acting as poll-watchers. Voters had their fingers dipped in red ink to prevent absent-minded repeat voting. General Moncado, running on the Liberal ticket, won the presidency by a narrow but honest plurality. By the first of the year the bandits were hard at it again in the northern mountains. Sandino lost a chief lieutenant, one Manuel Jirón, captured by none other than Herman Hanneken, executioner of Charlemagne and now a first lieutenant. Sandino himself slipped off to Mexico to raise funds. While he was gone, there was a corresponding reduction in banditry and in August 1929 the 11th Regiment went home to be deactivated. The Guardia Nacional was by now up to a strength of about two thousand but was still shaky and in the next two years there would be at least nine mutinies.

In May 1930 Sandino came back into northern Nicaragua. Three strong Marine columns went looking for him in the familiar hill country between the Coco and Bocay but he was as elusive as ever, although he was wounded in the leg on 19 June by an air strike. He was still at large in February 1931 when Secretary of State Stimson announced that the Marines would be reduced by 1 June to a battalion, plus supporting aviation, and confined to the Managua area. All were to be out by the inauguration of the next president.

One of Sandino's hardest-driving pursuers was Guardia captain (first lieutenant, USMC) Lewis B. ("Chesty") Puller. One forty-man patrol led by Puller fought four battles in ten days and killed thirty bandits. Another fight by Puller's company came the day after Christmas 1932. Puller was riding shotgun on the new El Sauce–León rail line when the bandits tried to take the train. Rebel losses were thirty-one killed.

Liberal Juan Sacasa was inaugurated on 1 January 1933. Next day the last elements of the Marine brigade sailed in the old *Henderson* from Corinto for home. In six years of campaigning, forty-seven marines had been killed, sixty-seven more wounded. A year later Sandino returned once again to Nicaragua. He was captured and shot on order of the new Jefe Director of the Guardia Nacional, Marine-trained Col. Anastasio ("Tacho") Somoza.

## CHINA SERVICE (1927–1938)

More pleasant than the Second Nicaraguan Campaign was the 1927 expedition to China. With the Kuomintang on the march in the south and the warlords contesting for control in the north, there had been reason for reinforcement of the Legation Guard in Peking and intermittent landings at Shanghai throughout the 1920s. In February 1927 Chiang Kai-shek marched on Shanghai. A provisional Marine battalion was hurriedly put together from the Asiatic Fleet and detachments in the Philippines and landed to help protect the International Settlement. Two weeks later, the 4th Marines arrived from San Diego, and along with the other foreign troops was put under the coordinate control (but not command) of Maj. Gen. John Duncan, British Army.

General Lejeune designated the skinny old war-horse, Smedley Butler, to command all U.S. Marines in China. The 6th Marines, disbanded in 1925, was hurriedly reorganized at Philadelphia and sent by rail to San Diego, where Butler set up the 3d Brigade headquarters, and together the regiment and brigade headquarters sailed for Shanghai, arriving there 2 May 1927. In his brigade, Butler had the 4th and 6th Regiments; 1st Battalion, 10th Marines (armed with French 75-mm field guns); some engineers and light tanks; and a Marine squadron rescued from a lonely vigil on Guam.

The war was now raging in the north. Butler left the 4th Marines in Shanghai (continuing a tenure which would last until Pearl Harbor) and went north with the rest of the 3d Brigade to Tientsin, piously explaining his mission as "solely for the defense of life and property." With his old companions, the 15th U.S. Infantry in Tientsin and the Legation Guard at Peking, there were about fifty-two hundred Americans in the north. Chiang Kai-shek had Peking by midsummer 1928 and there was no real fighting for the marines, neither for the brigade nor the 4th Marines in Shanghai. The 3d Brigade, less the 4th Marines, was pulled out in January 1929 and returned to San Diego. The Legation Guard in Peking was kept at about five hundred, including the famous troop of "Horse Marines" mounted on sturdy Mongolian ponies and armed, along with their '03s, with heavy, straight-bladed swords designed by a U.S. Army cavalryman named George S. Patton.

In 1932 the clash between the Japanese and Nationalists in Shanghai occasioned the 4th Marines to be joined briefly by the 31st U.S. Infantry from the Philippines, and in September 1937 the 2d Marine Brigade, under handsome Brig. Gen. John C. ("Johnny Beau") Beaumont, came out from San Diego with the 6th Marines. Brigade headquarters and the Sixth stayed on until February 1938 and then went home again. The 15th U.S. Infantry also departed, ending their long-term stay in Tientsin, and a detachment of the Legation Guard fell heir to their soot-gray barracks.

The uniform regulations of 1928 copied the British roll-collar coat with shirt and tie ("field scarf") for the green and khaki uniform, but the standing collar persisted for the blue uniforms and the officers' white uniforms. The officers had also brought back from France pegged riding breeches, field boots, and the Sam Browne belt.

## LEJEUNE AND BUTLER DEPART THE SCENE

Major General Commandant Lejeune was reappointed, first by Harding and then by Coolidge, for a total of nine years as commandant. He retired in 1929, at age 62, and became superintendent of the Virginia Military Institute. His successor was his long-time friend and World War I comrade Wendell Neville, but big, robust Buck Neville served little more than a year as major general commandant before dying in office on 8 July 1930.

Smedley Butler, the senior general in the Corps, was a strong contender for next commandant, but Ben Fuller was less controversial and had more years' commissioned service, so, as a safe choice, Fuller was named commandant in August 1930. A year later Butler went roaring off into noisy retirement. "Uncle Ben" Fuller served competently but quietly and for the last half-year before his retirement for age on 1 March 1934 he was off inspecting posts and stations, foreign and domestic. The real hands holding the reins of the Corps were those of John Russell, now the assistant commandant. Russell had come up from Haiti in 1930 after nine years as high commissioner. (On 21 August 1934 the last remnant of the 1st Marine Brigade marched out of the Casernes Dessalines in Port-au-Prince and sailed for Quantico.)

By 1932 Navy Department war plans were calling for a Marine expeditionary force of eighteen thousand to be ready within thirty days after mobilization and the General Board made the statement that:

> The Marine Corps should be so organized as to be capable of performing its mission in the seizure of an advanced base and in providing for its initial defense. The Army would in general relieve the Marine Corps of the permanent defense, thereby permitting the latter to resume operations with the Fleet for further expeditionary work.

In 1933 Russell, who disliked the term "expeditionary," persuaded the secretary of the Navy that the Expeditionary Force should be redesignated the Fleet Marine Force and made an integral part of the U.S. Fleet. The 1st Marine Brigade was to be home-ported at Quantico and the 2d Brigade at San Diego, and each was to have an infantry regiment; an artillery battalion

(75-mm pack howitzers); an anti-aircraft battalion; companies of engineers, light tanks, and chemical troops; and an aviation group.

Russell became major general commandant on 1 March 1934. In 1935, stating that the Corps should "be alive to the significance of the authorized designation (Fleet Marine Force) and avoid obsolete, less-inclusive terms," he ordered the use of "expeditionary" to be discontinued altogether as applied to Marine Corps units. During World War II the term would creep back in.

Russell served only two years as commandant before reaching the statutory age limit, but before retiring in December 1936 he instituted selection boards for officer promotions. President Roosevelt went much deeper for the next commandant, picking the relatively junior Brig. Gen. Thomas Holcomb, who, as a young officer, had distinguished himself first as a team shot and later as a battalion commander in France.

At Quantico an Equipment Board was established in 1933 and together with the Marine Corps Schools continued to test doctrine and materiel. The thinkers had collected their findings into a *Tentative Manual for Landing Operations,* published in 1934. The Navy issued the revised manual in 1938 as FTP-167, *Landing Operations Doctrine, U.S. Navy* , and in 1941 the U.S. Army brought out its own edition, almost identical, as FM 31-5, *Landing Operations on Hostile Shores.* From 1935 on, there were annual Fleet Landing Exercises. By 1938 all the basic types of landing craft used in World War II were well along in their development. The Roebling "Alligator," invented for rescue work in the Florida Everglades, was adopted by the Marine Corps in 1940 and became the progenitor of the LVT family of amphibian tractors. The problem of getting from ship to shore was well on its way to solution. And so were the related problems of command relationships, ship-to-shore communications, naval gunfire support, combat loading, and air cover.

After World War I, General Barnett had tried to return to the policy that all appointments to the rank of second lieutenant would be made from Naval Academy graduates or the enlisted ranks, but there were many vacancies to be filled, and in May 1921 Lejeune arranged with the War Department to commission twelve graduates from "Distinguished Military Colleges" having Reserve Officer Training Corps. One of the dozen commissioned that year was Randolph McCall Pate, who would one day be commandant. In 1927 a stocky farm boy from Battle Ground, Indiana, named David M. Shoup, was commissioned from the DePauw University ROTC. His year at the Basic School was interrupted by a tour with the 6th Marines in Tientsin,

Butler needing junior officers to fill out his brigade. In 1930 a short, trim, black-haired Vermonter, Wallace M. Greene Jr., whose ancestor Nathaniel Greene had done so well against Cornwallis, came into the Corps from the Naval Academy. He was followed four years later by the diminutive Victor H. Krulak, nicknamed "the Brute," who had been coxswain of the Annapolis crew. Next year among the lieutenants from the Naval Academy was burly Robert E. Cushman Jr., of Minnesota, and also in 1935 Leonard F. Chapman Jr., who was commissioned from the University of Florida. In those Depression years, the prospect of $125-a-month second-lieutenant's pay and the promise of sea duty and China service attracted the best the country had to offer. In 1936 barrel-chested Lewis W. Walt, a great football player and wrestler at Colorado State University, came into the Corps and a year later was looking across the sandbagged barricades of the International Settlement in Shanghai in company with "Wally" Greene. In 1937 the taciturn and brilliant Keith B. McCutcheon took his commission in the Corps after graduating from Carnegie Institute of Technology. The next year would see Raymond G. Davis coming in from Georgia School of Technology and tall, good-looking Donn J. Robertson commissioned from the University of North Dakota.

Beginning in 1935, there was another source of Marine officers called the Platoon Leaders Class. In the PLC a college student spent two six-week periods in summer training as a private first class in the Reserve and on graduation was commissioned a second lieutenant, U.S. Marine Corps Reserve. William K. Jones of Joplin, Missouri, was commissioned in 1938 after two summers in the PLC and graduation from the University of Kansas. That same year, Marion E. Carl, who had graduated from Oregon State College, resigned an Army Reserve commission to become a Marine aviation cadet.

## American Defense Service (1939–1941)

On 30 June 1939, there were 18,052 active-duty marines, which made the Corps about the same size as the New York City police force. On 8 September, seven days after Germany marched into Poland, Roosevelt proclaimed a "limited national emergency." For the Marine Corps this meant an increase in enlisted strength of twenty-five thousand and authority to recall volunteer officers and men from the retired list. A year later, on 5 October 1940, the secretary of the Navy ordered the Organized Marine Corps Reserve to active duty. There were twenty-three Reserve battalions totaling 232 officers and 5,009 enlisted men. The battalions were broken up and the personnel used as fillers for the regular establishment.

On 1 December 1940, "Tommy" Holcomb was named to a second term as major general commandant. Defense battalions were being dispatched to Samoa, Midway, Johnston, and Palmyra islands. The 1st Marine Brigade had departed from Quantico in the fall for Guantánamo. On 1 February 1941, while at sea en route to Culebra for Fleet Landing Exercise 7, it was redesignated the 1st Marine Division, with Maj. Gen. Holland M. Smith commanding. When the division came back from maneuvers in May 1941, it had three infantry regiments, the 1st, 5th, and 7th, and it had outgrown Quantico as a base, so some of the division went to Parris Island, while a new amphibious base was being readied at New River, North Carolina. Onslow Beach was used for landing exercises in the summer, and in September 1941 the division began moving into Tent Camp One of what would eventually become Camp Lejeune.

On the West Coast, the burgeoning 2d Marine Brigade had spread out to a temporary camp, first called Camp Holcomb, then Camp Elliott, on the sandy flats of Kearny Mesa outside San Diego. On 1 February 1941, the 2d Marine Brigade, like the 1st, was expanded to a division and the reactivated 9th and 2d Marines, in that order, joined ranks with the 8th Marines. More training area was needed and on 10 March 1942 the vast Rancho Santa Margarita, 132,000 acres, twenty miles of Pacific beach, and one-time scene of Gillespie's adventures, would be purchased.

In 1939 the General Board of the Navy had stated Marine Aviation's mission as follows:

> Marine Aviation is to be equipped, organized, and trained primarily for the support of the Fleet Marine Force in landing operations and in support of troop activities in the field; and secondarily as replacements for carrier-based aircraft.

It was a good statement of mission. The aircraft groups followed the brigades in their expansion. On 7 July 1941 the 1st Marine Aircraft Wing was activated at Quantico and three days later the 2d Marine Aircraft Wing came into being at San Diego. While this was going on, a brigade of marines was landing in Iceland.

## ICELAND INTERLUDE

In May 1941 there were twenty-five thousand British troops in Iceland and Churchill, needing them elsewhere, invited Roosevelt to take over the occupation as a kind of extension of the Monroe Doctrine. About this time the 6th Marines had sailed from San Diego with orders to join the 1st Marine Division in the Caribbean. The intention was to send a U.S. corps consisting of the 1st Marine Division and the 1st U.S. Infantry Division to secure the Azores. Then, on 5 June 1941, President Roosevelt directed the chief of naval operations to sail a Marine brigade in fifteen days' time to Iceland. The occupation of the Azores was shelved, and the 6th Marines, after passaging the Canal, were diverted northward to be the nucleus of the 1st Provisional Marine Brigade, under command of Brig. Gen. John Marston. The 4,095 marines sailed from Charleston on 22 June, tarried at Argentia while last-minute negotiations nudged the unenthusiastic Iceland government into accepting their protection, and then on 7 July reached Reykjavík.

The marines moved into British camps or built new ones using British Nissen huts, most of them in the southwest corner of the island near Reykjavík. The brigade adopted the British "Polar Bear" shoulder patch and the 6th Marines picked up the custom of singing in the mess, but even a rum ration could not make English rations palatable, so the marines ate U.S. Navy rations—when they could get them—along with locally purchased mutton and fish.

Churchill, meeting with Roosevelt in mid-Atlantic (the meeting which produced the Atlantic Charter), paused at the island and reviewed the brigade. He remembered later that "there was a long march past in threes, during which the tune 'United States Marines' bit so deeply into my memory that I could not get it out of my head."

The first element of a U.S. Army brigade arrived on 6 August 1941 and the last battalion of marines sailed away 8 March 1942. By that time the war with Japan was already three months old.

# 12

## *1941-1944*
### From Shipboard to Small Islands

### Pearl Harbor

At 0759 on Sunday morning, 7 December 1941, the sergeant of the guard at the Marine Barracks, Naval Ammunition Depot, Oahu, made a careful entry in his log: "Twenty-eight Japanese planes flew over Depot toward Schofield Barracks." Within minutes the USS *Arizona* had taken the first bombs of the Pearl Harbor attack. Maj. Alan Shapley, senior Marine officer, was thrown from the foremast a hundred feet into the water but managed to swim to Ford Island. At the Navy Yard, marines from the barracks and 3d Defense Battalion went to their battle stations. At Camp Catlin the 4th Defense Battalion tried to get its 3-inch AA guns into action. At Ewa Air Station, Marine Aircraft Group 21 (MAG-21) was caught on the ground and had all of its fighters and dive bombers knocked out.

Farther west, Midway, Johnston, and Palmyra islands, each with its Marine defense battalion detachment, were all bombarded by Japanese naval gunfire. The shelling of Guam began on 8 December; two days later six thousand Japanese came ashore and overwhelmed the 153-man Marine garrison and eighty-man Insular Guard.

Most of the 1st Defense Battalion was at Wake Island under Maj. James P. S. Devereux. Marine Fighting Squadron 211 (VMF-211) had arrived on the island four days earlier with twelve brand-new F4F-3 Grumman Wildcats. Seven were destroyed on the ground in the first attack on 8 December. The remaining five were used up one by one until 22 December, when the last two took off on a final mission. The next day, before dawn, the Japanese rammed two old destroyer-transports onto the reef and put ashore a thousand men from the Special Naval Landing Force. The island commander, Navy Cdr. Winfred S. Cunningham, decided further resistance was without purpose. At

0730 he sent out Major Devereux under a white flag to meet the Japanese and submit to surrender.

The 4th Marine Regiment, under white-haired Col. Samuel L. Howard, had arrived in the Philippines from Shanghai on 1 December. They were put under Gen. Douglas MacArthur's command and ordered to Corregidor to take over the beach defenses. The final Japanese assault came the night of 5 May 1942. At noon the following day Maj. Gen. Jonathan M. ("Skinny") Wainwright, USA, sent out a Marine captain and a field music under a white flag to arrange a parley. Colonel Howard sadly told his adjutant to burn the 4th Marines' colors.

By then other Marine forces were already moving westward. The 2d Brigade, stripped out of the 2d Marine Division, sailed from San Diego on 6 January 1942 for American Samoa. A 3d Brigade similarly was pulled from the East Coast 1st Marine Division in March and sent to Western (British) Samoa, then thinly garrisoned by New Zealanders. The 4th Defense Battalion moved forward into the malaria-ridden New Hebrides the end of March, and on 30 April the Efate airstrip (crushed coral rolled out with water to almost concrete consistency) was ready to receive MAG-24 aircraft.

The 6th Defense Battalion and Marine Aircraft Group 22 were on Midway. MAG-22 had two squadrons, Maj. Floyd B. Parks's VMF-221 with twenty-one near-useless Brewster Buffalo F2As and Maj. Lofton R. Henderson's VMSB-241 with seventeen old Vought Vindicator SB2U-3s. On 26 May the aircraft transport *Kitty Hawk* brought in seven new Grumman Wildcat F4F-3s and nineteen Douglas Dauntless SBD-2s.

The tactical zone for Western Samoa was extended to include Wallis Island, a French possession, some three hundred miles to the west. Elements of the 3d Brigade, accompanied by two Free French frigates and a party of French marines, made an unopposed landing at Wallis on 27 May and the 8th Defense Battalion took over its defense.

For MAG-22 the Battle of Midway began at dawn on 4 June. VMF-221 engaged a striking force of 108 aircraft headed for Midway. Thirteen F2As and two F4Fs were lost. Parks was among those killed. VMSB-241, attacking without escort, made a glide-bombing attack with the SBDs against the carriers *Akagi* and *Soryu* (or perhaps it was the *Kaga*). Eight of the attacking SBDs, including Henderson's, were shot down by the protecting Zeroes. At the end of the day only two Marine fighters and eleven dive bombers were still operational, but by then the U.S. fleet was fully in position. By 6 June, four Japanese carriers had been sunk and the Battle of Midway was won.

In Washington, the Joint Chiefs of Staff had decided that the Pacific, with its large watery spaces, was the obvious place for the two Marine divisions then being readied for deployment. On 9 April 1942 Lt. Gen. Joseph C. McNarney, acting Army chief of staff, had sent a memorandum to the chief of naval operations, Adm. Ernest J. King, stating the proposition that Army amphibious operations would be "merely the spearhead of a prolonged, heavy, land operation," whereas "in the Pacific, offensive operations for the next year or more promise to comprise a series of landing operations from shipboard to small islands with relatively minor forces. This is the type of amphibious warfare for which the Marines have apparently been specially organized. . . . It might be wise to recognize these differences."

In mid-May the 1st Marine Division, under the command of Maj. Gen. Alexander A. ("Sunny Jim") Vandegrift, left the East Coast for New Zealand. The Japanese were well into New Guinea and threatening Darwin. Rabaul, in Northern New Britain, had been developed into a major air and naval base. In the Solomons they had taken Tulagi, seat of the British colonial government, and had begun to build an airfield on neighboring Guadalcanal.

## GUADALCANAL

On 26 June, two weeks after his arrival at Wellington, Vandegrift was abruptly summoned to Auckland to meet with Vice Adm. Robert L. Ghormley, Commander South Pacific Area, and told there was to be a landing against the Japanese in the Guadalcanal-Tulagi area with a target date of 1 August. The division's third regiment, the 7th Marines, was to stay in Samoa and its place taken by the 2d Marines (still in San Diego). Also he would get the 1st Marine Raider Battalion (from New Caledonia) and the 3d Marine Defense Battalion (still at Pearl Harbor). The brilliant but often difficult Rear Adm. Richmond Kelly Turner would be Attack Force Commander; Rear Adm. V.A.C. Crutchley, Australian Navy, would have the Screening Force; and Rear Adm. Frank J. Fletcher, with three carriers, would have the Support Force.

The division intelligence officer, Col. Frank B. Goettge, went off to Australia to find out what there was to know about Guadalcanal and Tulagi and learned his best sources would be ex-missionaries, planters, and other persons of more dubious island trades. The Australians also had a well-established coast watcher system, set up in 1939 to watch the Germans and now in

place to watch the Japanese. While Colonel Goettge was reading the *Pacific Island Handbook* and fishing through British Colonial Office files, the division operations officer, Lt. Col. Gerald Thomas (of Belleau Wood) and the logistics chief, Lt. Col. Randolph McC. Pate, had gone back with Vandegrift to Wellington to get on with the planning and to start out-loading. An unexpected exasperation was coping with the longshoremen's union and finally troop labor had to do it, working the docks in pelting rain, to the tune of "Bless 'Em All," ankle-deep in soggy corn flakes.

On 17 July a B-17 took off for a visual and photo reconnaissance. The photos taken were pieced together into a kind of photo mosaic (with great gaps where the clouds were). Altogether, the intelligence-collection effort indicated that the Japanese were concentrating at Lunga Point and that an airfield was being built. It was guessed that there was an infantry regiment and an antiaircraft battalion on Guadalcanal, say five thousand Japanese, and fifteen hundred more on nearby Tulagi.

Admiral Turner agreed to delay the landing until 7 August. The Amphibious Force sailed on 22 July, arrived in the Fijis for the rehearsal on the twenty-eighth, and sortied for the objective area on the thirty-first. Tulagi was a banana-shaped island about three miles long tucked under the belly of Florida Island which, in turn, lay twenty miles north of the bigger Guadalcanal. Gavutu and Tanambogo were two fly specks a mile east of Tulagi, connected to each other by a causeway.

The 1st Raider Battalion, under Col. Merritt ("Red Mike") Edson, came to Tulagi on 7 August on board four APDs—World War I four-piper destroyers converted into high-speed transports—and landed at 0800 across Blue Beach on the southwest end of the island. They were to be followed by the 2d Battalion, 5th Marines. There was a patter of small-arms fire when they landed, but it was almost noon before a serious fight developed. By evening Edson had pushed the defenders back into a deep ravine lined with coral caves. During the night the Japanese came boiling back out in four banzai attacks. In the morning the marines learned, after counting the dead, that there had been about five hundred defenders, most of them members of the 3d Kure Special Landing Force.

Gavutu and Tanambogo were assigned to the 1st Parachute Battalion, with their landing scheduled for four hours after the touchdown at Tulagi. (It was a surface landing; in the course of the war the parachute marines would never make a combat jump.) The parachutes were a light battalion, about a third the size of an infantry battalion. Resistance was stiff and the 3d Battalion, 2d Marines, had to be landed next morning to finish the job.

The main landing on Guadalcanal itself began at 0910, five miles east of Lunga Point. There was no opposition. (There were only 2,230 Japanese, not five thousand, on the island and most of these were naval construction workers— "termites," the marines would call them—busy at work on the airfield.) Col. LeRoy P. Hunt's 5th Marines went ashore first, followed an hour later by the 1st Marines under Col. Clifton ("Lucky") Cates, who had been wounded six times and also gassed in World War I. Two air raids in the afternoon lent urgency to the unloading. Gear came ashore faster than the shore party could handle it and by nightfall the beach was chaotic. Night found both the 1st and 5th Marines holding a line along the Tenaru (or what they thought was the Tenaru—it was really the Ilu; their maps were wrong).

In the morning the advance began with a kind of pincer movement, the 5th Marines going straight for the airfield and the 1st Marines hooking around to the south and coming in from the jungle. The airfield was taken without difficulty but at 1230, forty Japanese bombers came over, going for the transports. There was a council of war that night aboard the Amphibious Force flagship *McCawley*. Fletcher had lost twenty-one of his ninety-nine fighters, was running short of fuel, and was pulling his carriers out to the south. Crutchley was concerned about his cruisers in the confined seas. Kelly Turner stated his transports could not stay unprotected in the objective area. Vandegrift said he had to check on the situation at Tulagi before he could possibly concur. It was then about midnight and Vandegrift was scarcely aboard the mine sweeper that was to take him to Tulagi when a Japanese task force came into Sealark Channel at flank speed, all guns blazing. It was the Battle of Savo Island and before morning Crutchley's force was nearly gone, sunk in what forevermore would be called Ironbottom Sound.

In the morning what was left of the fleet sailed away and the marines were left on the beach, short of supplies and badly disposed, with 11,145 men on the big island and 6,805 on Tulagi and Gavutu-Tanambogo. Vandegrift fanned out a defensive perimeter running from the Tenaru (or Ilu) south and west around the airfield and then up to Lunga Point, giving more attention to the coast line than to the inland jungle, and put his engineers to work completing the nearly finished runway.

## Japanese Reinforcements

In Tokyo on 8 August the Imperial General Staff informed Lt. Gen. Haruyoshi Hyakutake, commander of the Seventeenth Army, that his mission was to retake Guadalcanal. To do this he would be given fifty thousand men, including the 2d Sendai Division, the 38th Division, the Kawaguchi Brigade, the Ichiki Detachment, the 8th Tank Regiment, and an artillery group. The troop list was impressive but the assigned units were scattered from Guam to Manchuria. No matter; Imperial doctrine said to move fast and attack quickly. Hyakutake flew down to his headquarters on Rabaul and began day-and-night bombing. The Ichiki Detachment (actually the 2d Battalion, 28th Infantry, reinforced) had fought well in the Philippines and at Singapore and on 12 August it arrived at Truk from Guam. Hyakutake thought a surprise landing near the mouth of the Ilu, almost at the point where the Americans had landed, and a quick march onto the airfield might do the trick. Col. Kiyono Ichiki agreed. He started forward from Truk on 17 August.

On 13 August, Capt. Martin Clemens, one of the Australian coast watchers, had come in through the lines and announced that there were Japanese scattered throughout the hinterlands, disorganized, many weaponless, and without much fight in them. Clemens was using some of the old members of the Solomon Islands Police Force as scouts, and they were good at it. One brought in a report of a Japanese radio station, and a company of the 1st Marines was sent out on 19 August to get it. The patrol made contact, won the fight, and when they searched the bodies of the dead Japanese were surprised to learn that they were not Naval Landing Force but Imperial Army. The marines had made first contact with the Ichiki Detachment.

On 12 August, Vandegrift had sent a message: "Airfield Guadalcanal ready for fighters and dive bombers." On 20 August the escort carrier *Long Island* launched its aircraft from a position two hundred miles southeast of Guadalcanal. Capt. John L. Smith's VMF-223 had brand-new Grumman Wildcat F4F-4s. Maj. Richard C. Mangrum's VMSB-232 had the SBD-3, latest version of the Douglas Dauntless. First planes began to land at about 1700 on Henderson Field, named for Maj. Lofton Henderson, who had been killed at Midway.

That same night Colonel Ichiki sent his men across the Tenaru, hitting the 2d Battalion, 1st Marines. Marine machine guns and mortars, with the help of the artillery, chopped them down. The 1st Battalion, 1st Marines, moved upstream at daybreak, crossed, and came down on the Japanese flank. Ichiki was caught between the two battalions and the sea. He burned his colors and shot himself through the head.

At noon on the twenty-first, steely-eyed John Smith brought down his first Zero. On the twenty-fourth, VMF-223 intercepted a raid and got sixteen of the twenty-seven attackers, including three shot down by Midway veteran Capt. Marion Carl. The marines shot down thirteen of sixteen bombers on the twenty-sixth, Smith and Carl each getting two. Mangrum's dive bombers caught four destroyer-transports coming down the Slot on the twenty-eighth, and only one got away undamaged. On the twenty-ninth, VMF-223 got eight more enemy planes, and on the thirtieth they got fourteen, four by Smith and three by Carl.

They called themselves the Cactus Air Force after the code name for Guadalcanal. The Wildcats were neither as fast nor as nimble as the Zeroes but they were tougher. Marine fighter tactics were to come down from 25,000 or 30,000 feet in one screeching pass onto the backs of the Japanese—their fighters and bombers both flamed easily—and then dive for home. Col. William J. Wallace arrived on 30 August at Henderson as MAG-23 commander and with the group's remaining two squadrons, VMF-224 and VMSB-231.

## MAKIN RAID

Three weeks earlier, on 8 August—the same day that Edson's raiders were mopping up on Tulagi and Hyakutake was getting his orders to retake Guadalcanal—two companies of the 2d Raider Battalion, under Evans Carlson, loaded out of Hawaii in two big mine-laying submarines, the *Nautilus* and *Argonaut*. Carlson's executive officer was the president's son, Maj. James Roosevelt. Target for Carlson's raiders was Makin atoll in the British-mandated Gilbert Islands. The two subs got there before midnight 16 August. Intelligence had 250 Japanese on the atoll and a shore battery covering the entrance to the lagoon (but again intelligence was wrong; there were only seventy Japanese on the island and no shore battery). The raiders put their rubber boats in the water. Everyone got ashore safely, although not exactly where they had intended. The Japanese strung themselves across the coastal road in a fierce show of strength and about dawn a fire fight developed. With daylight a 3,500-ton merchant ship and a small patrol craft could be seen in the lagoon. The *Nautilus*, firing blind, sank both vessels. Two Japanese Type 95 scout planes came over, dropped a few bombs, and left. Twelve more planes came over at 1320 and bombed things in earnest. Two seaplanes sat down in the lagoon to off-load reinforcements and the marines sank them with antitank fire. The Japanese then boldly counterattacked, three times in all that afternoon, and managed to convey to Carlson the notion that he was greatly outnumbered. He decided to get off the beach after dark but had all kinds of trouble with the rubber boats and their cranky outboard motors. At midnight Carlson said every man was free to make his own choice: try to get through the surf to the subs or stay on the beach. By dawn he was ready to surrender, and he sent out a captain and corporal to parley. The captain and corporal, after some adventures of their own, came to the conclusion that there were no live Japanese left on the island. Heartened by this intelligence, Carlson reorganized his two scrambled companies, swept the island, shot two Japanese survivors, blew up the radio station, and burned what supplies he could find. The subs then came into the mouth of the sheltered lagoon to pick up the raiders. (In the confusion nine marines were left behind. The Japanese found them when they reoccupied the island and later cut off their heads.) The *Nautilus* got back to Pearl Harbor on 25 August and *Argonaut* came in a day later.

## EDSON'S RIDGE

Meanwhile Edson's raiders (two sister battalions were never less alike) had moved from Tulagi to Guadalcanal. One of their precious destroyer-transports, the *Calhoun,* was hit unloading rations at Lunga on 30 August and went down. On the night of 2 September two more APDs were sunk. On 7 September the raiders went on board two of the three remaining destroyer-transports, the *Manley* and *McKean,* for a raid west of Tasimboko. They attacked at daylight, captured a full battery of 75-mm guns, and more importantly, gathered a poncho full of documents that confirmed that Maj. Gen. Kiyotake Kawaguchi's heavily reinforced brigade had arrived and was poised for an attack against Henderson Field.

The raiders and what was left of the 1st Parachute Battalion were consolidated into a single battalion under Edson and on 12 September they occupied a low grassy ridge a mile south of Henderson Field. That night Kawaguchi, supported by naval gunfire, made three assaults against Edson's line. Next night, there were two more attacks against the center, then Kawaguchi switched his attention to the parachutists on the left flank. Edson's battalion, down to four hundred effectives, bent back but did not break. The 2d Battalion, 5th Marines, came up to help and in the morning eight hundred dead Japanese were counted on the ridge.

On 3 September stocky, cold-eyed Brig. Gen. Roy Geiger (who had commanded Squadron 7 in France) had arrived to be ComAirCactus, with headquarters in the Japanese-built wooden shack called "the Pagoda." By the 1st of October nearly all the original pilots of VMF-223 and VMSB-232, except for the iron men Mangrum, Smith, and Carl, were gone. Maj. Leonard K. ("Duke") Davis's VMF-121 arrived on 9 October and what was left of the original two squadrons could be pulled out. One of Duke Davis's captains, Joseph J. Foss, would get his first kill on 13 October. (The war would end with Smith and Carl the sixth- and seventh-ranking Marine aces, with nineteen and eighteen and one-half Japanese aircraft shot down respectively. Foss would be No. 2, with twenty-six planes to his credit.)

On the ground side, the 1st Marine Division, after over a month without reinforcement or substantial resupply (and often down to two meals a day, including captured Japanese stores), was joined by 7th Marines, fresh from Samoa. The commanding officers of the 1st and 2d Battalions, 7th Marines, were those two eminent bush fighters, Chesty Puller and Herman Hanneken. Puller was sent with his battalion on 23 September to swing through the Mount Austen area (the kind of reconnaissance in force he particularly enjoyed) with orders to link up with the 1st Raider Battalion at Kokumbona. Lt. Col. Samuel B. Griffith (a Chinese-language student who had translated the words of an obscure Chinese revolutionary named Mao Tse-tung) had moved up from executive officer to command of the raiders. Puller on his second day out developed a fight on the slopes of Mount Austen and the 2d Battalion, 5th Marines, was sent to reinforce him. Edson, now commanding officer of the 5th Marines, was dispatched to take command of the three battalions. There was some confused fighting along the Matanikau. It did not go well and the three battalions had to be pulled back.

On 7 October, Edson was given five battalions with which to try again beyond the Matanikau. They met Col. Tadamasu Nakaguma's 4th Infantry Regiment, intent on raiding the airfield, and the fight coalesced around the mouth of the river. Nakaguma broke off on the ninth after losing about seven hundred men.

General Hyakutake arrived at Guadalcanal that same day to take personal command. The 2d (Sendai) Division was present and reinforced up to about twenty thousand men. The night of 13–14 October was as bad as it got on the 'Canal. To cover the landing west of Koli Point, the battleships *Kongo* and *Haruna* pounded Henderson Field with their 14-inch guns. The airfield was left in a shambles. The Pagoda was leveled, forty-one marines were killed, and forty-eight of the ninety airplanes were knocked out. Everything that could still fly went up in the air, going after the Japanese transports unloading near Tassafaronga. Fortunately a fresh squadron of Wildcats, VMF-212 under Maj. Harold W. ("Indian Joe") Bauer, arrived during the day and immediately joined the fight.

Hyakutake, coming from the direction of Kokumbona, set his ground attack in motion on 16 October, probing first along the Matanikau, then swinging deeper and coming against the center of the American line. The 164th U.S. Infantry had arrived on 13 October, and, with this reinforcement, Vandegrift had divided his perimeter into five defense sectors, roughly along regimental lines. The center where the Sendai struck on the twenty-third was assigned to the 7th Marines but only Puller's 1st Battalion was manning the 2,500 yards of jungle front. Puller asked for help and the 3d Battalion, 164th Infantry, was fed in to reinforce. It was in this fight that Sgt. John ("Manila John") Basilone performed prodigies with two sections of heavy machine guns and became the first enlisted marine of World War II to receive the Medal of Honor. The Japanese came again the next night. This time it was Hanneken's 2d Battalion that bore the brunt of the attack. On the morning of 26 October, the Sendai, with some thirty-five hundred dead, began withdrawing into the interior.

There was a changing climate in the South Pacific. On 18 October Vice Adm. William F. ("Bull") Halsey succeeded Admiral Ghormley as area commander. On 28 October, I Marine Amphibious Corps was formed, with headquarters at Noumea, to coordinate all Fleet Marine Force units in the South Pacific. Reinforcements converged on Guadalcanal. On 4 November, the 8th Marines arrived from Samoa. On the same day, Carlson's raiders and the 1st Battalion, 147th U.S. Infantry, landed at Aola Bay, forty miles east of Lunga.

Geiger left the 'Canal on 4 November upon the arrival of Brig. Gen. Louis E. Woods. He received a second Navy Cross (his first Navy Cross was for World War I). The citation credited the Cactus Air Force with shooting down 268 Japanese aircraft during the period 3 September to 4 November.

## MATANIKAU

Beginning 1 November, Vandegrift made another attack across the Matanikau, the 5th and 2d Marines reinforced under Edson moving out toward Kokumbona five and a half miles to the west. After three days the advance was stopped short of Kokombona by Vandegrift because of events taking place east of the Lunga perimeter. On 1 November Hanneken had been sent with his battalion to see what was happening at Koli Point, well east of Vandegrift's perimeter but short of Aola Bay. Hanneken reached his objective coincident with the landing of the 230th Imperial Infantry. Hyakutake as well as Vandegrift was receiving reinforcements. Substantial parts of the 38th (Hiroshima) Division were being brought down the Slot by the Tokyo Express. Vandegrift decided to call off Edson's attack and concentrate on an envelopment of the Koli Point force. He sent out the rest of the 7th Marines and the 164th Infantry. The trap was somewhat porous. Some of the Japanese were caught in a pocket at Gavaga Creek, others oozed out. Carlson had been ordered to move his battalion out of Aola Bay to cut off any Japanese who might escape the Koli Point envelopment. He made his first solid contact on 12 November. Staying in the jungle until 4 December, he marched his battalion 150 miles, fought a dozen actions, killed five hundred enemy, and shunted the remainder into the inhospitable interior—at a cost of sixteen raiders killed, eighteen wounded.

With Koli Point resolved, Vandegrift had turned his attention once again to Kokumbona. On 10 November, the 2d Marines, reinforced with elements of the 8th Marines and the 164th Infantry, moved out to the west but after one day's advance were halted because of intelligence of another strong attack in the making. The main body of the 38th Division, ten thousand men embarked in eleven transports, escorted by a dozen destroyers, started down the Slot on 12 November. Patrol planes reported a huge Japanese task force two hundred miles to the northwest. That day, 12 November, the American Division's second regiment, the 182d Infantry, landed at Guadalcanal. Their escort, Rear Adm. Daniel J. Callaghan with five cruisers and eight destroyers, went out to meet the Japanese task force. The gun duel began during the early morning hours of the thirteenth at three thousand yards. Admiral Callaghan in the *San Francisco* and Rear Adm. Norman Scott in the *Atlanta* were killed, but the Japanese task force got the worse of it and was forced to retire. Planes from Henderson Field caught the crippled battleship *Hiei* and battered her further, so that she had to be scuttled.

Next day, 14 November, Marine and Navy air got to the transport group and sank seven of the eleven transports. The remaining four transports continued doggedly on toward Guadalcanal. There was another big-gun naval action in Sealark Channel. The U.S. battleship *South Dakota* was badly damaged; the Japanese battleship *Kirishima* was sunk. The four remaining Japanese transports drove themselves aground between Cape Esperance and Tassafaronga and the four thousand survivors went off to join Hyakutake.

On 18 November, Vandegrift moved out once again to the west, this time with the 8th Marines, the 164th Infantry, and two battalions of the newly arrived 182d Infantry. Once again there was a meeting engagement. Hyakutake, reinforced at such terrible cost, was coming against the airfield in yet another attack. The head of his column collided with two American battalions the night of 19–20 November and a two-day battle followed. On the twenty-third, the 8th Marines passed through the 164th Infantry to continue the attack, but the advance was still not conclusive.

On 29 November, Japanese efforts to resupply their forces by sea touched off yet another naval battle. A torpedo attack by eight Japanese destroyers sank the *Northampton* and put three other U.S. cruisers out of action, but even this brilliant attack could not reverse the swing of the pendulum. As December began, the Japanese came to the reluctant conclusion that they had lost the contest for Guadalcanal. By this time, Vandegrift was insisting that the 1st Marine Division be relieved and moved to a healthier climate. The surgeons estimated that a third of the division, ranks riddled with malaria and malnutrition, was medically unfit for combat.

On 8 December, the American Division's third regiment, the 132d Infantry, arrived. Next day command of the island passed from Vandegrift to Maj. Gen. Alexander M. Patch, USA. That same day, the 5th Marines sailed for Australia, followed shortly by the 1st Marines and 7th Marines. First elements of the U.S. 25th Division arrived on 17 December. On 2 January, Patch's force was designated the XIV Corps. Two days later, the 6th Marines landed, making the 2d Marine Division essentially complete (although commanded by the ADC, Brig. Gen. Alphonse De Carre, so as not to have a Marine major general ashore who was senior to Patch.) For a brief time, then, XIV Corps had three divisions—the Americal, the 25th, and the 2d Marine—some fifty thousand strong with which to fight the Japanese remnant.

Hyakutake was thought to still have about twenty-five thousand men. Patch's plan was to have the American Division hold the perimeter while the 25th Division and the 2d Marine Division attacked to the west. But Patch had the services of the 2d Marine Division only briefly. The 2d Marine Regiment embarked for New Zealand on 15 January, followed shortly by the 8th Marines. Patch then combined the newly arrived 6th Marines with the 147th and 182d Infantry Regiments into a provisional CAM (Composite Army-Marine) Division and the final drive began 22 January. U.S. Army elements closed on Cape Esperance on 9 February but the Japanese were gone. Hyakutake had begun his evacuation on 1 February and had completed it on the eighth, taking off some thirteen thousand men.

The six-month campaign had cost Hyakutake perhaps twenty-five thousand dead. Another thousand Japanese soldiers (admittedly mostly laborers) had been taken prisoner. Six hundred Japanese planes had been destroyed. The naval battles had cost each side twenty-four fighting ships: 126,240 tons for the Allies, and 134,838 tons for the Japanese. Ashore, U.S. Marine losses were 1,044 dead, 2,894 wounded, 55 missing, and 8,580 recorded cases of malaria. The U.S. Army lost 446 dead, 1,910 wounded. Marine air had lost 55 killed, 127 wounded, 85 missing.

## NEW GEORGIA

On 26 December, Brig. Gen. Francis P. ("Pat") Mulcahy, CG of the 2d Marine Aircraft Wing, arrived at Henderson Field to relieve Louis Woods as ComAirCactus. As a captain in France in World War I, Mulcahy had been one of the few marines to get a confirmed German aircraft kill. On 15 February 1943 the conglomeration of Army, Navy, Marine, and New Zealand air units in the Solomons was combined under Commander, Aircraft, Solomons (ComAirSols).

In December the Japanese had been discovered hard at work on an incredibly well-camouflaged airfield at Munda on the northern end of New Georgia. Across the Kula Gulf, another field was being completed on Kolombangara. The Japanese already had four fields operational on Buka and Bougainville and five on New Britain in the vicinity of Rabaul. Fortunately,

on 12 February, VMF-124 arrived at Henderson Field with twelve new gull-winged Vought Corsair F4Us. They were faster and had twice the range of any fighter the Japanese had. Within six months all eight Marine fighter squadrons in the South Pacific would have the Corsair.

From Henderson Field northwest to Rabaul was 565 air miles. From Port Moresby in New Guinea northeast to Rabaul was 445 miles. MacArthur would advance along the latter axis, Halsey along the former. Halsey's first move up the Solomons was the fifty-five-mile jump to the Russell Islands, halfway to New Georgia from Guadalcanal. Two new raider battalions, the 3d under Lt. Col. Harry B. ("Harry the Horse") Liversedge and the 4th under Maj. "Jimmy" Roosevelt, had come forward to Espiritu Santo. On 21 February, Liversedge's battalion made an unopposed landing on rain-soaked Pavuvu in the Russells. An airstrip was begun on neighboring Banika and beginning 14 March, MAG-21 set itself up in business with three squadrons of Wildcats.

On 15 March, at Espiritu, all four raider battalions were brought together into the 1st Raider Regiment under Liversedge. In the next weeks raider reconnaissance patrols were sent out to scout the middle Solomons.

Maj. Gen. Noboru Sasaki arrived to take command of the Kolombangara–New Georgia sector on 31 May. He had the 229th Infantry, reinforced, on New Georgia and a battalion of the 13th Infantry on Kolombangara. Rear Adm. Minoru Ota, who was already there, had the Kure 6th Special Naval Landing Force on New Georgia and the Yokosuka 7th SLNF on Kolombangara.

The U.S. plan for New Georgia was inordinately complex, six or seven landings in all, of which the Marines would take part in four. The Japanese were reported closing in on a New Zealander coast watcher at Segi Plantation at the southeastern end of the island. Accordingly, Lt. Col. Michael S. Currin landed there on 21 June with two companies of his 4th Raider Battalion (Roosevelt had gone home), rendezvoused with the coast watcher, and then made a four-day jungle march to Viru Harbor, which he took on 1 July. Meanwhile, his other two companies had landed with a larger Army outfit on nearby Vangunu Island.

The main landings came on 30 June. The 9th Marine Defense Battalion landed on Rendova across Blanche Channel from Munda behind the 43d Division's 103d U.S. Infantry. D-Day was violent in the air if not on the ground. American planes shot down 101 Japanese aircraft (fifty-eight by Marine pilots) out of 130 engaged. On 3 July, the 43d Division began shuttling across Blanche Channel to Zanana Beach, six miles east of Munda, while the

9th Defense Battalion and the Army artillery banged away at Munda airfield.

On the other side of the island, New Georgia was linked to Kolombangara by barge terminals at Enogai and Bairoko. From there, an overland trail led to Munda. Liversedge with his regimental headquarters, 1st Raider Battalion, and two battalions from the 37th Division landed at nearby Rice Anchorage in the predawn of Independence Day, 4 July, then made a wet march through mangrove swamps to Enogai Inlet, developing a fight on the seventh which lasted until the tenth. He paused until the eighteenth, when he was joined by Currin's battalion. On the twentieth, Liversedge moved out with his two Marine and two Army battalions against Bairoko (through which Japanese reinforcements, including the 13th Regiment, were funneling to Munda) and got into a hornet's nest of well-emplaced machine guns and 90-mm mortars for which he had nothing heavier than 60-mm mortars. After taking 243 casualties he fell back on Enogai to wait for heavier-calibered help. (When Army patrols went into Bairoko on 23 August they found it deserted.)

Meanwhile, most of the 37th and 25th Divisions had to be committed to help the 43d Division (while the 9th Defense Battalion's 155-mm "Long Toms" continued to pound the strip) before Munda was eventually secured on 5 August. Marine Fighter Squadrons 214 and 221 moved onto the field on 14 August. The Japanese still had a good airfield and perhaps ten thousand men on Kolombangara. It was decided to bypass it and move on to Vella Lavella. The 4th Marine Defense Battalion followed the Army's 35th Regimental Combat Team ashore there on 15 August. This gave the Allies control of the whole New Georgia group.

## BOUGAINVILLE

The next step up the ladder of the Solomons would be a big one, to Bougainville, largest of the islands, much like Guadalcanal, only wilder. There were supposed to be about thirty-five thousand Japanese on Bougainville, most of them clustered around the airfields. It was decided the marines would set up their own airfield behind a force beachhead line. Midway down the west side of the island, in Empress Augusta Bay, there were two miles of what looked like good beach in the lee of the fishhook formed by Cape Torokina. An airstrip there would be only 210 miles from Rabaul.

D-Day was set for 1 November 1943. Landing force would be the I Marine Amphibious Corps, until now an administrative headquarters at Noumea,

New Caledonia. Commanding general was Vandegrift, promoted to lieutenant general. He would have the 3d Marine Division for the assault and the Army's 37th Division in reserve. The 3d Marine Division, commanded by Maj. Gen. Allen H. ("Hal") Turnage, had come out to New Zealand in April 1943 and had gone into camps near Auckland. From there, after strenuous training, it had moved up to Guadalcanal.

To support the Bougainville operation AirSols had fifty-two squadrons (fourteen of them Marine) totaling 728 aircraft. Maj. Gen. Ralph J. Mitchell had arrived in the South Pacific in April to take command of the 1st Marine Aircraft Wing from Geiger and on 20 November he became ComAirSols.

A diversion was needed to put the Japanese off as to the real target. A discarded operation order for a division landing on Choiseul was dusted off. The 2d Parachute Battalion, under Lt. Col. "Brute" Krulak, reinforced to about 725 men, landed there the night of 27–28 October from the hardworked destroyer transports. The parachutists rendezvoused with a coast watcher and some natives, and pretended to be the 3d Marine Division. The Japanese started to reinforce Choiseul from Bougainville, which was what was wanted, and Radio Tokyo announced that twenty thousand Americans were ashore. On the night of 3–4 November, with the real landing at Empress Augusta Bay already accomplished, Krulak's battalion was lifted off by landing craft. Another part of the diversion was the landing of the New Zealand 8th Brigade Group on 27 October in the Treasury Islands sixty-five miles southeast of Empress Augusta Bay. Fighting there would go on until 12 November.

H-Hour at Cape Torokina was 0645 on 1 November. The beach was bisected by the Koromokina River. The 9th Marines were to land on the left of the Koromokina and the 3d Marines, reinforced with the 2d Raider Battalion, were to land on the right. The 3d Raider Battalion was to take Puruata Island. The plan was to put all eight battalions ashore at once, so the transports could go back for the 21st Marines and the 37th Division. There was more resistance than expected. The 1st Battalion, 3d Marines, landing inside the hook of Cape Torokina on the extreme right flank, was caught in a vicious crossfire including a 75-mm gun that knocked out six landing craft before it was eliminated by a brave sergeant. On the left flank surf conditions were bad. Something like eighty-six landing craft broached and were smashed, so that the beach was abandoned and the 9th Marines came in behind the 3d Marines. Nevertheless, by nightfall the Marines had fourteen thousand troops and 6,200 tons of supplies ashore despite the interruption of a 120-plane raid from Rabaul.

The Japanese defenses were under the overall command of the old antagonist, General Hyakutake, headquartered at Rabaul. In addition to the mauled formations that had escaped from Munda, he had the full-strength 6th Division and the splendid Kure 7th Special Naval Landing Force. The 23d Infantry Regiment was sent marching to Torokina under command of a Colonel Kawano. Hyakutake's plan was to send down elements of the 17th Division from Rabaul to land beyond the American left flank, while Kawano came down the trails against the perimeter. Only four destroyers got through from Rabaul. On the night of 6–7 November about 475 Japanese landed off to the left of the beachhead; they dug in behind the Koromokina River and it took two days and three battalions to kill them all.

General Geiger, after a brief tour as director of aviation at Headquarters, arrived on 4 November to relieve General Vandegrift of command of I Marine Amphibious Corps. Vandegrift left for Washington, where he was to become the next commandant on the first of the year.

The raiders moved out to the northeast on Piva Trail and on 5 November set up a blocking position where it intersected with Numa Numa Trail. A Japanese battalion bounced off the block and withdrew to Piva village. On the morning of 10 November, the Marine Corps Birthday, two battalions of the 9th Marines passed through the raiders and went on into Piva village behind a carpet of 100-pound bombs laid 120 yards in front of them by two Marine torpedo squadrons putting to practical test the "yard-a-pound" rule of thumb. By now the 21st Marines were ashore and the 37th Infantry Division was in the process of landing. The 37th Division took over the left half of the perimeter. There were twenty-two air raids in November, offering plenty of targets for the 3d Defense Battalion's 90-mm guns. The 3d Marines were now out in front. From 19 to 24 November they fought six actions, called the Battle of Piva Forks.

On the twenty-ninth the 1st Parachute Battalion went off on a raid down the coast, to a place called Koiari. They ran into a thousand or more Japanese and it turned out badly. They had to be taken out under covering fire from three destroyers and 155-mm guns firing at extreme range from Torokina.

What was left of the 23d Imperial Infantry had consolidated on some high ground the marines called Hellzapoppin Ridge. The 21st Marines finished them off in a series of fights that went from 12 to 23 December. Except for the

3d Defense Battalion (which would stay until June 1944) it was now time for the Marines to leave Bougainville. The Americal Division had arrived to relieve the 3d Marine Division, and on 15 December the Army's XXIV Corps had taken over from I MAC. Bougainville had cost the Marines 423 dead, 1,418 wounded. It also marked the end of ground action in the South Pacific for the Marines. Halsey's line of advance in the South Pacific had now merged with that of MacArthur's drive up through the Southwest Pacific.

To pound Rabaul, Mitchell, as ComAirSols, planned to use his medium and heavy Army bombers and also fighter sweeps, a technique that had worked well at cleaning out Kahili. His star performer at fighter sweeps was Maj. Gregory R. ("Pappy") Boyington. Flying P-40s with the Flying Tigers in China, Boyington had claimed six Japanese planes. Now thirty-one years old, he had gotten no victories in his first Solomons tour as CO of VMF-112 during the summer of 1943. In September he was given the chance to reorganize VMF-214. They took the name "Black Sheep" because the squadron had been filled out with pool pilots and other odds and ends. By the first of the new year Boyington's score, by his own count, stood at twenty-five. On 3 January he took his squadron over Rabaul at 20,000 feet. About fifty Japanese fighters came up to meet them. Boyington got three more planes before his Corsair's main gas tank caught fire. Several hours later a Japanese submarine picked him up from his rubber raft and took him into Rabaul. Boyington survived a harsh captivity and emerged at the end of the war as the Marine Corps' ranking ace with twenty-eight claimed air-to-air victories.

The Japanese took their remaining aircraft out of Rabaul in February and the Marine SBD dive-bombers and TBF torpedo-bombers were able to go in earnest against the shipping servicing the Japanese base. After the big ships were sunk or driven off, the light bombers went after the all-important barges and did so well that by March the Japanese at Rabaul were no longer even receiving their mail.

After Bougainville I Marine Amphibious Corps became the III Amphibious Corps and Geiger would remain its commander for the remainder of the war.

## CAPE GLOUCESTER

MacArthur had decided that Cape Gloucester on New Britain would be the next target for the 1st Marine Division, which had been rebuilding slowly in Australia since arriving there from Guadalcanal. It had been re-equipped (the beloved bolt-action Springfield '03 giving way to the semiautomatic Garand M-1) and in August a Sixth Army inspection team had given them a combat efficiency rating of "excellent." William H. Rupertus now had the division. The new ADC was Brig. Gen. Lemuel C. Shepherd Jr. In late December 1943 the division moved to staging areas on the east coast of New Guinea. Across the Straits was crescent-shaped New Britain, 330 miles long, mountainous, wild, heavily jungled. At the northwestern corner of the island was Cape Gloucester, where there was an airfield. At the other end of the crescent was Rabaul itself. There were an estimated seventy thousand Japanese on New Britain, most of them in the north. Marine amphibious scouts and some Australians had gone into the objective area several times and there were the usual ubiquitous coast watchers. Division Intelligence came up with a minimum-maximum of 7,416 to 9,816 Japanese, which was pretty close. Command of western New Britain was under Maj. Gen. Iwao Matsuda. He had the 65th Brigade with the 53d and 141st Regiments.

D-Day, several times postponed, was finally set for 26 December. The 1st Marine Division embarked the day before Christmas. No big transports were available but none were really needed for the short inter-island haul. The assault echelons went in APDs, the much-used destroyer-transports, from which they would go ashore in landing craft. The support groups were in LCIs (landing craft, infantry) which hopefully would be able to beach. The reserve and the heavy equipment and vehicles were in LSTs (landing ships, tank). Christmas was spent at sea and at 0300 on the twenty-sixth the troops were broken out for "steak-and-eggs" (a taste developed in Australia), which would become the traditional D-Day breakfast.

There was a fringing reef but there were breaks in it and the plan was to pass through the reef in two places. The 7th Marines were to land across Yellow Beach, about seven miles down the east coast from the cape. The 1st Marines (less its 2d Battalion) would then land behind the 7th, and, on order, pass through and attack toward the airfield. The 5th Marines would be in reserve. Meanwhile, the 2d Battalion, 1st Marines, would land on the other side of the cape over Green Beach at Tauali, to block either reinforcement or withdrawal by the Japanese along the west coast trails.

H-Hour was 0745. Initially there was no enemy, nothing behind the narrow beach but a dense wall of jungle, but within an hour 3d Battalion, 7th Marines, had developed a line of bunkers beyond Yellow One. The 3d Battalion, 1st Marines, passed through and by midmorning had developed a good-sized fight. That afternoon there was an air raid by eighty-eight planes from Rabaul. Most of them were knocked down by Army P-38s, but a U.S. destroyer was sunk and three others damaged. Across the cape, the 2d Battalion, 1st Marines, had landed at Tauali with no more resistance than a brush with a Japanese patrol but could not make radio contact with the division ten miles away because of the hill mass, dominated by 6,000-foot Mount Talawe, which separated them.

The monsoon rains began in earnest that night. There was also an attack against the center of the Marine perimeter by the 2d Battalion, 53d Imperial Infantry. In the morning the 1st and 3d Battalions of the 1st Marines moved up the axis of the coast road against no opposition to within a mile and a half of the airfield. In front of them the 1st Battalion, 53d Infantry, had a line of defenses which the marines would call Hell's Point. The Japanese were pushed back from there on the twenty-eighth. That same day the 5th Marines was landed and next day both regiments went forward, the 5th Marines moving up on the left of the 1st Marines, and by nightfall most of the airfield had been taken.

Even so, Matsuda still had most of his brigade intact, including the 141st Regiment, and he was thought to be in the high, heavily jungled ground south and west of the beachhead. On the twenty-ninth, Rupertus told Shepherd to take the 7th Marines plus the 3d Battalion, 5th Marines, and destroy Matsuda. Three battalions were to advance abreast through the rain-sodden hills until contact was made, then the reserve battalion would hook around in an envelopment. A captured order told the marines that "Aogiri Ridge" was to be held at all costs. This ridge was reached on 8 January. Lt. Col. Lewis Walt now had the 3d Battalion, 5th Marines. He put his shoulder to a 37-mm gun and, using canister, blasted his way to the top. Matsuda tried a counterattack on the night of the ninth, failed, and fell back. There was one more hill, a big one, 660 feet high. The 3d Battalion, 7th Marines, under Lt. Col. Henry W. ("Bill") Buse, Naval Academy '34, went forward against Hill 660 on the thirteenth. The first assault failed, Buse dug in for the night, and next morning worked around the west face of the hill and came down on the Japanese. By dusk he had the ridge. The Japanese counterattacked with two companies at daybreak on the sixteenth. Matsuda then broke off contact but it was not known if he was moving east or south.

Chesty Puller, now executive officer of the 7th Marines, took a 384-man "patrol" across the island to Gilnit on the south coast and back again, but he found nothing except a few stragglers. Matsuda was not in the interior but moving along the north coast, leaving behind a trail of dead and dying Japanese. The 5th Marines went after them and paused at Iboki, sixty miles from Cape Gloucester. Then under a new regimental commander, the slender and quiet Col. Oliver Prince Smith, they made a fifty-seven-mile shore-to-shore amphibious move on 6 March to take Talasea airfield at the tip of Willaumez Peninsula. On 28 April 1944, the 1st Marine Division was relieved by the 40th Infantry Division. New Britain had cost the Marines 310 killed, 1,083 wounded. The division, reembarked, hoped they were going back to Australia. Instead they were headed for a muddier camp at Pavuvu in the Russell Islands, and perhaps even more rain than in New Britain.

# 13

## *1943‑1945*
### All Organized Resistance Has Ceased

Tarawa

At the Quebec Conference in August 1943 the line of advance for the Central Pacific offensive was marked out as from the Gilberts, to the Marshalls, to the Marianas, and thence to the Carolines. First objectives, then, would be the Gilbert Islands, stretching loosely across the equator like so many carelessly flung coral necklaces.

The V Amphibious Corps—two divisions, one Army, one Marine—under Maj. Gen. Holland M. Smith (whom the press was beginning to call "Howlin' Mad") would be the landing force. The 27th Infantry Division, led by Maj. Gen. Ralph C. Smith, USA (a name to remember), would land at Makin. The 2d Marine Division, which had been resting in New Zealand since coming out of Guadalcanal, would land at Tarawa under command of a third Smith, this one the soft-spoken, gentlemanly Julian C. Smith.

Tarawa atoll is an extended thumb and forefinger. Betio island is the thumbnail, two miles long, half a mile wide, and at no point more than ten feet above sea level. Three runways forming a flat letter A filled most of the island. The rest was fortifications: coconut logs, coral, a lot of reinforced concrete, and over two hundred guns of all calibers up to four fine 8-inch guns (later mistakenly reported as having come from Singapore). There were 5,236 souls on the island, 2,619 combatants in the Sasebo 7th Special Naval Landing Force and 3d Special Base Force, the rest airfield specialists and labor troops; all were under command of bombastic Rear Adm. Keichi Shibasaki, who was of the opinion that the Americans could not take the island in a million years.

The Marines chose to land on the north shore, which faced on the lagoon. There was a fringing reef on that side, five hundred to a thousand yards of coral. Landing craft couldn't cross it; amphibian tractors might. The 2d Division had something over a hundred of them, thin-skinned Alligators, enough to lift the first three waves. A pier, solidly built of coconut logs and coral, bisected the north beach, jutting out five hundred yards. Any guns left intact on the pier would enfilade the waves coming into the beach. The three-day prelanding bombardment called for fifteen hundred tons of bombs and two thousand tons of naval shells.

H-Hour was to be 0830, 20 November 1943, but when that hour came the shore batteries were not yet quiet and so H-Hour was postponed until 0900. The assault waves began taking 37-mm and 76-mm fire three to four thousand yards off the beach. A scout-sniper platoon reached the pier and began burning out gun emplacements with flame throwers. About fifteen minutes later, first elements of the 2d Battalion, 8th Marines, touched down on Red Beach Three just east of the pier. The 2d Battalion, 2d Marines, coming in west of the pier on Red Beach Two got badly shot up; its battalion commander was killed in the water. Farther west, at some distance, 3d Battalion, 2d Marines, landed on the extreme right flank of Red Beach One. The battalion had gotten separated from its command group and the senior company commander, Maj. Michael P. Ryan, took charge.

The 1st Battalion, 2d Marines, waded in across the fire-swept reef behind 2d Battalion, 2d Marines. The 3d Battalion, 8th Marines, which was to follow the 2d Battalion, 8th Marines, onto Red Three was caught unloading from landing craft at the edge of the reef and was badly shelled. Col. David M. Shoup, commanding the 2d Marine Regiment, landed about 1030 and set up his command post in a blasted Japanese blockhouse. As night fell, Shoup, with parts of four battalions, held a shallow box-shaped perimeter around the base of the pier. Separated from him and over on the right flank, two Sherman tanks had landed and with these Ryan had started toward Green Beach on the western tip of the island. During the night, made bright with star shells and burning gasoline, some guns from the 10th Marines got ashore. The 1st Battalion, 8th Marines, spent the night out in the water in landing craft, started in at daybreak, and took heavy losses. Needing more troops, Julian Smith got the release of the 6th Marines, which was in corps reserve.

On D-Plus-One, Shoup, already wounded, attacked south across the waist of the island, his four battalions in two columns. By nightfall he had reached the south shore. Ryan, still separated from the rest of the landing force, had

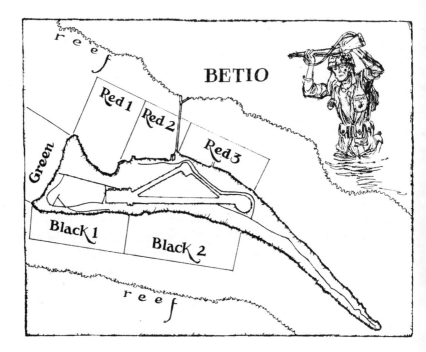

secured Green Beach by noon. The 1st Battalion, 6th Marines, under Maj. William K. Jones, got ashore late in the afternoon. Sometime during the day Shibasaki had expired. His last message to Tokyo ended, "May Japan exist for ten thousand years."

Next morning, Jones attacked at right angles to Shoup's position and by dark the Marines had the western two-thirds of the island. That night the Japanese tried three desperate and futile banzai attacks. The following morning the fresh 3d Battalion, 6th Marines, passed through the Marine line and pushed to the eastern tip of the island. At 1321, 23 November, Julian Smith declared the island secured. The seventy-six hours of fighting had cost 984 Marine dead and 2,072 wounded. The only enemy left alive were seventeen wounded prisoners and 129 Korean laborers.

The 27th Infantry Division landed on Butaritari island in the Makin atoll on schedule on 20 November. Ralph Smith used a 6,472-man regimental landing team built around the 165th Infantry Regiment. There were 848 Japanese on Butaritari, about a third of them first-class fighting troops, and these were taken care of in four days.

After Tarawa, Holland Smith recommended the "assignment of at least one Marine Aircraft Wing specifically for direct air support in landing operations." What were needed were escort carriers to provide the platforms from which to operate, but the Navy was chary about giving these decks to the Marines. So, for the time being, Marine aviation in the Central Pacific would be limited to rear-area missions. The 4th Marine Base Defense Aircraft Wing had been activated in August 1942 and on Christmas Day 1943 Brig. Gen. Lewie G. Merritt brought the forward echelon forward to Tarawa.

## THE MARSHALLS

Next objective in the Central Pacific would be Kwajalein (the world's largest atoll) in the Marshall Islands, a part of Japanese trust territories since World War I. The V Amphibious Corps would again be the landing force, this time with the Army's 7th Division and the new 4th Marine Division under Maj. Gen. Harry ("the Dutchman") Schmidt. The Army was to take Kwajalein island itself at the southeast corner of the atoll. The Marines were to land on the twin islands of Roi and Namur at the northeast corner. D-Day was set for 31 January 1944.

Roi-Namur was supposed to have three thousand defenders but was nowhere near so well fortified as Betio had been. Heaviest guns were a pair of twin 5.5-inch dual-purpose naval rifles. As at Tarawa, the landing would be made on the lagoon side of the islands. Amphibian tractors were now coming off the assembly lines in quantity and 4th Marine Division had three times the number the 2d Division had had at Betio. There were to be two days of heavy, deliberate bombardment.

D-Day operations called for the 25th Marines to make five separate landings on the mellifluously named islets of Mellu, Ennuebing, Ennugarret, Ennumennet, and Ennubir, which flanked the "big" islands of Roi and Namur (neither of which measured much more than a mile along its longest axis). The 25th Marines would be followed by the 4th Division's artillery regiment, the 14th Marines, which would set up to cover the main landings the following day. These landings went well except for troubles with the amphibian tractors. There were plenty of them but their crews were half-trained, relations with their mother LSTs were acrimonious, their radios were unreliable, their sea-keeping ability marginal; when their engines stopped, so did their pumps, and they had a distressing habit of sinking.

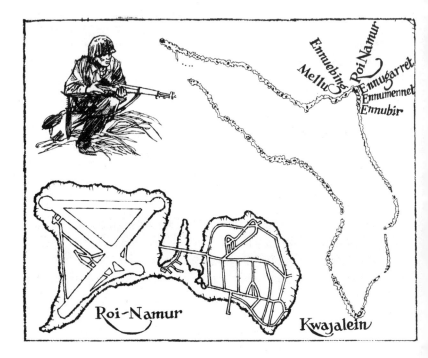

D-Plus-One's plans called for the 23d Marines to land on Roi and the 24th Marines to land on Namur. (The two islands were linked by a causeway.) Roi was skinned clean of vegetation and most of it was taken up by an X-shaped airfield. Namur to the east had most of the supply installations and was still pretty well covered with pandanus and such. H-Hour was delayed until 1100. The 23d Marines, which had a fresh amphibian tractor battalion to lift it, was on the mark, but the 24th Marines were to use yesterday's tractors and there seemed to be only sixty-two of them left. The 23d Marines landed on Roi against virtually no opposition, raced across the island in a pell-mell formless attack, slaughtering dazed and bewildered Japanese (half of the defenders were already dead from the naval bombardment), and secured the island by nightfall.

The 24th Marines found it tougher going. At dark, with two-thirds of Namur in their possession, they halted for the night. The Japanese tried a half-hearted banzai attack. Next morning the 24th Marines went forward supported by tanks and half-tracks, and at 1428 on 2 February Namur was declared secure. The 4th Marine Division plus naval gunfire had killed 3,563

Japanese at a cost of 313 dead, 502 wounded. Meanwhile, the 7th Infantry Division had landed on Kwajalein island itself on 1 February and in four days killed 4,823 enemy, losing 173 soldiers dead, 793 wounded.

## ENIWETOK

The next objective would be Eniwetok atoll at the northwest edge of the Marshalls. Ready at hand was the unused V Phib Corps reserve, a brigade-size force, called Tactical Group 1, under hot-tempered Marine Brig. Gen. Thomas E. ("Terrible Tommy") Watson, consisting of two regiments: the 22d Marines and the 106th U.S. Infantry. There were three islands in the atoll to be taken. Engebi, a triangular piece of coral, had the airfield and was at the northern curve of the necklace. Twenty miles south of Engebi, across the lagoon, was Eniwetok island itself, and northeast of Eniwetok island was Parry island. Once again, the landing was to be made from inside the lagoon.

On 17 February 1944, behind a curtain of naval gunfire, the amphibian tractors ground ashore on three islets adjacent to Engebi to secure support-ing artillery positions. The next morning the 22d Marines made the main landing, its three battalions in the classic "two up and one back" formation. Touchdown was at 0842, 18 February. There was a fairly wild night (the defenders had a new trick—a "spider web" of tunnels made up of buried oil drums laid end to end) but in the morning it was all over and the U.S. flag went up while someone sounded colors on a captured Japanese bugle.

Next morning, the 106th Infantry landed at Eniwetok at 0915, found it tougher going, and were joined at 1330 by the 22d Marines' 3d Battalion. After two days of hard fighting, Eniwetok island was declared secured on the twenty-first, and next day the 22d Marines went on to take Parry island. Sixty-six prisoners had been taken and about 3,400 Japanese killed. The Marines had lost 254 killed and 555 wounded. U.S. Army casualties were ninety-four killed and 311 wounded.

There were four more big Japanese bases in the Marshalls—Mille, Jaluit, Wotje, and Maleolap—but if they were cut off from reinforcement and kept neutralized by air attacks, they would be impotent and could be left to wither away. To this end MAG-31 started flight operations from Roi on 15 March and MAG-13 began flying from Majuro on the twenty-first. The 4th Marine Base Defense Aircraft Wing echeloned its headquarters forward to Kwajalein on

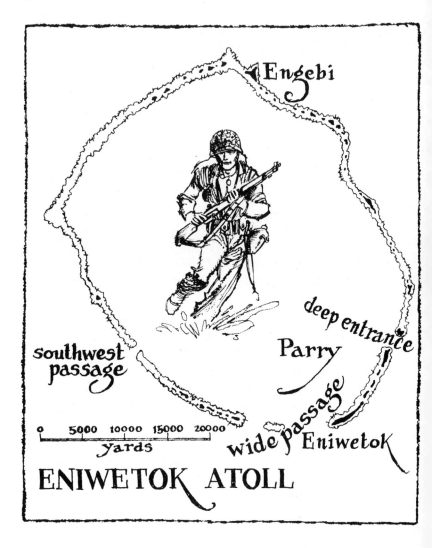

Engebi

deep entrance

Parry

southwest passage

wide passage  Eniwetok

0   5000   10000   15000   20000
yards

ENIWETOK ATOLL

9 March. Later MAG-22 from Midway would join the wing. Ten fighter and four bomber squadrons would continue the long-term, monotonous, but necessary task of neutralizing the bypassed Marshall atolls. (How well they would do the job was revealed after the war: of the 13,701 Japanese on the four atolls, 7,440 would die, 2,564 from the bombing, the rest from disease and starvation. Ninety percent of the damage was attributed to the Marine squadrons.)

## THE MARIANAS

The Air Force needed airfields in the Mariana Islands, fifteen hundred miles from Japan, if the new B-29s were to reach the Empire. The Navy wanted advanced bases there for future moves against the Philippines and eventually against the Japanese home islands, and also hoped that such an attack would bring out the Japanese main battle fleet, absent since Guadalcanal, to a final decisive action. There were three main islands to go after: Saipan, Tinian, and Guam.

Some eight hundred ships and 162,000 men rendezvoused in the Marshalls for the long step to the Marianas. All this made up Spruance's Fifth Fleet. The Joint Expeditionary Force was under Kelly Turner. Holland Smith, now a lieutenant general, had two jobs: Expeditionary Troops, and Northern Troops and Landing Force. NTLF had the 2d Marine Division, commanded by newly promoted Tommy Watson, and the 4th Marine Division, still under Harry Schmidt. Saipan was first, fourteen miles long by six wide, rugged, mountainous, ringed with a coral reef, and with a Japanese and Chamorro civilian population. D-Day for Saipan was 15 June 1944. The assault on Guam, for which there was a Southern Troops and Landing Force, was to be three days later, on the eighteenth. Tinian was then to follow. Ralph Smith's 27th Infantry Division was in floating reserve and the 77th Division was to be held in Hawaii as strategic reserve.

Saipan was the headquarters of the Japanese Central Pacific Fleet under Adm. Chiuchi Nagumo, who had been Commander Striking Force at Pearl Harbor and Midway. The headquarters of the new 31st Army was also there, under elderly Lt. Gen. Yoshitsugo Saito. The 31st Army was subordinate to the Central Pacific Fleet but the command lines were convolute and the admiral and the general did not get along. Nagumo thought the landing would be on the east coast, in Magicienne ("Magazine") Bay, and soon. Saito thought it would be on the west coast near Charan-Kanoa but not until November. By careful count there were 29,662 defenders on Saipan. Army troops included the 43d (Nagoya) Division, the 47th Independent Mixed Brigade, the 9th Tank Regiment, two engineer regiments, and an antiaircraft regiment. Most of the soldiers had come recently from the Kwantung Army in China. Naval defenses, chiefly the 1st Yokosuka Special Naval Landing Force, were concentrated around Tanapag Harbor on the northwest coast. Key terrain feature was Mount Tapotchau, 1,552 feet high, in the center of the island. The one important airfield was Aslito field at the southern end of the island.

Saito had been right; the Marines were going to land across the beaches north and south of the sugar-mill town of Charan-Kanoa. The 2d Division was on the left, 6th and 8th Marines in the assault. The 4th Division was on the right, farther south, with the 23d and 25th Marines in the lead. Seven hundred amtracks were to carry the assault waves, coming in behind new armored amphibians mounting 75mm guns. H-Hour was 0840. There was much mortar and artillery fire as the tractors came across the reef. The Marines took two thousand casualties the first day. Five of the original battalion commanders were hit. One battalion—the 2d Battalion, 6th Marines—had four different commanders before dark.

The situation ashore was not good, but the Navy got one reaction they wanted: the Japanese Combined Fleet came out from its hiding places to meet the Fifth Fleet. Spruance met with Holland Smith and Kelly Turner the morning of 16 June on board the *Rocky Mount*. He was sending Marc Mitscher's Task Force 58 out to meet the Japanese fleet. The Guam landing would be postponed. The 27th Division would be landed on Saipan and the 77th Division would be brought forward from Hawaii.

Ashore, by noon on the sixteenth, two battalions of the 2d Division had gotten through Charan-Kanoa. Meanwhile, the 4th Division was attacking straight ahead, clearing the beach so that the 165th Infantry could come ashore. At about 0330 the next morning the 9th Tank Regiment hit the 2d Division; the tanks got almost to the 6th Marines command post before being stopped. With daylight on the seventeenth the Marine attack started forward slowly. Marshy Lake Susupe lying behind Charan-Kanoa separated the two divisions and proved troublesome. Momentum picked up on the eighteenth. The 4th Division, with its regiments abreast, pushed across the island to Magicienne Bay. On the 4th Division's right flank, the 165th Infantry had curled south and taken Aslito airfield, and on 165th's right, the 105th Infantry had moved to the cliffs on the southern tip of the island, so that by the nineteenth a Japanese battalion had been compressed into a pocket at Nafutan Point.

It was on 19 June that Task Force 58 shot down 346 Japanese aircraft off Guam in the "Marianas Turkey Shoot." Next day Spruance pressed home the attack and, although it cost a hundred American planes, took out three Japanese aircraft carriers in the Battle of the Philippine Sea.

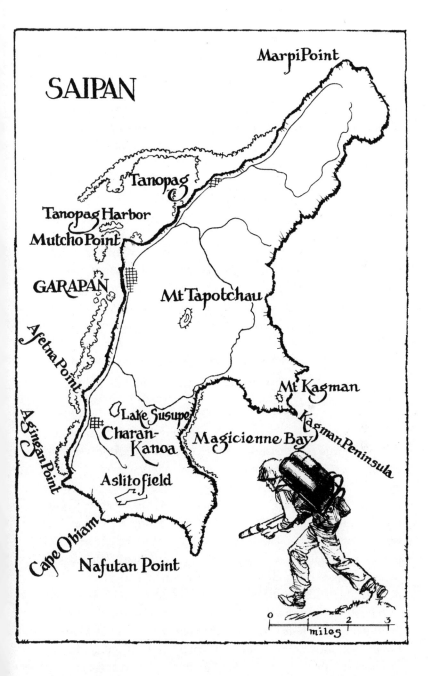

SAIPAN

MarpiPoint

Tanopag

Tanopag Harbor
Mutcho Point

GARAPAN

Mt Tapotchau

Afetna Point

Agingan Point

Lake Susupe
Charan-
Kanoa

Aslito field

Mt Kagman

Kagman Peninsula

Magicienne Bay

Cape Obiam

Nafutan Point

0        2      3
miles

On the twentieth, while the 2d Division held fast as a pivot, the 4th Division swung around so that there was a line facing north. Holland Smith now ordered the 27th Division to leave one battalion in the south to clean out Nafutan Point and to move in between the 2d and 4th Divisions. On the twenty-third, the three divisions jumped off behind a preparation laid down by eighteen battalions of artillery. On the left, in the 2d Division's zone, the 2d Marines on 24 June entered Garapan, once a town of fifteen thousand, now empty and nearly flattened. The 8th Marines started up the slopes of Mount Tapotchau. On the right, the 4th Division took Hill 600 (and renamed it "Hot Potato Hill") which covered Kagman Peninsula, which in turn formed the northern lip of Magicienne Bay.

In the center, the 27th Division had bogged down. After conferring with Spruance and Kelly Turner, Holland Smith relieved Ralph Smith of his command. A Marine general named Smith relieving an Army general named Smith was a ready-made newspaper sensation and the effects of it on interservice relations would be felt for years. Next day Lt. Col. Rathvon McC. ("Tommy") Tompkins, who had the 1st Battalion, 29th Marines (a separate battalion attached temporarily to the 2d Division), made a brilliant flanking attack to the top of Mount Tapotchau, getting above the Japanese defenders.

On the night of 26 June the Japanese in the Nafutan Point pocket (they were the 317th Battalion, 47th Brigade) came boiling out, punched through the 2d Battalion, 105th Infantry, and reached the flight line on Aslito (renamed IDly) airfield. Some five hundred were eventually killed by the 25th Marines, who were in reserve, and the artillerymen of the 14th Marines.

In the north, as the island narrowed, the 4th and 27th Divisions continued in the assault and the 2d Division passed into reserve. On 6 July, Saito pressed his samurai sword to his breast, drew blood, and was ceremoniously shot by his adjutant. At about the same time Admiral Nagumo put a bullet through his own brain. By now Maj. Gen. George W. Griner, USA, had arrived from Hawaii to take over the 27th Division. Holland Smith told him to expect a banzai attack. It came early on the morning of 7 July. Two to three thousand Japanese found a 300-yard gap separating the 1st and 3d Battalions of the 105th Infantry, poured through, and were finally stopped by the 3d Battalion, 10th Marines, firing at pointblank range with 105s. Next day General Smith sent in the rested 2d Division to relieve the 27th Division. By 9 July Marpi Point was reached at the northern tip of the island. It was a 220-foot cliff honeycombed with caves. Urged on by the remaining Japanese soldiers, many of the civilians committed mass suicide by leaping from the cliff. The alternate method preferred by most of the soldiers was to blow themselves up with hand grenades.

American casualties for Saipan numbered 16,525, of whom 12,934 were marines. Of the nearly thirty thousand Japanese defenders, all but about a thousand perished. On 18 July, Premier Hideki Tojo, mortified by the defeat in the Battle of the Philippine Sea and the loss of Saipan, submitted his resignation to the Emperor.

## GUAM

Peanut-shaped Guam, largest and southernmost of the Marianas, twenty-eight miles long, four to eight miles wide, was not unlike Saipan, but bigger, with more jungle, and no cane fields. The southern half of the island, where not cultivated, was high jungle country. The northern half was flatter, less lush, but covered with dense brush and undergrowth. The natives of Guam were called Chamorros, a brown people, their aboriginal blood liberally mixed with Spanish, Filipino, and Japanese. On the western side of the island were two coral fingers, Cabras Island and Orote peninsula, sticking out into the sea and forming Apra harbor. North of Cabras, along the coast road, was the town of Asan and then the capital, Agana, about twelve thousand souls in normal times. South of Orote the road ran to Agat and then petered out to little more than a track that went on around the island. Behind Apra harbor was Mount Tenjo, going up to a thousand feet.

Lt. Gen. Takeshi Takashina, a vigorous veteran of Manchuria, was the senior Japanese officer present. His command included the 38th Infantry Regiment, reinforced, the 48th Independent Mixed Brigade, and the 10th Independent Mixed Regiment, about thirteen thousand army troops altogether. There were also fifty-five hundred members of the Imperial Navy, under Capt. Yutaka Sugimoto, the most significant unit being the 54th Naval Guard Force (whom the U.S. Marines would call "Imperial Marines" and who would fight exceedingly well). Tumon Bay, north of Agana, was the most obvious landing site and Takashina had fortified it heavily. There was the usual large inventory of artillery of mixed calibers and origins, the most formidable being nineteen 8-inch guns, not all of which were in position, the Japanese not having gotten down seriously to the business of fortifying Guam until after the Marshalls had fallen.

Maj. Gen. Roy Geiger would be Commander, Southern Troops and Landing Force. His headquarters was the III Amphibious Corps, a redesignation of what had been I Marine Amphibious Corps. He had the 3d Marine Division under Maj. Gen. Allen H. ("Hal") Turnage, the 1st Provisional Marine Brigade under Brig. Gen. Lemuel Shepherd, the usual corps troops including plentiful artillery, the 9th and 14th Defense Battalions (with which to garrison the island after the assault), and, in reserve, the 77th U.S. Army Division.

Landing day, called W-Day for this operation, originally to have been 18 June, now was set for 21 July. There was the usual problem of a fringing reef but this was becoming almost routine—the amphibian tractors would take the assault waves into the beach, then come back to transfer line at the reef's edge and pick up the succeeding waves from the landing craft. There would be two landings, about five miles apart. Turnage's 3d Marine Division would make the northern landing, avoiding Tumon Bay, and going in on a wide crescent-shaped beach between Adelup and Asan points. Shepherd's brigade would land just south of Agat. H-Hour was 0830. Air and naval gunfire had flattened Agana, Asan, Agat, and nearly everything above ground on Orote peninsula. Most of the big-caliber coastal guns had been knocked out or neutralized; not so with the lighter guns. The 3d Marine Division landed with three regiments abreast behind a barrage of rockets fired from LCI gunboats, the first waves being armored amphibians mounting 37-mm and 75-mm guns. As they came across the reef the Japanese started dropping artillery and mortar fire on them, and then brought them under crossfire from machine guns hidden in the cliff faces. The 3d Marines, on the left, met stiffening resistance as they moved forward into a vise formed by the Chonito Cliff and the Fonte heights. The 21st Marines, in the center, went through the town of Asan and continued west against the higher ground farther inland. The 9th Marines, on the right flank and on easier ground, swung south, secured Asan point, and reached the causeway to Cabras Island by evening.

Shepherd's brigade had harder fighting. Put together on Guadalcanal, the brigade had two regiments, the 22d Marines, veterans of Eniwetok, and the new 4th Marines, made up of the raider battalions, reorganized into infantry, and given the designation of the regiment lost at Bataan. The brigade landed with the 4th Marines on the right, 22d Marines on the left, both with two battalions abreast. Separating the two regimental beaches was Gaan point. The Japanese had hollowed it out and in the nose were two short-barreled 75-mm guns that piled up two dozen amphibian tractors landing the 22d Marines.

GUAM

0  2000 4000 6000 8000 10000
yards

Ritidian Point

Tumon Bay

Mt Barrigada

Adelup Point

Asan Point

Cabras

Agana

Asan

Fonte hill

Apra Harbor

Pacific Ocean

Pago Bay

Orote
Point

Sumai
airfield

Mt Tenjo

Gaan Point

Agat

Bangi Point

Mt Alifan

Facpi Point

Gaan point stayed "hot" most of the day. Alifan ridge was a mile behind the beach; the 4th Marines got halfway there before nightfall. The 22d Marines went through Agat and curled toward the base of Orote peninsula. The 305th U.S. Infantry, on temporary loan from the 77th Division as brigade reserve, came into the beach about dark.

Sometime after midnight the Japanese came out of their caves and boiled toward the brigade beachhead. Takashina used up two battalions of the 38th Regiment in the attack. When morning came, the 4th Marines resumed the advance and by nightfall had reached the crest of Mount Alifan. The 305th Infantry moved into the center of the brigade beachhead and the 22d Marines started north astride the Agat-Agana Road. By 23 July they had cut across the base of Orote peninsula to Apra harbor.

The 3d Division was also heavily engaged. In the first three days, the 3d Marines had been held stalled in front of Fonte hill; the 21st Marines had doggedly made their way inland against successive ridgeline positions; and the 9th Marines had taken Cabras Island. The 9th Marines could now spare a battalion to come to the help of the 3d Marines. Lt. Col. Robert Cushman arrived with the 2d Battalion, 9th Marines, the night of 24 July. The next morning, his battalion passed through the 3d Marines' leading edge, crossed the Mount Tenjo Road, and went up the slope of Fonte hill, driving a wedge into the Japanese defenses. That same day, the twenty-fifth, patrols from the 9th and 22d Marines made contact on the rim of Apra harbor and the two beachheads were tenuously linked. Most of the 77th Division was ashore by now and the 4th Marines had come up on the left of the 22d Marines on Orote peninsula.

That night, 25–26 July, Takashina made his big effort. On Orote peninsula, the naval defenders came charging out of a mangrove swamp in a saki-inflamed, suicidal extravaganza. In the north what was left of the 10th Independent Mixed Regiment came against Cushman's battalion on Fonte hill. Company F, under a tall Mississippian, Capt. Louis H. Wilson, was at the apex of the Marine salient, and during the night seven separate attacks were beaten off. Elsewhere on the division perimeter there were two penetrations and some of the attackers got back to the field hospital, where there was a weird scene of wounded marines fighting in bandages and underwear. By morning, the fire was out of the attack on both fronts and Takashina had used up the equivalent of ten battalions. On Fonte, Lou Wilson, three times wounded, collected a patrol and tidied up his company position before allowing himself to be evacuated. He would receive the Medal of Honor.

Takashina himself was killed on the twenty-eighth. That same day, the 22d Marines reached the fire-blackened skeleton of the old Marine barracks and next day took Orote airfield. During the last days of the month the 77th Division moved up on the right of the 3d Marine Division and on 31 July the two divisions started forward in a shoulder-to-shoulder sweep. MAG-21 began flight operations at Orote airfield on 4 August and eventually grew to twelve squadrons. On 7 August the rested brigade came in on the division's left flank, and three days later the last Japanese defenders were pushed over the northern cliffs.

American casualties were 1,919 killed, 7,122 wounded, 70 missing; a total of 9,111. Japanese losses were put at 17,300 killed, 485 prisoners, although for months, even years to come (as late as 1972), hardy survivors would be killed or captured, running up the count.

## TINIAN

Tinian is just south of Saipan, separated by about two and a half miles of water. Smaller than Saipan (about twelve miles long, north to south), Tinian is also less rugged, mostly a fairly regular low plateau, densely planted in those days in sugar cane. The cane fields in the center of the island promised room for six 8,500-foot runways for the B-29s that were to bomb the Japanese home islands.

The Japanese commander was Col. Keishi Ogata, a veteran of the Kwantung Army. He commanded the 50th Infantry Regiment, 29th Division, plus a battalion of the 135th Infantry and the usual reinforcements. Also under Ogata's orders was the 56th Naval Guard Force. In all there were 4,700 army and 4,110 navy.

Near the northern tip of the island there were two beaches, both very small, one about sixty yards wide and the other with a usable length of about seventy-five yards. Reconnaissance showed mines between the high- and low-water marks, but obviously the Japanese did not expect a landing over such narrow beaches.

The plan was for the 4th Marine Division (now commanded by Clifton Cates—Harry Schmidt had moved up to command of V Amphibious Corps) to make a shore-to-shore landing while Tommy Watson's 2d Division demonstrated off Tinian Town in the south. By 15 July, all the artillery on Saipan had been grouped in the south of the island from where it could cover

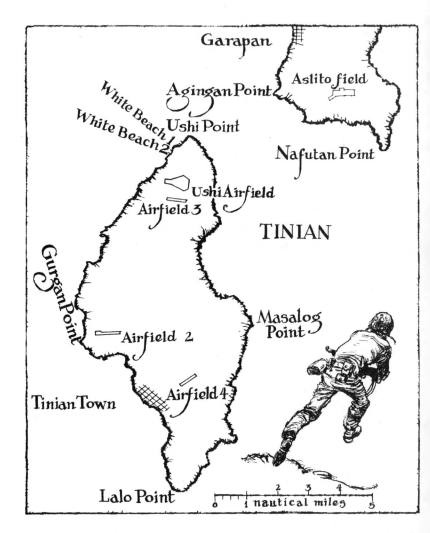

Tinian. Naval gunfire support was also plentiful. Air support would come from Army and Marine squadrons already in place on Saipan, as well from carrier-based naval aviation.

J-Day was 24 July. At 0745, the 24th Marines came across White One, the northern, more narrow beach, in columns of battalions, while the 25th Marines landed with two battalions abreast on White Two. Opposition was "light" on White One, "moderate" on White Two. About midday the 23d Marines moved into line on the right flank.

Colonel Ogata, still committed to a doctrine that said to defend at the waterline, started his counterattack in motion that afternoon. At 0200 in the morning the 1st Battalion, 135th Infantry, hit the center of the Marine line. The 25th Marines were very solidly in position on good ground and the attackers made no impression. At 0300, the 50th Infantry attacked, found the boundary between the 25th Marines and the 23d Marines, and a couple of hundred of them got through as far as the light artillery positions. About this same time the 56th Naval Guard Force was destroying itself against the 24th Marines on the left flank.

The next day, 25 July, the 2d Marine Division came ashore, took Ushi airfield, swung around and came up on the 4th Division's left flank. The 24th Regiment went into reserve and the two divisions started a shoulder-to-shoulder systematic sweep southward. On 31 July the 4th Division moved through Tinian Town. Early next morning, there was a banzai attack of sorts and at daylight the body of a colonel was found hanging on the wire. It might have been Ogata. As the Japanese were compressed into the southern part of the island, there was a repetition of the death hysteria that had gripped Saipan. On 1 August American patrols reached the southern coast and Harry Schmidt was able to announce that "all organized resistance had ceased." By 12 August, 13,262 civilians had been rounded up and put safely into stockades. By count, 6,050 Japanese defenders were dead, 255 others were prisoners. The Marines had lost 290 killed, 1,515 wounded, and 24 missing.

PELELIU

The Palaus are about midway between the Marianas and the southern Philippines, say five hundred miles from Mindanao—easy medium-bomber range. The biggest island is Babelthuap but the Americans were interested more in Peleliu, at the southern end of the group. Six miles long, two miles wide, shaped something like a lobster's claw, Peleliu had a big airfield filling most of its flat lower end. Off the northern end was the smaller island, Ngesebus, connected to Peleliu by a causeway. The backbone of Peleliu, north of the airfield, was a coral-limestone ridge, going up to about two hundred feet and forming the upper half of the lobster's claw. The natives called the ridge Umurbrogol.

The Palaus were to be another III Phib Corps operation. Expeditionary troops would be the 1st Marine Division, coming up from muddy Pavuvu, and the untried 81st U.S. Division from Hawaii. The Marines would take

Peleliu, while the Army demonstrated off Babelthuap and then moved on to take Angaur, seven miles southwest of Peleliu. Maj. Gen. William Rupertus still had the 1st Marine Division, which was reinforced for the operation to a strength of 28,484.

A very canny lieutenant general named Sadea Inoue commanded the Palau Sector Group. On Peleliu he had the 2d Infantry Regiment from his own 14th Division (one of Japan's oldest and best), two more infantry battalions, and reinforcements which included tanks and a mixture of guns, among them a new 200-mm rocket launcher. That made about six thousand Japanese soldiers. There were also forty-one hundred Imperial Navy, including the usual Naval Guard Force.

D-Day was set for 15 September 1944. The bombardment began on D minus 3. Afterward it was called the "least adequate" of the Pacific War, partly because of the length of time, partly because of poor targeting, but, in fairness, mostly due to the Japanese soldier's skill with pick and spade. Rupertus's scheme was to land all three infantry regiments abreast on the wide beach on the west side of the island right off the airfield. The 7th Marines (now commanded by Herman Hanneken) would land on the southernmost beach and clear out the lower end of the island. The 5th Marines, under Col. Harold D. ("Bucky") Harris, would land in the center and drive straight across the airfield. The 1st Marines, under Chesty Puller, would land on the left and swing to the north along the axis of Umurbrogol ridge. Four days, someone suggested, would be all it would take.

H-Hour was 0830. Conduct of the defense devolved upon Col. Kunio Nakagawa, commander of the 2d Infantry Regiment. The first wave of marines was met at the beach by nothing heavier than small-arms fire and then, in accordance with Inoue's plan, the guns and mortars opened up and it was a repeat of Saipan and Guam. Twenty-six LVTs were knocked out. At about 1630, Nakagawa hit between the 1st and 5th Marines in a tank-infantry thrust. His attack was stopped cold, but by dark less than half the Marines' D-Day objectives had been taken. During the night there were probes but no major counterattacks, no senseless, drunken banzais. Next day, in the south, Hanneken's marines moved well against what appeared to be one battalion. Bucky Harris's 5th Marines drove straight across the airfield, hurt most by artillery and mortars dropping on them from the ridge. Puller's 1st Marines butted their heads against what was already being called the "Bloody Nose." There was a general advance on 17 September, the 7th Marines finished clean-

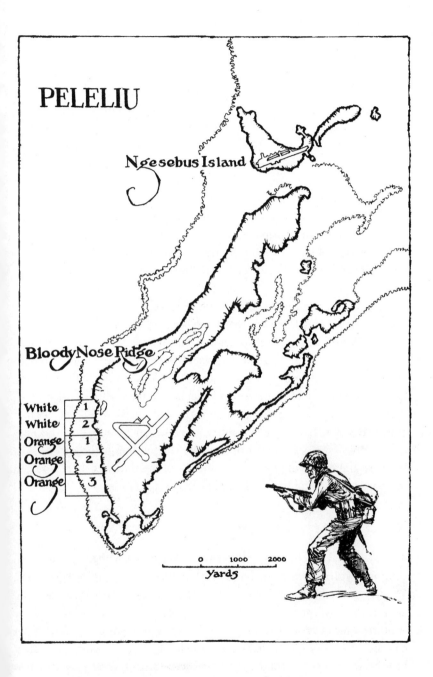

PELELIU

Ngesebus Island

Bloody Nose Ridge

White   1
White   2
Orange  1
Orange  2
Orange  3

0    1000    2000
yards

ing out the southern tip, the 5th moved north of the airfield (130 ruined Japanese aircraft were counted), and the 1st Marines, at terrible cost, clawed a few yards farther up the slopes of Bloody Nose. On the twentieth, Geiger met with Rupertus and over Rupertus's objections told him to get ready to reembark Puller's regiment; Geiger was bringing in the 321st RCT. The battered 1st Marines, with 1,749 casualties (56 percent) was relieved by the 7th Marines and started back for Pavuvu. The 321st (which, with the 322d RCT, had taken Angaur in three days of fighting) landed on the twenty-third, moved up the coast road on the left of Bloody Nose ridge, and, using the road as a line of departure, attacked up the ridge on a broad front. It was decided to add a third prong to the attack by passing Harris's 5th Marines behind the 321st, having Harris clear the northern end of the island, and then attack south along the ridge. By nightfall on 26 September, the 5th Marines had swept the northern end but were bothered by heavy mortar fire coming from Ngesebus Island. On 28 September the 3d Battalion, 5th Marines, made a shore-to-shore landing onto Ngesebus behind sixteen Sherman tanks and thunderously supported by naval gunfire, artillery, and close air support from VMF-114. (The Marine Corsair squadron had arrived two days earlier.)

This left just the center section of the Umurbrogol. By 1 October another Corsair squadron, VMF-122, had arrived and Marine Aircraft Group 11 was in place. Delivering their ordnance a thousand yards from takeoff, the Corsairs had two novelties to offer: rockets and napalm. On the twelfth the island was declared "secure," and a few days later the 81st Division relieved the 1st Marine Division. In a battle in many ways worse than Tarawa, Rupertus had taken 6,265 casualties, 1,241 of them dead. The marines had buried 10,695 Japanese and taken 301 prisoners. Ironically, MacArthur was already on his way back to the Philippines and Peleliu wasn't really needed.

## NIGHT FIGHTERS AND MARINE CARRIERS

Also present at Peleliu was VMF(N)-541, a Marine night-fighter squadron equipped with Grumman F6F Hellcats. The first night-fighting squadron, VMF(N)-531, had been activated at Cherry Point in November 1942. The only aircraft then available were surplus PV-1s—twin-engined Lockheed Vega Venturas which were really patrol aircraft. Later squadrons were given radar-equipped Corsairs and Hellcats, but a single-place fighter wasn't the complete answer either. A second man was needed to work the radar. Even so, the one Japanese aircraft shot down in the Palaus by a marine was on the night of 31 October by VMF(N)-541.

Two more Marine fighter squadrons and a torpedo-bomber squadron arrived on Peleliu in October and, after the island was finally secured, took up the sometimes dangerous "milk run" neutralization of the remaining Palaus and bypassed Yap. The 2d Marine Aircraft Wing, coming up from the New Hebrides, was designated Garrison Air Force, Western Carolines, with two operating groups, MAGs 11 and 25.

In April 1944, a 9th Marine Aircraft Wing had been activated at Cherry Point and in May the 3d MAW had come out to Ewa. As of the end of June, Marine aviation had a strength of 5 wings, 28 groups, 126 aircraft squadrons, and 112,626 personnel, of whom 10,457 were pilots. In August, General Vandegrift went out to Pearl Harbor to confer with Adm. Chester Nimitz on the question, once again raised, of putting Marine squadrons back on board aircraft carriers. It was decided that Marine aircraft would be put on a certain number of escort carriers, or CVEs, of which the Navy now had thirty-five.

In October 1944, Marine Carrier Groups, Aircraft, Fleet Marine Force Pacific, was activated in Santa Barbara, California, to get on with the implementation of the Nimitz-Vandegrift decision. There were to be eight carrier air groups, each with an eighteen-plane fighter squadron and a twelve-plane torpedo-bomber squadron. The fighters would be F4Us (greatly improved since rejected by the Navy as carrier fighters in 1942) and the torpedo bomber TBMs, the latter being the General Motors model of the Grumman Avenger. The Marine Corps had also gotten into the medium-bomber business, apparently for no reason other than that the Army Air Force was overstocked with North American Mitchell B-25s (which the Navy called PBJs). Eventually, five squadrons of Marine PBJs would serve in the South and Southwest Pacific and two in the Central Pacific. In the Central Pacific the 4th MBDAW, with Louis Woods, now a major general, as its commander, dropped the "Base Defense" from its designator and became simply the 4th Marine Aircraft Wing.

## THE PHILIPPINES

The reoccupation of the Philippines began on 20 October 1944 with landings on the east coast of Leyte by X and XXIV Corps. On loan to XXIV Corps were 1,528 marines, mostly from V Phib Corps artillery, and a sign sprang up on

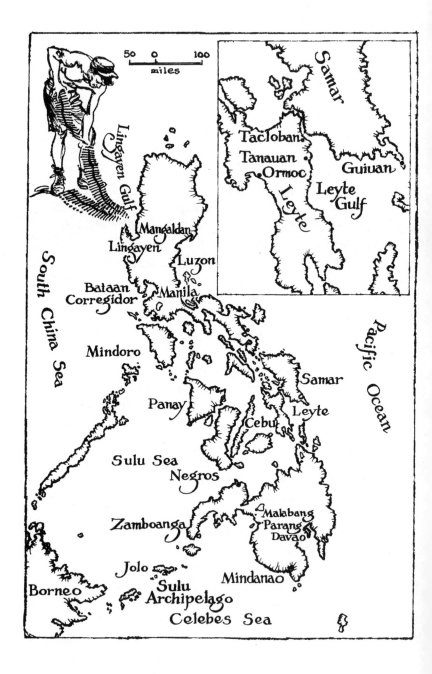

the beach, "By grace of God and a few Marines, MacArthur's back in the Philippines." Also present was Maj. Gen. Ralph Mitchell, who was looking for work for his underemployed 1st Marine Aircraft Wing, which was still in the northern Solomons.

The Leyte landings caused the Japanese Combined Fleet to sortie and the Battle for Leyte Gulf resulted, a decisive affair fought in three parts and one in which the new Japanese kamikaze tactic of slamming aircraft into ships caused much consternation. General Mitchell, ashore at muddy Tacloban airfield on 25 October, worked a pair of signal flags to help bring in forty Navy planes that had lost their carrier decks. But when the battle was over, the Imperial Navy, in the postwar words of one Japanese reporter, "as a Navy, had ceased to exist."

MacArthur wanted the Marine night-fighter squadron at Peleliu moved up to Leyte and on 3 December, VMF(N)-541 came in at Tacloban with its F6F Hellcats. MAG-12's four squadrons of FG-1s, the Goodyear version of the Corsair, began arriving a few hours later, and, by the end of the first week of December, five Marine squadrons totaling eighty-seven aircraft were trying to operate from the mud of Tacloban. On 7 December, Marine air helped cover a landing by the 77th Division on the west side of Leyte south of Ormoc. The Japanese made a desperate effort to reinforce and there were transports and destroyers to sink as well as bombers and fighters to battle.

The Army landed on Mindoro on 15 December against no opposition, Marines contributing to the air cover and also flying interdiction strikes against Japanese fields on Luzon. Late in the month MAG-12 moved from muddy, crowded Tacloban seven miles south to Tanauan, an airstrip made of Marston matting laid over beach sand. MAG-14, meanwhile, was in the process of moving north from Green Island to a coral strip at Guian on Samar. When the Sixth Army's landings at Lingayen on Luzon began 9 January 1945, both MAGs 12 and 14 were in support.

Col. Clayton C. Jerome, CO of MAG-32, and Lt. Col. Keith McCutcheon, operations officer of MAG-24, went ashore at Lingayen on 11 January with a jeep and a driver and found a seasonally dry rice paddy at Mangaldan. Bulldozers went to work, the first Marine SBDs began to arrive on 25 January, and by the month's end, seven squadrons of Marine dive bombers—174 aircraft in all—were present and ready for operations. Preparations for the move of

MAGs 24 and 32 to the Philippines had begun in October at Bougainville, dedicated to the principle, in McCutcheon's words, that "close air support aviation is only an additional weapon to be employed at the discretion of the ground commander."

Colonel Jerome, as senior Marine officer present, commanded MAGS-DAGUPAN ("Marine Aircraft Groups, Dagupan"). First strikes were flown on 27 January. MAGSDAGUPAN was to give priority of support to the 1st Cavalry Division in its drive for Manila. The dash got under way on 1 February and the cavalrymen reached the city in sixty-six hours (although complete reduction of the Japanese defenses would require almost a month's more hard fighting). Twelve miles northwest of Manila General Yamashita had eighty thousand troops invested in the twenty-five-mile-long Shimbu Line. MAGSDAGUPAN would pound this line for the next several weeks and give some measure of support to all ten U.S. divisions operating on Luzon plus five "regiments" of guerrillas who were roaming the mountains and jungles.

Next came Zamboanga, a tail-like appendage extending southwest from the big island of Mindanao. The U.S. 41st Infantry Division put two regiments ashore there on 10 March. Jerome and McCutcheon followed the GIs to San Roque field, a mile inland. The first Corsair landed on 14 March, and the next day marines were flying missions. The new aggregation—MAGs 12, 24, and 32—was called MAGZAM (Marine Aircraft Groups, Zamboanga) and it would eventually total 293 aircraft. MAG-14 would stay on Samar but would furnish close support to operations on neighboring Panay and Cebu, as well as longer-legged missions to Mindanao.

There was a series of Army D-Days to be supported: the 40th Division's landing on Panay on 18 March, the Americal Division's landing on Cebu on 26 March, the 40th Division's landing on Negros on 29 March, the 41st Division's operations in the Tawatawi group stretching to the southwest (particularly the Jolo island landing on 9 April), and, toughest nut of all, the main landings on Mindanao. X Corps was to land at Parang on the south coast on 17 April. MAG-24, still in Luzon, was to support from Mala-bang field, which was held by guerrillas. Flight operations stopped at Man-galdan on 14 April (which was just as well—spring rains were dissolving the rice-paddy airstrip) and the group staged down to Malabang on Mindanao. The 24th Division, covered by Marine air, took Davao, Mindanao's principal city, on 3 May.

IWO JIMA

Think of a bad-smelling pork chop, burned black, five miles long and two and a half miles wide, about eight square miles in all, and that was Iwo Jima. It lay in the Volcano-Bonin archipelago, almost at the midpoint of a line drawn from the B-29 bases on Tinian and the home islands—700 miles from the Marianas, 660 miles from Tokyo. The Japanese had completed two airfields on the island and were working on a third. Although the bony knob at the shank end of the pork chop, 556-foot-high Mount Suribachi, was itself extinct, the core of the island was still hot. The volcanic rock tunneled easily and the loose black sand combined well with cement to make a first-class concrete.

Short, squat, fifty-four-year-old Lt. Gen. Tadamichi Kuribayashi commanded at Iwo. In what was nominally the 109th Infantry Division, he had the 2d Independent Mixed Brigade, the 145th Infantry Regiment, a battalion of the 17th Regiment, a brigade artillery group, and the 26th Tank Regiment. In the artillery group there were five antitank battalions, also batteries ranging from 70-mm to 8-inch coast defense guns, all kinds of mortars, including a new 320-mm spigot mortar, and rockets improvised from 8-inch naval shells. There was also a naval force, mostly antiaircraft and construction. Suribachi, with seven successive galleries of defenses, was a fortress in itself.

North of Suribachi a broad belt of fortifications passed across the island between Airfields 1 and 2 and another belt filled the space north of Airfield 2. Kuribayashi had published a set of "Courageous Battle Vows" and these were pasted to the inner walls of the pillboxes. One of the vows was "Each man will make it his duty to kill ten of the enemy before dying." In all, there were about twenty-three thousand Japanese defenders.

For the assault against Iwo Jima, Lt. Gen. Holland Smith would again be Commanding General, Expeditionary Troops. Landing Force was the V Amphibious Corps under Maj. Gen. Harry Schmidt and there would be three Marine divisions. The 4th Division, commanded by Maj. Gen. Clifton Cates, would come forward from Hawaii as would the 5th Marine Division, new and untried but well-salted with combat veterans including former parachutists, commanded by Maj. Gen. Keller E. Rockey (sometimes called "the Great Stone Face"). In floating reserve would be the 3d Division coming from Guam and led by Graves B. ("the Big E") Erskine. D-Day was first set for 20 January 1945 but when the Fleet got involved in the Philippines this was post-

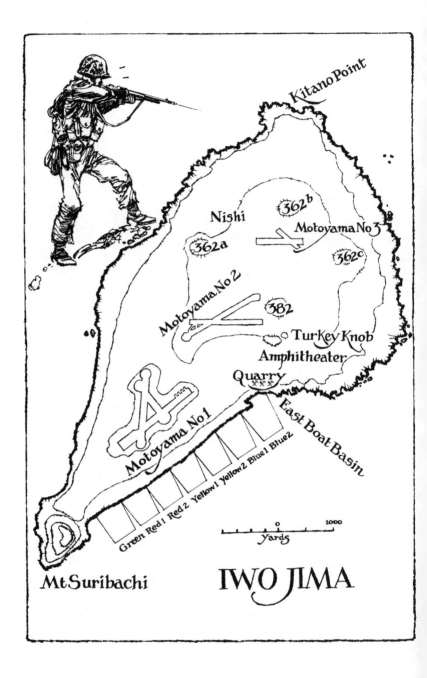

Nishi

362b

Motoyama No 3

362a

362c

Motoyama No 2

382

Turkey Knob

Amphitheater

Quarry

Motoyama No 1

East Boat Basin

Green  Red 1  Red 2  Yellow 1  Yellow 2  Blue 1  Blue 2

Kitano Point

o          1000

Yards

Mt Suribachi

IWO JIMA

poned, first until 3 February, and then a second time until 19 February. The photo interpreters had pegged a total of 642 blockhouses, pillboxes, and gun positions. There was a drumfire of carefully targeted Army and Navy air attacks for the seventy-four days before the landing. The immediate prelanding preparation was limited to three days, not as much time as the marines would have liked. Prevailing winds dictated the choice of the eastern beaches, left flank almost at the foot of Suribachi, right flank at East Boat Basin. As there was no fringing reef, landing craft would be able to beach. There were to be seven assault battalions and the beaches from left to right were Green, Red One, Red Two, Yellow One, Yellow Two, Blue One, and Blue Two. The first wave of armored amphibian tractors touched down at 0902 and the troop-carrying tractors began disgorging their passengers three minutes later. There was nothing to oppose them except some small-arms fire and an occasional mortar shell. Rockey's 5th Marine Division landed across the Green and Red Beaches, the 28th Marines on the left, 27th Marines on the right. The 28th Marines were to turn left and take Suribachi while the 27th Marines cut across the island. Cates's 4th Division, meanwhile, with the 23d and 25th Marines landing across Yellow and Blue Beaches, would move against Airfield No. 1. That was the plan and by 0945 all seven assault battalions were ashore.

Then the pounding started as Kuribayashi brought all his carefully ranged guns and mortars to bear along with the deadly scissors of crisscrossing automatic fire. Gy. Sgt. "Manila John" Basilone, now commanding a machine-gun platoon in the 1st Battalion, 27th Marines, said, "Come on, you guys, we got to get these guns off the beach," started over the rise, and was killed. From late morning until early afternoon virtually no landing craft could make the shore. Wheeled vehicles could not move through the sand. Tracked vehicles did little better. Tanks ran into deadly 47-mm fire. What artillery was ashore had to set up in the open, almost abreast of the infantry. Not until late afternoon did the reserves begin to land. At 1800, when the advance ended for the day, the Marine beachhead swung in an undulating line from the base of Suribachi around the southern edge of the airfield to the East Boat Basin just beyond the right flank of the landing. Bypassed defenders popped up here and there but there was no big wild banzai. In the morning the Marines continued the attack. Cates's 4th Division was to wheel northward. Rockey's 5th Division was to go in two directions: the 27th Marines were to hook around to the north on the west side of

Airfield No. 1 in coordination with the 4th Division while the 28th Marines went against Suribachi.

Liversedge of the Raiders had the 28th Marines. He started up Suribachi at 0830 on 20 February, his 2d and 3d Battalions in the assault, the 1st in reserve. A day's fighting gained the regiment 200 yards. Next morning they were at it again, all three battalions in line. The Japanese erupted from the mountain in a counterattack. It failed. The attack against Suribachi beat its way uphill again on the twenty-second. Next morning the mountaintop seemed silent. A squad-sized patrol went forward, feeling its way. It was followed by a larger, platoon-sized patrol. There was a short hard fight and the crest was taken. It was about 1015, 23 February. The lieutenant had a small American flag. He and his marines put it on the end of a piece of Japanese pipe and stood it up on the hilltop. A couple of hours later a four-man patrol brought up a larger flag from LST 779. It was fastened to another pipe; the four marines had trouble getting it into position so another marine and a hospital corpsman gave them a hand. Associated Press photographer Joe Rosenthal took their picture.

Suribachi had been taken, but the attack to the north had come almost to a halt. The belt of fortifications between Airfields No. 1 and No. 2 had no flanks and it was worse than Suribachi. On D-plus-1, the 27th Marines on the left had made good gains. In the center, the 23d Marines stayed abreast, but on the right, against the toughest resistance, the 25th Marines had barely made two hundred yards. Next day, 21 February, the 26th Marines passed through the 27th Marines in the 5th Division's zone, while the 21st Marines came ashore and relieved the 23d Marines. Harry Schmidt decided the main effort against Airfield No. 2 would be in the zone of the fresh 21st Marines. They attacked on the twenty-fourth, behind a thunderous preparation by naval gunfire, artillery, and carrier-based air, and supported by all the tanks that could be mustered from both the 4th and 5th Divisions. Fifteen tanks got loose on Airfield No. 2, and in an hour and a half the 21st Marines ("fighting on a pool table") had advanced half a mile.

Erskine was now ashore with the rest of the 3d Marine Division (except for the 3d Marines which stayed afloat as a last reserve) and Schmidt put him into the center of the line. The 9th Marines (the "Striking Ninth") passed through the 21st Marines and after three days of hard fighting held two hills north of Airfield No. 2. Next afternoon, 28 February, the 21st came back into the attack, took the ruined rubble of Motoyama village, and started up into the hills overlooking unfinished Airfield No. 3. On 3d Division's right, Cates's 4th Division was fighting hard for Hill 382 and on their left, Rockey's 5th Division was stopped by Hill 362A. Schmidt now shifted the weight of his attack to his flank divisions. The 28th Marines were brought north from Suribachi, attacked Hill 362A on 1 March, and by nightfall had the crest. The 4th Division called Hill 382 the "Meatgrinder." It was 2 March before the 2d Battalion, 24th Marines, succeeded in sticking to the top of the hill.

Two more hills were numbered "362," quite separate from Hill 362A. Hill 362B, in the 5th Division zone, was taken on 3 March by the 26th Marines. Hill 362C, in the 3d Division's zone, was defended by the dismounted Japanese 26th Tank Regiment. They fought hard and were compressed into Cushman's Pocket (named for Bob Cushman's heavily engaged 2d Battalion, 9th Marines). On 7 March, Erskine's 3d Division made a silent predawn attack with no artillery preparation, took the tankers by surprise, and made a good advance. Two days later the 3d Division plunged forward again and broke their way through to Iwo's northeastern shore. The 9th Marines faced east toward the 4th Division, the 21st Marines faced west toward the 5th Division, and the final compression began. The remaining defenders made a last wild counterattack against the 4th Division the night of 8 March, getting at the juncture of the 23d and 24th Marines. After that it was simply a case of mopping up. The last die-hards were eliminated on Turkey Knob and in the Amphitheater on 10 March, and 4th Division patrols pushed on to the northeast coast.

Rockey's 5th Division still had a powerful Japanese remnant under Kuribayashi's personal command in front of them at Kitano Point, the northwestern tip of the pork chop. With help from Erskine's 3d Division, Kitano Point was taken on 26 March and the island was declared secured. That night a shapeless last-ditch counterattack hit the 5th Pioneer Battalion near Airfield No. 2. There were many Japanese officers among the attackers (forty samurai swords were picked up later) and it was rumored that one of the 223 dead was Kuribayashi. On 16 March he had sent a last message to Imperial General Headquarters: "I humbly apologize to His Majesty that I have failed to live up to expectations. . . . Bullets are gone and water exhausted. . . . Permit me to say farewell. . . ."

Of the 71,245 Marines who had gone ashore, 5,931 had been killed, 17,372 wounded. Admiral Nimitz could well have been speaking for both attacker and defender when he said of this bitterly fought battle, "Uncommon valor was a common virtue."

## OKINAWA

One of the consequences of heavy Navy losses to the kamikazes was to put Marine fighter squadrons on board the big attack carriers. VMFs 124 and 213 in the *Essex* took part in Admiral Halsey's great raid against the Indo-China ports and airfields in January 1945, and when Adm. Raymond A. Spruance sent his fast carrier task force against the Japanese home islands during Iwo Jima, there were eight Marine squadrons on board the *Bennington, Bunker Hill, Essex,* and *Wasp.* In mid-March, the Marine squadrons in the *Essex* and *Wasp* were replaced with all-Navy air groups, but the *Franklin* had come out with two fresh Marine squadrons. She had just joined Vice Adm. Marc A. Mitscher's task force when on 19 March, a little after daybreak and fifty-five miles off Japan's coast, a Japanese plane put two bombs into her flight deck. She was gutted and VMFs 214 and 452 were knocked out of the war after only two days' carrier combat. This left four squadrons operational in the *Bunker Hill* and *Bennington.* Both carriers would have a part to play in the seizure of Okinawa.

Okinawa would be the point of final intersection of Nimitz's drive across the Central Pacific and MacArthur's march up from the Southwest Pacific. The island was about sixty miles long and from two to eighteen miles wide, looking something like a long skinny insect with a number of peninsular legs sticking out each side. The northern part was wild and mountainous; the south, below the narrow Ishikawa waist, was more open, heavily cultivated, but still hilly, with several ridges crossing the island from east to west.

Spruance would be in overall charge of the operation. Kelly Turner, with 1,213 ships, would once again have the Joint Expeditionary Force. Lt. Gen. Simon Bolivar Buckner Jr., USA, who had the Tenth Army, would command the Expeditionary Troops ashore. Under him he would have as Northern Landing Force the III Amphibious Corps, still commanded by Roy Geiger, with the 1st and 6th Marine Divisions. Southern Landing Force would be the XXIV U.S. Army Corps under Maj. Gen. John R. Hodge, USA, with the 7th, 77th, and 96th Divisions. The 2d Marine Division would go along as a demonstration force and the 27th Division would be in floating reserve.

All the land-based air support was grouped under Tactical Air Force, Tenth Army, with Marine Maj. Gen. Francis Mulcahy as tactical air commander. Carrier-based air support came more directly under Turner and included eighteen escort carriers (of which four had Marine squadrons on

OKINAWA

Iheya Retto

Ii Shima

Motobu Peninsula

East China Sea

Nago Wan

Nago

Yontan

Chimu Wan

Kadena

Hagushi Beaches

Hagushi

Philippine Sea

Naha

Shuri

Buckner Bay

Oroku Peninsula

Yonabaru

miles

Chantan

Machinato airfield

Dakeshi

Wana

Shuri

Naha

Yonabaru

airfield

Oroku

Kokuba

Chinen

Iwa

Kunishi

Yuza

Mezado

Makabe

Hanagusuku

Ara Point

miles

board) and also the planes from the big carriers of Task Force 58 when they were sent in to help.

By official count there were 182,112 men in the Tenth Army of whom 81,165 were marines. L-Day was to be Sunday, 1 April 1945, which was both Easter and April Fool's Day. Naval gunfire and air preparation began seven days before the landing. On 26 March a Marine reconnaissance battalion and two regiments of the 77th Division took five islands of the Kerama Retto group thirty miles west of Okinawa against light resistance. On L-Day the 2d Marine Division was to feint a landing in the extreme south while the two corps landed abreast over what the Americans called the "Hagushi" (actually, the Japanese name was "Tagushi") beaches on the western side of the island close to Yontan and Kadena airfields. After cutting the island in half, III Corps would swing north and XXIV Corps, making the main effort, would go south toward Shuri Castle and Naha.

The 2d Marine Division under Maj. Gen. LeRoy P. Hunt lost a transport and an LST to a kamikaze attack shortly after dawn while getting into position for the demonstration. The landing craft embarked their troops, made their run in toward the beach, and then turned away. Meanwhile, the real landing was underway, with touchdown scheduled for 0830. From left to right, the 6th and 1st Marine Divisions were landing on the northern or Blue Beaches and the 7th and 96th Infantry Divisions were coming across the southern or Purple Beaches, each division with two regiments abreast. By noon Shepherd's 6th Division had taken Yontan airfield. (After Guam, the 1st Provisional Marine Brigade had added the 29th Marines and became the 6th Marine Division, under command of Lem Shepherd, promoted to major general.) By 4 April Maj. Gen. Pedro del Valle's 1st Marine Division had cut across the island and secured Katchin peninsula. XXIV Corps on his right flank had taken Kadena airfield on 2 April and by 4 April had swung to the right into a line of four regiments stretching across the narrow waist of the island. So far the fighting had been negligible. The Japanese were believed to have from fifty-five to sixty-five thousand troops on the island. Where were they?

The highly capable Lt. Gen. Mitsuru Ushijima had elected not to defend the beaches or the airfields. In his "Battle Instruction Number 8," issued 8 March 1945, Ushijima said: "We must make it our basic principle to allow the enemy to land in full . . . until he can be lured into a position where he cannot receive cover and support from the naval gunfire and aerial bombardment, we must patiently and prudently hold our fire. Then, leaping into action, we shall open fire and wipe out the enemy." His 32d Army included two divisions, a brigade, a tank regiment, and a great deal of artillery. He had concentrated his strength in the south. Using the east-west ridges, he had organized three defense lines. The first followed Kakazu ridge. The second and strongest was in front of Shuri Castle and covered the capital city of Naha. The third line was well to the south and passed through Kunishi ridge. Ushijima himself was in a command post dug in under Shuri Castle. (It had been nearly a hundred years since Commodore Perry had marched his blue-jackets and marines to Shuri Castle—to the consternation and ultimate undoing of the elderly regent.)

It was against Ushijima's first line that XXIV Corps moved on 4 April, 7th Division on the left and 96th on the right. The advance ground to a stop on the slopes of Kakazu ridge and by the twelfth, the day of Roosevelt's death, all forward momentum had been lost. The 27th Division was moved into line on the right of the 96th and a three-division attack jumped off on 19 April. A mile-wide gap opened between the 27th and the 96th, and it took eight days of hard fighting before Kakazu ridge was cleared.

On the northern end of the island, Shepherd's 6th Division had swung to the left to take Motobu peninsula, above Nago Bay, beginning the attack on 12 April with his new regiment, the 29th Marines. The key piece of terrain, 1,200-foot Yae Take, proved more than the 29th Marines could handle by themselves. The veteran 4th Marines moved up to help, got to the top of the Yae Take on 16 April, and by the nineteenth the fight for Motobu was over. The 22d Marines in the meantime had reached the northern end of the island.

Buckner's problem now was how to get things moving in the south. The Marines were urging an amphibious landing to turn the enemy position. The 2d Marine Division was available and General Vandegrift, who visited Okinawa on 21 April, seconded Geiger's nomination that it be used, but Buckner decided in favor of a shoulder-to-shoulder frontal assault. On 27 April Del Valle's 1st Marine Division was assigned to XXIV Corps and on 1 May relieved the badly battered 27th Division. The 77th Division also moved into line, relieving the 96th Division, so that the corps front, from left to right, was 7th Division, 77th Division, and 1st Marine Division.

On 4 May, Ushijima "leaped into action" all along the line, his tanks and infantry coming in close behind a drumfire artillery preparation. The XXIV Corps front was briefly punctured at the 7th and 77th Division boundary. Buckner ordered Geiger to join him on the southern front with the rest of III

Phib Corps. Mopping up in the north was turned over to the 27th Division and the 6th Marine Division moved in on the extreme right flank of the line, the 1st Division sliding over to the left. It was now a two-corps front: Geiger's III Amphibious Corps on the right, Hodge's XXIV Corps on the left. In front of the 1st Marine Division was Dakeshi ridge and beyond that was Wana ridge. In front of the 6th Marine Division was the western anchor of the Shuri line, a complex of low, rounded hills dominated by "Sugar Loaf." A general advance began on 11 May.

The 22d Marines crossed the Asa Kawa by footbridge and two days later were clawing their way up Sugar Loaf. They were joined by the 29th Marines, and by the eighteenth the Shuri line had been breached. The 4th Marines relieved the 29th Marines, threw off a night counterattack, and continued to advance, crossing the Asato, and by 23 May, as the spring "plum rains" began to fall, the 6th Marine Division was on the outskirts of Naha.

Meanwhile, the 96th Division had taken Conical Hill, the eastern bastion of the Shuri line, and the 77th Division and 1st Marine Division were converging on Shuri Castle itself. On 12 May, the 7th Marines had gotten to the top of Dakeshi ridge and on 15 May started against Wana ridge. By the twenty-first, the 1st and 5th Marines were within assaulting distance of Shuri castle itself.

Ushijima now decided to withdraw to his third and final defensive line. His columns on the roads south of Shuri were cut into bloody ribbons by air and naval gunfire; nevertheless, Ushijima completed his withdrawal in good order. The rear guard left at Shuri had been ordered to hold until 31 May. On the twenty-ninth, Company A, 5th Marines, entered Shuri Castle and at 1015 reported it secured.

With a solid week of rain, the whole front had turned soggy. The naval garrison, commanded by Rear Adm. Minoru Ota (who had defended Bairoko against Liversedge's raiders), was still intact on Oroku peninsula. Shepherd, ordered to take the peninsula (a problem not unlike the one he had faced on Guam in taking Orote peninsula), elected to make a shore-to-shore landing. With the 22d Marines attacking on the landward side to seal off the base of the peninsula, the 4th Marines led off in the landing, touching down at 0600 on 4 June, followed later in the day by the 29th Marines. All three Marine regiments joined to compress the naval defenders into one last pocket near Oroku village. (Ota signaled: "The Naval Base Force is dying gloriously.") The Ota Force was eliminated on 14 June.

Ushijima's remnants on Kunishi ridge still showed fight. Del Valle's 1st Marine Division started against the ridge. The 7th Marines crossed half a mile of flat paddy land on 11 June in a night attack and four days later got to the crest. On the eighteenth, the 8th Marines, brought in from Saipan, relieved the 7th. General Buckner, watching them jump off from the division observation post, was struck by fragments of a Japanese shell and ten minutes later was dead. Geiger, by seniority, became as of that minute Commanding General, Tenth Army, the first marine to command a field army.

## MARINE AIR AT OKINAWA

III Phib Corps' four "VMOs" (or light observation squadrons) with their "Grasshoppers" had moved into Yontan and Kadena airfields immediately after the landing. Within a week Marine Aircraft Group 31 was operating its F4U Vought Corsairs from Yontan, and a few days later MAG-33 was at Kadena, so that within ten days of the landing, two hundred Marine aircraft were shore-based. MAG-22 arrived in May from Midway and was put in at Ie Shima, an offshore island taken by the 77th Division. In June, MAG-14 came up from the Philippines. In all, at final count, there were twenty-two Marine squadrons ashore.

In addition, there was some support from ten Marine squadrons at sea. The escort carrier *Block Island,* with its squadrons of Corsairs, Hellcats, and Avengers, flew its first strike on 10 May, and was joined on 21 May by the *Gilbert Islands.* Both carriers, however, were used more to neutralize the airfields in Sakishima Gunto, midway between Okinawa and Formosa, than in direct support of the ground fighting. Two kamikazes got to the attack carrier *Bunker Hill* on 11 May. This left just the two squadrons in the *Bennington:* VMFs 112 and 123. In almost continuous combat from 16 February to 8 June 1945, the two squadrons had shot down 82 enemy planes, destroyed 149 more on the ground, dropped over 100 tons of bombs, and fired more than 4,000 rockets. Their own losses were eighteen pilots killed, forty-eight planes lost.

## THE END

On 21 June General Geiger announced that "all organized resistance has ceased" and next morning, at 1000, there was a formal flag-raising in front of Tenth Army headquarters. That same day, Lt. Gen. Mitsure Ushijima dressed himself in full uniform, and told his chief of staff, Lieutenant General Cho, "I'll take along my fan since it is getting warm." The two generals made the ceremonial abdominal cuts and then their adjutant took off their heads with his sword. Three days later patrols from the 32d Infantry found their graves.

In all its dimensions Okinawa had been the biggest amphibious operation of the Pacific war. An official total of 107,539 Japanese and Okinawans had been killed on the island (and some estimates go much higher); 7,401 had been taken prisoner. The Japanese had lost 7,830 airplanes, 3,041 of them shot down by Navy and Marine pilots. The United States had lost 768 planes. The U.S. Navy had lost 36 ships sunk, 368 damaged—more than at Pearl Harbor—and the number of Navy dead—4,907—exceeded the total of either the Army or Marines. The Marines had lost 2,899 killed, 345 dead of wounds, and 11,677 wounded.

On 2 September 1945, the Japanese officially surrendered on board the battleship *Missouri* in Tokyo Bay. Standing little-noticed on a deck filled with U.S. and foreign dignitaries was Lt. Gen. Roy Geiger, who had succeeded Holland Smith as Commanding General, Fleet Marine Force, Pacific.

When Commo. Matthew G. Perry landed at Yokohama on 8 March 1854 much of the accompanying pomp and circumstance was provided by Maj. Jacob Zeilin— a future commandant—and the two hundred marines with the squadron. *painting by Wilhelm Heine*

The Marine detachment and ship's company in the USS *Vandalia* are turned out for inspection in 1886. The Navy was in a slow, sometimes reluctant transition from sail to steam with Marine shipboard duties subject to challenge.

The ubiquitous Lt. Col. L. W. T. ("Tony") Waller, seated front row center, arrived in Panama with his battalion in January 1904. The equally ever-present Capt. Smedley D. Butler is in the light shirt, rear rank.

The landing at Veracruz, Mexico, in April 1914 was a full-fledged brigade action complete with mule-drawn 3-inch field pieces. Three Marine regiments were involved in the brief but violent street fighting.

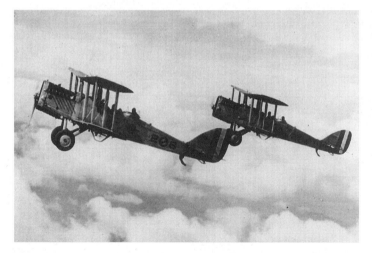

The British-designed, American-built DeHaviland DH-4 overcame its early reputation as a "flying coffin" and gave good service as a light bomber from the end of World War I through the "banana wars" of the 1920s.

Marine column at rest on its way to the front. In World War I the Marines arrived
in France in field hats, forest green uniforms, and leggings. These, at General Pershing's insistence, were exchanged for the tin hat, olive drab, and wrap puttees of
the doughboy. As part of the 2d U.S. Division, the 4th Brigade of Marines
blunted the German drive on Paris in June 1918, counterattacked, and fought its
way through Belleau Wood.

Marines were put to guarding the U.S. mails after a series of daring train robberies in 1921 and again in 1926. In both cases after the Marines were so assigned the robberies came to an abrupt halt.

Two Vought Corsair F-4Us take off from the airstrip on Banika in the Russell Islands in August 1943. The F-4U, with its unmistakable inverted gull wing, was more than a match for the vaunted Japanese Zero and would continue to serve the Marine Corps throughout the Korean War. *photo by Sgt. W. G. Wilson*

No beachhead of World War II offered more concentrated horror than Betio in Tarawa atoll. It took the 2d Marine Division seventy-six hours and cost over three thousand American casualties to capture the minute coral island.

Mt. Suribachi dominated the landing beaches at Iwo Jima. The sulphur smell and loose black volcanic sand gave the beachhead a special nightmarish quality. Three Marine divisions would be used in the battle. *photo by S.Sgt. Lou Lowery*

Joe Rosenthal's famous photograph of the flag-raising over Mt. Suribachi, taken 23 February 1945, became a national icon symbolizing victory over Japan and inspiring the Marine Corps War Memorial in Arlington, Virginia, sculpted by Felix de Weldon. Five marines and a Navy pharmacist mate raised the flag; three would be killed before the battle ended. *AP photo by Joe Rosenthal*

Armored amphibian tractors, making up the first waves of the III Amphibious Corps, churn their way ashore at Okinawa on 1 April 1945. The Japanese 32d Army did not elect to defend the landing beaches.

Each island battlefield in the Pacific had its own unique characteristics. Okinawa would be remembered for its Japanese pine covered ridge lines and the tombs and cemeteries that occupied so much of the island.

Maj. Gen. Keller E. Rockey, commanding III Amphibious Corps, accepts the surrender of Lt. Gen. Ginosu Uchida and his garrison at Tientsin, China, on 6 October 1945. Marines would remain in North China until 1949.

Corsairs of VMF-323 being armed with rockets on board the USS *Badoeng Strait* off Korea, September 1950. These fighter-bombers, supporting the 1st Provisional Marine Brigade, did much to save the Pusan perimeter.

Marines on the southern edge of the Hagaru-ri perimeter watch a Corsair deliver napalm on a Chinese position on 6 December 1950. The break-out of the 1st Marines Division southward to Koto-ri began that day. *photo by Sgt. Frank C. Kerr*

In July 1966, 3d Marine Division marines moved north from Da Nang to Quang Tri province to meet the threat of North Vietnamese regulars crossing the Demilitarized Zone. Large-scale battle followed. *photo by Sgt. Finnell*

Leadership in July 1967, from left to right: Lt. Gen. Robert E. Cushman, CG III Marine Amphibious Force; Maj. Gen. Bruno A. Hochmuth, CG 3d Marine Division; Army Gen. Creighton W. Abrams, Deputy ComUSMACV; and Brig. Gen. John R. Chaisson, MACV operations officer.

Gen. Leonard C. Chapman, as commandant, went first to Viet Nam in January 1968. On his last trip in January 1971 he enjoined his marines to bring out everything "worth more than five dollars."

A Vertol CH-46 helicopter on 9 February 1968 delivers marines from the 2d Battalion, 4th Marines, to Hill 674 in Thua Thien province. Hill 674 was a typical fire support base used by the Marines to support mobile operations.

Lebanese rescue workers remove a body from the wreckage of the Beirut barracks. The suicide explosion of a truck bomb, Sunday morning, 23 October 1983, killed 242 Americans, 218 of them marines. *photo by S.Sgt. Robert E. Kline*

A Marine LAV (light armored vehicle) moves past a Dairy Queen in Santiago, Panama, in December 1989. The newly acquired LAVs proved their worth in an urban environment during Operation Just Cause. A year later they would demonstrate their value on a larger battlefield: Desert Storm. *photo by Sgt. Robert C. Jenks*

A Marine CH-53E Super Stallion comes in to land on the flight deck of the USS *Raleigh*, an amphibious transport dock (LPD), during Desert Shield, the buildup in the Persian Gulf. Frequent landing exercises acquainted Saddam Hussein with the Navy–Marine Corps potential for an amphibious assault against his coastline. *U.S. Navy photo by Capt. Rick Mullen, USMC*

A marine escorts a section of a long string of Iraqi prisoners to the rear. By best count, marines took 22,308 prisoners in the four days of ground action.

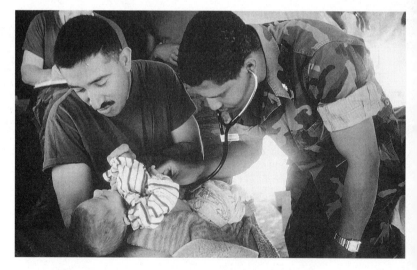

Hospital Corpsman Charlie Alva and Lt. Ronald Buckley, a Navy doctor, check a child's heart in a medical tent in Zakhu in northern Iraq. They were members of the 24th Marine Expeditionary Unit, deployed as part of Operation Provide Comfort to protect Kurdish refugees from a vengeful Saddam Hussein. *U.S. Navy photo by PH2 Milton R. Savage*

# 14

## 1945‑1950
### A Very Serious and Urgent Matter

### Occupation of Japan

On 10 August 1945 Japan sued for peace under the terms of the Potsdam Declaration and on 14 August President Truman announced that the war had ended. The war had cost the Marines 86,940 dead and wounded and there had been eighty Medals of Honor. The Corps' main effort was in the Pacific, but there had been diverse employment for Marines around the globe. Marine detachments had continued to serve afloat in the capital ships of the Fleet. A few marines had served with the British in Europe and the Middle East. Others had been with the partisans in Yugoslavia and some with the guerrillas in the Philippines and China. Among those serving in China was a tall young lieutenant from Louisiana named Robert H. Barrow.

If Japan had not sued for peace, both the III and V Amphibious Corps would have been involved in the invasion of the Japanese home islands. As it was, when the war ended, Halsey's Third Fleet was the closest Allied force to the Empire. Task Force 31 was formed to land at Yokosuka naval base near Tokyo. The 4th Marines came forward from Guam. Two other regiments, provisional ones, were formed the old-fashioned way from ships' crews and Marine detachments: a three-battalion Fleet Marine Landing Force and a three-battalion Naval Landing Force. The British carrier task force contributed a battalion of sailors and Royal marines.

The reception they would get ashore was an unknown quantity; there was considerable apprehension as to possible treachery and last-ditch fanaticism. Task Force 31 dropped anchor in Tokyo Bay off Yokosuka on 28 August. After some cautious preliminaries, the 1st and 3d Battalions, 4th Marines, touched down on the beach in the main landing at 0930 on 30 August. White flags were everywhere and the few Japanese in sight wore white arm bands. That afternoon Nimitz and MacArthur also came ashore—MacArthur to stay for six years as Japan's virtual ruler.

A week later the provisional units were dissolved and their component parts went back to the Fleet. MAG-31 came up from Okinawa to be the supporting aircraft group. The survivors of the "old" 4th Marines, captured at Corregidor, were found and released from their captivity, and there was a formation at which they received the colors of the "new" 4th Regiment. By the end of December redeployments had brought the regiment down to a single battalion. In January 1946 the regimental headquarters left for Tsingtao to rejoin the 6th Marine Division and the remaining battalion was converted into the 2d Separate Guard Battalion and had little to do but police the Yokosuka naval base.

The V Amphibious Corps, still commanded by Harry Schmidt, was assigned the responsibility of occupying Kyushu. Major objectives were Nagasaki, still reeling from history's second atomic bombing, and Sasebo naval base. On 22 September the 5th Marine Division's transports arrived off Sasebo and were courteously directed to safe berths by Japanese pilots. The next day, the 2d Marine Division landed at Nagasaki. MAG-22 arrived from Okinawa and was operational before the month's end.

The Japanese were as docile and cooperative in defeat as they had been fanatical and intransigent in battle. The 5th Marine Division left for home in December, followed in January by V Phib Corps headquarters. Both were deactivated in February 1946. The 2d Marine Division stayed on in Japan until June 1946.

## OCCUPATION OF CHINA

Occupation of North China proved less tranquil. Nominal mission for III Amphibious Corps, now under Keller Rockey, would be to disarm and repatriate the Japanese (there were 630,000 of them); more importantly—though unwritten—the Marines were to get to North China before the Russians could come sweeping down from Manchuria and were to hold it against the Chinese Communists until the Chinese Nationalists could redeploy northward.

The 1st Marine Division, having come from Okinawa through the tail of a typhoon and an adventuresome passage through the mine-strewn Yellow Sea, arrived off Taku Bar during the early hours of 30 September 1945, landed

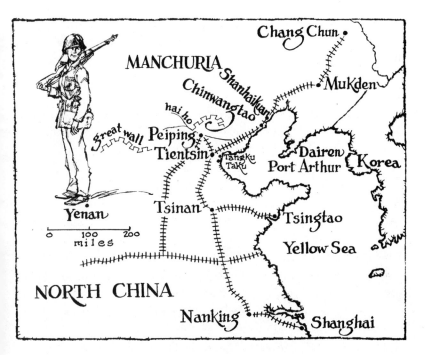

administratively, and started their way up the Taku-Tientsin rail line, the same line traveled in 1900 and 1927 by Smedley Butler. The line was guarded by well-uniformed Chinese soldiers. The Marine rank-and-file thought them Chinese Nationalists; they were not. They were "puppet" troops under Japanese control. The 2d and 3d Battalions, 7th Marines, moved on into Tientsin without incident. The next day, 1st Battalion, 7th Marines, sailed from Taku for Chinwangtao, shipping point for the coal mines in Tangshan. It was held to be vital that 100,000 tons of coal be shipped to Shanghai each month, or else the public utilities and factories would shut down.

The headquarters of III Phib Corps and 1st Marine Division found opulent billeting in the European quarter of Tientsin; the 1st and 11th Marines were in and around the city. On 6 October General Rockey received the official surrender of fifty thousand troops in front of Tientsin's municipal building. The 5th Marines had gone on up to Peiping, the regimental headquarters establishing itself in the old Legation Guard barracks. On 10 October, fifty thousand more Japanese were surrendered there. The Japanese prisoners were not immediately disarmed; the Americans were learning that they were the one disciplined force upon which they could depend.

Farther south, Lemuel Shepherd's 6th Marine Division had arrived at Tsingtao on 10 October. The Japanese garrison of ten thousand was surrendered at the race course on 25 October. Beyond the city limits, except for roads and rail lines held open by the Japanese, Shantung peninsula was under Communist control.

During October, the U.S. Fourteenth Air Force brought into Peiping the Ninety-second and Ninety-fourth Chinese Armies (some fifty thousand men—a Chinese Nationalist army equated to a U.S. division) and U.S. Navy amphibious shipping ferried the Thirteenth CNA to Chinwangtao. The Chinese Nationalists controlled the cities; the legendary Communist Eighth Route Army dominated the countryside. Also adrift were the puppet troops cast loose by the Japanese and independent "people's armies," indistinguishable from outright bandits. Against U.S. advice Chiang Kai-shek started moving his new strength north into Manchuria.

The 1st Marine Aircraft Wing set up its headquarters in the old French arsenal outside of Tientsin. MAGs 12 and 24 were at Peiping and MAGs 25 and 32 were at Tsingtao. On 31 October, Maj. Gen. Claude E. Larkin passed command of the wing to Louis Woods.

By the first of November the Marines had formally accepted the responsibility for guarding all railroad bridges over a hundred meters in length and Marine guards were riding virtually all trains. On 14 and 15 November, Maj. Gen. DeWitt Peck (who now had the 1st Marine Division) on an inspection trip from Tangshan to Chinwangtao had his train stopped twice by firing incidents, presaging more serious events to come.

## BLACK MARINES

Up until World War II, the Corps had thought of itself, not quite accurately, as all-male and all-white. Actually, the pay rolls of Captain Mullan's company show that he enlisted an "Isaac Walker, Negro" on 27 August 1776 and another recruit was shown in October 1776 as "Orange . . . Negro." There were probably others. Hard-pressed recruiters in the Revolution were not apt to be finicky as to pedigree. But when the Marine Corps was re-created in 1798, the recruiting regulations, directed toward shipboard service, provided that "No Negro, Mulatto or Indian to be enlisted . . ." and there were specific instructions "not to enlist more Foreigners than as one to three natives." These precautions were thought necessary to insure the reliability and loyalty of the

Marine guard. As late as 1852, a Navy commander would write Archibald Henderson: "It is useless to disguise the fact that the crews of our ships are now composed of foreigners and the most worthless class of our native population; with such materials to manage, a large guard of Marines is, in my judgment, highly desirable, if not absolutely necessary."

By mid-1941 President Roosevelt had taken steps to erase discrimination in the armed forces and General Holcomb, eyeing the probability that Negroes would be coming into the Corps, directed a study be made as to how they could best be used. A board headed by Keller Rockey, then a brigadier general, recommended they be used in a composite defense battalion.

Soon after the war began, the Corps was ordered to accept Negro enlistments. Col. Samuel A. Woods Jr. (who had entered the Marine Corps from the Citadel, Charleston, South Carolina, in 1916) was named to head the program. A training camp was built at Mumford (later changed to "Montford") Point across the New River from Camp Lejeune and the first recruits arrived in late August 1942. The new unit was designated the 51st Composite Defense Battalion.

In January 1943 a commissary or steward's branch was established. There were also to be Negro "pioneer infantry"—a euphemism for labor troops. At first, all black marines were to be trained by the 51st Defense Battalion, but this load was lightened in March 1943 when a Recruit Depot Battalion was activated. Initially, all drill instructors and officers were white but the white NCOs were to be replaced as fast as black NCOs could be trained. Intermingling of "colored and white enlisted personnel" was to be avoided and in no case were "colored" NCOs to be senior to white men in the same outfit.

The 51st Defense Battalion left Montford Point on 20 January 1944, its departure a riotous affair which was later investigated and blown up out of all proportion. The battalion, its strength on 31 January standing at 1,478, sailed from San Diego and on 27 February arrived at Funafuti, Ellice Islands, a backwater of the war, where it relieved elements of the 7th Defense Battalion. In September 1944 it moved on to Eniwetok, where it relieved the 10th Antiaircraft Battalion, and in June 1945 a composite group from the battalion went to Kwajalein. In late November the battalion returned to the United States, arriving at Montford Point the day after Christmas. The men were put on leave and the battalion disbanded at the end of January 1946.

There was also a 52d Defense Battalion, organized 15 December 1943, which departed from Montford Point on 19 August 1944, staged through San

Diego and Pearl Harbor, and arrived at Roi-Namur on 22 October, relieving the 15th Antiaircraft Battalion. The 52d echeloned forward to Guam in May 1945 and in November, after the war's end, was divided into two groups. One went to Eniwetok, the other to Kwajalein—to defend against what threat is not clear. In January 1946, the men with the longest periods of obligated service remaining were put into a heavy antiaircraft group and sent to Saipan. The remainder of the battalion reassembled at Guam, sailed for San Diego in March, arrived at Montford Point in April, and were redesignated the 3d Antiaircraft Battalion in May. The Saipan group was disbanded in February 1947, its remaining personnel being transferred into provisional depot companies.

Fifty-one black Marine depot companies and twelve black Marine ammunition companies were formed during the war. Assigned to Service Command, their job was to serve as shore party labor during landings and to work supply points in forward field depots. By one of the vagaries of the war, these black Marine units saw more combat than the more selective black defense battalions. They did notably well, beginning at Saipan, through Guam, Tinian, Peleliu, and Iwo, and on to Okinawa.

In truth, there was no great rush of black volunteers into the Marine Corps. Of a total of 19,168 black Americans who served during World War II, 16,039 were drafted. As late as April 1944, a Headquarters Marine Corps study was recommending against "colored" officers. A year later, the first three black officer candidates reported to Quantico. One was a sergeant major, two were first sergeants; all three were college graduates, but all three failed the course—one physically, the other two academically. The first black second lieutenant in the Marine Corps Reserve was commissioned on 10 November 1945. The war was over and with the rest of his class he was placed immediately on the inactive list. Not until 28 May 1948 did a black attain a regular commission (but by 1996 there would be 288 black officers on active duty, including a brigadier general).

For the peacetime Marine Corps, General Vandegrift approved a quota, not to exceed 10 percent, of blacks in the Corps, but it was a puzzling problem as to where these segregated units could fit into the structure of the shrinking postwar Marine Corps. Then, in June 1949, the secretary of the Navy decreed that "no distinction" was to be "made between individuals wearing the uniform." The segregated boot camp at Montford Point closed in September 1949. By the eve of the Korean War, June 1950, of a strength of about 74,000 marines in the Corps, some 1,500 were blacks, some in the steward's branch but most on general duty.

## WOMEN MARINES

There had been "Reservists (Female)" in World War I. Authorized on 12 August 1918, three months before the Armistice, they had been recruited up to 305 members and called, by a bit of cloying whimsy, the "Marinettes." Despite, or perhaps because of this experience, the Marine Corps was the last of the four armed services to organize a Women's Reserve in World War II. Pressed and prodded on the issue, General Holcomb, with undisguised reluctance, wrote to the secretary of the Navy on 12 October 1942: "In furtherance of the war effort, it was believed that as many women as possible should be used in noncombatant billets, thus relieving a greater number of the limited manpower available for essential combat duty."

By Holcomb's own frequently recounted story, when he went home that night to the Commandant's House and announced his decision to bring women into the Corps, Archibald Henderson's portrait fell off the wall. President Roosevelt was more approving, and on 7 November 1942 the U.S. Marine Corps Women's Reserve was authorized. Mrs. Ruth Cheney Streeter of New Jersey was selected to head the program and was commissioned a major. Public announcement of the new Reserve was made on 13 February 1943. Total strength, to be attained by 30 June 1944, was set at a thousand officers and eighteen thousand enlisted women.

Women officer candidates initially went to Mount Holyoke College in Massachusetts, and enlisted recruits went to Hunter College in the Bronx, New York. Uniforms were adaptations of regulation Marine "greens" and "blues." Lipstick was to match the winter cap cord and muffler, and was known to the trade as "Montezuma Red." Girdles were required articles of dress. In midsummer 1943, training of both officers and enlisted women was shifted to Camp Lejeune and, at Mrs. Roosevelt's instigation, weapons instruction was included. Women marines could be assigned to any of over two hundred job classifications ranging alphabetically from "accountant" to "woodworking-machine operator," but the great majority filled clerical billets, and by June 1944 constituted 85 percent of the enlisted personnel at Headquarters Marine Corps. When the war ended in August 1945, there were 820 women officers and 17,640 enlisted women, serving as far west as Hawaii;

General Vandegrift would remark they "could feel responsible for putting the 6th Marine Division into the field."

By December 1945 two-thirds of them (including Ruth Streeter, promoted to colonel) had been released from active duty. It was planned that all would be gone by September 1946, but then a decision was made to keep a small cadre on active duty. In June 1948 integration of women into the Regular Marines was authorized.

## DEMOBILIZATION

Congress in 1945 set the peacetime strength of the Corps at 107,000, nearly six times its prewar size but less than a quarter of its peak wartime strength of 485,053. In the wartime structure, weighted entirely in the direction of the Pacific, there had been two corps, six divisions, and five aircraft wings. For peacetime it was decided that there would be a Fleet Marine Force, Atlantic, as well as a Fleet Marine Force, Pacific, each with a division and wing (albeit at peacetime strengths) plus supporting combat and combat service units.

Discharges were regulated by a point system based on length of service, time overseas, wounds, and medals. The wartime formations as they came home were shrunk to cadres. The 4th Division (Saipan, Iwo Jima, Tinian) was deactivated in November 1945, followed by the 3d Division (Bougainville, Guam, Iwo Jima) in December. The 5th Division (Iwo Jima), home from Japan, went off the active list in January 1946.

The 6th Division (Okinawa) would be disbanded in April 1946. The 2d Division (Guadalcanal, Tarawa, Saipan, Tinian) on coming back from Japan in June 1946 was home-ported at Camp Lejeune with the 2d Wing close by at Cherry Point. The 1st Division (Guadalcanal, Cape Gloucester, Peleliu, Okinawa) on coming out of China would go to Camp Pendleton and its companion, the 1st Wing, to El Toro. There would also be a brigade on Guam.

In late 1946 the U.S. Mediterranean Squadron (later to be the Sixth Fleet) was re-established. Afloat with the squadron was a battalion landing team from the 2d Marine Division. Rotated at six-month intervals, it would see much use and service in the next half century. The arrangement by which the Marines provided security guards to embassies and legations was formalized. (By 1997, a total of 119 diplomatic posts would have such guards, usually a seven- or eight-man detachment commanded by a staff noncommissioned officer, all trained and administered by the Marine Security Guard Battalion headquartered in Quantico.) The Basic School for new second lieutenants (and for some older ones whose wartime training had been slighted) was reestablished, not at Philadelphia Navy Yard, but at Quantico. The more advanced courses at Quantico were regularized into an Amphibious Warfare School with junior and senior courses. Personnel strengths had not yet bottomed out. By the end of 1946 they were plunging below the hundred thousand mark. There was a brief experiment, under the peculiar "J" tables of organization, with a division and brigade structure which would have separate battalions and no regimental echelon.

## UNIFICATION AND THE MARINE CORPS

Following U.S. Army blueprints, there were strong pressures, endorsed by President Truman, for the "unification" of the U.S. Armed Forces, all services to be merged under a single Department of War, with a single chief of staff and a national general staff, and perhaps even a common uniform. In the spring of 1946, a series of Congressional hearings was held on a bill encompassing most of the War Department's merger plan. The bill was beaten down, largely because of the stalwart counter-testimony of General Vandegrift, but another, similar bill appeared in 1947. The National Security Act, as it was passed in 1947, created the Department of Defense with the subordinate Departments of the Army, Navy, and Air Force. The future status of the Marine Corps was left unclear.

General Vandegrift's term as commandant ended on 31 December 1947. The choosing of the next commandant was up to President Truman. The two leading contenders, Clifton B. Cates and Lemuel C. Shepherd Jr., offered remarkably similar credentials. How to choose between two such men? President Truman called them to the White House and told them that as a military man he had always believed in seniority. Said President Truman to General Shepherd: "General Cates is senior to you and he's older than you are. I'm going to make him commandant this year, and I trust that I'll be able to have you follow him four years from now."

Clifton Bledsoe Cates, urbane, given to wearing a trench coat, and seldom without a cigarette in a lengthy holder (perhaps out of kindness to his gas-injured lungs), thus became the nineteenth commandant. Cates, who in combat had commanded every size unit, from platoon to division, now had a new battlefield, Capitol Hill, and the fight would be to keep the Marine Corps alive.

On 11 March 1948, James Forrestal, the first secretary of Defense, assembled the chiefs of the Army, Navy, and the new Air Force at Key West, Florida, for a four-day discussion of roles and missions. General Cates was not invited. After the conference, the press was informed that the Marines were not to constitute a second land army; that there would be a four-division ceiling on their wartime strength; and that a marine would not exercise tactical command higher than corps level. A few days later, the ailing James Forrestal was replaced as secretary of Defense by a West Virginia politician, Louis A. Johnson, who had little love for the Navy and none for the Marine Corps. Unopposed by a complaisant secretary of the Navy, he directed sharp cuts in Fleet Marine Force strength for fiscal years 1949 and 1950 (the budget dollar is the device by which Congress regulates the size of the U. S. military establishment) so that FMF force structure came down to eight infantry battalions and twelve aircraft squadrons. (In a bit of pettiness, Johnson in 1949 also forbade the future official observance of the Marine Corps Birthday on 10 November. This prohibition was observed in the breach by round-the-world "private" parties. Even the most minuscule Marine Security Guard sponsors a party; these have come to rival, in foreign capitals, the U.S. ambassador's traditional Fourth of July reception.)

In the fall of 1949, there was another series of hearings before the House Armed Services Committee. In his testimony, Cates pointed out that the Marine Corps had no voice or vote in Joint Chiefs of Staff proceedings and that Secretary Johnson had quashed a proposal that the commandant be allowed to sit in on JCS meetings treating items dealing with the Marine Corps. Sympathetic congressmen drafted a bill making the commandant of the Marine Corps a member of the JCS. The bill was not acted upon that year but the seed was sown.

## END OF THE CHINA EXPERIENCE

In December 1945, General of the Army George C. Marshall went out to China at President Truman's behest to attempt to mediate the differences between the Nationalists and the Communists. There was a brief cease-fire beginning 13 January 1946; then the situation worsened. For the Marines it meant dealing with blown bridges, derailments, and ambushes. Under the point system, combat veterans were going home by the thousands and for every two that went home there was only one replacement.

On 1 April 1946, the 6th Marine Division was deactivated and its remaining pieces reorganized into the 3d Brigade, its infantry core being the 4th Marines, whose colors had come over from Japan. (Symbolically, if not actually, the 4th Marines, the old China regiment, had returned to China.) The brigade did not last long. On 10 June, III Amphibious Corps was redesignated Marine Forces, China. Authorized strength was set at 24,252—less than half the strength of III Phib Corps when it landed in September 1945. The 3d Brigade was disbanded and the 4th Marines put under the 1st Marine Division. MAGs 25 and 32 left for home.

On 29 July 1946, a platoon-size motorized patrol from the 11th Marines, escorting a supply convoy, was ambushed at An Ping (where Seymour's column had turned back in 1900). Three marines, including the lieutenant, were killed; twelve more were wounded. On 1 August, the Tsingtao garrison was reduced to just the 3d Battalion, 4th Marines, and the rest of the regiment sailed for home. On 18 September, General Rockey turned over command of Marine Forces, China, to Maj. Gen. Samuel Howard (who had commanded the 4th Marines when it was surrendered at Corregidor). In December, the 7th Marines left for the States and the reduced 11th Marines departed for Guam.

On the night of 4 April 1947, there was a stiffish raid against the ammunition supply point at Hsin Ho, near Tangku. Five marines were killed, sixteen wounded. Soon thereafter, the headquarters of the 1st Marine Division and 1st Marine Aircraft Wing departed and on 1 May a new consolidated command, Fleet Marine Force, Western Pacific, was created. The 5th Marines sailed away in April and May and by the first of September 1947, all remaining marines were concentrated at Tsingtao. Down to two infantry battalions, they were charged with the defense of the Seventh Fleet naval base and also with having a battalion ready for airlift to Shanghai, Nanking, or Tientsin, to go to the aid of American nationals if need be. (Under the short-lived "J" tables of organization that did away with the regimental echelon yet tried to keep the regimental numbers alive, the 2d Battalion, 1st Marines, had become the "1st Marines" and the 3d Battalion, 4th Marines, the "3d Marines.")

By the fall of 1948 Tsingtao was an island in a Communist sea; the imminent collapse of the Chinese Nationalists was obvious to even the most sanguine. In December the battalion-size 9th Marines came forward from Guam, staged through Tsingtao, and went to Shanghai to assist in the evacuation of American nationals. The 1st Marines left Tsingtao in February 1949 and the 3d Marines went afloat in the harbor. They sailed for home in May, and by June 1949 the last Marine element had cleared Tsingtao and China.

## VERTICAL ENVELOPMENT

Amphibious assaults against fortified beaches had been written off by many military experts as a nuclear age improbability. Gen. Omar Bradley, USA, chairman of the Joint Chiefs, gave his opinion to the House Services Committee that amphibious operations were a dead letter and that there would never again be another major amphibious assault.

In the Marine Corps the thinking was otherwise. In July 1946, six months before his death, General Geiger, having viewed the Bikini bomb tests, wrote to General Vandegrift from his headquarters in Hawaii, "It is trusted that Marine Corps Headquarters will consider this very serious and urgent matter and will use its most competent officers in finding a solution to develop the technique of conducting amphibious operations in the atomic age."

A board to study the matter was convened under General Shepherd, who had returned from China to become assistant commandant. Shepherd's report, delivered on 16 December, recognized that wide dispersion had to be reconciled with control, flexibility, and concentration of striking power. It concluded that carrier-based helicopters offered the best possible solution to the critical ship-to-shore movement and it recommended the activation of an experimental helicopter squadron at Quantico. Within three days, Vandegrift had approved the report, but helicopters came more slowly.

On paper, there was a requirement for ten helicopter aircraft carriers and 240 helicopters, each capable of lifting a squad. The Corps' first helicopter squadron, HMX-1, organized at the end of 1947, got its first five helos early in 1948. Each would lift, somewhat precariously, two passengers. In May, in a Marine Corps School's amphibious command post exercise at Camp Lejeune, these early choppers simulated the landing of a regiment. Later in the year the Piasecki HRP-1, the "Flying Banana," and the first true transport helicopter, came into the inventory, and in November, Quantico published a slender pamphlet, bound in blue paper, "PHIB-3 1, Employment of Helicopters (Tentative)."

In June 1950, ten days before the North Koreans crossed into South Korea, President Truman came to Quantico to see a simulated helicopter assault. Not greatly impressed, the old National Guard battery commander grinned, patted the barrel of a 75-mm pack howitzer, and said, "I like this best."

# 15

## 1950-1953
### IF I ONLY HAD THE 1ST MARINE DIVISION

### GAINING THE RIGHT TO FIGHT

Before dawn on Sunday, 25 June 1950, Far Eastern time, seven infantry divisions and one armored division of the North Korean People's Army crossed the 38th Parallel into South Korea. In Washington, in the frantic first hours that followed, no one seemed to have time for General Cates. The stock of the Marine Corps was at its lowest post–World War II ebb. The commandant was not included in the urgent councils of war taking place in the White House and Pentagon. President Truman's position was that the chief of naval operations represented both the Navy and Marine Corps. On 29 June Cates buttonholed the CNO, Adm. Forrest Sherman, in the halls of the Pentagon and offered a regimental combat team and aircraft group for immediate service. Sherman was only mildly interested. The next day, Cates got to see Navy Secretary Matthews, who said he couldn't recall any discussion on the possibility of using Marines in Korea. But at Cates's urging, Sherman on 1 July sent Vice Adm. C. Turner Joy, commanding U.S. Naval Forces Far East, an eyes-only message authorizing him to offer the Commander in Chief Far East a Marine air-ground brigade. General MacArthur, CinCFE, fired back a dispatch to the Joint Chiefs of Staff asking for the Marines. MacArthur's request was put on the JCS agenda for 3 July. Cates arrived at the meeting uninvited but was allowed to sit in. That night he was able to write on his desk calendar, "Attended JCS meeting. Orders for deployment of FMF approved."

The next day, 4 July, Lemuel Shepherd, now a lieutenant general who had taken command of Fleet Marine Force, Pacific, just two days earlier, left Honolulu for Tokyo to confer with MacArthur, taking with him his G-3, Col. "Brute" Krulak.

At Pendleton, on 7 July, the 1st Provisional Marine Brigade was stripped out of the skeleton 1st Marine Division and put under slender, white-haired Brig. Gen. Edward A. Craig. Then fifty-four, Craig had been commissioned in 1917, had commanded the 9th Marines at Guam, and had been Schmidt's G-3 at Iwo. It would be an air-ground brigade. The core of the ground element would be the 5th Marines, commanded by Lt. Col. Raymond L. Murray, a tall, rangy Texan who had fought exceedingly well at Guadalcanal. The air element of the brigade would be Marine Aircraft Group 33 under Brig. Gen. Thomas H. Cushman. Cushman, who was also deputy brigade commander, was fifty-five and like Craig had come into the Corps in 1917. He had been one of the aviation pioneers in Haiti and Nicaragua and during World War II had commanded a wing. Three carrier-qualified fighter-bomber squadrons, equipped with late model F4U Corsairs, were assigned to the group; joining them was a light observation squadron, VMO-6, just activated. VMO-6 was taking eight light OY airplanes (in the hope that four could be made to fly) and four two-place HO3S-1 Sikorsky helicopters hastily brought west from Quantico.

In Tokyo, MacArthur, meeting with Shepherd on 10 July, moved to his wall map of Korea and stabbed at the port of Inchon with the stem of his corncob pipe: "If I only had the 1st Marine Division under my command again, I would land them here." Shepherd told him that the rest of the 1st Marine Division could be ready by the first of September.

MacArthur had Shepherd draft a message to the JCS for his signature asking for the 1st Marine Division. After two more messages from MacArthur, the JCS directed the deployment of the 1st Marine Division accompanied by the 1st Marine Aircraft Wing to Korea.

The 1st Provisional Marine Brigade, strength 6,534, sailed from San Diego on 12 July. Craig and Cushman, who had gone on ahead by air with an advance party, met with MacArthur on the nineteenth. MacArthur reiterated that if the 1st Marine Division could be assembled by September he would land at Inchon, march to Seoul, cut North Korean lines of communication, and isolate the North Korean People's Army. Walker's Eighth Army would then break out of the Pusan perimeter and the North Korean invasion would be crushed in classic hammer-and-anvil fashion three months after it had begun.

The perimeter was roughly a quarter circle drawn at a radius of a hundred miles from Pusan although the front was by no means as definite or solid as lines on the map would indicate. By the last week of July, the whole business threatened to collapse and on the twenty-fifth MacArthur ordered the brigade to Pusan as the last available reserve. The 24th Infantry and 1st Cavalry Divisions, badly understrength, were in the process of falling back to new positions along the Naktong, while the 25th Infantry Division had been shifted to the western flank to cover Chinju. The brigade would have to act as kind of a fire brigade.

## PUSAN PERIMETER

First elements of the brigade came ashore at Pusan on 2 August. At dawn the next day, the 5th Marines moved west some forty miles by truck and rail to an assembly area at Changwon. By now the NKPA were pressing close to Masan and the brigade was given Sachon as its objective as part of a 25th Division counterattack. The 5th Marines jumped off on 7 August, eighth anniversary of their landing at Guadalcanal. The soldiers of the 25th Division watched with outspoken envy and admiration the quality of close air support delivered by the Corsairs. Cushman's two-day fighter-bomber squadrons, VMF-214 and VMF-323, with their gull-winged F4Us, were working from the escort aircraft carriers *Sicily* and *Badoeng Strait*. The night fighter squadron, VMF(N)-513, was at Itazuke in Japan, under Fifth Air Force control, and was being used for night heckler missions.

On 13 August, with the 5th Marines about to enter Sachon, Craig received sudden orders to disengage and move seventy-five miles north to the "Naktong Bulge," a salient created by the 4th NKPA Division crossing the river near Obong-ni. The 5th Marines were given "No-Name Ridge" to take. Murray assaulted in columns of battalions on the fifteenth and on the fourth try reached the crest. That night the NKPA counterattacked. The Marines made their first acquaintance with the vaunted Russian-built T-34 tanks and tore them up with rocket launchers, recoilless rifles, and 90-mm tank fire. Next morning the 4th NKPA Division, badly battered, retired across the river, harried by Cushman's Corsairs.

The NKPA came across the Naktong again on 3 September, this time with their 9th Division, hitting the newly arrived 2d U.S. Infantry Division's 9th Regiment. The 5th Marines came charging up and in three days the 9th NKPA Division had been pushed back six miles with heavy losses. On 5 September the brigade went into reserve to load-out for Inchon.

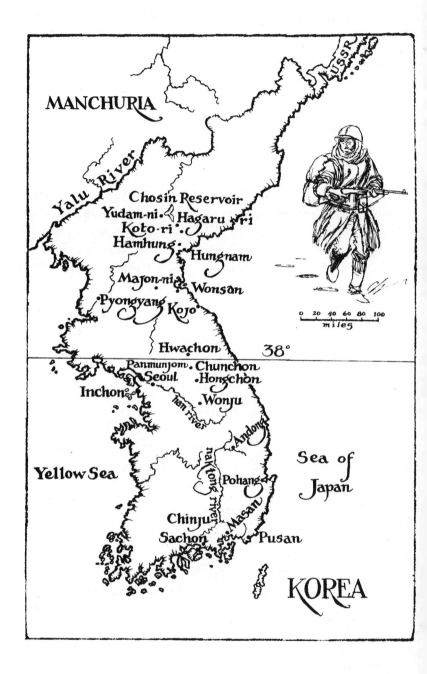

MANCHURIA

USSR

Yalu River

Chosin Reservoir
Yudam-ni · Hagaru-ri
Koto-ri ·
Hamhung ·
Hungnam
Majon-ni · Wonsan
Pyongyang Kojo

Hwachon      38°
Panmunjom · Chunchon
Seoul · Hongchon
Inchon · Wonju
han river

Andong

Yellow Sea
naktong river
Pohang

Sea of
Japan

Chinju · Masan
Sachon · Pusan

KOREA

0  20  40  60  80  100
miles

There had been 74,279 marines on active duty, 27,656 of them in the Fleet Marine Force (with further cuts planned for fiscal year 1951 by Louis Johnson), when Cates made his proposal that a brigade go to Korea. On 19 July, after a nudge from the chairman of the House Armed Services Committee, President Truman authorized the call-up of the Marine Corps Reserve's "citizen-marines." Mobilization of the Organized Marine Corps Reserve brought in 33,528 well-qualified officers and men, many of them World War II combat veterans. Three understrength battalions were dispatched from Lejeune to Pendleton to serve as the cadre for the 1st Marine Regiment. Hearing that his old regiment was being put on a war footing, Col. Chesty Puller, now CO of the Marine Barracks at Pearl Harbor, pestered the commandant with telephone calls and cables asking for its command. Maj. Gen. Oliver P. Smith, who had been assistant division commander at Peleliu, had just taken command of what was left of the 1st Marine Division. He acceded to Puller's request. The two men, Smith and Puller, were very different—Smith, tall, ascetic, professorial—Puller, bandy-legged, gnarled, always outspoken, often profane—but the two worked well together. The division headquarters and the 1st Marines (put together in ten days from the Lejeune battalions, filled out with reserves and drafts from posts and stations) sailed from San Diego in mid-August.

Orders reached El Toro on 16 August telling Maj. Gen. Field Harris (Naval Academy, class of 1917) to take the headquarters of his 1st Marine Aircraft Wing and MAG-12 with Corsair squadrons VMF-212, VMF-312, and VMF(N)-542 to the Far East. All cleared the West Coast by 1 September.

Meanwhile, Col. Homer L. Litzenberg, commander of the 6th Marines at Lejeune, having sent his battalions off to Pendleton, was ordered to take his depleted command to Camp Pendleton, where it would be a cadre for the 7th Marines, reactivated on 17 August and filled out with reserves and odds and ends pulled in from other commands.

## INCHON

MacArthur, in his *Reminiscences,* says:

> The target date, because of the great tides at Inchon, had to be the middle of September. This meant that the staging for the landing at Inchon would have to be accomplished more rapidly than that of any other large amphibious operation in modern warfare. . . . My plan was opposed by powerful military influences in Washington. The essence of the operation depended upon a

great amphibious movement, but the chairman of the Joint Chiefs of Staff, General Omar Bradley, was of the considered opinion that such amphibious operations were obsolete—that there would never be another successful movement of this sort.

The Attack Force would have come up to Inchon from the Yellow Sea through the narrow and tortuous Flying Fish Channel. When the tides went out they ripped through the channel at seven or eight knots, leaving vast mud flats across which even amtracks could not expect to crawl. The hydrographers said the best date would be 15 September. Morning high tide (an incredible 31.2 feet) would be at 0659, evening high tide at 1919. The landing would have to accommodate to these times.

Much of the Navy's Amphibious Force was a rusty travesty of the great World War II amphibious armadas. Many of the LSTs to be used in the landing had to be reclaimed from Japanese charters. Some came complete with Japanese crew. Other crews had to be made up from Navy reserves flown to Japan.

Now came an aggravation from another quarter. On 21 August, Congressman Gordon L. McDonough of California had written President Truman urging that the commandant of the Marine Corps be given a voice in the Joint Chiefs of Staff. Truman answered with a tart personal note: "For your information the Marine Corps is the Navy's police force and as long as I am President that is what it will remain. They have a propaganda machine that is almost equal to Stalin's. . . . The Chief of Naval Operations is the Chief of Staff of the Navy of which the Marines are a part."

The story got into the newspapers on 5 September. Great cries of outrage went up from the public. Next day Truman sent a contrite apology to Cates regretting his choice of language and then manfully appeared at a Marine Corps League banquet by chance being held in Washington, but he did not recant his fundamental beliefs as to where the Marine Corps should fit in the national military establishment.

The 1st Marines, staging out of Kobe for Inchon, read about the incident in the *Stars and Stripes* and chalked on their trucks and tanks, "Horrible Harry's Police Force." The 1st Marine Division would literally form on the battlefield. The 5th Marines were loading out of Pusan. The 7th Marines were still on the high seas (one of its battalions had been in the Mediterranean and was coming by way of Suez). On 3 September the 1st Korean Marine Corps Regiment was assigned to the 1st Marine Division.

Lifting the Landing Force would be Amphibious Group 1, under Rear Adm. James H. Doyle. Superimposed on top of the Landing Force was X Corps, under Maj. Gen. Edward M. Almond, USA, MacArthur's chief of staff. The 7th U.S. Infantry Division would be in reserve. Pyramided over X Corps was Joint Task Force 7.

There were estimated to be about 2,200 second-rate North Korean troops in Inchon. Inland, in the vicinity of Seoul, there were thought to be about 21,500 enemy of better quality. A battalion of the 5th Marines would land at daybreak on Green Beach on Wolmi-do, an island separated from Inchon itself by a 600-yard causeway. Then there would be a long wait of twelve hours until the evening tide was in and the main landings could be made. The rest of the 5th Marines would then land across Red Beach to the north and the 1st Marines across Blue Beach to the south—although calling them "beaches" was a misnomer; the harbor was edged with sea walls which would have to be scaled with ladders.

Air and naval gunfire preparation of the target area began on 10 September. L-Hour for Wolmi-do was 0630 on 15 September. BLT 3/5 scrambled ashore and twenty-five minutes later ran up the flag over Radio Hill.

"That's it," said MacArthur, watching from the bridge of the command ship *Mount McKinley* along with Shepherd, Almond, Doyle, and Smith. "Let's get a cup of coffee."

During the day the target area became increasingly smudged with smoke from the burning city, mixed with rain and fog. H-Hour for the main landings was 1730. No landmarks could be seen in the grayish-green pall, the assault waves crisscrossed during the run into the sea wall, and all the sorting out wasn't complete before it was pitch black. The X Corps' plan was to move inland following the landing, capture Kimpo airfield, cross the Han, recapture Seoul, and then act as the anvil against which the NKPA would be crushed by an Eighth Army drive up from the south. The axis for the twenty-mile advance to Seoul was the intertwined road and railroad. In the morning the division moved out, 1st Regiment astride and right of the road, 5th Regiment on the left. On the morning of 17 September, MacArthur and other notables came ashore to visit the front. On the highway they saw the still-smoking hulks of a column of T-34s which had tried a counterattack at dawn. MacArthur gave Craig, Murray, and Puller Silver Stars, and Smith was told that the 7th Infantry Division would land next day and move in on the right of the 1st Marines.

That same day, 17 September, Murray's 5th Marines took Kimpo airfield. Swimmers were put across the Han and Lt. Col. Robert D. Taplett's 3d Battalion went over in amtracks at dawn on the twentieth, followed a few hours later by the 2d Battalion. This put the 5th Marines in position on the high ground north of Seoul.

The 1st Marines, coming up along the Inchon-Seoul Road, had found it tougher going. There had been a hard fight at Sosa, and it was the nineteenth before they reached the hills overlooking Yongdong-po, the city that lies across the Han from Seoul. All three battalions of the 1st Marines went in the final attack beginning on 21 September against Yongdong-po. Capt. Bob Barrow with Company A, 1st Battalion, was first in the town and held it in an all-night fight in an action reminiscent of Cates at Bouresches. Things were tidied up in the morning and this finished the enemy west of the Han.

On the twenty-fourth, Puller's 1st Marines crossed the river. The next day the 1st and 5th Marines went into Seoul itself, the 1st Marines attacking up Ma Po Boulevard toward Ducksoo Palace, the traditional seat of government. Supporting arms had to be used sparingly because of the civilian populace and the fighting was largely grenade and rifle, barricade-to-barricade, and house-to-house. That night the NKPA tried a final tank-infantry counterattack with everything they had left in the city. It failed, and by the twenty-seventh Seoul was secure. Two days later Syngman Rhee, escorted by MacArthur, made a triumphal reentry into the capital. On 30 September Litzenberg's 7th Marines, who had joined the 1st Division in Seoul, moved out along the Seoul-Pyongyang highway, reaching Uijongbu, ten miles to the north, under the approving eye of visiting General Cates. The 1st Cavalry Division, new armor and vehicles gleaming, now passed through the 1st Marine Division, which then made a motor march back to Inchon to reembark.

## WONSAN

The next objective was Wonsan on the east coast, north of the 38th Parallel. The harbor had been sown extensively with Russian-made mines. By the time these were cleared, there was no need for an amphibious assault; the port had been taken from the land side by resurgent Republic of Korea forces. The 1st Marine Division landed administratively across the beach on 26 October and found the checkerboard-nosed Corsairs of VMF-312 already operating from Wonsan airfield.

General Almond's X Corps was conducting these operations on the eastern coast independently of the Eighth Army. The 1st Marine Division was given a zone of action three hundred miles from north to south, fifty miles deep. The 5th and 7th Marines were to go north to Hamhung to prepare for a further advance to the Yalu. The 1st Marines were to stay behind in the vicinity of Wonsan and scoop up the supposedly shattered remnants of an NKPA division. In Tokyo they were saying the war would be over by Christmas. O. P. Smith was not so hopeful. He thought his division badly overextended.

Immediately after landing at Wonsan on 26 October, the 1st Battalion, 1st Marines, had been sent south by rail to the picture-book little seaport of Kojo, almost undisturbed by the war, forty miles down the coast. A still-intact NKPA regiment hit the 1st Battalion the night of 27 October, causing heavy casualties in a fight that went on until midmorning on the twenty-eighth. Having weathered that storm, the 1st Battalion stayed at Kojo until 1 November when it was relieved by the 3d Battalion, Korean Marines.

A sister unit, the 3d Battalion, 1st Marines, had been sent twenty-six road miles west of Wonsan on 28 October to secure the mountain town of Majon-ni, important because it was where the cross-peninsula roads from Seoul, Pyongyang, and Wonsan came together. Once in position the battalion found itself surrounded by the 15th NKPA Division, many members of which were more than ready to surrender (the 3d Battalion took more prisoners than its own total strength while at Majon-ni), but there was still considerable fight left in the rest. Convoys could get through to Majon-ni only with major effort (Captain Barrow with Able Company brought one convoy through) and the 3d Battalion was kept supplied chiefly by free-fall airdrop with casualties going out by helicopter. On 10 November (the Marine Corps Birthday, celebrated with a makeshift cake) the 3d Battalion was joined by the 3d Battalion, Korean Marine Corps, and on the afternoon of the thirteenth the 1st Battalion, 15th U.S. Infantry, fresh from Fort Benning, arrived. The 3d Battalion, 1st Marines, turned the Majon-ni perimeter over to the Army and left next morning by truck for Wonsan.

## CHOSIN RESERVOIR

There was hard intelligence that the Chinese Communist Forces were across the Yalu but CinCFE in Tokyo at first denied and then minimized their presence, insisting that it was too late for the Chinese to intervene effectively in the war. The 1st Marine Division was to advance northwest of Hungnam along a mountain road to "Chosin" Reservoir, site of an important hydro-electric plant, and thence to the Yalu. (The marines took the name "Chosin" from their Japanese-based maps; the Koreans knew it as "Changjin.")

Hungnam and Hamhung; the names are confusingly similar. Hungnam is the seaport. Hamhung is the road and railroad nexus, some eight miles to the northwest. The 7th Marines under Litzenberg moved out of Hamhung on 2 November and by midnight were in heavy contact with the 124th CCF Division near Sudong-ni. The Marines reported the capture of Chinese prisoners, but GHQ in Tokyo passed these off as volunteers. General MacArthur had assured President Truman at their Wake Island meeting a few weeks before that it was too late for the Chinese to intervene effectively.

The fight now went uphill through tortuous Funchilin Pass to a high plateau. The 124th broke contact on 7 November and on 10 November the 7th Marines entered Koto-ri. Three days later they were in Hagaru-ri at the southern tip of Chosin Reservoir. Marine engineers began to scrape out air strips at Koto-ri and Hagaru-ri. General Almond, X Corps commander, planned to bring his flag forward to Hagaru-ri and some Army engineers and signal troops were detailed to begin the construction. The brief autumn was almost over and the weather was turning bitterly cold. The nearest Eighth Army unit was eighty miles to the west. The Chinese, underestimated at MacArthur's headquarters in Tokyo if not by the Marines above Hungnam, had used an ancient stratagem: reconnaissance in force, then a pull-back to lure their enemy into a trap.

On 24 November, the day after Thanksgiving (special holiday menu including roast turkey, cranberry sauce, fruit cake, and mincemeat pie), the 7th Marines moved out along the road west of Chosin Reservoir through Toktong Pass to Yudam-ni. Fox Company was dropped off at Toktong Pass to keep it open. Two days later the 7th Marines were joined at Yudam-ni by Murray's 5th Marines. Puller's 1st Marines had been relieved at Wonsan by the newly arrived 3d U.S. Infantry Division and his battalions were strung out along the road to keep the lines of communication back to Hungnam open: 1st Battalion at Chinhung-ni at the foot of Funchilin Pass, 2d Battalion and the regimental command post at Koto-ri, and 3d Battalion at Hagaru-ri.

On 24 November, Smith had received a warning order that his division would make a wide sweeping envelopment to the west to form the northern arm of a giant pincer of which the Eighth Army would be the southern arm.

H-Hour was to be 0800 on the twenty-seventh. This gave the 1st Marine Division the bleak prospect of crossing the near-roadless and mountainous backbone of Korea in weather that was already subzero.

Then, on 25 November, the II ROK Corps, forming the Eighth Army's right wing, was struck seventy miles southwest of Yudam-ni by a Red Chinese counterattack. The ROK Corps gave way, the right flank and rear of the 2d U.S. Infantry Division was exposed, and by the twenty-sixth the Eighth Army advance had come to a disastrous halt.

On the twenty-seventh, with the X Corps operation order unmodified, the 5th Marines dutifully attacked to the west from Yudam-ni, went a mile, and were stopped. That night it snowed and the temperature went down to twenty degrees below zero. Gen. Sung Shih-lun came out of the mountains with eight CCF Divisions in a carefully planned counterstroke with the express mission of destroying the 1st Marine Division. Three CCF Divisions hit at the 5th and 7th Marines at Yudam-ni. Other elements cut the MSR to Hagaru-ri and struck at Fox Company, holding Toktong Pass. Another division attacked Hagaru-ri, defended by two-thirds of 3d Battalion, 1st Marines, two batteries of 105s, and odds and ends of service and combat support troops. The road south to Koto-ri was also cut and Koto-ri attacked by still another division.

## HAGARU-RI

The situation was most precarious at Hagaru-ri. The high ground, called East Hill, that dominated the town and also the exit south to Koto-ri, had been lost to the Chinese. The unfinished 2,900-foot airstrip had been penetrated and, although the line there was restored, the strip continued to be fire-swept.

On 28 November, O. P. Smith flew in to Hagaru-ri and opened his command post there. He ordered the 5th Marines to hold where they were and the 7th Marines to reverse direction, attack southward, and clear the MSR from Yudam-ni to Hagaru-ri. On the twenty-ninth, the remnants of Task Force Faith, three Army battalions, badly cut up east of the reservoir, were attached to the 1st Marine Division. Few of the survivors, limping across the ice into Hagaru-ri, were in fit condition to fight.

Hagaru-ri had to be held until the division could be reconstituted. On the twenty-ninth, Puller at Koto-ri, at Smith's instruction, put together a relief column to come up to Hagaru-ri. Lt. Col. Douglas B. Drysdale, RM, had reported to the 1st Marine Division on 20 November at Hungnam with the 41 Independent Commando, Royal Marines. In addition to the commando (fourteen officers and 221 enlisted men) there was Company G, reinforced, 1st Marines, on its way to rejoin its parent battalion at Hagaru-ri; Company B, 31st U.S. Infantry; and two Marine tank companies with twenty-nine tanks—altogether over nine hundred men and a headquarters train of some 141 vehicles. Twice Task Force Drysdale was ambushed and halted. The armor could cut through and the infantry could handle itself; the truck convoy got the worst of it. Drysdale was told to push on "at all costs." By midnight on the twenty-ninth he was in Hagaru-ri with 41 Commando, Company G, and one of the tank companies. On the road behind them the truck column had been cut up into four different segments. Their situation was hopeless and by morning (except for a few hardy individuals who made their way either back to Koto-ri or forward to Hagaru-ri) all were killed or captured.

## FROM YUDAM-NI TO HUNGNAM

On 30 November, "Ned" Almond flew in to Hagaru-ri to see Smith. He said the situation had changed radically for the worse all across the front and there would be no attack to the west; X Corps would fall back to Hungnam. Weapons, equipment, and vehicles were to be abandoned as necessary. Smith demurred; he told Almond his marines would fight their way out.

Next day Lt. Col. Raymond G. Davis with the 1st Battalion, 7th Marines, started across country from Yudam-ni to relieve Fox Company, still grimly holding on to Toktong Pass. He reached there on 2 December, and found only eighty-two of the original two hundred marines still combat-effective; twenty-six had been killed, three were missing, and eighty-nine wounded. Meanwhile, Taplett's 3d Battalion, 5th Marines, led the main body out of Yudam-ni along the road, carefully shepherded overhead by Marine air.

Transports, mostly Marine R4Ds, a military version of the Douglas C-47, began using the Hagaru-ri strip on 1 December, bringing in supplies and taking out the wounded. Five hundred replacements were eventually flown in, many of them direct from hospitals in Japan, barely recovered from earlier wounds. The column from Yudam-ni reached Hagaru-ri on 3 December, having done fourteen miles of fighting and marching in seventy-nine hours.

The breakout southward from Hagaru-ri began on 6 December, led by Litzenberg's 7th Marines, followed by Murray's 5th Marines with 41 Commando and 3d Battalion, 1st Marines, attached. The Marines were bringing everything out and there was a solid mass of vehicles on the road. On the flanks, the rifle companies leapfrogged from one piece of critical terrain to the next. Overhead was close air support, Marine air reserving for themselves a corridor a mile wide over the column with Navy and Air Force working farther out. Last elements from Hagaru-ri had completed the eleven-mile march and entered the perimeter at Koto-ri by midnight on the seventh.

Next morning the division resumed its march to the sea. Funchilin Pass was now held by the Chinese and had to be cleared. The 1st Battalion, 1st Marines, led by Capt. Bob Barrow's Able Company, made a successful uphill attack from Chinhung-ni, taking the high ground overlooking the pass on 8 December. By the morning of 12 December the division had closed at Hungnam. The weather along the coast seemed almost balmy to the marines. The Reservoir had cost them 4,400 battle casualties (730 killed or dead of wounds) and uncounted cases of frostbite and pneumonia. All the fight was out of the Chinese. They had lost perhaps twenty-five thousand dead and did not press the perimeter as X Corps prepared to evacuate Hungnam.

A curious rumor circulated that the Marines were going to Indochina to help the French. Chesty Puller, aboard the MSTS transport *General Collins,* reviewed for some of his junior officers the events of the Russo-Japanese 1904–1905 war in Korea and was gloomy in his prognostications. The Marines unloaded at Pusan, jolted down the road, and spent Christmas in the Bean Patch at Masan.

## KILLER AND RIPPER

As the new year began, some semblance of order emerged from the chaos. Lt. Gen. Matthew B. Ridgway, USA, had come out to take command, replacing Walton Walker, who had been killed in a vehicle accident. The Eighth Army had succeeded in establishing a line south of Seoul. The 1st Marine Division was given a sector in the rear stretching from Pohang on the east coast northwest to Andong and spent an easy month, from 12 January to 15 February, in antiguerrilla operations, experimenting with such things as inserting reconnaissance patrols by helicopter.

Ridgway planned a buttoned-up shoulder-to-shoulder United Nations counteroffensive (unlike Walker's freewheeling, hell-for-leather operations) called Operation Killer. The 1st Marine Division moved to the center of the line, under IX Corps, far from blue water. The Marines jumped off from

Wonju on 21 February and with the 1st and 5th Marines in the assault took their objective, Hoengsong, eight miles to the north, three days later. That same day, the IX Corps commander died of a heart attack and O. P. Smith, by seniority and with Ridgway's endorsement, became corps commander. Puller, now a brigadier general, moved up to temporary command of the division. But the press inevitably confused the quiet and courtly O. P. Smith with the sulphurous H. M. Smith. Saipan was remembered, and O. P. Smith remained in command of IX Corps only as long as it took the Army to get a more senior major general to Korea.

Operation Killer was succeeded by Operation Ripper on 7 March. In the Marines' zone of action, the attack was led off by the 1st Marines (now commanded by Col. Francis M. McAlister) and the 7th Marines (also with a new commander, Col. Herman ("Herman the German") Nickerson Jr.). The marines liked Ridgway's way of fighting. By April the Eighth Army's line was generally north of the 38th Parallel. Political considerations outweighed military momentum and there now came a pause.

## HWACHON RESERVOIR

The 1st Marine Division was at Hwachon Reservoir when the Chinese spring counteroffensive materialized on 21 April. In one night's fighting the 6th ROK Division on the Marines' right flank was swept away and a gap opened in the line ten miles wide by ten miles deep. McAlister's 1st Marines, in reserve, was flung into action on the twenty-second, battalion by battalion, to seal off the penetration. The 7th Regiment was withdrawn and echeloned to the left. The division was joined by the British Commonwealth 27th Brigade and by 26 April the situation was once again stabilized. On that day O. P. Smith turned over command of the division to "Jerry" Thomas of Belleau Wood and Guadalcanal, now a major general. By 30 April, the 1st Marine Division was once again part of Almond's X Corps, and in a defensive position at Hongchon.

The second phase of the Chinese spring offensive came in mid-May. This time they hit heavily on the Marines' right, rolling back the 2d U.S. Infantry Division. The 1st Marines, now under Col. Wilburt S. ("Big Foot") Brown, went to the aid of the 2d Division, which in turn was able to echelon to the right to retake ground lost by another collapsed ROK division. The Chinese attack ran out of steam and it was the turn of the United Nations to take the offensive. (Another fighting general, James Van Fleet, had replaced

Ridgway, who had moved up to take MacArthur's place as CinCFE.)

The 1st Marine Division found itself back in the Hwachon Reservoir sector, moving up to Yanggu through rugged mountain country. There were North Koreans in front of them and they fought more tenaciously than the Chinese. By the first week in June all three Marine regiments were abreast on line and by 20 June the division had taken its portion of the corps' objective, a ridgeline overlooking a deep circular valley which was promptly nicknamed the "Punchbowl." Truce negotiations now began and the UN forces settled down into a defensive line.

## THE PUNCHBOWL

Summer 1951 was quiescent. Then in September the division was ordered to take the rest of the Punchbowl. The attack began 5 September. There were eighteen days of hard, inconclusive fighting. Thomas said flatly that the air support meted out by the Fifth Air Force was "unsatisfactory." Over Marine Corps protests, the 1st Marine Aircraft Wing had been put under operational control of the Fifth Air Force with mission assignments coming from the Joint Operations Center. This was in accordance with Air Force doctrine of a single air commander and centralized control of tactical air operations, but it did great damage to the Marine Corps' air-ground team concept. While the general level of air support across the whole front for all divisions may have improved, that received by the 1st Marine Division was down in both quantity and quality.

Strategically, the Fifth Air Force began Operation Strangle on 5 June, an interdiction attack against the enemy's rear designed to dry up his ability to fight. Maj. Gen. Christian Schilt, hero of Quilali, had succeeded Field Harris as commanding general of the 1st Marine Aircraft Wing. During July some concessions were wrung out of the Fifth Air Force as to the assignment of Marine aircraft to Marine-requested missions.

In September 1951, HMR-161, the first transport helicopter squadron, arrived in Korea. Equipped with the Sikorsky HRS-1, the squadron put theory to practice and demonstrated that it could supply an infantry battalion in combat, lift a rocket battery, and move the division reconnaissance company to a mountaintop.

Winter 1951 found the 1st Marine Division holding eleven miles of front on the north side of the Punchbowl. On 10 January 1952, Thomas returned to

Washington to become the assistant commandant and Maj. Gen. John T. Selden took over the division. Planners dreamed of amphibious "end runs," but they never came about.

On 23 March the division was pulled out of the Punchbowl sector and moved 180 miles west to the left flank of the United Nations line, thirty-five miles of front that overlooked Panmunjom and included the defense of the Pyongyang-Seoul corridor. The British Commonwealth Division tied in on their right flank. The lines had solidified and it was trench warfare now, very much like World War I. There were no general offensives or big attacks, just nasty localized actions growing out of patrols and raids, or the loss or capture of an outpost.

In mid-August 1952, there was hard fighting at "Bunker Hill" outpost. In October, there was a fight for the "Hook." In early 1953 there was a contest for "Berlin" and "East Berlin" and in March particularly hard fighting for possession of "Reno," "Carson," and "Vegas." (Vegas was lost and recaptured by 5th Marines, now commanded by Col. Lew Walt.)

During 1952 and 1953, the F9F Panther jet gradually replaced the prop-driven Corsair as the Marine Corps first-line fighter-bomber and the Douglas R4D transports were augmented by Fairchild R4Q "Flying Boxcars."

In June 1953, Maj. Gen. Randolph Pate took command of the division. Firing ceased at 2200 on 27 July as the truce argued out at Panmunjom went into effect. During the Korean War 4,262 marines were killed and 21,781 wounded, twice the totals of World War I. Of the 7,190 Americans taken prisoner, however, only 227 were marines. The 1st Marine Aircraft Wing had flown 127,496 combat sorties and lost 436 aircraft.

Korea had been fought largely with World War II weapons drawn from the vast stores held by the Marines at Barstow in California's desert. There were few new innovations in equipment. The basic rifle was still the M-1. Leggings, which like the bayonet had grown shorter, gave way to combat boots. For cold weather a thermal-insulated "Mickey Mouse" boot replaced the treacherous shoe-pac used during the first winter. An armored vest, or "flak jacket," developed at Camp Lejeune proved particularly effective against grenades and mortars and became general issue. A cold weather training camp was opened at Pickel Meadow in California's High Sierras and all replacements passed through it. A huge artillery range was acquired at Twentynine Palms in California. An East Coast counterpart of the supply center at Barstow was developed at Albany, Georgia.

# 16

## 1952-1965
### A Separate Service, Distinct and Apart

The armistice in Korea did not signal victory but rather a shift from a war of movement to a gray kind of war of position which never really ended. The 3d Marine Division had been reactivated in January 1952 and in August 1953 it had come out to Japan to be in strategic reserve for the Far East. The 1st Marine Division stayed on in Korea until 1955 and then came home to Camp Pendleton. The 1st Marine Aircraft Wing went to bases in Japan. The 3d Marine Division, crowded out of Japan, sent the 4th Marine regiment to Hawaii and the remainder of the division began moving to Okinawa.

President Truman had fulfilled his promise and on 1 January 1952 Lemuel Cornick Shepherd Jr. had become commandant. One of Shepherd's first actions was to reorganize Headquarters Marine Corps along general staff lines with a G-1 (Personnel), G-2 (Intelligence), G-3 (Operations and Training), and G-4 (Logistics).

The political battle for the survival of the Marine Corps was still being waged. In January 1951 Senator Paul H. Douglas of Illinois and Congressman Mike Mansfield of Montana (both former marines) had introduced in their respective bodies of the Congress the Douglas-Mansfield Bill, which would have made it a matter of law that there would be four Marine divisions and four Marine air wings in the active structure. There had been committee hearings, sometimes acrimonious, in the Senate and the House in April and May of 1951. The proponents of the bill emphasized the "force-in-readiness" or expeditionary status of the Corps. The House Armed Services Committee in its report reaffirmed that the Marine Corps "is and has always been since its inception a separate service, distinct and apart from the United States Army, United States Navy, and United States Air Force." The bill went through various permutations and as signed by President Truman (not altogether enthusiastically, it can be assumed) it became Public Law 416, 82d Congress, and it provided for three active Marine divisions and three air wings, and co-equal status for the commandant with the Joint Chiefs of Staff when matters of direct concern to the Marine Corps were under consideration.

The 1st Provisional Marine Brigade that had gone into Korea had been a Marine air-ground team. In January 1953, its near-namesake, the 1st Provisional Air-Ground Task Force, was activated at Kaneohe Bay, Oahu, under Brig. Gen. James P. Riseley. General Shepherd, in his commandant's annual report, written in August 1955, spoke of each of the two Fleet Marine Forces as being "a flexible, mobile, integrated force of ground and air elements comprising a single weapons system." He cited the 1st Provisional Air-Ground Task Force as an example of how the FMF structure made "it easy to form special air-ground task forces tailored to meet the specific needs of an emergency or continuing nature." In May 1956 the 1st Provisional Marine Air-Ground Task Force was redesignated the 1st Marine Brigade, FMF.

In the Far East there were various demands requiring the attention of the 3d Marine Division and the 1st Marine Aircraft Wing. In February 1955, when the Chinese Communists seized Ichiang island and the adjacent Tachen Islands became untenable for the Chinese Nationalists, marines with the Seventh Fleet assisted in the evacuation of twenty-four thousand Nationalist soldiers and civilians to Taiwan. In the same year they also helped in the larger evacuation of three hundred thousand refugees from North Viet Nam to South Viet Nam.

Shepherd retired on 31 December 1955 and was recalled to active duty to be chairman of the Inter-American Defense Board. His successor as commandant, appointed by President Eisenhower, was Gen. Randolph McCall Pate. Born in Port Royal, South Carolina, in 1898, Pate had served briefly as a soldier in World War I, then had gone to Virginia Military Institute (as had Shepherd), where he graduated in 1921. In the 1920s he had served in Santo Domingo and China. He was the logistic planner for Guadalcanal and had spent World War II as a staff officer. In Korea, he had commanded the 1st Marine Division in the last days of the war. Like Shepherd, he was a traditionalist. There was much emphasis on the fit of uniforms, the length of trousers, and proper civilian dress. (Secretary of Defense Charles E. Wilson testily decreed that officers serving in the Washington area should wear civilian clothes. General Pate said that Marine officers must wear hats.) Pate also brought back the swagger stick and made it near-compulsory for officers and staff noncommissioned officers.

A drill instructor at Parris Island on 8 April 1956 took his platoon on an unauthorized night march and six of them drowned in marshy Ribbon Creek. There was a court-martial and national attention focused on recruit-training methods. David Shoup of Tarawa, now a major general, was ordered to make a searching investigation of what went on in boot camp. Recruit training would remain hard but not harsh; the "head-in-the-bucket" era was over.

In the same year the unstable situation in the Middle East came unhinged with the Suez crisis. On 31 October 1956, the 3d Battalion, 2d Marines, afloat with the Sixth Fleet, landed at Alexandria and covered the evacuation of fifteen hundred civilians from thirty-three different countries. Marines also evacuated some U.N. truce team members caught between the Israelis and Egyptians, and, in an action somewhat removed from the main event, the Marine garrison at Port Lyautey was reinforced because of the fighting between the French and Moroccans.

There were also occasions for the controlled use of amphibious power in the Caribbean. In January 1958, after the overthrow of Dictator Pérez Jiménez in Venezuela, and with mobs running rampant in Caracas, the cruiser *Des Moines* with a company of marines embarked took station off-shore in time-honored fashion. In May, after Vice President Richard Nixon's goodwill visit to Caracas turned sour, a battalion of marines was put on board the cruiser *Boston*. In neither case did they land.

## LEBANON INTERVENTION (1958)

The largest Marine operation in these years, however, was in Lebanon. On 14 July 1958 the equilibrium of the Arab world was once again tipped violently, this time by the coup d'état in Iraq and the murder of pro-Western King Faisal. In half-Christian, half-Moslem Lebanon, President Camille Chamoun, confronted with open rebellion supported by Syrian troops poised on Lebanon's borders, asked for U.S. and British intervention. That same day, 14 July, President Eisenhower met with the JCS, listened to their recommendations, and made his decision: "All right, we'll send them in."

There was a contingency plan, nicknamed Bluebat, which called for two Marine battalion landing teams, one to land north, the other south of Beirut, while a British airborne brigade came in from Cyprus. As of 14 July, three battalion landing teams were present in the eastern Mediterranean, partly by coincidence, partly by design. BLT 1/8 was just north of Malta, its return to the United States delayed because of the unsettled conditions. BLT 3/6, newly arrived as relief for BLT 1/8, was steaming from Crete toward Athens. BLT 2/2 was off the southern coast of Cyprus and closest to Beirut. Also present was the headquarters of a brigade equivalent, the 2d Provisional Marine Force. This headquarters had been formed in January under Brig. Gen. Sidney S. Wade for a combined exercise to be held at Sardinia with the British Royal Marines and the Italian Navy. After rioting broke out in Lebanon, General Wade and his staff had come forward into the Mediterranean.

BLT 2/2 was ordered to land at 1500 on 15 July over Red Beach, four miles south of Beirut, half a mile from the International Airport, and a mile north of the village of Khalde. At 1330, U.S. Ambassador Robert McClintock informed Gen. Fuad Chehab, commander of the Lebanese Army, of the impending landing. Chehab, visibly upset, asked that the Americans remain on board their ships. Ambassador McClintock had no radio link with the Fleet so he dispatched his naval attaché to Red Beach to stay the landing. The attaché arrived at Khalde at 1520; by that time the landing had been in progress for twenty minutes, battle-clad marines picking their way through sun-bathers and soft-drink vendors, toward the beach road and the airfield. Lt. Col. Harry A. Hadd, commanding the 2d Battalion, 2d Marines, opined to the attaché that he knew of no way to reverse a landing ordered by the president of the United States. By evening, with four rifle companies ashore, Hadd's battalion had taken over the airport from the bemused Lebanese airport guards and had established a defensive perimeter.

Next morning, before dawn, Adm. James L. ("Lord Jim") Holloway arrived from London as Commander in Chief, Specified Command, Middle East. At 0730, BLT 3/6 began landing across Red Beach and 2d Battalion, 2d Marines, formed up into column to move into Beirut. After several false starts (Chamoun thought the Marines should come into the city; Chehab thought they should not), the column got under way about 1230 and by 1900 the battalion had control of the dock area and had put guards on the critical bridges and the U.S. embassy. The "Basta," the rebel stronghold in the center of the city, was left alone. There were some minor confrontations with both the Lebanese Army and the rebels, a few shots were exchanged, but there were no casualties.

The next day the cooperation of the Lebanese Army improved markedly and on the eighteenth, BLT 1/8 landed over Yellow Beach four miles north of the city while air-transported elements of 2d Battalion, 8th Marines, began arriving at the International Airport from Camp Lejeune. The earmarked British brigade from Cyprus had gone into Jordan at the request of Faisal's cousin, King Hussein. Its place was taken in Bluebat by the U.S. 24th Airborne Brigade, which began to arrive from Germany on 19 July. Maj. Gen. Paul D. Adams, USA, was named CinC American Land Forces, Lebanon, and arrived on 26 July. Afterward, General Wade paid Adams the oblique compliment of being "as fair to the Marine Corps as any Army general I've ever dealt with."

Lebanese national elections were held on 31 July and General Chehab was elected president. He took office on 23 September, having formed a coalition government with the rebels. Chamoun, who had asked the Americans to intervene, was out, and Chehab, who had walked the fence, was in. In the interim, three Marine battalions had departed for home and by 18 October all the marines were gone.

The Lebanon intervention of 1958 would be the last time the chief of naval operations, then the redoubtable Adm. Arleigh A. Burke, would actually be the *chief* of *naval operations*. The Reorganization Act of 1958, pushed by President Eisenhower, had moved the organization of the defense establishment closer to the original Marshall-Collins plan. The chiefs of service (CNO for the Department of the Navy) were removed from the operational chain of command where they had acted as "executive agents" for designated unified and specified commands. Their residual operational authority rested in their membership in the Joint Chiefs of Staff. The powers of the secretaries of the military departments were reduced essentially to those of business managers. The powers of the secretary of Defense were clarified and broadened, not only in the logistical area but also in the operational chain of command, which was now drawn clearly from the secretary of Defense through the Joint Chiefs of Staff to the unified and specified commands. By the time of Lebanon, Admiral Burke's legal authority had actually lapsed; he exercised it through sheer force of will. He liked to boast that he had set the intervention into motion with two phone calls: one to CinCNELM (Admiral Hollaway's other hat) in London and one to CinCLant in Norfolk.

Beginning in 1958, a battalion landing team was kept afloat in the Western Pacific with the Seventh Fleet as a Special Landing Force, and late in the same year MAG-11 went to Taiwan for an extended stay. The Communist-provoked civil war in Laos began in earnest in 1960. As a countermove, a Marine helicopter squadron went into Thailand in 1961, followed in May 1962 by a sizable exercise involving the 3d Marine Expeditionary Unit (made up of a battalion landing team, a helicopter squadron, and an attack squadron). Marine involvement in Southeast Asia had begun.

## SHOUP AS COMMANDANT

David Monroe Shoup succeeded Pate as commandant. In naming him, President Eisenhower went past five lieutenant generals and four major generals. Shoup, the first Midwesterner to become commandant, delighted in playing the earthy Indiana farm boy. In his baptismal speech in January 1960 he said, "It is good to feel the grips of the plow in my hands," and he promised that "the furrow will be straight and true." He also announced, with respect to the swagger stick, "It shall remain an optional item of interference. If you feel the need of it, carry it." Shoup continued the modernization of Headquarters Marine Corps begun by Shepherd. A shrewd fundamentalist, he was skeptical of the counterinsurgency doctrines then in vogue. In private he was critical of the U.S. policy toward Castro's Cuba. Viet Nam he considered a rat hole and he sought to keep the Marine commitment to the advisory effort down to a minimum.

In October 1962, after President Kennedy's ultimatum to the Soviets that the offensive missiles must be removed from Cuba, the garrison at Guantánamo was reinforced to regimental strength. The rest of the 2d Marine Division went to sea in amphibious shipping and was joined in the Caribbean by the 5th Marine Expeditionary Brigade, drawn from the 1st Marine Division, which had come through the Panama Canal from California. To support them, much of the 2d Marine Aircraft Wing deployed forward to airfields in Florida and Puerto Rico.

Budget constraints kept the strength of the Corps down to about 175,000, so that the Fleet Marine Forces were chronically understrength; nevertheless, the operating forces reached perhaps their highest peacetime level of effectiveness. During these years technical capabilities had caught up with doctrinal aspirations. There was now a family of dependable helicopters in fairly sufficient quantity. The Fleet also was gaining in the number of platforms from which they could be launched. The Fleet Marine Force had been restructured in 1956 and 1957, so that division elements were now largely helicopter transportable, with heavier units, such as tank battalions, being moved out of the division and into Force Troops. The USS *Thetis Bay*, an old escort carrier, had been recommissioned for testing as an LPH (Landing Platform Helicopter Carrier). These experiments led to the reconfiguration of a number of former attack carriers (including the *Boxer* and *Princeton*) as LPHs. These, in turn, were followed by new-construction LPHs, beginning with the *Iwo Jima*, commissioned in 1961.

The problem of establishing high-performance tactical aircraft ashore quickly and early in an amphibious operation was approached by something called the SATS or "Short Airfield for Tactical Support." SATS, approved for development in 1958, applied aircraft-carrier components to an expeditionary airfield whose "flight deck" consisted of a new type of aluminum matting. Less esoterically, in 1962 the M-14 rifle, chambered for the 7.62-mm "NATO" cartridge, replaced the M-1, and the M-60 machine gun replaced the vintage Brownings.

Marine Corps Order 3120.3, published in December 1962, formalized the creation of Marine air-ground task organizations, emphasizing that:

> A Marine air-ground task force with separate air-ground headquarters is normally formed for combat operations and training exercises in which substantial combat forces of both Marine aviation and Marine ground units are included in the task organization of participating Marine forces.

The organizational structure of a Marine Air-Ground Task Force (MAGTF or "Mag-taff"), said the order, included four major elements: command, ground combat, aviation combat, and combat service support. Four types (or sizes) of MAGTFs were prescribed: a Marine Expeditionary Unit (MEU) built around a battalion landing team and a helicopter squadron; a Marine Expeditionary Brigade (MEB) with a regimental landing team and a provisional Marine aircraft group as its core; a Marine Expeditionary Force (MEF), basically a reinforced division and an aircraft wing; and a less well-defined Marine Expeditionary Corps (MEC). One variety of a MEC was to have it as a headquarters superimposed over two MEFs.

## GREENE BECOMES COMMANDANT

Wallace Martin Greene Jr., of Vermont succeeded General Shoup as Commandant on 1 January 1964. A graduate of the Naval Academy (class of 1930), his career before World War II had followed the familiar pattern of Basic School, sea duty, China duty, schools, and Guantánamo. At the beginning of the war he was an observer in Britain. In the Pacific he served as an operations officer in the Marshalls and at Saipan and Tinian. After the war came more operations-planning experience at successively higher echelons. After Ribbon Creek he was sent to Parris Island to take command of the Recruit Depot. When Shoup became commandant in 1960, he made Greene his chief of staff.

More of an internationalist than his predecessor, Greene set up, as one of his first actions, Operation Steel Pike. Held in concert with the Spanish Marine Corps in the fall of 1964, it was the largest combined amphibious exercise since World War II.

## DOMINICAN INTERVENTION (1965)

In the spring of 1965, there was a testing of a different sort of the Atlantic Fleet's amphibious capability. Since the days of the 1916–1924 occupation, the Dominican Republic had been the subject of special, almost sentimental, Marine Corps interest. Before and after Trujillo's assassination in May 1961, ships' visits and a showing of the flag had helped keep a highly inflammable situation from bursting into a conflagration. In November 1961, when a civil war threatened, an adroit amphibious demonstration dampened it down. Similar actions were effective in 1963, but in April 1965 the situation got out of hand.

Late on Saturday, 24 April, word reached the 6th Marine Expeditionary Unit (then on board amphibious shipping, anchored south of Puerto Rico's Vieques Island) that a Communist-inspired coup was under way in Santo Domingo. Orders were to take station off the southern coast of the troubled republic, hull-down, but prepared to move in to evacuate up to twelve hundred U.S. citizens. By 0200, 25 April, the task group was off Haina, the sugar port and minuscule naval base just west of Santo Domingo city. The 6th MEU included Battalion Landing Team 3/6 and Medium Helicopter Squadron 264. Fixed-wing support would have to come from Roosevelt Roads in Puerto Rico. By this time the rebels had gained substantial control of downtown Santo Domingo, the loyalist troops had been pushed out of the National Palace, and Donald Reid Cabral had quit as president. The number of U.S. citizens and foreign nationals to be evacuated had grown to three thousand.

The evacuation site was the Hotel Embajador on the western edge of the city, with a polo field, once used by the Trujillos, offering an elegant helicopter-landing zone. Evacuation began at 1300 on 27 April. Downtown, the U.S. embassy, defended by an eight-man Marine security guard and thirty-six national policemen, was receiving sporadic sniper fire. Next morning, 28 April, the National Police announced they no longer could guarantee the security of either the evacuation site or the embassy. Accordingly, a platoon of marines was put in at each place. The loyalists, having lost most of the city, had concentrated at San Isidro air base some eight miles away. At midafternoon, the military junta at San Isidro asked that a battalion of marines be landed to help restore order. At about 1900, authority came back from Washington to land five hundred marines to protect the lives of Americans and foreign nationals. Within two hours, 526 marines had come into the Embajador landing zone.

Early the next afternoon, 29 April, the U.S. embassy came under heavy small-arms fire. From Washington came word that the Organization of American States was considering an International Safety Zone. By nightfall all of BLT 3/6 was ashore. During the early morning hours of 30 April, the 3d Brigade, 82d Airborne Division, began arriving at San Isidro. The day's operation plan called for 3d Battalion, 6th Marines, to move east from the polo field to a north-south line just beyond the U.S. embassy so as to establish the International Safety Zone agreed to by the OAS. The 2d Brigade, 82d Airborne, was to come in from San Isidro as far as the vital Duarte Bridge across the Río Ozama. The loyalists, relieved at the bridge, were to go forward and patrol the center of the city. All parts of the plan worked, except the last. Instead of advancing, the loyalists fell back to San Isidro, where a three-cornered negotiation for a cease-fire was taking place. Next morning the Marines and Airborne pushed forward their patrols and linked up shortly after noon. Then they got orders from the U.S. negotiators to withdraw to their original positions.

Lt. Gen. Bruce Palmer, USA, arrived that morning with the 2d Brigade, 82d Airborne, and took over command of all U.S. ground forces. Other arrivals that day at San Isidro were Brig. Gen. John H. Bouker, USMC, as Commanding General, 4th Marine Expeditionary Brigade, and air-lifted BLT 1/6. A five-man peace commission from the OAS also arrived. The Marines and Army were now permitted to link up once again, which they did shortly after midnight on 3 May. Later on the third BLT 1/8 came into San Isidro by air, while BLT 1/2 arrived on board the LPH *Okinawa* to serve as floating reserve.

On 6 May, after bitter debate, the OAS voted to create an Inter-American Peace Force. On 7 May, tough and wily Brig. Gen. Antonio Imbert Barreras, one of the two surviving assassins of Trujillo, took over as head of the San Isidro group. He energized the faltering loyalist effort and began the cleanup of the remaining pocket of rebel resistance in the old part of the city.

With three BLTs ashore and one afloat, Marine strength had peaked at eight thousand. On 25 May, the first contingent of Brazilians arrived. Eventually, Paraguay, Honduras, Nicaragua, and Costa Rica would all send small units and more than a thousand troops would come from Brazil. On 26 May the Marines began to withdraw. Last elements had gone by 6 June and the Dominican intervention, as far as the Marines were concerned, was over. Marine casualties had been nine killed and thirty wounded. U.S. Army casualties were about the same. There were those who would say that the threat of a Communist takeover was never so great as assumed by President Lyndon B. Johnson and that the amount of U.S. forces sent ashore went far beyond that required. Others would say that the Dominican situation had been exploited as a laboratory opportunity for testing the respective strategic mobility systems of amphibious and airborne forces. Elsewhere in the world, by this time, an even more ambiguous and infinitely more costly involvement had already begun.

# 17

## 1965-1972
### BATTLES WOULD BE FOUGHT
### AND REFOUGHT

### DA NANG AND III MAF

On 8 March 1965, under Brig. Gen. Frederick J. Karch, the 9th Marine Expeditionary Brigade, after standing off the coast for two months, landed across a fine sandy beach in the Bay of Da Nang, the first American ground-combat forces to come into Viet Nam. Battalion Landing Team 3/9 had hit Red Beach Two at 0902, looking very fierce in camouflaged helmets and armored vests, and were met with speeches and flowers from the official South Vietnamese welcoming committee. Two hours later, BLT 1/3 began landing at Da Nang Air Base in Marine KC-130 transports.

Marine operational involvement in the Viet Nam War had begun three years earlier when on Palm Sunday, 15 April 1962, Medium Helicopter Squadron 362 had arrived at Soc Trang in the Delta south of Saigon with its Sikorsky UH-34s. The task unit was called "Shu-fly" and its first operational employment, lifting Vietnamese Army "little people" into battle, had come a week later, on Easter. In September 1962 Shu-fly had moved north to Da Nang, South Viet Nam's second largest city, and set itself up on the west side of the airfield in a run-down French compound. By early 1965 half the medium helicopter squadrons in the Marine Corps had rotated through Da Nang for a tour of duty. Then in 1964 the Marines began to supply advisors for service with the Vietnamese Army in addition to those already with the Vietnamese Marine Corps.

Once ashore, 9th MEB was given the mission of reinforcing the defenses of the air base and such other installations as might be agreed upon with Maj. Gen. Nguyen Chanh Thi, the tigerish commanding general of I Corps and I Corps Tactical Zone. The 3d Battalion, 9th Marines, moved out to a ridgeline west of the field dominated by Hill 327. Behind it was the Bay of Da Nang, formed by the embracing arms of Hai Van peninsula on the northwest and Tiensha peninsula on the southeast. The Trans-Vietnam Railway was still intact north to Hue, going behind Red Beach, across Nam O Bridge and then up through the blue-green Hai Van mountains by way of a half-dozen tunnels to Thua Thien province. Highway One, the old Mandarin Road, roughly paralleled the railroad, zigzagging through the Hai Van Pass, which the French, for good reason, called *Col des Nuages* ("Pass of the Clouds"). Tiensha peninsula was flat and sandy but at its end was Monkey Mountain, 621 meters high and once an island. Below Monkey Mountain, beautiful China Beach curved southward for some twelve kilometers to Marble Mountain, monoliths of marble jutting up out of the sand, and highly regarded as a Buddhist shrine.

Looking south from Hill 327 the Marines could see virtually all the rest of the populated area of Quang Nam province, the hamlets like dark-green islands in a checkerboard sea of green and brown rice paddies. The rivers twisted and turned through the lowlands, following a hundred different courses and changing their names a dozen times, but the main ones were the Thu Bon and the Vu Gia. Thirty kilometers due south were the Que Son mountains, another spur coming out of the Annamites and, as the Marines would learn, honeycombed with a thousand caves which would serve the Viet Cong well.

The 1st Battalion, 3d Marines, stayed on the airfield to provide close-in security. At that time Da Nang had one of only three jet airfields in South Viet Nam, a crazy quilt of activities, some military, some civilian, some Vietnamese, some American. Northernmost of the four Vietnamese corps areas, I Corps Tactical Zone included five provinces: Quang Tri, Thua Thien, Quang Nam, Quang Tin, and Quang Ngai, stretching some 225 miles from north to south and as narrow as thirty miles. General Thi's corps headquarters was in a handsome French compound on the east side of the field.

On 11 April the first fixed-wing Marine squadron arrived, VMFA-531, flying the superb McDonnell F4B Phantom. That same day, BLT 2/3, which had been on an exercise in Thailand, landed across Red Beach, and three days later BLT 3/4 arrived from Hawaii and was put in at Phu Bai, seven miles southeast of Hue, Viet Nam's third-largest city and the old imperial capital.

Maj. Gen. William R. ("Rip") Collins, commander of the 3d Marine Division, moved his flag to Da Nang on 3 May and three days later 9th MEB was dissolved to be replaced by the III Marine Expeditionary Force. Ground elements were grouped under the 3d Marines and air elements under Marine

North Viet Nam

DMZ
ConThien
Khe Sanh   Dong Ha
QUANG   Quang
TRI    Tri

DMZ
Gio Linh
ConThien
cua Viet River
9  Cam Lo
Camp Carroll
Rock Pile
Khe Sanh
Combat Camp
Ca Lu  Quang Tri
9   Khe Sanh
Dong Ha
1
Quang Tri River

Hue
THUA THIEN
PhuBai
VIET NAM
I CORPS TACTICAL
ZONE
A Shau

Hai Van
Tiensha
DaNang
Marble Mt
QUANG NAM
ThuongDuc  ThanhQuit
An Hoa
Hoi An
Thang Binh
KhamDuc  QueSon
Hiep Duc
QUANG TIN
Tam Ky
ChuLai

SOUTH CHINA SEA

LAOS

Van Tuong
Batangan
Quang Ngai
QUANG NGAI
II CTZ
Duc Pho

25
0   miles   50

Aircraft Group 16. On 11 May, Maj. Gen. Paul J. Fontana, one of the Guadal-canal air aces, arrived with the advance headquarters of 1st Marine Aircraft Wing. All three headquarters—Force, Division, and Wing—were crowded into the same ramshackle compound that had been occupied by Shu-fly.

One or two back-page news stories, datelined "Saigon," pointed out that the term "Expeditionary" was not apt to be regarded fondly by South Viet-namese who remembered the French Expeditionary Corps of the First Indo-China War (1946–54). Alarm bells went off in the Saigon headquarters of the U.S. Military Assistance Command, Viet Nam. ComUSMACV, Gen. William C. Westmoreland, got off a message to the Joint Chiefs of Staff urging a unit designation less likely to upset Vietnamese sensibilities. Unit designations are a service prerogative and the Joint Chiefs asked General Greene to come up with a more neutral term. Greene's staff worked up a list of possibilities. "III Amphibious Corps," the designation of the ancestor of the III Marine Expe-ditionary Force, was a leading contender because of its World War II battle honors, including Guam, Peleliu, and Okinawa. Someone cautioned that the Vietnamese might find "Corps" offensive (even though they used it for their own major tactical units). The new title factored down to "III Marine Amphibious Force." (In 1970, "Amphibious" would be substituted for "Expe-ditionary" in all MAGTF designations.)

On 4 June, Maj. Gen. Lewis Walt (in the intervening years "Silent Lew" of World War II had become "Uncle Lew" to the troops) took over command of III MAF and 3d Marine Division from General Collins in a ceremony held rather furtively in the Officers Mess because the display of U.S. national colors was not yet permitted. Next day, Brig. Gen. Keith McCutcheon (the brilliant theoretician of close air support and helicopter tactics) relieved General Fontana.

## CHU LAI

A second jet-capable airfield was urgently needed in I Corps Tactical Zone, and on 7 May the 3d Marine Expeditionary Brigade, commanded by Brig. Gen. Marion Carl (the same Carl who had scored eighteen Japanese aircraft in World War II), had landed the 4th Marines at "Chu Lai," a sandy pine bar-ren fifty-five miles south of Da Nang. They were promptly absorbed into III MAF. By Memorial Day four thousand feet of aluminum matting had been laid and on 1 June eight Douglas A4 Skyhawks arrived from the Philippines and flew their first combat mission.

The steady parade of Marine battalions and squadrons into Viet Nam continued. On 1 July the Seventh Fleet's Special Landing Force, then BLT 3/7, landed at Qui Nhon, 175 miles south of Da Nang, to cover the impending arrival of the 1st Air Cavalry Division. A week later BLT 3/7 was reembarked, having been relieved in place by 1st Battalion, 7th Marines. On 6 July the headquarters of the 9th Marines arrived at Da Nang and was given the area immediately south of the airfield. On 14 August the headquarters of the 7th Marines landed at Chu Lai. Thus by late summer 1965, four Marine infantry regiments—the 3d, 4th, 7th, and 9th Marines—were in Viet Nam. In this new war Marine regimental headquarters would tend to function as brigade headquarters with battalions moving in and out of regimental operational control, as available and as required, much the same way squadrons moved in and out of Marine aircraft groups.

There were four Marine aircraft groups: MAG-12 with its A-4s was at Chu Lai; MAG-11, a fixed-wing group, came into Da Nang from Japan on 7 July; MAG-16 detached its fixed-wing squadrons to MAG-11, and in September moved with its helicopters to the new Marble Mountain Air Facility on China Beach; at about the same time, MAG-36, also a helicopter group, arrived from California and set itself up on Ky Ha peninsula northeast of the Chu Lai strip.

## Operation Starlite

By 15 August good intelligence indicated that the 1st Viet Cong Regiment, some two thousand strong, was concentrated on Van Tuong peninsula, fifteen miles south of Chu Lai, with intentions of attacking the airfield. To thwart those ambitions, Operation Starlite was launched on 18 August, the first regimental-size battle fought by U.S. forces since Korea. The 7th Marines converged on the 1st Viet Cong Regiment, one battalion making a river crossing from the north in LVTs, another landing to the west in helicopters, and a third battalion coming in from the sea in an amphibious landing. By 24 August nearly a thousand Viet Cong had been killed.

## Pacification

South of Da Nang, the 9th Marines had cleared one-third of the way to Hoi An by October. The theory of pacification was deceptively simple. A hamlet or village would be liberated from VC domination, would be provided security, the seeds of Government of Viet Nam control would be sown, and then nurtured with a carefully-worked-out civic-action program. The test zone would be the nine villages of the Hoa Vang district that lay south of the Song Cau Do. By October 1965 this area had been cleared by the 9th Marines and the province chief had developed his Nine Village program. Until sufficient Popular Forces were ready to take over, the specially formed 59th Regional Force Battalion would provide close-in security while Marines provided an outer ring of tactical protection.

The same kind of thing was happening at Chu Lai and Phu Bai as the Marines moved out from their base areas in clearing operations. Drawing on tribal memories of Nicaragua, Haiti, and Santo Domingo, the Marines recognized that the key to pacification was an effective grass-roots gendarmerie. They therefore set about to improve the quality of the Popular and Regional Forces. The Vietnamese rule-of-thumb called for providing a PF squad to each hamlet and a PF platoon to each village or township. Weapons were scarce, mostly carbines and festoons of grenades. Many units were no more than the personal bodyguards of the hamlet or village chiefs.

During the summer the 3d Battalion, 4th Marines, at Phu Bai had organized something called a "Joint Action Company" (later the name would be changed to the more accurate "Combined Action Company"). A squad of marines, all volunteers, was assigned to work with each of five Popular Force platoons in the hamlets north and east of Phu Bai. The combination seemed to work. From the PF the marines got a feel for the local situation and the marines gave the PF the stiffening provided by good communications, adequate fire support, and a little basic military training. When 3d Battalion, 4th Marines, came down to Da Nang in January 1966 to serve as air-base defense battalion, it brought along the Combined Action concept and Marine squads were paired off with the seven Popular Force platoons located around the airfield. From these beginnings the Combined Action Program would grow eventually into a regimental-size force.

The night of 27 October 1965 was an unhappy one for Marine aviation. Viet Cong sappers, under cover of a mortar barrage, got onto the air facility at Marble Mountain. Forty-one were killed but six reached the flight line with bangalore torpedoes and satchel charges, destroying twenty-four helicopters and damaging twenty-three more, almost all of MAG-16's aircraft. That same night at Chu Lai there was a similar attack and two A-4s were destroyed and six damaged before the raiders could be cut down. It was an embarrassment, but later, as the war wore on, it would come to be accepted that no number of American defenders could guarantee an absolute defense against rockets or mortars or even determined sappers.

BLT 2/7 at Qui Nhon was finally released by the Army and loaded out in amphibious shipping on 7 November, it having been decided to combine the move to Chu Lai with a tactical landing. A Vietnamese Marine battalion was also embarked in the Amphibious Task Group and on 10 November, the Marine Corps Birthday, the two battalions landed northeast of Tam Ky, midway between Da Nang and Chu Lai. There was no opposition and the chief result was historical: the first combined landing by U.S. and Vietnamese marines. The Vietnamese Marine Corps, shaped in the U.S. Marine Corps mold, had been formed after the departure of the French in 1954 and had grown to five infantry battalions, an artillery battalion, and an amphibious support battalion. The brigade was highly valued by Saigon as a strategic reserve, and before the war's end it would grow to a light division.

Meanwhile, the northeast monsoon had begun to blow and by November the rain was averaging an inch a day. Outlines of the Viet Cong monsoon strategy were soon clear. After Starlite they avoided stand-up battles against the Marines in anything larger than a company-size formation, but small units—fire teams and squads, even platoons and companies if they were unwary—would be surprised and struck and there would be attacks by fire and sappers against the major bases. As for the ARVN, the Viet Cong were still willing to take them on in battalion or even regimental strength. But the main targets for the monsoon season were the isolated district capitals and market towns garrisoned by the RFs and PFs.

Hiep Duc, a district headquarters twenty-five miles west of Tam Ky, was overrun the night of 16 November. Two ARVN battalions were flown by Marine helos through a solid wall of cotton-wool clouds and rain and then through a gantlet of ridgeline machine guns into the valley. After a bitter fight the ARVN retook the town. Then General Thi, because he had too few regular troops to leave them there, ordered the town abandoned.

After Hiep Duc, the Viet Cong moved next against Que Son district headquarters. Beleaguered Que Son lay in a valley completely dominated by the Viet Cong. To remove the pressure against Que Son it was planned that an ARVN column would move southwest along the axis of one of two roads entering the valley. After the ARVN had developed a contact, two Marine battalions would heli-lift behind the enemy with a third battalion held ready in reserve. The operation was called Harvest Moon.

The ARVN 5th Regiment with two battalions started down the road from Thang Binh the morning of 8 December. About 1330 the right-flank battalion was knocked out of the fight by a heavy close-in attack. Marine helicopters brought in another ARVN battalion before dark. Next morning the commanding officer of the 5th ARVN Regiment (a brave man who had done well at Hiep Duc three weeks earlier) was killed and his faltering regiment driven south and east. To salvage the fast-disintegrating situation, General Walt landed the 2d Battalion, 7th Marines, west of the line of contact and put the 3d Battalion, 3d Marines, in southeast of the battle area. Next morning the Special Landing Force—in this case, the 2d Battalion, 1st Marines—landed midway between them and the Marine battalions were put under Task Force Delta with headquarters at Que Son. Meanwhile the shaken ARVN had caught their breath. They came back into the valley under the personal command of Maj. Gen. Hoang Xuan ("Ho Ho") Lam, commander of the 2d ARVN Division, and moved against the northern rim while the Marines moved south. The Marine climb into the hills was prefaced by four B-52 strikes, the first to be delivered in direct support of Marine operations. By 16 December Viet Cong resistance had faded and three days later the Marines were out of the valley.

An ambitious operation, Double Eagle, was begun on 28 January 1966, targeted against the 325A NVA Division, which was believed to be straddling I Corps' southern boundary. Task Force Delta, which had been formed for the Que Son operation, was given four battalions for the new job. It was a hopscotch kind of battle, played in concert with the 1st Air Cavalry Division, which was operating across the Corps boundary in Binh Dinh province. Task Force Delta returned to Que Son valley in Quang Tin province in mid-February and for the next several months, with a changing array of subordinate battalions, did some hard fighting against the 36th NVA Regiment and the reconstituted 1st Viet Cong Regiment.

## 1ST MARINE DIVISION ARRIVES

The 1st Marine Division had moved its flag forward from Camp Pendleton to Okinawa in August. Its 7th Marine regiment and the 1st and 2d Battalions, 1st Marines, were already in country as 1966 began. The rest of the division, including the 5th Marines, was now scheduled to come into country. In March, with two-thirds of his division in place, Maj. Gen. Lewis J. ("Jeff") Fields opened his command post at Chu Lai. He was given the southern two provinces of the Corps area, Quang Tin and Quang Ngai, as an area of operations to be shared with General Lam's 2d ARVN Division.

## BUDDHIST REVOLT

General Thi had been running I Corps Tactical Zone almost semi-independently of Saigon. He and Premier Ky were old rivals, and on 10 March, Thi was relieved of his command and ordered out of the country. Pro-Thi, anti-government protests under Buddhist leadership bubbled up in Saigon, Da Nang, and Hue. The dissidents coalesced into something called the "Struggle Force." By 3 April the 1st ARVN Division was in the streets of Hue demanding the overthrow of the Saigon government. Ky responded by bringing three battalions of Vietnamese marines to Da Nang the night of 4 April.

On 9 April a Struggle Force column started up Route 1 from Hoi An toward Da Nang. It was met at Thanh Quit bridge, twelve kilometers south of the air base, by Company F, 9th Marines. For several tense hours, U.S. marines stood gunpoint to gunpoint with the Struggle Force but the Hoi An column did not seek to force the bridge. Elsewhere, General Walt was using his good offices to help negotiate a solution.

A kind of accommodation was reached which lasted until 15 May when Ky landed four battalions at the airfield and overran the semi-abandoned corps headquarters (the deposed Thi was in Hue). A week of confused, nasty fighting in and around Da Nang followed. On 22 May active resistance in Da Nang collapsed. Government troops then marched north to Hue and on to Quang Tri, and by 22 June the Buddhist revolt was over and Thi was on his way to exile.

All of this played havoc with the pacification program south of Da Nang, which in late February and early March, before the internecine troubles, had begun to pick up momentum. The 9th Marines had developed several new techniques. One was the "County Fair," a kind of elaborate cordon-and-search operation. Another was "Golden Fleece," in which they protected the rice harvest.

The chronic enemy south of Da Nang was the R-20, or Doc Lap Battalion, a Viet Cong Main Force formation which in the first year showed great willingness to accept appalling losses in night attacks against Marine company and battery positions. The enemy then settled down to sapper and terrorist activities and in his use of mines, both antipersonnel and anti-vehicular, he had a cheap and effective means of exacting Marine casualties. Throughout the six years that Marines would work south of Da Nang, the percentage of casualties caused by these insidious devices would hang at 50 percent.

In March, just before the Buddhist Revolt began, General Walt had returned from Washington where he had gone for a month's leave and promotion to lieutenant general. He continued as Commanding General, III Marine Amphibious Force, but command of the 3d Marine Division now went to Maj. Gen. Wood B. Kyle (they had been in the same Basic School, and had also served together in Shanghai and on Guadalcanal). General Kyle started a deliberate, systematic advance to Hoi An, a kind of scrubbing action, using first the 9th Marines and then moving the 3d Marines in on the right flank and the 1st Marines in on the left.

## NORTH TO THE DMZ

General Kyle's careful campaign was interrupted in July 1966 by solid intelligence that the 324B NVA Division had crossed over the DMZ into Quang Tin province. Task Force Delta was dispatched north with three battalions and on 15 July Operation Hastings began. By the end of the week three more U.S. battalions and five Vietnamese battalions had been fed into the action and the Marines became acquainted with the "Rockpile," a seven-hundred-foot hill which formed a cork to the valleys leading down from the north and west. The Marines met a new kind of enemy: fresh, well-equipped North Vietnamese regulars fighting with secure supply lines to their rear. There was a pause the first week in August, then the 324B tried again, this time accompanied by the 341st NVA Division. The new action was called Operation Prairie; it would be fought in four phases, and it would last until 31 May 1967.

The battleground was the strip between Route 9 and the DMZ. In general the Marines were west of Route 1 and the ARVN east of the road. Fortunately the 1st ARVN Division had recovered from the Buddhist Revolt and was once again a first-class fighting division.

In October 1966, General Kyle moved his 3d Marine Division command post northward to Phu Bai with an advance CP at Dong Ha where Route 9 intersects with Route 1. Essentially, General Kyle had his 3d and 9th Marines in Quang Tri province, fighting the main battle of the DMZ from a series of combat bases along Route 9. Kyle's other regiment, the 4th Marines, was in Thua Thien province covering the western approaches to Hue.

Maj. Gen. Herman Nickerson Jr., a flinty native of Maine who had had the 7th Marines in Korea, now commanded the 1st Marine Division. With the shift of the 3d Marine Division northward, he moved his headquarters up from Chu Lai into the bunkered command post vacated by General Kyle on the reverse slope of Division Ridge. The 1st Marines were now in Quang Nam province, the 5th Marines in Quang Tin, and the 7th Marines in Quang Ngai. Also in Quang Ngai was the 2d Korean "Blue Dragon" Marine Brigade with three battalions and very much like the U.S. Marines in organization, training, and equipment.

On Okinawa the 9th Marine Amphibious Brigade was organized to be CinCPacFlt's strategic amphibious reserve. In addition to overseeing the refitting of the battalions and squadrons briefly rotated out of Viet Nam, the brigade also provided the BLTs and helo squadrons which served afloat as the 7th Fleet's Special Landing Force. On 1 April 1967, 7th Fleet activated a second Amphibious Ready Group, doubling its Special Landing Force capability. The two SLFs, each a battalion landing team and a medium helicopter squadron, were designated Alpha and Bravo.

In California, the 5th Marine Division had been reactivated as a temporary division and by late 1966 its first infantry regiment, the 26th Marines, was echeloning its battalions forward to the Western Pacific.

In the south of I Corps Tactical Zone, the U.S. Army's 196th Light Infantry Brigade landed at Chu Lai on 9 April. It was joined later by the 3d Brigade, 25th Infantry Division. Both were placed under Task Force Oregon, commanded by Maj. Gen. William B. Rosson, USA. TF Oregon in turn was put under III MAF and for the first time since the Smith vs. Smith unpleasantness at Saipan, a Marine corps-size headquarters had the equivalent of an Army division subordinate to it. The two battalions of the 5th Marines in Quang Tin province, joined later by their 1st Battalion, which was then Special Landing Force Alpha, had heavy fighting in Que Son valley during late April and through the month of May, called Operation Union.

Meanwhile, there was even bloodier fighting going on in the northwest corner of Quang Tri province. On 20 March, tall, athletic Maj. Gen. Bruno A. Hochmuth replaced General Kyle as Commanding General, 3d Marine Division. In late March the enemy pounded Gio Linh and Con Thien with rockets, artillery, and mortars. In early April, most of the fighting centered around Cam Lo. Then on 24 April a patrol from 1st Battalion, 9th Marines, bumped into an NVA force five miles northwest of Khe Sanh. Next day 3d Battalion, 3d Marines, arrived from Dong Ha by helicopter and by nightfall was in contact with at least a battalion on Hill 861. On 26 April, the 3d Marines command group came in along with the regiment's 2d Battalion. Hill 861 was secured by the evening of 27 April and next day the 2d and 3d Battalions went forward in a two-pronged attack against Hill 881 North and Hill 881 South. Hill 881 South was taken in a one-day assault but 2d Battalion fought until 3 May before winning Hill 881 North.

On 12 May, with the First Battle of Khe Sanh over, the 26th Marines arrived and relieved the 3d Marines. East of Khe Sanh the Marines now went on the offensive with the mission of ridding the DMZ south of the Ben Hai of the enemy. A complicated maneuver began on 18 May 1967. Five battalions of the 1st ARVN Division worked along the axis of Highway 1 between Gio Linh and the Ben Hai while three Marine battalions plus the Special Landing Force worked along the river itself. The Prairie series came to a close on 31 May with a hard action on Hill 174 southwest of Con Thien.

## CHANGES

On 1 June 1967, Lieutenant General Walt, after two years of commanding III MAF, was relieved by Lt. Gen. Robert E. Cushman, a big, bluff fifty-two-year-old, former military assistant to Vice President Nixon and holder of the Navy Cross from Guam. Two years of fighting in Viet Nam had brought visible changes in the appearance of the Marine rifleman. He had begun the war with the M-14 rifle, essentially an improved M-1, rechambered for the 7.62-mm NATO cartridge and with a 20-round box magazine. In the spring of 1967, in time for the fighting at Khe Sanh, he had been rearmed with the M-16. A 5.56-mm weapon of terrific velocity (3,250 feet per second), the M-16 was at its best in delivering high-volume fire at short ranges.

The Marine rifleman had worn the standard green utility uniform into Viet Nam and with General Greene's permission had cut off the sleeves at the elbow. There had been some experimentation with lightweight, quick-drying materials and now there was a loose-fitting camouflaged cotton uniform reminiscent of that worn by the French paratroopers. There was also a "South-East Asia" boot with molded rubber soles and canvas uppers instead of the leather combat boot.

Robert Strange McNamara was the first secretary of Defense to make full use of his operational powers as clarified by the Reorganization Act of 1958. Civilian *control* of the military had become detailed civilian *direction*. He directed that a "fire break" be cut from Con Thien through Gio Linh to the sea. It was to be filled with barbed wire heavily seeded with sensors and mines and was to link a series of hardened strong points along Route 9. There was no great enthusiasm amongst the Marines for the barrier and the press quickly pounced upon it as "McNamara's Wall," comparing it with the Great Wall of China and the Maginot Line.

Violent fighting broke out around Con Thien on 2 July, marked by massive supporting fire. With the NVA pushed back from Con Thien, three battalions of marines and three battalions of ARVN on 14 July went into the southern half of the DMZ for a two-day sweep while the 1st Amphibian Tractor Battalion worked the sandy area between Route 1 and the sea.

At this time, the 3d Marine Division had three infantry regiments in Quang Tri province. The 9th Marines were in "Leatherneck Square," formed by Gio Linh and Con Thien up along the border and Dong Ha and Cam Lo along Route 9. West of Leatherneck Square, the 3d Marines were operating in the vicinity of Camp Carroll, the Rockpile, and Ca Lu. Farther west, the defense of Khe Sanh continued under the 26th Marines. There was hard fighting that September going on around Con Thien. The press was calling it "little Dien Bien Phu." The hill itself, 158 meters high and scraped down to the bare laterite, was never occupied by much more than a battalion and, while it was a continuing target for enemy artillery and mortars, most of the fighting was some distance away as the enemy tried to get within attack range.

The 4th Marines in Thua Thien province were having a relatively quiet time of it, but it was becoming increasingly apparent that A Shau valley, empty of Allied effort since March 1966, was being developed as a major NVA logistical base. The introduction of 122-mm and 140-mm rockets into the enemy's arsenal had increased the problems of defending the base areas from stand-off attacks. Dong Ha, Da Nang, and Chu Lai continued to be regular targets. Nevertheless, security of the populated coastal area was steadily improving. It was now possible to drive along Route 1 from Dong Ha south to the Binh Dinh province border. In all, it was a strange, blurry kind of war where every scrap of statistical evidence—enemy killed, weapons captured, rice caches found—had to be collected and fed into a computer so that

Washington could measure progress. Sometime in midsummer 1967 total Marine casualties in Viet Nam went past the total for the Korean War and Viet Nam had become the second largest war in Marine Corps history.

On 14 November Major General Hochmuth was killed when his UH-1E helicopter exploded and crashed. Maj. Gen. Rathvon Tompkins, holder of the Navy Cross from Saipan, came out from Parris Island to be the new 3d Marine Division commander. Donn J. Robertson, who had his Navy Cross from Iwo Jima, was now in command of the 1st Marine Division and in September there had been heavy fighting in Que Son valley.

## Tet Offensive (1968)

Farther south, additional brigades joined TF Oregon which in late September was re-designated the Americal or 23d U.S. Infantry Division. This new Army strength set in motion a whole sequence of moves which the Marines called "Operation Checkers." The Korean Marine Brigade moved up from Chu Lai in late December 1967 to an area of operations radiating out from Hoi An. This made it possible to start sending some additional 1st Marine Division battalions north. The idea was to allow the 3d Marine Division to concentrate on the defense of the DMZ and Quang Tri province and have the 1st Marine Division take over responsibility for Thua Thien and the approaches to Hue. The 1st Marine Regiment's headquarters had already moved to Quang Tri and it was supposed to flip-flop with the 4th Marines headquarters in Thua Thien, thus getting the regiments realigned with their parent divisions. On the enemy side, six NVA divisions threatened Quang Tri and Thua Thien.

The second battle of Khe Sanh began on 20 January 1968 with a sharp fight between the 3d Battalion, 26th Marines, and an NVA battalion entrenched in the saddle between Hills 881 North and South two miles northwest of the base. Next day the enemy overran the village of Khe Sanh and pushed against the base itself. An ammunition dump went up under the barrage. General Tompkins sent the 26th Marines a fourth battalion, the 1st Battalion, 9th Marines, and on 26 January the lightweight 37th ARVN Ranger Battalion joined the defenders. Cushman's battle plan was to put no more troops than necessary into Khe Sanh, realizing that they must be resupplied by air through the tag end of the monsoon, and to put his dependence upon massive air and ground firepower to destroy the attackers.

The Tet holiday was about to begin and the Viet Cong announced a nationwide truce to run from 27 January until 3 February 1968. This illusory truce was interrupted on 29 and 30 January by rocket attacks against Da Nang, Marble Mountain, and Chu Lai. On the thirtieth and thirty-first there were ground attacks against all five province capitals. In Da Nang, before dawn on 30 January, infiltrators reached the I Corps headquarters compound; their mission was to disrupt command and control while the 2d NVA Division launched its attack from south and west of the city. The 2d NVA columns which were to make the main effort were caught by Marine air and artillery as they came down from the hills west of An Hoa. Some North Vietnamese made it almost to the river south of the Da Nang airfield where they were engaged by Marine infantry.

The enemy had more success, at least temporarily, at Hue. Several regiments had been infiltrated into the city in civilian clothing. At midnight, 30 January, they changed into their uniforms, let go a rocket and mortar barrage, and revealed themselves as essentially in control of the city. There were pockets of Allied resistance. First ARVN Division headquarters was still intact as was the MACV advisers' compound south of the Perfume River.

Early next morning, 31 January, 1st Battalion, 1st Marines, at two-company strength, started up the road to Hue from Phu Bai, fought their way through scattered resistance, and arrived at the MACV compound in the early afternoon. They were then ordered to open a route to the 1st ARVN Division headquarters. There was a hard fight getting over the bridge, they reached the Citadel wall, could not breach it, and withdrew south again to the MACV compound. On 1 February the battalion was given the task of clearing the part of the city that lay south of the river. By 4 February, 2d Battalion, 5th Marines, had also arrived. The counterattack was put under command of the 1st Marines. It was house-to-house street fighting of a kind that Marines had not done since Seoul in 1950. By 9 February the city south of the river had been cleared.

Across the river, the ARVN had been attacking from the northeastern corner of the city toward the Citadel. On 12 February the 1st Battalion, 5th Marines, went in on the ARVN left flank. The 3d ARVN Regiment was in the center and the Vietnamese Marines were on the right flank. After ten grinding days the U.S. Marines reached the southeast wall of the Citadel. Mopping up continued for another week and on 2 March the Battle for Hue was declared over. Three understrength U.S. Marine battalions and thirteen Vietnamese battalions had virtually destroyed at least eight, and possibly eleven, North Vietnamese battalions. In retaliation, thousands of civilians had been executed by the enemy or marched off into oblivion. Much of the beautiful old city lay in ruins.

In Washington, on 1 January, Gen. Leonard Fielding Chapman Jr. had succeeded General Greene as commandant. An artillery battalion commander in World War II and Greene's chief of staff, Chapman would give the Marine Corps four years of leadership characterized by cool managerial efficiency.

## SECOND BATTLE OF KHE SANH

At Khe Sanh, during the early morning of 5 February, sensors told the 26th Marines that the enemy was coming. The NVA attempted to assault Hills 881 South and 861A, were hit heavily with air and artillery, and thrown back. Next day the enemy continued the attack, coming in from the west along the axis of Route 9, and successfully overran the Special Forces camp at Lang Vei, six miles from Khe Sanh, using Russian-built PT-76 amphibian tanks.

On 9 February, Westmoreland sent his deputy, fifty-three-year-old, cigar-chewing Gen. Creighton W. Abrams, to Phu Bai to establish a MACV forward command post (which later became XXIV Corps). Many interpreted this as a questioning of Marine generalship at Hue and Khe Sanh. Not so, said General Westmoreland—and General Abrams was scrupulously correct in his dealings with General Cushman.

Regimental Landing Team 27, the second RLT to be drawn off from the new 5th Marine Division, began arriving on 17 February and went into the still-troublesome area south of Marble Mountain, permitting the rest of the 5th Marines to go north to Phu Bai. Brigades from the 101st and 82d Divisions also arrived in Thua Thien province. By the end of February there were twenty-four U.S. Marine and twenty-eight U.S. Army infantry battalions in I Corps Tactical Zone and General Cushman was commanding the equivalent of a field army.

On 10 March, Westmoreland made Gen. William W. Momyer, CG, Seventh Air Force, the "single manager" for tactical air and gave him "mission direction" of the 1st Marine Aircraft Wing's fixed-wing strike aircraft. The Marines had fought this assignment on doctrinal grounds, but found in practice it could be accommodated and Marine ground operations continued to get first priority for Marine tactical air support. Tactical air had gotten its greatest testing of the war in its support of the Khe Sanh defenders. Unprecedented tonnages of bombs churned the green hillsides into a red-orange moonscape. Aerial resupply by C-123s and C-130s and by helicopter transports continued in what Westmoreland called the "premier air logistical feat of the war." On 18 March the NVA tried to crack the portion of the perimeter held by the Vietnamese 37th Rangers and failed. On the thirtieth, the 1st Battalion, 26th Marines, counterattacked and dislodged an NVA battalion from the hills a mile south of the airstrip.

## Spring Counteroffensive (1968)

Cushman's plan for a spring counteroffensive had three phases: relief of Khe Sanh, a raid into A Shau valley, and an attack into the DMZ. The relief of Khe Sanh, called Operation Pegasus, got under way 1 April 1968. The 1st Marines and three Vietnamese battalions moved westward along Route 9 while the 1st Air Cavalry Division and an ARVN airborne battalion leapfrogged toward the beleaguered base. On 4 April the twenty-sixth Marines attacked southeast from Khe Sanh and two days later made contact with the Air Cav. By 12 April, Route 9 was open to truck traffic. Next came a spoiling attack by the 1st Air Cavalry and 101st Airborne Divisions into the A Shau valley, from 19 April until 16 May, costing the enemy the largest materiel losses he had yet suffered in Corps Tactical Zone.

The thrust into the DMZ was delayed by an attack by the 320th NVA Division beginning 29 April against 3d Marine Division elements at Dong Ha. There was a bitter six-day seesaw action at Dai Do hamlet northeast of Dong Ha and heavy fighting continued through most of May. The enemy's attack on Dong Ha was part of his second major offensive for the year. The Marines called this new offensive "mini-Tet." In Quang Nam province four NVA regiments were south and west of Da Nang. The 1st Marine Division's defense of the Da Nang vital zone had resolved itself largely into a thickly-manned, heavily-patrolled "rocket belt" arcing around the city. In early May, to keep the NVA regular formations at arm's length, the 7th Marines were sent on a sweep through "Go Noi Island," a delta west of Hoi An formed by the many-channeled, many-named Ky Lam or Thu Bon river, and then on westward into the Thuong Duc corridor.

During May, Maj. Gen. Raymond Davis, Medal of Honor holder from Korea, took command of the 3d Marine Division and Tompkins moved up to deputy commander, III MAF. Tactical headquarters at Khe Sanh was now Task Force Hotel under Brig. Gen. Carl W. Hoffman. Earlier in May there had been a series of sharp actions with the rejuvenated 304th NVA Division in the hills and along Route 9. At the end of the month, the 304th was replaced by the 308th, which had two regiments—the 88th and 102d—fresh from Hanoi. Davis gave Hoffman the 1st and 4th Marines for a fast-moving, high-mobility operation. The objective area was a salient south of Khe Sanh formed by a loop in the Laotian border. Two fire-support bases, Robin and Loon, were blasted through the canopy. The first battalions were inserted on 2 and 3 June and when it was over on 19 June, the 308th NVA Division, after only two weeks in combat, was on its way back north for refitting.

Next mission assigned Task Force Hotel was the evacuation of Khe Sanh. Cushman had argued for such a move immediately after Operation Pegasus. Westmoreland agreed militarily but was concerned over the timing politically and asked that the decision to execute be deferred until Abrams had taken over as ComUSMACV. This occurred on 11 June. The planned evacuation got into the press prematurely and caused much speculation and debate. Why, if Khe Sanh had been worth defending at all costs just a few months before, was it being abandoned now? The White House quickly announced that it was a military decision, not President Johnson's. Hanoi equally quickly claimed that the "fall" of Khe Sanh was a "grave defeat" for the Americans. The official MACV explanation stressed the switch-over to more mobile tactics, making "the operation of the base at Khe Sanh unnecessary." Meanwhile, the 1st Marines and the 11th Engineer Battalion had razed Khe Sanh and withdrawn east along Route 9, almost without incident.

In July, General Cushman got on with the third phase of his spring counteroffensive, a general cleansing of the area between Route 9 and the DMZ. The 3d and 9th Marines led off with a series of convoluted attacks coordinated with actions by the 2d ARVN Regiment. Contact was frequent but small-scale. At the end of July the 1st Brigade, 5th U.S. Mechanized Division, arrived in Quang Tin as the numerical relief for the temporarily deployed RLT-27, which would return to Camp Pendleton in September.

West and south of Da Nang, the 1st Marine Division, now commanded by artilleryman Maj. Gen. Carl A. Youngdale, fought sharp actions near Hill 55 and in and around Go Noi Island, and it became increasingly obvious that the enemy was preparing the battlefield for another major attack. The enemy's "Third Offensive" of 1968 began on 18 August with rocket and mortar attacks and some sapper action against provincial and district headquarters. The main target, though, was Da Nang. Before dawn on 23 August a VC sapper battalion got across the Cau Do River and into the Hoa Vang district headquarters and also seized the southern end of the Cam Le bridge, one of two bridges which carry Route 1 into Da Nang. The ARVN Rangers threw the VC out of Hoa Vang district headquarters and those on the bridge were caught between two companies of marines. Four miles south of the bridge, the 38th NVA Regiment was badly mauled in a three-day battle with three Vietnamese battalions and elements of the 27th Marines. It was the enemy's last serious effort to enter Da Nang by force. As part of the August offensive, the 320th NVA Division came across the DMZ but was ejected in a counteraction by the 9th and 3d Marines west and north of the Rockpile, followed by a sweep through the DMZ, which gutted the 320th NVA Division's carefully positioned ammunition stockpiles.

## MONSOON (1968)

September and October were quiet months, the coming of the monsoon causing seasonal problems for both sides. The 1st Cavalry Division (AirMobile) was redeployed to III Corps Tactical Zone and the 3d Marine Division and 101st Airborne Division adjusted their boundaries accordingly. The 3d Marine Division and the 1st Brigade, 5th Mechanized, would continue to work in Quang Tin province and the 101st in Thua Thien province.

Thuong Duc Special Forces Camp lay in the valley of the Song Vu Gia about halfway between Da Nang and the Laotian border. On 28 September 1968 the NVA attacked the camp, briefly held two outposts, were driven out by air and artillery, and then settled down to a more deliberate siege. On 6 October, the 7th Marines launched a relief column down the axis of Route 4, feinted an attack, developing the enemy positions, while other battalions went in deeper by helo. The fight coalesced into a struggle for Hill 163, two miles from the camp. This was taken and held and by 19 October the road to Thuong Duc was once again open. The 5th Marines, meanwhile, were operating close by in the "Arizona" territory south of the Vu Gia and Thu Bon. Almost half of the 1st Marine Division kills that summer and fall were attributed to the 1st Reconnaissance Battalion using what were called "Sting

Ray" techniques, quiet insertions of six-man patrols who watched for enemy movement and then called in Marine air and artillery.

November saw the beginning of the Accelerated Pacification Plan, designed to win back all that had been lost in territorial confidence and security as a result of the Tet offensive. Operation Meade River, an enlarged County Fair, was begun by the 1st Marine Division on 20 November. The target area was "Dodge City," ten miles south of Da Nang and lying between the La Tho and Ky Lam rivers, where there had been much hard fighting since the 9th Marines first went there in 1966. Six Marine battalions were used for the cordon which worked out to one marine for every five meters along the perimeter. Inside the box there were thought to be thirteen hundred NVA and about a hundred VCI. When the operation ended on 9 December, the total enemy body count was put at 1,210.

## NEW YEAR (1969)

As 1969 began, it was estimated that there were about ninety thousand enemy either in I Corps Tactical Zone or poised on its borders. South and southwest of Da Nang, the 1st Marine Division, now commanded by Maj. Gen. Ormond R. Simpson, followed up the success of Meade River with a deep thrust into the enemy's mountainous base areas. Farther south, on 13 January, the 2d and 3d Battalions, 26th Marines, landed on the northern face of Batangan peninsula, the old Starlite battlefield, in what was the largest Special Landing Force operation of the war. In an amphibious application of the County Fair concept, the two SLF battalions closed a cordon formed on the land side by two battalions of the Americal Division, and together the joint operation killed 239 enemy and screened twelve thousand Vietnamese, of whom 256 were identified as Viet Cong cadre.

To the north, in Quang Tri province's southwest corner, the 3d Marine Division had begun Dewey Canyon, perhaps the most successful high-mobility regimental-size action of the war. On 22 January the 9th Marines, commanded by Col. Bob Barrow (who had done so well in Korea), went into the enemy's Base Area 611 in Da Krong valley. Depending entirely upon helicopters for logistic support, the battalions leapfrogged from fire-support base to fire-support base, these quickly hacked out of the jungle to provide a helo landing zone and room for a mixed battery of artillery. By 18 March the enemy's base area had been cleaned out, 1,617 enemy dead had been counted, and 1,461 weapons and hundreds of tons of ammunition and supplies had been taken.

Tet 1969 in mid-February was only a pale shadow of the violence of Tet 1968. The enemy sought once again to mount a full-scale attack against Da Nang. The attack was launched on 23 February and in three days it had petered out.

Pacification seemed to be going well. The goal for the year was to bring all the populated area under government control and to raise the security level of the population to 90 per cent. III MAF's largest contribution to the security of the rural areas continued to be the Combined Action Program. The program had grown to four battalion-size Combined Action Groups, with headquarters at Da Nang, Chu Lai, Phu Bai, and Quang Tri. These groups totaled nineteen Combined Action Companies. Under the companies, in turn, were 102 Combined Action Platoons—the specially selected and trained Marine rifle squads which were paired off with Popular Force or Regional Force platoons to provide hamlet and village security.

On 26 March 1969, Lt. Gen. Herman Nickerson Jr., who on his previous Viet Nam tour had commanded the 1st Marine Division, relieved General Cushman as the CG, III MAF. Cushman on his return to the States became the deputy director of the Central Intelligence Agency.

## Troop Withdrawals Begin

In April the arrival of a fresh NVA regiment in the vicinity of Cam Lo caused some sharp exchanges with the 9th Marines. In May, the 9th Marines passed this sector to the 3d Marines and went back into Da Krong valley in a replay of Dewey Canyon. Finding it virtually empty, in June they moved up into the salient formed by the Laotian border south of Khe Sanh. This is where the war ended for the 9th Marines. The first major U.S. troop withdrawal had been announced and the 9th Marines were to return in July to Okinawa. Proportional slices of combat support and service support as well as elements of the 1st Marine Aircraft Wing also left. At this time the wing was operating from five major airfields with six aircraft groups and twenty-six tactical squadrons with a total of 186 helicopters and 242 fixed-wing aircraft.

The 1st Marine Division continued its less spectacular but arduous operations west and south of Da Nang. Battles would be fought and refought against the almost invisible enemy on the same ground: "Barrier Island," the sandy waste south of Hoi An dotted with poverty-stricken fishing villages; the "Arizona Territory," the piedmont agricultural area northwest of An Hoa made desolate by the war; "Dodge City," south of Da Nang; and "Go Noi Island," one-time center of silkworm and mulberry culture. At the end of August the boundary between the 1st Marine Division and the Americal Division was realigned and the Marines were again given responsibility for Que Son valley, first entered by them in December 1965. The 7th Marines began moving back into the valley on 15 August, displacing the 196th Light Infantry Brigade.

In September, the second increment of the U.S. troop withdrawal was announced. By mid-October the rest of the 3d Marine Division was gone, Headquarters and the 4th Marines to Okinawa, the 3d Marines to Camp Pendleton. All helicopter squadrons remaining in country were consolidated under MAG-16 at Marble Mountain.

The last Special Landing Force operation was conducted in September 1969, one more sweep of Barrier Island. Since 1965, Seventh Fleet had carried out seventy-two of these SLF landings, of which fifty-three were in I Corps Tactical Zone. No beaches had been assaulted in World War II style; the enemy never did more than lightly harass the landing force. The SLFs were most profitably used as highly mobile reserves with which to exploit opportunities presented by ongoing operations. This was particularly true of the big battles fought along the DMZ by the 3d Marine Division in 1967 and 1968. Coastal operations, such as the repeated visits to Barrier Island and Batangan Peninsula, helped keep those areas free of the enemy and aided the U.S. Navy's Market Time blockade of infiltration from the sea.

By this time the enemy in Quang Nam and Quang Tin provinces had reverted almost completely to guerrilla and terrorist operations and it was once again monsoon season. In December, Maj. Gen. Edwin B. Wheeler, who as a colonel had commanded the 3d Marines, the first regiment to come in-country in 1965, succeeded General Simpson as Commanding General, 1st Marine Division. The division had just ended a six-month effort to clean out, once again, the Dodge City–Go Noi Island areas. By the end of the year, in the northern five provinces, the percentage of the population judged to be living in secure areas had climbed to an optimistic 94 percent and a goal of 100 percent was set for 1970.

## XXIV CORPS TAKES OVER

It was now time for another troop withdrawal. Between January and April 1970, the Marines reduced their in-country strength another 12,600 "spaces." The 26th Marines went back to Camp Pendleton and eventual deactivation. A helicopter squadron and three fixed-wing squadrons also departed. With these reductions, the U.S. Marines were no longer the dominant U.S. service in I Corps. On 9 March 1970, upon the detachment of Lieutenant General Nickerson, the roles of III MAF and XXIV Corps were reversed. Lt. Gen. Melvin Zais, USA, shifted his headquarters from Phu Bai down to Da Nang and into the old III MAF compound on the Tourane River. The new III MAF commander was Keith McCutcheon, now a lieutenant general. McCutcheon moved his headquarters to Red Beach, close to where the Marines had originally landed in 1965.

The "tactical area of responsibility" of III MAF had shrunk to that held by the 1st Marine Division, essentially Quang Nam province. The division was now down to its three organic infantry regiments, the 1st, 5th, and 7th Marines, and its artillery regiment, the 11th Marines. It had lost some of its amphibious elements but was heavy with engineer and motor transport reinforcements. The division's overriding mission was still to keep the enemy at arm's length from Da Nang. Ed Wheeler broke his leg in a helo crash on 18 April and was succeeded by Charles F. ("Chuck") Widdecke, who had earned a Navy Cross at Guam and who had commanded the 5th Marines in Viet Nam in 1966.

On 2 July 1970, I Corps Tactical Zone was redesignated Military Region 1. There were sweeping organizational changes with more responsibility for territorial security going to the province chiefs. General Lam, commanding in Military Region 1 and knowing that further U.S. troop withdrawals were imminent, planned a last large-scale broad-front combined offensive westward into enemy base areas. In Quang Nam province a Vietnamese Marine brigade was added to the 51st ARVN Regiment and the Ranger Group so that a division-equivalent was available. The 7th Marines followed behind Lam's attack in a supporting operation, Pickens Forest, 16 July to 24 August. The results were not great, but the pattern was significant: the ARVN were out in front and the Marines were in a supporting role. Marine strength was scheduled to go down 18,600 more "spaces" by 15 October. The 7th Marines would begin one more operation before leaving for home. On 31 August, behind a thunderous air and artillery preparation, they went back into the Que Son mountains, beginning Operation Imperial Lake, the Marines' last effort to clean out that enemy stronghold.

The 7th Marines went home to Camp Pendleton in September and the 5th Marines took their place in the Que Sons. The 1st Marines, alone now in the Da Nang area, fanned out to take over the 5th Marines' zone north of the Thu Bon. The great combat base at An Hoa, most of it razed, was turned over to the ARVN just as the monsoon rains began.

On the air side, Maj. Gen. Alan J. Armstrong now commanded the 1st Marine Aircraft Wing. As part of the withdrawals, VMCJ-1, the hard-working reconnaissance and electronic countermeasures squadron, left for Iwakuni. MAG-13 turned Chu Lai over to the U.S. Army and left for El Toro. Remaining in country were two aircraft groups, MAG-11 at Da Nang with about eighty fixed-wing aircraft, and MAG-16 at Marble Mountain with about 150 helicopters.

In October, Typhoon Kate caused the worst floods in Quang Nam since 1964. Strenuous rescue efforts by the Marines—particularly by the Marine helicopters—evacuated perhaps thirty thousand civilians. The province chief estimated that, otherwise, as many as ten thousand might have died.

There was a big celebration of the Marine Corps Birthday on 10 November, capped by a pageant in one of the hangars on the west side of Da Nang Air Base. General McCutcheon officiated, but he wasn't feeling well, and on 13 December he left for the U.S. Naval Hospital at Bethesda. The Marine aviator who had done so much to develop close air support and to bring helicopters and vertical-lift aircraft into the Marine Corps was terminally ill. He was placed on the retired list on 1 July 1971 in the grade of four-star general and died of cancer two weeks later.

## Phase Out

Donn Robertson, who had commanded the 1st Marine Division in 1967 and 1968, came out to Viet Nam just before Christmas as a lieutenant general to take command of III MAF. The next troop reduction was being negotiated and the days of the III MAF in-country were literally numbered. The intensity of combat experienced by the 1st Marine Division continued to decline. In 1969, the division had had 1,051 killed and 9,286 wounded. In 1970, casualties were down to 403 killed and 3,626 wounded. They continued to trail off in the first months of 1971. General Chapman paid his last visit as commandant to the combat zone in January. He charged the remaining Marines to come out of Viet Nam in good order, leaving behind nothing worth more than "five dollars."

In February, General Lam launched the major incursion into Laos, called Lam Son 719. It was supposed to be a spoiling action to prevent a large-scale enemy offensive into the northern province. Unlike the Cambodian offensive of the year before, U.S. ground forces did not go into Laos. For many reasons, including bad weather and the lack of American advisors with the ARVN units, the operation went badly. U.S. Marine participation was limited to tactical air support, a few heavy-lift helicopters, and some engineer and transportation help on the Vietnamese side of the border.

The 5th Marines started its stand-down on 15 February, coming out of the Que Son valley and mountains. Two fixed-wing and one helicopter squadron also departed. Just the 1st Marine regiment remained in the field. In January, the 1st Marines had put a battalion for the last time up onto Charlie Ridge west of Da Nang to look for the NVA's elusive rocketeers, who were still sporadically shelling the city and air base. Another bobtailed battalion was put up into the Que Sons. Any marine finding a rocket was rewarded with a short leave, if he wished to go, to Hong Kong or Bangkok.

On 14 April 1971, General Robertson took the flag and headquarters of III MAF to Okinawa. That same day the headquarters of the 1st Marine Aircraft Wing left for Iwakuni in Japan and the flag of the 1st Marine Division departed for Camp Pendleton. The remaining combatant elements were briefly combined into the 3d Marine Amphibious Brigade under General Armstrong. Ground and air operations stopped on 7 May and by 26 June 1971 all elements of the brigade had been redeployed. The Marines' place in Quang Nam province was taken by the U.S. 196th Light Infantry Brigade.

## EASTER OFFENSIVE 1972

This left about five hundred marines in Viet Nam—embassy guards, air and naval gunfire spotters, and advisors to the Vietnamese Marines—and this was about the number that was present when the North Vietnamese began their Easter offensive at the end of March 1972. The four-division NVA thrust across the DMZ and sliced through the new and green 3d ARVN Division. The brigades of the Vietnamese Marine Division were hurriedly moved into blocking positions. At sea, by the end of the first week in April, the 9th Marine Amphibious Brigade had taken station in amphibious shipping with four battalion landing teams and two composite helicopter squadrons. At Da Nang air base, MAG-15 had begun arriving with four squadrons of F4 Phantoms. Most of this air support was used in Military Regions I and II; some strikes were flown north into Laos and North Viet Nam. Farther south, at Bien Hoa, a field not previously used by the Marines, MAG-12 moved in during mid-May with two squadrons of A-4 Skyhawks to support Military Regions III and IV, with some sorties into Cambodia.

From on board the USS *Coral Sea*, VMA(AW)-224, with the A-6 Intruder, flew most of its missions in Laos and North Viet Nam. HMA-369, with the new AH-1J Sea Cobra, arrived off the coast on 20 June and began flying armed helicopter strikes from the decks of the USS *Denver*.

No Marine ground-combat troops went ashore, but with this kind of air and naval gunfire support—every available cruiser and destroyer in the Seventh Fleet took its turn on line—the crack Vietnamese Airborne and Marine divisions, widely held to be the two best divisions in South Viet Nam's armed forces, fought a series of delaying actions, finally stopped the North Vietnamese drive at My Chanh, north of Hue, and then counterattacked. The Marine advisors to the Vietnamese Marine Division—some forty-one officers and thirteen enlisted men—never left the side of their counterparts. Helicopters from the 9th MAB were used to lift the Vietnamese marines, and in one operation U.S. Marine amphibian tractors landed a battalion across the beach.

Task Force Delta, reactivated for the occasion, went to Nam Phong in Thailand in late May to set up an expeditionary airfield. In June, MAG-15 moved from Da Nang to Nam Phong, promptly naming it "the Rose Garden," in a derisive reference to the then-current recruiting slogan, "The Marine Corps didn't promise you a rose garden."

## RESTRUCTURING FOR PEACE

The Viet Nam War was the longest and, in some dimensions, the biggest war in the history of the Marine Corps. At its peak strength in 1968, III Marine Amphibious Force had a total of 85,755 marines, more marines than had been ashore at Iwo Jima or Okinawa. By mid-1972, 12,926 marines had been killed, another 88,542 marines wounded (about half of whom required hospitalization), casualties that compare to the 19,733 marines killed and 67,207 wounded in World War II.

Overall strength of the Corps during the Viet Nam War peaked at 317,400, far under the 485,053 peak reached in World War II. But because Viet Nam was fought using peacetime personnel policies, more marines actually served in the Corps during the seven years of major involvement in Viet Nam than served during the four years of World War II, roughly eight hundred thousand as opposed to six hundred thousand.

# 18

## 1972-1975
### GETTING BACK IN THE
### AMPHIBIOUS BUSINESS

RESTRUCTURING FOR PEACE

On 1 January 1972, Gen. Robert Everton Cushman Jr. took over as commandant from General Chapman. Gen. Ray Davis retired as assistant commandant on 1 April. The new assistant commandant was Gen. Earl E. Anderson, the first Marine aviator to reach four stars on active service. The Corps, by then, was down to about two hundred thousand men. The post–Viet Nam redeployments had put the 3d Marine Division back on Okinawa, and the 1st Marine Brigade had been reconstituted in Hawaii. The 1st Marine Division was back in Camp Pendleton and the 3d Marine Aircraft Wing remained at El Toro. On the East Coast, the 2d Marine Division continued at Camp Lejeune and the 2d Wing at Cherry Point.

At Quantico, as after previous wars, the lessons of Viet Nam were being analyzed and digested. In April 1971, at about the same time that President Nixon was welcoming the 1st Marine Division home from Viet Nam, VMA-513 at Beaufort, South Carolina, received its complement of AV-8As, the British-built Hawker-Siddeley Harrier. With its vertical take-off and landing capability, the Harrier promised to be as revolutionary in the area of close air support as the helicopter had proved for tactical troop lifts. "Sea-basing" was the name given to the new concept aimed at greatly increasing seaborne logistic support, so that future operations would not need the great sprawling logistics complexes such as had grown up in Viet Nam. General Cushman said in April 1972, "I don't want to give the impression that we are rewriting the book on amphibious warfare. Sea-basing represents an evolutionary refinement, not a revolutionary new concept. We have deployed forces which were essentially sea-based since the end of World War II, including our Caribbean and Mediterranean ready forces and our Special Landing Forces in Viet Nam."

Then, in words that Nicholas, Henderson, and Lejeune would have appreciated, Cushman said tautly: "We are pulling our heads out of the jungle and getting back into the amphibious business. . . . We are redirecting our attention seaward and re-emphasizing our partnership with the Navy and our shared concern in the maritime aspects of our national strategy."

The numbers of amphibious ships had shrunk with the overall contraction of the U.S. Navy, but the quality was good, if aging, and the objective of a 20-knot speed of advance for the amphibious forces had been attained. The new capital ship for the amphibs was to be the LHA, a multipurpose amphibious assault ship that could handle helicopters from its flight deck and amphibian vehicles from its hold. The first of these, USS *Tarawa* (LHA-1), began its operational tests in 1975. It was to be followed shortly by USS *Saipan* (LHA-2). The three remaining ships of the class were to have delivery dates stretching out through the late 1970s.

## PARIS PEACE ACCORDS

In Paris, on 27 January 1973, after four frustrating years of negotiation, the "Peace Accords" were signed by four parties: South and North Viet Nam, the Viet Cong, and the United States. Fighting was to stop while the Vietnamese themselves worked out South Viet Nam's political future. Until free general elections could be held, the Saigon government was to remain in power. The U.S. and other foreign troops were to be out of country in sixty days (most had already departed) and their bases dismantled. No requirement was imposed, however, for the pull-back of the 150,000 North Vietnamese soldiers then encysted in South Viet Nam. The cease-fire was to go into effect at midnight, Greenwich Mean Time, 27 January.

For the United States, the Peace Accords offered a face-saving formula: they permitted the release of U.S. prisoners of war and the end of participation in an unbearably unpopular war—without the appearance of utterly abandoning an ally. The Nobel Peace Prize for 1973 went jointly to U.S. Secretary of State Henry A. Kissinger and North Vietnamese negotiator Le Duc Tho. Kissinger accepted his prize, but Tho said he would be able to consider it only after "real peace is established in South Viet Nam."

In February and March 1973, 649 American prisoners of war came home from Hanoi. Only twenty-six of them were marines. Twelve other marines had either escaped or were exchanged earlier. Three were known to have died in captivity.

The cease-fire was to be monitored by a four-nation International Commission of Control and Supervision (ICCS)—1,160 members to be drawn equally from Canada, Indonesia, Hungary, and Poland. Almost immediately, violations began to be reported on both sides. The work of the commission was effectively blocked by Hungarian and Polish intransigence and North Vietnamese obstructionism. In July 1973 Canada withdrew in frustration from the ICCS and was replaced by Iran. North Vietnamese forces continued to march into South Viet Nam. Much of northernmost Quang Tri Province was now in Communist hands, and heartsick American marines read in the newspapers that Khe Sanh and Dong Ha, scene of their hard-won victories, were now North Vietnamese airfields.

## ISRAEL AND CYPRUS (1973–1974)

On the other side of the world, on 6 October 1973, Syria and Egypt launched their twin offensives against Israel in what quickly came to be called the October or Yom Kippur War (it was not only the Jewish holy day but was also the tenth day of Islam's sacred month of Ramadan). Afloat in the eastern Mediterranean was the Landing Force, Sixth Fleet—the 34th Marine Amphibious Unit (34th MAU) and the headquarters of the 4th Marine Amphibious Brigade (4th MAB) under the command of Brig. Gen. Andrew W. O'Donnell. The skeleton brigade was quickly reinforced by the arrival of the 32d MAU, so that O'Donnell had under his command forty-four hundred marines, organized provisionally into a regimental landing team, a helicopter group, and a logistics support group. But this was not 1956, when the mere presence of the U.S. Sixth Fleet could halt a Suez war. Ashore, out of sight of the marines, the greatest tank battles of history were being fought, and from these battles the marines would derive certain lessons as to their own anti-tank and antiaircraft defenses.

The following summer, in July 1974, the 34th MAU, then consisting of Battalion Landing Team 1/8 and Medium Helicopter Squadron 162, was engaged in a landing exercise in Lakinikos Gulf, about a hundred miles southwest of Athens, when word reached them that Archbishop Makarios of Cyprus had been overthrown on the fifteenth by Greek Cypriot factions seeking *enosis,* or union, with Greece. On 20 July, in a countermove, the Turks landed on the north coast of Cyprus. The next day, the 34th MAU, in its amphibious shipping, took station off the south coast of the embattled island and, on 22 July, began the evacuation of U.S. citizens and other foreign nationals. Some were evacuated from Dhekalia airfield by Marine helicopters; others were delivered to the ships by the British. In all, 752 persons, 498 of them Americans, were taken out and given safe passage to Beirut. The warm glow of this successful evacuation was chilled a month later, on 19 August, when a Cypriot mob attacked the U.S. embassy in Nicosia and, despite the best efforts of a handful of Marine security guards, ransacked the building while a sniper's bullet killed U.S. Ambassador Rodger P. Davies.

## Viet Nam (1975)

In January 1975 the North Vietnamese boldly took possession of Phuoc Long province, only forty miles north of Saigon. The United States did nothing and President Nguyen Van Thieu accepted the loss. Having tested South Vietnamese resolve and U.S. reaction, North Viet Nam followed up this initial probe with a full-scale offensive, pressing forward on a broad front that swung in a great arc from the DMZ in the north, through the Central Highlands, down Route 14 to Tay Ninh in the south. To meet the attack, the South Vietnamese had, on paper, an imposing numerical superiority: 850,000 combatants to North Viet Nam's 305,000. But the South Vietnamese had only thirteen divisions in the field and these were widely dispersed as compared to the eighteen to twenty lean and concentrated North Vietnamese divisions.

In March, Ban Me Thuot, montagnard city and capital of Dar Lac province in the Highlands, fell after a week's fighting. This apparently triggered a decision on Thieu's part to withdraw from both the Highlands and the north so as to concentrate his regular forces in the vital coastal regions and around Saigon. (The word "enclave," much discussed in the strategic debates of 1965 and 1966, was rediscovered.) On 14 March, Thieu met secretly at Nha Trang with Lt. Gen. Pham Van Thu, commander of Military Region 11. Thu was to evacuate the Highlands and shift his corps headquarters from Pleiku to Nha Trang on the coast. Thieu then flew north to Da Nang to meet with Lt. Gen. Ngo Quang Truong. Truong, admired by the U.S. marines, had the reputation of being the best fighting general in the South Vietnamese army. He had already lost most of the Airborne Division, which had been ordered back to Saigon. His best remaining troops were the ARVN 1st Division and the Vietnamese Marine Division. Thieu ordered him to pull back from Quang Tri, the northernmost province.

All along the front, from north to south, the withdrawal became a rout. Provinces were lost at the rate of one a day. Kontum, Pleiku, and Dar Lac were the first to go, then Quang Tri, and in the south, Binh Long and Quang Duc. In Military Region 1, the old battleground of the III Marine Amphibious Force, General Truong was outflanked and overextended. He thought he could hold Hue. Then he changed his mind and withdrew. American marines, listening to the news and watching their maps, waited for their old comrades, the Vietnamese marines, heroes of the 1972 counteroffensive, to make their stand. A defense line, swung in an arc around Da Nang from the Hai Van peninsula (what the marines had called "the Rocket Belt") to Hoi An seemed feasible. The Vietnamese marines were marched and counter-marched as orders changed, but there was no stand. This time there were no U.S. advisors, no U.S. close air support, no B-52 raids in the north, no mining of Haiphong harbor, no seemingly endless onrush of U.S. logistical support. Da Nang fell without a fight.

## Cambodia (1975)

The end was also fast approaching in neighboring Cambodia. The Khmer Rouge had begun their dry-season offensive, and by March had completed the encirclement of the capital, Phnom Penh, cutting off the vital Mekong River supply line. Only a 1,500-ton-a-day airlift of ammunition, food, and medical supplies—flown into Pochentong airport by U.S. civilian pilots in chartered U.S. Air Force C-130s—kept the city alive. The Khmer Rouge noose tightened around Phnom Penh and Pochentong came within easy range of Soviet-supplied rockets and artillery.

On 1 April ailing President Lon Nol left his capital for an "official visit" to Indonesia (and thence to exile in Hawaii). His departure signaled the irreversible collapse of his government. Out in the Gulf of Siam, amphibious ships of the Seventh Fleet, with the 31st Marine Amphibious Unit embarked, waited for President Ford's decision to execute Operation Eagle Pull, the evacuation of the few remaining Americans and such foreign nationals who chose to leave. The order came on 12 April 1975.

It was a Saturday and in the early morning hours a Ground Combat Force (GCF) of about three hundred marines came in by helicopter and threw a perimeter around the soccer field (near the U.S. embassy), which had been designated as the evacuation site. Two Marine helicopter squadrons, flying

CH-53 Sea Stallions from the decks of amphibious assault ship *Okinawa* (LPH-3) and attack carrier *Hancock* (CVA-19), swiftly shuttled 276 Americans, third-country nationals, and high-ranking Cambodians to safety. The operation went smoothly and was over in a little more than two hours. The marines from the embassy guard then brought down the U.S. flag and left in the last helicopter. As it lifted from the landing zone, three Khmer Rouge recoilless rifle rounds impacted on the soccer field, killing or wounding, it was reported, several Cambodian children who had been watching the evacuation.

## THE END IN SAIGON

In South Viet Nam, the collapse of the Thieu government was accelerating. The Communists had taken the coastal cities of Qui Nhon, Tuy Hoa, Nha Trang, and Cam Ranh. Only at Xuan Loc, forty miles east of Saigon on Route 1, and covering Bien Hoa, South Viet Nam's next-to-last jet air base, was there determined resistance to the invaders. The Vietnamese marines (those who weren't captured or surrendered) had left Da Nang in great disorder, many on board the SS *Pioneer Commander,* which took them to the great base at Cam Ranh Bay, where the breakdown in order and discipline seemed complete. Only a single brigade of combat-effective Vietnamese marines could be fed in at Xuan Loc to reinforce the battered ARVN 18th Division.

On 21 April 1975 President Thieu resigned, leaving office with bitter words of denunciation for the United States. He was replaced by feeble seventy-one-year-old Vice President Tran Van Huong. After a week, Huong transferred the presidency to Gen. Duong Van ("Big") Minh, the neutralist Buddhist who had helped engineer the overthrow of Ngo Dinh Diem in 1963 and who was now eager to turn over the Saigon government to the North Vietnamese. Xuan Loc fell; the Communists were in the outskirts of Saigon and were playing cat-and-mouse, perfectly able to enter the city whenever they wished.

As so many times before in those waters, the 9th Marine Amphibious Brigade (which had made the original landing at Da Nang ten years before) was standing by in its amphibious ships, waiting for the order to go ashore and take out the Americans. The brigade was commanded by Brig. Gen. Richard E. Carey, a Marine aviator who had cut his combat teeth as a rifle and machine-gun platoon leader in Korea. He had under him Regimental Landing Team 4 (commanded by stocky, hard-talking Col. Alfred M. Gray

Jr.), Provisional Marine Aircraft Group 39, a Brigade Logistical Support Group, and an Amphibious Evacuation Security Force. The last was made up of hastily organized security platoons, which were to preserve some semblance of order and discipline on board the Navy and merchant ships which were carrying off distraught Vietnamese refugees by the tens of thousands.

A five-man advance party from the brigade went ashore at Saigon on 20 April to assist in the evacuation planning and was dismayed by the "business-as-usual" attitude of the American community. Some six thousand Americans, it was thought, were still in the city; no one was sure. The number of potential Vietnamese evacuees was astronomic. Most of the Americans and some of the Vietnamese were evacuated in fixed-wing transports, some chartered, some U.S. Air Force, from Tan Son Nhut airport before Communist rockets and artillery closed down flight operations. On 26 April a platoon from Company C, 9th Marines, was landed at Tan Son Nhut to augment the thinly spread Marine Security Guard from the embassy. Before dawn on Tuesday, 29 April, Communist rockets killed two marines standing guard at the Defense Attaché Office compound at Tan Son Nhut. By Washington time, it was the evening of the twenty-eighth. President Ford convened the National Security Council and at 2245 ordered Operation Frequent Wind, the final evacuation of Saigon, to begin.

Shortly after noon, Saigon time, 29 April, 9th MAB received the order to execute Frequent Wind. An hour and a half later, Dick Carey arrived at the DAO compound at Tan Son Nhut from the amphibious command ship *Blue Ridge* (LCC-19) and opened his command post ashore. Two heavy helicopter squadrons, HMH-462 and HMH-463, began shuttling in the Ground Security Force (GSF). (After Phnom Penh, someone had decided that Ground *Combat* Force was too warlike.) Some 865 marines from BLT 2/4 came into the tennis court landing zone in the DAO compound. In the early evening, three platoons were heli-lifted from there into the city to help out the Marine Security Guard. This brought a total of 171 marines at the embassy.

Meanwhile, the outbound flights of the CH-53s were carrying the evacuees back to the ships. Things went smoothly at the DAO compound. In all, 395 Americans and 4,475 Vietnamese were safely gone by midnight. The last marines to leave set the buildings, once known as "Pentagon East," on fire.

Things went less well at the U.S. embassy. Besieged by a combination of frantic would-be refugees and anticipatory looters, the gates had to be locked and late-arriving Americans lifted over the walls. Helicopters could be landed at two spots: The embassy roof could take the medium CH-46s and the heavy CH-53s could go in, one at a time, at the embassy parking lot. Plans had called for only a hundred Americans to be taken out of the embassy, but the evacuation went on all night and, before it was over, 978 Americans (including some rather strange ones who had come out of the "woodwork") and 1,120 foreign nationals and Vietnamese were evacuated. The Vietnamese mob used a fire truck to bash its way into the embassy. The Marine guards withdrew to the roof, floor by floor. The last CH-46 lifted off at 0753 with the last eleven marines on board. The North Vietnamese were already into the heart of the city, primed for a May Day takeover of South Viet Nam.

Overhead, the Marine helicopters had been covered by U.S. Air Force jets flying from Thailand bases and U.S. Navy jets from offshore carriers. There had been much harassing ground fire, apparently from both the Communists and disgruntled South Vietnamese. Because of the dense civilian population, and with iron discipline, the Americans did not return the fire. There were also a number of reported surface-to-air missiles; but there were no U.S. combat casualties, either in men or aircraft. Two Marine helicopters were lost to operational causes: one, a CH-46 with its pilot and copilot, the other, a UH-1E.

An aftermath to the collapse of the Thieu government was the influx of some 150,000 refugees into the United States. A mixture of the high and the low, the threatened, the desperate, the opportunistic, and the simply frightened, they were staged through three principal areas: Guam, Wake Island, and Clark Air Base in the Philippines. Retired Gen. Leonard Chapman was the director of the Immigration and Naturalization Service. A large share of the processing of the refugees fell to him and he handled it with the same cool efficiency that had marked his years of active Marine Corps service. Temporary camps for the arriving refugees were opened at three military bases—Camp Pendleton, California; Fort Chaffee, Arkansas; and Eglin Air Force Base, Florida—and later a fourth one, at Indiantown Gap, Pennsylvania. The tent camp at Pendleton (immediately and predictably nicknamed "Little Saigon") was closest to the points of arrival and was soon filled to its 18,000-person capacity. Among the temporary guests was the flamboyant and controversial former premier, Air Marshal Nguyen Cao Ky, still wearing his lavender scarf, familiar to thousands of marines who had seen him in his frequent visits to I Corps.

## THE *MAYAGUEZ* INCIDENT

At 1420 on Monday, 12 May 1975, a Cambodian gunboat fired across the bow of the thirty-one-year-old, 10,766-ton container ship SS *Mayaguez,* tramping her way from Hong Kong to Sattahip, Thailand. The *Mayaguez* prudently hove to, a boarding party came over the side brandishing weapons, and the American ship was ordered to follow the Cambodian gunboat at half-speed. The ship was led to an anchorage off Koh Tang, a two-by-three-mile, heavily jungled island thirty-four miles from the Cambodian mainland port of Kampong Som. The thirty-nine-man crew was taken ashore and then, on the fourteenth, moved to Kampong Som. En route, their gunboat was strafed and tear-gassed by American jets. The attacking aircraft were U.S. Air Force F-4s, A-7s, and F-111s sent up from Thai bases to interdict any Cambodian boats moving between Koh Tang and the mainland. The jets sank five gunboats and hit at least two others. The sight of Caucasian faces had saved the gunboat carrying the *Mayaguez* crew from sinking or more serious damage.

The National Security Council had met on Tuesday, 13 May, and President Ford had decided upon a rescue mission. The decision had gone from the president through the secretary of Defense and the Joint Chiefs of Staff to Commander in Chief, Pacific, in Hawaii, and thence for execution to Lt. Gen. John J. Burns, Commander, Seventh Air Force, at his headquarters in Nakhon Phanom air base in Thailand. Marines were to make two assaults: one to board the *Mayaguez,* the other to land on Koh Tang, where the crew was thought still to be. Over the protests of the Thai government, 2d Battalion, 9th Marines, reinforced, was airlifted in Air Force C-141s from Okinawa to Utapao air base in Thailand. Meanwhile, the attack carrier *Coral Sea* (CVA-43), the guided-missile destroyer *Henry B. Wilson* (DDG-7), and four destroyer escorts were steaming into the Gulf of Siam. There were no amphibious assault ships or Marine helicopter squadrons in the vicinity, so helilift for the assault was to be provided by two Thai-based U.S. Air Force squadrons, eight CH-53s from the 21st Special Operations Squadron and eight HH-53 ("Jolly Green Giants") from the 40th Aerospace Rescue and Recovery Squadron. (During the marshaling, one of the CH-53s crashed thirty-seven miles west of Nakhon Phanom and all twenty-one airmen on board were killed.)

The first echelons of marines began arriving at Utapao at 0430 on 14 May. Their leaders made an air reconnaissance of Koh Tang that afternoon and saw nothing to cause them to think there would be any resistance. At midnight, General Burns decided that the raid on the island and the retaking of the *Mayaguez* would be undertaken simultaneously the following morning.

Lift-off from Utapao was made at 0415, Wednesday, 15 May, in six HH-53s and five CH-53s. The first part of the operation went well. Three HH-53s delivered sixty-nine marines from Company D, 1st Battalion, 4th Marines, to the destroyer escort *Harold E. Holt* (DE-1074) at 0550. The *Holt* came alongside the *Mayaguez* at 0830, the marines went over the rail, found the ship deserted, and ran the U.S. flag up over the fantail, Iwo Jima style. At this time, the *Mayaguez* crew was in fact being returned in a captured Thai fishing boat. This fishing boat was intercepted by the *Wilson* at 0945, the *Mayaguez* crew taken safely on board; and the Thai fishermen, also rescued, were separated from their Cambodian guards and allowed to head for home. Meanwhile, Navy A-6s and A-7s from the *Coral Sea* were pounding Ream airfield outside of Kampong Som.

The raid on Koh Tang was also under way. At 0600, under cover of U.S. Air Force fighter-bombers, the 210-man raiding force—Company G, 2d Battalion, 9th Marines—under Lt. Col. Randall W. Austin began to land and immediately ran into devastating ground fire. Heavy counterfires were brought to bear on the island and included the dropping of a 15,000-pound bomb—the kind that had been used to blow away jungle canopy in the Viet Nam War. The marines were divided between two landing zones and their position was precarious until their eventual evacuation the night of 16 May. By then the crew of the *Mayaguez* had her under way again and was headed for Singapore.

Of the fifteen U.S. Air Force helicopters employed, three had been shot down, ten others had received battle damage, and only two had escaped unscathed. Personnel casualties were also proportionately high: eleven marines, two sailors, and two airmen killed; three marines missing in action; and forty-one marines, two sailors, and seven airmen wounded.

# 19

## 1975-1989

## As Tough and Ready As Marines Have Ever Been

### Wilson Becomes Commandant

Morale of America's citizenry, battered by Viet Nam, would get a boost in 1976 with the celebration of the nation's bicentennial. Before then, on 10 November 1975, the Marine Corps would celebrate its own 200th birthday. A new commandant would ride the rising tide of national good feeling.

On 30 April 1975, the same day that the North Vietnamese marched into Saigon, President Ford announced the nomination of Lt. Gen. Louis Hugh Wilson, Commanding General, Fleet Marine Force, Pacific, to be the next commandant of the Marine Corps. General Cushman, harried by the problems of rebuilding the Corps and severely criticized for certain of his personnel policies, had elected to retire, six months early, on 1 July. As a captain, Wilson had been a company commander in Cushman's battalion during Bougainville and Guam, including the notable fight at Fonte that earned him the Medal of Honor.

Wilson was born in Brandon, Mississippi, in 1920 and had gone to Millsaps College. As a brigadier general, Wilson had been the legislative assistant to the then-commandant, General Chapman. He knew the workings of the legislative process. His courtly southern ways meshed with the manners and interests of the southern senators and congressmen who dominated the major defense-related committees.

### Rebuilding the Corps

One of Wilson's first actions was to appoint the "Haynes Board," named for its senior member, Maj. Gen. Fred E. Haynes Jr., to recommend answers to the big questions as to what should be the size, organization, and role of the Marine Corps in the future. During the Viet Nam conflict, the Marine Corps, with the pressure of the draft, filled its ranks in numbers but not always in quality. Strength reached a peak of 317,400. Throughout the early 1970s the Corps grappled with problems of drug abuse, drinking, racism, and unauthorized absence.

Wilson brought his long-time friend, Maj. Gen. Robert H. Barrow, up from Parris Island to be his deputy chief of staff for manpower, with a promotion to lieutenant general. The two men were in many ways very much alike. Both were big men, impressive physically, with courtly manners and a leadership style that was rooted in the landed aristocracy of the Old South. Both were convinced that the Corps was not getting the quality recruits it should. One of the first Wilson-Barrow actions was to bring recruiting under command of the recruit depot commanders, all recruiting east of the Mississippi under Commanding General, Parris Island, all west of the Mississippi under Commanding General, San Diego. For the next twenty years the Marine Corps would argue for a strength of about 204,000 and settle for a manning level of about 196,000.

Manpower plans were almost disrailed by two of the worst cases of recruit abuse since the Ribbon Creek tragedy of 1956. A recruit, possibly mentally deficient, died of injuries received in "pugil stick" exercises at San Diego. Another recruit was shot through the hand by a posturing drill instructor on the rifle range at Parris Island. The cases caused special hearings to be held by the House of Representatives' Subcommittee of Military Personnel. Impressive testimony by Wilson and Barrow saved the Marine Corps' traditional "boot camp," but both knew that more reforms and closer supervision were needed.

As CG, FMFPac, Wilson had seen larger possibilities for the "sleepy little artillery base" at Twentynine Palms. That vast tract of desert north of the oasis-hamlet of Twentynine Palms had been an Army training center during World War II. In the summer of 1952 it became a Marine Corps Training Center, more than a half-million acres ("Rhode Island squeezed dry"), owned and operated by Camp Pendleton, mostly for use as an artillery range. At first an expanse of unused emptiness except for live-fire exercises, it grew into and increasingly became an all-purpose training site, becoming an independent command, Marine Corps Base, Twentynine Palms, in 1957, with a brigadier general in charge.

Wilson had argued that infantry battalions should be passed through Twentynine Palms as they prepared for "transplacement" to the Western Pacific. On becoming commandant, he was determined to enlarge Twentynine Palms' mission to include training of all tactical units in the Marine Corps. Key to this expanded mission was the construction in 1976 of an expeditionary airfield with an adequate eight-thousand-foot runway.

On a projected schedule of ten per year, battalion landing teams, with supporting arms and air, would go to Twentynine Palms for Combined Arms Exercises (CAX). Headquarters of Marine amphibious units (MAUs) and brigades (MABs) would also be exercised. Doing a CAX at Twentynine Palms became "a Marine Corps-wide badge of honor." In 1979 Wilson redesignated the base as Marine Corps Air Ground Combat Center. By then he was extolling Twentynine Palms as "the best training area in the United States."

Wilson, who had strong ideas about uniforms, disliked the lightweight poplin jacket (all services had a similar jacket) which was much worn by Washington commuters, usually unzipped and hanging open. He directed that a substitute be found that could not be unzipped. The substitute turned out to be the off-the-shelf adoption of the British "woolly-pully" sweater with its distinctive cloth elbow and shoulder patches. Wilson made the purchase of the sweater "optional" (which translates roughly into "or else"). Wear of the sweater soon became universal and it was immensely popular. The Army, Navy, Air Force, and Coast Guard soon followed with their own sweaters in various colors.

The Marine Corps did not have a satisfactory raincoat and the stiff old-fashioned overcoat was seldom worn except in the coldest of climates. The Corps' uniform experts at Albany developed an "all-weather coat," its pattern a simplification of the British officer's trenchcoat of World War I. The coat proved a great success and was copied quickly by the Air Force and the Army.

Wilson moved Barrow to command of Fleet Marine Force, Atlantic, and II Marine Amphibious Force in 1976. A NATO mission was essential to get the dollars needed for force modernization. The Marine Corps concentrated on a reinforcing mission on NATO's northern flank—Norway and Denmark's Jutland peninsula. A 4th Marine Amphibious Brigade was created, under command of Al Gray, now a brigadier general. The 4th MAB deployed regularly for NATO exercises in Norway and northern Germany.

The Marine Corps had always viewed skeptically the Army's Reforger exercises that flew Army reinforcements across the Atlantic to marry up with prepositioned equipment and supplies at Kaiserlautern. Now they would do something of the same on a smaller scale. The winter exercises led to the prepositioning of a brigade's worth of supplies and equipment "in the rock" in Norway. Other NATO exercises were being conducted in the Mediterranean, particularly the Eastern Mediterranean.

In 1978 Wilson brought Barrow back to Headquarters, with a fourth star, to be his assistant commandant. It was about this time that Wilson, deftly using his political connections, achieved full membership on the JCS for the commandant of the Marine Corps.

## BARROW AS COMMANDANT

President Jimmy Carter, after a personal interview, chose Barrow to be the twenty-seventh commandant. The change of command came on Friday evening, 29 June 1979, at the traditional parade at Marine Barracks, Washington. By then more stringent recruiting standards and more demanding training had improved quality immensely, but the Carter years were lean ones for the military services. Personnel costs left little money for force modernization. During his first week as commandant, Barrow announced that he was willing to accept a decrease in end-strength in fiscal year 1980 from 189,000 to 179,000 in order to obtain funds to maintain combat readiness.

Among his initiatives to improve recruiting and reenlistment, Barrow gave his field commanders enlistment authority to grant substantial reenlistment bonuses. In certain occupational fields, a reenlistment bonus could be as much as fifteen to twenty thousand dollars.

Tragedy struck early in Barrow's tenure. On 19 October 1979 a typhoon caused a terrible fire at Camp Fuji, Japan. Thirteen marines of the 2d Battalion, 4th Marines, died of the burns they received.

Under pressure to increase the number of women marines, Barrow reported early in 1980 that women marines were then serving in 90 percent of all Marine occupational fields. He set a goal of ten thousand women marines, but remained staunchly opposed to the assignment of women to the combat arms.

Barrow was equally unflinching in his attitude toward drugs, launching a concentrated campaign to eliminate their use by marines, all of whom now became subject to random urinalysis testing. Detected drug use went down drastically.

## New Amphibious Ships

The chronic shortage of amphibious shipping continued. As General Shoup was wont to say, the Corps had "more fight than ferry." The introduction of "helicopter carriers," typified by the *Tarawa* class, first commissioned in 1976, as the primary amphibious ships, had revolutionized landing operations. But there could never be enough of these increasingly costly ships. The Marine Corps was faced with bloc obsolescence of amphibious ships in ten years' time. In his appearances before Congressional committees, Barrow hammered at his concern over the slowness with which obsolescent amphibious shipping was being replaced. The total of sixty-seven amphibious ships then in commission fell far short of the goal to lift one MAF and one MAB simultaneously. The Navy was reluctant to spend "blue" dollars for new amphibious ships. Barrow set about cultivating better relations with the Navy aimed at easing this reluctance. A consummate speaker, he preached to a wide range of audiences on the importance of a maritime strategy combining control of the sea and power projection (with amphibious forces as the "tip of the spear").

## Maritime Prepositioning

The Norwegian experience had won the Marines over to a somewhat begrudging acceptance of geographic prepositioning of stocks of equipment and supplies. Carter's brilliant secretary of Defense, Harold Brown, had moved the concept of prepositioning a step further by resurrecting the old notion of depot ships. In one of his few personal interchanges with Barrow, he asked the rhetorical question: "Do Marines always have to storm ashore?"

Barrow answered that amphibious assaults were just a means to an end and that marines did most of their fighting after getting ashore, by whatever means. Brown advanced the idea of ships being preloaded with necessary supplies and equipment to meet with marines at a safe port, where they could be unloaded. What evolved was an emphasis on the creation of Marine amphibious brigades that could "marry up" with the prepositioned ships at some safe port close to the projected area of operations. First step was "Near-Term Prepositioning Ships," an improvisation with readily available commercial cargo ships. The prototype brigade took shape as the 7th Marine Amphibious Brigade with headquarters at Twentynine Palms, California.

## GUARDING THE EMBASSIES

In the terrorist-ridden world of the late twentieth century, minuscule squads of marines assigned to "embassy duty" were frequently the front-line protection for the American diplomatic community abroad. Terrorists killed S.Sgt. Charles W. Turbeville in an attack against the U.S. embassy in Phnom Penh, Cambodia, on 25 September 1971. In March 1973 the Marines held the U.S. embassy at Khartoum after the ambassador and chargé d'affaires were abducted and murdered by Palestinian terrorists. When the Turks invaded Cyprus in the summer of 1974, the sixteen-man Marine security guard defended the embassy in downtown Nicosia. On 19 August hundreds of Greek Cypriots broke into the embassy grounds. Rounds from an AK-47 assault rifle mortally wounded a woman secretary and the American ambassador. On 21 November 1979, M.Sgt. Loyd G. Miller and his detachment, forbidden to use "deadly force," held off with tear gas an attack against the U.S. embassy in Islamabad, Pakistan. The embassy was set on fire. The 137 civilians took refuge in a third-floor vault. The heat of the flames forced them out. Miller led them to the roof. Cpl. Steven J. Crowley was killed manning his rooftop post. Miller carried his body out of the burning building. At noon on 30 October 1979, in San Salvador, two hundred leftists invaded the embassy. Two marines were wounded, but the crowd was held off with tear gas and by the marines firing over their heads until government forces could arrive and expel them.

On 14 February 1979, demonstrators attacked the U.S. embassy in Teheran, Iran, and abducted several marines. One sick marine was held for a week before being released. A worse attack against the embassy came on Sunday morning, 4 November 1979. Thirteen marines were among the sixty-five Americans taken hostage. Five off-duty marines were captured in their apartment house. The eight on-duty marines fought with tear gas. Four black marines and nine other Americans were released two weeks later. The other nine marines were among the fifty Americans who continued to be held under abominable conditions. The Iranian hostage crisis caused the bombing of the U.S. embassy in Bangkok, an attack against the embassy in Libya, and lesser violence around the world.

President Carter directed the Joint Chiefs of Staff to find a way to get the hostages out of Iran. The ill-fated effort to rescue the hostages had the brave name "Operation Eagle Claw" but is best known as "Desert One" for the desolate landing site two hundred miles from Teheran where everything went wrong. Marine fliers, headed by Col. Charles H. Pitman, were to fly eight long-range Navy RH-53 helicopters from the deck of the nuclear aircraft carrier USS *Nimitz* to Desert One, where they were to rendezvous with ninety-plus members of the Army's Delta Force coming in on C-130s being flown from an Egyptian airfield. Three of the helicopters developed engine trouble and had to turn back to the *Nimitz*. Only five reached Desert One. Six helicopters was the minimum required. The mission was aborted, but in refueling at Desert One another helicopter crashed into a C-130 and both aircraft burned. Three marines and five airmen were killed. Five more men were wounded, including two Marine majors who were badly burned. The hostages, including the nine marines, were finally released on 20 January 1981, the day of Ronald Reagan's inauguration, having endured 444 days of captivity.

## RAPID DEPLOYMENT FORCE

The debacle in Iran created a national imperative for a "rapid deployment" force to deal with such situations. The question: How could military force best be projected into the Middle East? In December 1979, Secretary of Defense Harold Brown announced that the new "Rapid Deployment Joint Task Force" would be headed by a Marine general. The appointment and a promotion to lieutenant general went to Paul X. ("P.X.") Kelley, a fast-riser in the Marine Corps, who had commanded both a battalion and a regiment in Viet Nam. Kelley activated the Rapid Deployment Joint Task Force (RDJTF or simply RDF) on 1 March 1980, with headquarters at McDill Air Force Base, Tampa, Florida. The all-service RDJTF was pointed primarily in the direction of the Middle East ("from Marrakesh to Bangladesh"), but when the boundaries were drawn, Israel and Lebanon were, for political reasons, excluded. At McDill, Kelley would be left for a considerable period with a skeleton staff and an empty headquarters.

There was, however, an immediately perceptible relationship between maritime prepositioning, the 7th Marine Amphibious Brigade, and the new rapid deployment force. In April 1982 some ten thousand marines and sailors from the 7th Marine Amphibious Brigade took part in Gallant Eagle '82 at Twentynine Palms, an exercise that involved an additional fifteen thousand members of the other services. The Gallant Eagle exercises became annual affairs and turned into veritable rehearsals for Desert Storm.

But by early 1981 the press was reporting a split among the Joint Chiefs of Staff over the Rapid Deployment Force. There was feuding, it was said, between the operational commander, Lieutenant General Kelley, and the theater commander, Army Gen. Volney F. Warner, commander of the Readiness Command. It became obvious that command arrangements would be changed. After much debate, some of it acrimonious, President Reagan in December 1982 announced the activation of the U.S. Central Command, the expected outgrowth of the RDJTF and the command that would fight the Persian Gulf War. Assignment as CinCCentCom would alternate between Army and Marine Corps generals.

## Looking Like a Marine

In August 1981 General Barrow stood before his generals at the opening of the year's General Officers Symposium (which brought in three-quarters of the general officers in the Corps from all parts of the world) and in his opening remarks asked: "Do I look like a Marine Corps general?"

Most present would have said that he looked the epitome of a Marine Corps general, but his question was rhetorical. He was referring to the short-sleeve khaki shirt he was wearing and compared it to a sport shirt. At that point he announced his "Let's dress up, not down" uniform policy. Later he stated his objectives as "Uniformity, quality, and availability." He decreed that the green service uniform would be the uniform of the day, short sleeve shirts were suitable for summer office wear but not for liberty, and wear of the woolly-pully would be limited to working hours. He emphasized the wearing of the dress blue uniform by those that had it and encouraged the wearing of both the green and blue uniforms after working hours. He disliked the wearing of slacks by women marines. The windbreaker, abhorred by Wilson and which no one was wearing, was officially terminated in 1982.

In his 1982 "posture" statement, Barrow reported to the Congress, "My personal observations of your marines convince me that they are as tough and ready as United States Marines have ever been."

## A New Commander in Chief

Ronald Reagan's election in November 1980 brought with it a growing optimism among the service chiefs. Not only were the services going to be better funded, but they now would have a commander in chief "with firm convictions about a strong America." Early on, the new secretary of the Navy, John Lehman, and Barrow had long, wide-ranging talks, with emphasis on the Marine Corps' contribution to a maritime strategy. Barrow was delighted with Secretary Lehman's decision to bring two battleships, with their 16-inch guns, out of mothballs, and that Lehman's shipbuilding program included new amphibs.

Both Wilson and Barrow had pushed for the procurement of the F/A-18 as the replacement for the aging McDonnell F-4 Phantoms of the Viet Nam era. The first Marine Corps F/A-18 "Hornet" rolled off the line at the Northrup plant on 13 January 1982 in Hawthorne, California. Eventually there would be twelve squadrons of F/A-18s.

By the first half of 1983 the Marine Corps was benefiting increasingly from the Reagan Administration's investment in new and improved weapons and equipment. In February the Marines began receiving the lightweight M198 155-mm artillery piece, which would replace both the self-propelled M109 155-mm gun and the venerable 105-mm howitzer (the 105s were providentially stored away for possible future use).

## PRELUDE TO LEBANON

Modern-day deployment of Marines to the Mediterranean had begun in 1948, when the 8th Marines (then at single battalion strength) sailed as part of a Sixth Fleet response, on orders of President Truman, to emerging crises in Greece and Turkey. The presence of a Marine battalion landing team in the Mediterranean became more or less continuous, with battalions rotating at six-month intervals. The BLTs, with an aviation element added, became Marine Amphibious Units or MAUs, the smallest-sized Marine air-ground task force or "MAGTF."

Since the Viet Nam War the I Marine Amphibious Force had been headquartered at Camp Pendleton, the II MAF at Camp Lejeune, and the III MAF on Okinawa. Several expeditionary brigade headquarters existed now, at least in cadre status. The numbered Marine amphibious units (MAUs) had become standing headquarters that would pick up their subordinate units, train, deploy, return, and repeat the process in order to deploy again.

By the 1980s the 8th Marine regiment was providing all the battalions for the MAUs deploying to the Mediterranean. The battalion landing team or

"BLT" configuration meant that the basic infantry battalion was reinforced with armor, artillery, reconnaissance, amphibious assault vehicles, and combat engineer detachments taken from the parent 2d Marine Division. Similarly, the aviation element of the MAU, usually a composite helicopter squadron, came from the 2d Marine Aircraft Wing and the logistic support element from the 2d Force Service Support Group.

The 32d (later renumbered the 22d) and 24th MAUs handled the Mediterranean deployments on a one-on, one-off basis. The MAUs deployed in an amphibious squadron or PhibRon. A PhibRon with a MAU embarked became an Amphibious Ready Group or ARG. As the amphibious task force of the Sixth Fleet, its designation was Task Force 61.

In June 1982, the Israeli Defense Force (IDF) invaded Lebanon. On 23 June, the 32d MAU, which had been standing offshore, successfully evacuated from the port city of Juniyah those U.S. citizens who wanted to leave Lebanon. On 2 July the Israelis put in place a military blockade of Beirut. One consequence was to force a concentration of Yasser Arafat's Palestinian Liberation Organization, better known as the "PLO," and their Syrian supporters in Beirut. The beleaguered Lebanese government, barely functioning outside of Beirut and controlling no more than half the city itself, asked for help.

The 32d MAU, under Col. James M. Mead, went into Beirut on 25 August 1982 to supervise, along with French and Italian contingents, the evacuation of the PLO. By 9 September some fifteen thousand PLO and their supporters, still armed and still defiant, were evacuated. Mission completed, the 32d MAU reembarked and rejoined the Sixth Fleet.

Then came the assassination of Lebanese president-elect Bashir Gemayel on 14 September and the massacre by rogue Israeli elements of Palestinian and Lebanese refugees a few days later in the Sabra and Shatila refugee camps. The Lebanese government asked for a multinational force to help restore order.

The 32d MAU landed on 29 September as part of the Multi-National Force (MNF), composed of American, French, Italian, and—somewhat later— British forces. The MNF mission was vaguely stated as being to assist the Lebanese government in establishing sovereignty and authority over the Beirut area.

The Marines took up positions on the Beirut International Airport, a commercial airport. The Marines did not control its flight operations or security, but they were responsible, of course, for their own defense. Efforts to clear the many thousand pieces of unexploded ordnance strewn around their zone caused the first Marine casualties.

The Marines began motorized patrols in east Beirut to give a clear demonstration of their "presence." They also began an informal training program for the Lebanese Armed Forces (LAF). On 1 November a three-hundred-pound car bomb, a portent of things to come, exploded on a main road close to the beach across which marines unloaded their supplies.

On 3 November the 24th MAU replaced the 32d MAU. Training of an LAF rapid-reaction force began on 21 December. In late December the Marines were ordered to limit their own patrolling to a radius not much beyond the boundaries of the airport itself. The troops were given cards outlining the "ROE" or "rules of engagement." The rules were ambiguous and poorly understood. They boiled down to an understanding by the marines that they could not shoot except in self-defense and that they could not even chamber a round in their weapons unless they were fired upon and had a clear target.

In January 1983, Israeli patrolling south of the airport caused increasing friction with the Marines. On 2 February, Marine Capt. Charles B. Johnson created an international incident (and admiration on the part of most Americans) by drawing his pistol while blocking an attempt by three Israeli tanks to push through his checkpoint near the Beirut University Library.

During February "presence" assumed a humanitarian face when Marines took a major part in rescue operations during a severe blizzard in the mountains east of Beirut. Along with French and Italian units they operated beyond the lines staked out by the Syrian forces, rescuing Christians and Moslems alike.

On 15 February the 22d MAU (the renumbered 32d MAU) relieved the 24th MAU. On 16 March a terrorist grenade slightly wounded five marines on patrol in south Beirut. On 18 April a pickup truck packed with explosives destroyed the U.S. embassy. Seventeen of the sixty-three fatalities were Americans, one of them a marine. The pro-Iranian terrorist group Islamic Jihad claimed credit for the bombing.

At the end of May the 24th MAU, commanded by Col. Timothy J. Geraghty, again relieved the 22d MAU. Lt. Col. Howard L. Gerlach commanded BLT 1/8, the battalion landing team with the 24th MAU. Combined Lebanese and Marine patrols began on 25 June. Rocket and mortar attacks, targeted against LAF positions at the airport, dropped some rounds onto Marine Corps positions. On 22 July, a shelling of the airport by Druze artillery shut down flight operations and wounded three marines. As the hot summer days slowly passed, intermittent shelling continued, killing two more marines and wounding another.

The marines hardened their positions with more sandbags, more barbed wire, more digging. During August the rocket attacks against the Lebanese increased, with more spillover into Marine Corps positions. Lieutenant Colonel Gerlach, with Colonel Geraghty's approval, decided to reduce exposure to this random fire by concentrating his headquarters and service support personnel in his four-story headquarters building. A year earlier the building had survived a furious shelling by the Israelis. It was gauged to be strong enough to offer protection from anything but direct rocket or artillery fire.

## KELLEY BECOMES COMMANDANT

On 24 March 1983, President Reagan announced the nomination of P.X. Kelley as Barrow's successor. Kelley, having left the Rapid Deployment Force, was now the assistant commandant and chief of staff with four stars. The turnover was held on a beautiful Sunday evening at Marine Barracks, Washington. President Reagan attended. On Barrow's last day as commandant, 30 June 1983, the strength of the armed forces was 2,223,400, of whom 193,993 were Marines.

Early in his tenure, exuberant, Boston-born P.X. Kelley announced that he wished to have a minimum of change in uniforms and uniform regulations while he was commandant. But he did want all-season fabrics developed so there could be an all-season service uniform, an all-season blue dress uniform, and an all-season evening dress uniform for officers. The "mess dress" or white dinner jacket for officers went out and so too, in time, did the white summer uniform. It was soon noticed, however, that Kelley often wore the "woolly-pully" sweater in circumstances where General Barrow would have worn the service coat. Restrictions on the wearing of slacks by women marines were relaxed. Lessened formality in uniform wear rippled down through the Corps.

## LEBANON DISASTER

Late in August the fighting between the Lebanese government forces and the Amal militia in West Beirut intensified. More fire fell on the airport, some of it obviously targeting the Marines. The Americans began to shoot back with Marine guns ashore and Navy guns afloat. Two more marines were killed and two more wounded by a shelling on 4 September. That same day the Israeli Defense Forces withdrew to the Awali River, opening the way to increasing factional fighting—largely Moslems versus Christians—in the hills above Beirut.

The artillery and mortar attacks against the Marine positions were now more or less constant. The arrival on station on 26 September of the battleship *New Jersey* with its 16-inch guns was credited with bringing about a cease-fire. By some accounts it was the 179th cease-fire since 1975. The cease-fire did not stop the sniping at marines which had become a daily occurrence. On 19 October a car bomb interrupted a Marine supply convoy on its way to the temporary U.S. embassy, about twelve kilometers from the airport.

At daybreak on Sunday morning, 23 October, a yellow five-ton Mercedes stake-bed truck roared into the parking lot adjacent to the headquarters building, circled the lot at high speed, and then crashed through a barbed-wire barrier. The truck then moved past two sentry posts, went through a gate in an iron fence, hurdled over an obstacle made of sewer pipe, plowed through a sandbag barrier, and crashed through a four-foot-wide door into the lobby of the building, whereupon the cargo, estimated to be the equivalent of six tons of TNT, detonated.

Two hundred and thirty-nine occupants of the building were killed immediately; three were U.S. Army, eighteen were U.S. Navy, and 218 were U.S. Marines. More than a hundred more were wounded. Of these, three would die. Lieutenant Colonel Gerlach, commander of BLT 1/8, was among those severely wounded. For the wounded, definitive medical care in U.S. hospitals in Germany was four hours away by air. The British immediately made available their military hospital in Cyprus. Air evacuation to both Cyprus and Germany was done by U.S. and Royal Air Force aircraft. Medical assistance offered by France was considered unnecessary. Medical aid extended by the Israelis was refused.

At almost exactly the same time as the attack on the Marine headquarters, a smaller vehicle approached the eight-story apartment building north of the airport that housed the French contingent. It took a sharp turn into the driveway, rammed its way into the underground garage, and exploded. Fifty-eight French soldiers died.

Replacements, including a fresh rifle company, began arriving the next day. The 22d MAU, routinely scheduled to arrive at Beirut about 10 November to relieve the 24th MAU, arrived a week late, on 17 November, because of a diversion to Grenada. Lebanese dissidents greeted the relief with small arms fire.

On 2 November Secretary of Defense Casper Weinberger announced the appointment of a commission "to inquire into the facts and circumstances surrounding the terrorist attack." Headed by recently retired Adm. Robert L. J. Long, the commission began its work on 7 November. On 20 December the Long Commission reported its findings, concluding that the attack "was tantamount to an act of war using the medium of terrorism." The commission did not find the security measures in effect in the MAU compound commensurate with the increasing level of the threat. The commission blamed the BLT commander for concentrating 350 persons in his headquarters building, a blame to be shared by the MAU commander who had condoned the concentration. But there was more blame, to be shared by others. The MAU had been faced with the "unique and difficult task of maintaining a peaceful presence in an increasingly hostile environment" and "the 'presence' mission was not interpreted the same by all levels of the chain of command." The chain of command that wound its way back to the U.S. Commander in Chief, Europe, was top-heavy and tortuous.

While the pros and cons of their "presence" continued to be debated at the highest national level, marines in Lebanon continued to die and be wounded, fortunately in small numbers, until they were pulled out entirely in late February 1984. The whole affair caused bitter recriminations and a reexamination of so-called "peace-keeping" missions.

## Grenada Excursion

On 25 October 1983, President Ronald Reagan announced to the American public that forces from six Caribbean nations and the United States had landed on the island of Grenada to "restore order and democracy" and to ensure the safety of approximately a thousand Americans on the island. Grenada, a member of the British Commonwealth, was the southernmost of the Windward Islands in the Caribbean Sea, 133 square miles in size, and with an estimated population of 111,000, mostly black. Prime Minister Maurice Bishop had been killed on 19 October. Since then the army chief, Gen. Hudson Austin, known to have close ties to the Soviet Union, had been in charge. There were reports of riots and looting.

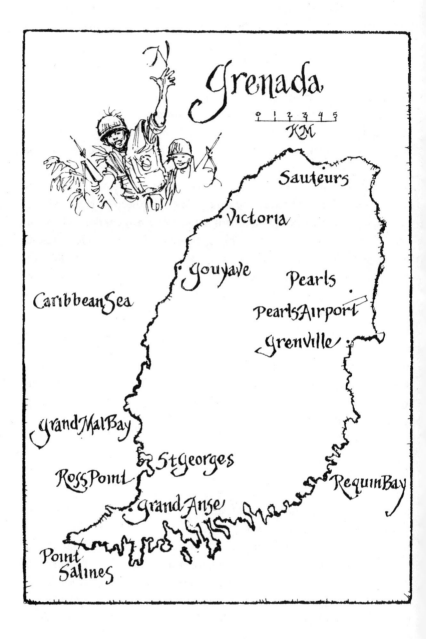

Grenada

Sauteurs

Victoria

Gouyave

Pearls

PearlsAirport

Grenville

Caribbean Sea

Grand Mal Bay

St Georges

Ross Point

Requin Bay

Grand Anse

Point Salines

The 22d Marine Amphibious Unit under Col. James P. Faulkner had embarked at Morehead City, North Carolina, on 17 October in Amphibious Squadron 4. The 2d Battalion, 8th Marines, core of the battalion landing team, had just been reorganized. Commanded by Lt. Col. Ray L. Smith, it was now smaller (forty-three officers and 779 enlisted) but more mobile and somewhat more heavily armed than the thousand-man battalions of the past. Rifle platoons which previously had forty-five men now had thirty-six, organized into three eleven-man squads, each with two five-man fire teams.

Phibron 4, which had five amphibious ships, including the amphibious assault ship *Guam,* sailed the next day. The 22d MAU's original destination was Lebanon, to relieve 24th MAU, with an amphibious exercise in Spain on the way. Toward midnight on 20 October, the Phibron commander received orders to change course to the south and take station five hundred miles northeast of Grenada. Faulkner supposed that an NEO—noncombatant evacuation operation—of American citizens was in the offing. Best information available indicated that the Grenadian People's Revolutionary Army (PRA) numbered about twelve hundred, supported by a militia of some two to five thousand and about three to four hundred police. About six hundred armed Cuban construction workers were reported on the island. Faulkner learned that the U.S. Army would make an airborne assault and assumed that the MAU would be in reserve. Not until late on 23 October did he find out that the Marines would have the task of seizing Pearls and the port of Grenville while the Army moved to capture the nearly completed jet airfield on the southern end of the island.

Vice Adm. Joseph Metcalf III, Commander, Second Fleet, and Commander, Joint Task Force 124, designated 25 October as D-day. Faulkner's 22d MAU was to make a combined air and surface assault in the Pearls-Grenville area. Two rifle companies, heli-lifted by the MAU's aviation element, HMM-261 under Lt. Col. Granville R. ("Granny") Amos, was to seize Pearls Airport and Grenville, to be followed by a daylight surface landing if a suitable beach could be found. At 0315 "Granny" Amos's first helicopters took off in radio silence from the *Guam.* Rain squalls delayed the landing at LZ Buzzard just south of Pearls. A sputtering of 12.7-mm antiaircraft fire came from the airfield. The Cobras silenced them with 20-mm cannon fire and 2.75-inch rockets.

An hour after the landing at LZ Buzzard, Company F landed on a soccer field ("LZ Oriole") in the Grenville area against no opposition and quickly seized the town. Most of the local populace greeted the marines as liberators.

U.S. Army Rangers, landing in the Salines area, had a harder time, taking heavy antiaircraft fire on the way in and, once on the ground, encountering considerable resistance from the Cubans. Nevertheless, they took the airfield and then proceeded to evacuate the bemused American students at St. George's University Medical School. A special force sent to rescue the governor general, Sir Paul Scoon, a vestige of British colonialism, reached his mansion but was immediately besieged by elements of the Grenadian army. Admiral Metcalf directed the amphibious task force to break the siege and rescue Scoon and also to send a flight of Cobras south to Salines to help the Rangers. Command and control was bad. Two Cobras were lost.

Ray Smith, ashore with two rifle companies at Pearls and Grenville, had only intermittent radio contact with the *Guam* and learned almost inadvertently that his Company G was being committed to a landing across Grand Mal beach to rescue Scoon. Hastening out to the *Guam* he succeeded in delaying the landing. Company G had spent most of the day afloat in amphibian tractors awaiting assignment to a beach. A heli-lift was considered, then canceled, and Company G was now told that it would land at Gouyave, about four kilometers south of Victoria, and well north of Grand Mal. This too was canceled and it was decided to land the company at a small fuel farm in Grand Mal Bay. The first amphibian tractors left the tank landing ship *Manitowoc* at 1830 and ground ashore against no opposition a half-hour later. Company G moved south and occupied a race track north of St. George's without incident.

By dawn Company F was also on the road south. Company F started up the mountain track that led to the governor general's mansion, dropping a squad off to outpost the late prime minister's vacant house. They found Sir Paul Scoon, his wife, and nine other civilians in the mansion and evacuated them to the *Guam*.

Smith then turned his attention to Fort Frederick, the crumbling eighteenth-century fort that dominated St. George's harbor. The defenders, perhaps a company in all, had decamped, leaving behind their uniforms and quantities of Soviet-made weapons.

"Granny" Amos's helicopters meanwhile were sent off to support an Army Ranger evacuation of American students at Grand Anse. The operation got underway at 1600 and the landing was made against scattered small arms and automatic weapon fire. One helicopter was lost when its rotor brushed a palm tree; another was damaged. Close to two hundred civilians were evacuated.

Company E was still at Pearls, holding the airfield. Reconnaissance patrols went out, responding to exaggerated reports of enemy forces from friendly but excited Grenadians. Some resistance from Cubans materialized near Mirabeau Hospital but was promptly squashed.

On D plus 2, Companies F and G moved against Richmond Hill Prison, Fort Adolphus, and Fort Lucas. Embarrassment was avoided when at the last moment it was discovered that "Fort Adolphus" was actually the Venezuelan embassy. With all the forts and dominating terrain in hand, Company F now marched into St. George's itself.

Meanwhile, a brigade of the Army's 82d Airborne Division was bogged down, more because of air traffic conditions at the uncompleted airfield than by Cuban resistance. Admiral Metcalf adjusted the boundary that separated the Army and Marine zones of action, moving it south to a line joining Requin Bay and Ross Point.

The Marines were given the objective of securing Ross Point Hotel where a reported four hundred Canadian, British, and American citizens were awaiting evacuation. Company F reached the seaside hotel about nightfall and found fewer than two dozen foreigners, mostly Canadians, notably unanxious to be evacuated. Next morning lead elements of the 82d Airborne, who had not been told of the boundary change, reached the hotel and were surprised to find the Marines present.

On D plus 4, in the north, Company E moved into Sauteurs. The only two towns of consequence not in American hands were Gouyave and Victoria on the northwest coast. Company F stayed in the St. George's area and Company G mounted amphibian tractors, rattled up the coast road, and entered the two towns without incident. In four days ashore the Marines had taken seven-eighths of the island.

On 31 October the scattered parts of the MAU were pulled together and reembarked in their shipping. There were reports of mysterious goings-on, possibly even the presence of North Korean soldiers, on Carriacou, a small island to the north of Grenada. On 1 November, hard-working BLT 2/8 landed on Carriacou, Company F going in by helicopter to Lauriston Point airstrip and Company G landing by tractor at Tyrrel Bay. The civilian populace gave them a delirious welcome; the platoon-sized PRA militia surrendered gladly. Next day the marines went back to their ships and 22d MAU resumed its voyage to Lebanon. For the Marines, Grenada hadn't been much more than a good training exercise with a smidgen of resistance to provide a bit of excitement.

## GOLDWATER-NICHOLS ACT

Latent discontent with the direction of the Viet Nam War caused many studies and examinations of the organization of the Department of Defense. Conclusions and recommendations gelled in the Defense Reorganization Act of 1986, commonly called the "Goldwater-Nichols Bill," for its Senate and House sponsors, the venerable Senator Barry Goldwater, Republican of Arizona (and himself a retired major general in the Air Force Reserve), and Congressman William F. Nichols, Democrat from Alabama (a wounded and decorated Army captain in World War II). It was the first significant statutory reform since the Reorganization Act of 1958.

As approved by the Ninety-ninth Congress and signed by President Reagan, the Goldwater-Nichols Act strengthened the authority of the chairman of the Joint Chiefs, the Joint Staff, and the unified commanders (that is, the theater commanders). The chairman became the "principal military advisor" to the president. The chiefs of service as members of the JCS were relegated to the status of advisors in operational matters. The service chiefs were to concentrate on the organization, training, and equipping of their individual services, and even these were subject to program surveillance by the chairman. This was not altogether a new role for the commandant of the Marine Corps. It was almost exactly the position he had held, sometimes chafingly, under the chief of naval operations prior to 1958. A not immediately perceived benefit was that Marine forces assigned to unified commands slipped out from Navy fleet control and became full-fledged "components."

## A ROUGH NEW COMMANDANT

On 1 July 1987, Gen. Alfred M. Gray, a tobacco-chewing, ex-enlisted man from New Jersey, took Kelley's place as commandant. The new commandant, always known as "Al Gray," had been outspoken in what he considered the softening of the Corps. Impatient, blessed with apparent total recall of everything that ever happened, stocky in build, and given to wearing his camouflage utility uniform on all appropriate, and sometimes inappropriate, occasions, he worked to restore the "warrior" image of the Marines.

Uniform wear became markedly less formal under General Gray. Camouflage utilities became the de facto uniform of the day for most of the Corps. Kelley had directed the development of an intermediate-weight jacket that could be worn with the service trousers in a mild to cool environment. An adaptation of the World War II tanker's jacket was adopted, but was not available for optional purchase until Kelley was gone and Gray was commandant. As they had the woolly-pully and all-weather coat, the other services were quick to copy the "tanker's jacket."

Gray had enlisted in 1950, reached the grade of sergeant, and served with the 1st Marine Division in Korea. As a junior officer in the early 1960s, he engaged in some highly interesting intelligence operations, having to do with radio intercepts, in Viet Nam. Immediately before becoming commandant he was the commanding general of Fleet Marine Force, Atlantic, and the II Marine Amphibious Force. Before that, he commanded the 2d Marine Division.

On 10 November 1987, the 212th birthday of the Corps, Quantico's Marine Corps Development and Education Command, at the direction of General Gray, became the Marine Corps Combat Development Command; "MCDEC" became "MCCDC." It was more than a slight change in words and acronyms. The traditional role of the Marine Corps Schools continued and the old designation of Marine Corps Base was reestablished. What was new was the creation of five functionally related centers: MAGTF Warfighting, Training and Education, Intelligence, Wargaming and Assessment, and Information Technology. He set a deadline of midsummer 1988 to have the reorganization completed. General Gray's pet was the Warfighting Center. As he told the Senate Armed Services Committee, "In short, the Warfighting Center will be our brainpower in the areas of operational concepts, studies, doctrine, and plans."

As a step in "streamlining" the acquisition of "hardware" process, Gray's proposal to create a Marine Corps Research, Development, and Acquisition Command at Quantico was approved by Secretary of the Navy James H. Webb Jr. (himself a Marine officer wounded in Viet Nam) in November 1987.

Early in 1988, Gray returned Marine air-ground task force designations to what they had been before 1965. "Amphibious" became "Expeditionary" once again: Marine *Expeditionary* Unit, Marine *Expeditionary* Brigade, Marine *Expeditionary* Force. Said Gray: "The Marine air-ground task forces which we employ around the world are not limited to amphibious operations alone ... Our Corps is an expeditionary intervention force with the ability to move rapidly, on short notice, to wherever needed to accomplish what is required."

A "university" concept for Quantico had been discussed at least since the 1960s; General Gray made it real on 1 August 1989 by the activation of the Marine Corps University at Quantico. Its first president was Brig. Gen. Paul K. Van Riper. The rather windy statement of the university's purpose began with: "to educate every Marine in the philosophical underpinnings of warfare, the art of war and its relevance to the security and well-being of the United States." Its primary function would be "to bring about a truly educational atmosphere in which students of different ranks and specialties would associate and learn from one another." The core of the university would be the existing resident schools: Command and Staff College, Amphibious Warfare School, Staff NCO Academy, Communication Officers School, and The Basic School. The faculty was expanded to include civilian professors, both resident and visiting. The hub of the university was to be the $12 million state-of-the art Marine Corps Research Center, the "jewel in the crown," completed and dedicated on 6 May 1993.

## PANAMA'S "JUST CAUSE"

Marines would have only a relatively minor role in Just Cause, the operation aimed at snatching Panama's dictator and drug dealer, Gen. Manuel Antonio Noriega. Relationships with Panama had fallen apart early in 1988 when Noriega was indicted in absentia in Florida for racketeering and drug trafficking. The pro-U.S. president, Arturo Delvalle, tried to depose him and instead was deposed himself, with Noriega taking over as unabashed dictator. Panama was credited with being able to field some three thousand to thirty-five hundred combat troops, largely trained and equipped by the U.S. Army, from the Panamanian Defense Forces (PDF). Noriega also had a paramilitary force of fourteen "Dignity Battalions," each numbering about two hundred to 250 persons, largely untrained and not capable of much more than some streetfighting and random acts of terrorism.

Panama would give the Corps a chance to employ its new light-armored vehicles (LAVs) and its anti-terrorist teams. In place was the Marine Corps Security Force (MCSF) Company, Panama, Maj. Eddie A. Keith, commanding, five officers and 125 marines, the diminished successor to what had been the long-time Marine Barracks, Fifteenth Naval District. On 14 March 1988 Keith was reinforced with a platoon from the new Fleet Anti-Terrorist Security Team Company (the clumsy title yielded the catchy acronym "FAST") from the Marine Security Force Battalion, Atlantic, based in Norfolk, Virginia. This new battalion was a kind of consolidation of what had been the Marine guards in major Navy ships and a substitute for the fast-disappearing Marine barracks at major naval bases. Major Keith assigned the platoon to the security of the Navy's Arraijan Tank Farm, which stored in underground tanks most of the fuel used by all the U.S. forces in Panama. The tank farm, looking something like a golf course, was sandwiched between the Pan-American Highway on the north and Howard Air Force Base on the south. The FAST platoon was soon reporting intruders and other suspicious activity.

Contingency plans called for the dispatch of a Marine expeditionary brigade to the Canal Zone when and if needed. The staff of the 6th Marine Expeditionary Brigade at Camp Lejeune poised itself for deployment. On 1 April three brigade staff officers flew to Panama to coordinate the movement. That same day the Pentagon announced that fifteen hundred additional troops were being sent to Panama, including three hundred marines.

Gen. Frederick E. Woerner, USA, Commander in Chief, Southern Command (SouthCom), had decided he did not need a Marine expeditionary brigade nor any Marine air assets. Instead of the 6th MEB, the Marine Corps would deploy a provisional MAGTF—a Marine air-ground team without its air element, essentially no more than a reinforced rifle company from the 2d Marine Division. Company I, 3d Battalion, 4th Marines, arrived on 6 April. Col. William J. Conley, who had been the brigade's chief of staff, was designated commander of this rump MAGTF. On 9 April operational control of what was now Marine Forces Panama shifted from U.S. Navy South to the newly established Joint Task Force Panama (JTF Panama) under Maj. Gen. Bernard Loeffke, USA.

Company I took over the defense of the tank farm. There was an argument with the Army as to whether the marines should patrol with a round in the chambers of their weapons. FMFLant, remembering Beirut, insisted on it. On 11 April, Company I sensed a probe against its lines and sent a out a squad-sized patrol to investigate. The patrol split into two groups to converge on the suspected area. A flare popped. There was an exchange of shots and Cpl. Ricardo M. Villahermosa, the patrol leader, was mortally wounded.

Next evening, at about dusk, battlefield sensors picked up the movement of about forty persons coming from the Pan American Highway toward the tank farm. The marines used their 81-mm mortars, mostly illumination rounds but some high-explosive, and received return fire from a ravine to their front. The marines sent back more fire including a long string of 40-mm rounds from an M-19 chain gun.

About two hours later, General Loeffke arrived on the scene. Unconvinced that there had been opposition, he ordered a cease-fire, suggesting that the marines had fired at shadows. He replaced the Marine company with a reinforced Army battalion. The soldiers had their own fire fight with the phantom enemy on the night of 14 April.

Later in the month Colonel Conley's Marine Forces Panama was reinforced with an Army rifle company and a large military police detachment. Company I went back to the tank farm. Company L, 3d Battalion, 4th Marines, relieved them in June and on 19 July would have another phantom fire fight. This time General Loeffke was overhead in a helicopter monitoring the affair. There would be more sightings and sporadic fire fights, but not much evidence as to who the intruders were.

On 31 October there was a good-sized fire fight. Company M, 3d Battalion, 8th Marines, was now on the tank farm. Again the results were inconclusive. The marines were informed that their primary duty, henceforth, would be to conduct training, not security of the tank farm. They were to adopt a less aggravating stance.

Much later it was confirmed that the intruders had been members of the "Macho de Monte," a Panamanian special operations company. Noriega apparently seized on an opportunity to harass and embarrass the Americans and at the same time give his force a bit of live-fire training.

Col. Thomas W. Roberts arrived and took over command of Marine Forces Panama from Colonel Conley. He ordered that the field fortifications at the tank farm be razed and that the Marines adopt light infantry tactics. Operation Rabbit Hunt, conducted in December by the Marines and the 1st Battalion, 508th Infantry, swept the whole tank farm area—grand training, but no tangible results.

The new year, 1989, started quietly. Then Noriega lost the 7 May election and his response was to send his Dignity Battalions into the streets. More Army and Marine reinforcements arrived. General Woerner liked the Marines' light armored vehicles, something the Army did not have. Company A, 2d Light

Infantry Battalion, arrived by Air Force airlift with its LAVs, their turrets housing a 25-mm chain gun and a 7.62-mm machine gun. The Panamanians called them *tanquitos*. The LAVs transformed Marine Forces Panama from a stationary base defense force into a maneuver force and security operations gained the name "Sand Fleas." To demonstrate their capabilities the LAVs repeatedly "swam" across the Canal from one bank to the other. On 7 August the Panamanian Defense Forces made the mistake of detaining one of the LAVs near Arraijan. A full LAV platoon went to the rescue. The marines took into custody a PDF squad and relieved them of their weapons and ammunition.

In October an element of the Panamanian military failed in an attempt to dislodge Noriega. SouthCom and the JCS reexamined their options and gave the XVIII Airborne Corps under Lt. Gen. Carl W. Stiner, USA, the decisive role. Marine Forces Panama, with the contingency designation of "Task Force Semper Fi," was given the mission of defending the western approaches to Panama City, including the Bridge of the Americas over which the Pan American Highway crosses the Canal. Col. Charles E. Richardson now was the Marine commander.

On Saturday, 16 December, 1st Lt. Robert Paz and three other officers went to dinner in Panama City. They were stopped at a PDF checkpoint, tried to drive away, and Paz died in a fusillade of AK-47 rounds. Next day the JCS met at the quarters of the chairman, Gen. Colin L. Powell. General Gray offered the immediate use of the 11th Marine Expeditionary Unit. It was not considered needed. General Powell secured President Bush's approval to proceed. H-hour was set at 0100 on 20 December. The operation was given the name "Just Cause."

The JTF commander was now Maj. Gen. Marc A. Cisneros, USA. Colonel Richardson gave a final briefing to his Marine commanders on 19 December. Company D, 2d LAI Battalion, was now the LAV unit. The LAVs moved out ten minutes before H-hour to sweep up some PDF detachments. Cpl. Garreth C. Isaak was killed in the fight for a PDF station. Another marine was wounded. By dawn the Marines had accomplished their original missions. Meanwhile the eight marines of the security guard at the U.S. embassy, armed with shotguns, successfully repelled an attack.

Early on 20 December, Richardson received a fresh mission: to take the headquarters of the 10th Military Zone in La Chorrera, Panama's third-largest city. He gave the assignment to Company D. By afternoon the LAVs had rolled into La Chorrera after going through a road block. Once they reached the headquarters, only a few snipers remained. The rest of the PDF had fled.

By 21 December the Marine mission had become the stabilization of Arraijan and La Chorrera, chiefly the prevention of looting. By Christmas Eve the fighting was all but over. On 3 January 1990 Noriega surrendered to members of the Army's Delta Force. Operation Just Cause became Operation Promote Liberty. The Marines calculated that they had captured 1,320 PDF and Dignity Battalion members, about one-quarter of the total number detained. By 1 June all detachments still deployed in the countryside were pulled back into the Canal Zone. Two weeks later, all remaining marines except for the company-size Marine Security Force departed by way of the USS *Trenton*. Their numbers had never exceeded 650.

## VIOLENCE AND DISGRACE IN THE EMBASSIES

Elsewhere in the world violence against the embassy marines continued. Three marines were wounded in San José, Costa Rica, when their vehicle was blown up by a command-detonated mine. On the evening of 19 June 1985, four off-duty marines were among the thirteen persons killed while seated at a San Salvador sidewalk cafe when a dozen men opened fire on them.

The proud traditions of the Marine Security Guards, however, were badly tarnished by the revelation in 1986 of shameful events in Moscow. Seven Marine guards were taken into custody for unlawful conduct such as allowing Soviet citizens into classified areas of the embassy. For most the charges were dismissed for lack of evidence, but Sgt. Clayton J. Lonetree became the first U.S. Marine ever to be tried for espionage. Infatuated with a Soviet woman agent who worked in the embassy, he was enmeshed by the KGB and continued his espionage even after being transferred to the U.S. embassy in Vienna, where at last he turned himself in to a CIA officer. Conviction by general court-martial sentenced him to thirty years' confinement. He was released in 1996, after serving eight years.

## THE TANKER WAR

In 1984 the Iraqis, with their war with Iran at a stalemate, started the so-called "Tanker War" by targeting Iranian oil tankers operating in the Persian

Gulf. In retaliation, the Iranians began attacking the shipping of Iraq's chief supporters, Kuwait and Saudi Arabia, using armed speed boats operating from Bushier and Farsi islands. Iranian oil platforms in the southern Gulf served as observation posts and command and control facilities.

On 23 December 1986, Kuwait formally requested that some of her tankers be reflagged under United States registry so as to qualify for U.S. Navy protection. A similar request had been made of the Soviets. Eleven supertankers were put under the American flag. Six months passed before the first convoy proceeded up the Gulf. On 24 July 1987 the tanker *Bridgetown* hit an Iranian mine. Central Command and its regional surrogate, Middle East Force, under Navy command, took a more aggressive stance which became Operation Earnest Will.

The 24th Marine Amphibious Unit, under Col. Gordon W. Keiser, had just left a liberty visit to Kenya, when, at sea, orders were received to detach the *Guadalcanal*. The big 18,825-ton amphibious assault ship, with its Marine helicopters, was to proceed at maximum speed to Diego Garcia to pick up the Navy's Air Mine Countermeasure Squadron HM-14.

For the next several months Marine and Navy helicopters flew cover for the American-flagged tanker convoys, searching the water for mines and challenging Iranian naval vessels if they came too close. On 21 September the Navy–Marine Corps force caught the Iranian ship *Iran Air* in the act of laying mines across a convoy route. Marine helicopters provided cover for Navy SEALS who boarded the ship the following day.

In late November 1987, Contingency MAGTF 1-88, under Col. Frank Libutti, arrived in the Gulf to relieve the elements of 24th MAU. Libutti had six hundred marines including a rifle company which gave the Middle East Force an amphibious raid capability. Contingency MAGTF 2-88, much of it drawn from experienced members of the 24th MEU and embarked in the *Trenton*, came out in February 1988, under Col. William Rakow, to relieve Libutti.

On 14 April the U.S. frigate *Samuel B. Roberts* hit a mine, damaging her badly and injuring ten crew members. Retaliation was swift. SEALS were to attack *Sirri* oil platform. Navy surface ships were to search out an Iranian warship in the Straits of Hormuz and sink it. Rakow's mission was to neutralize the gas and oil separation platform *Sassan*. At 0800 on 18 April the defenders of the *Sassan*, estimated to be twenty to thirty Iranian marines, were warned to abandon the platform. After allowing time for the evacuation, the Navy opened fire with 5-inch guns spotted by a Marine ANGLICO team. An Iranian 23-mm gun returned fire but was quickly silenced. At 0930 four Marine Sea Cobras closed on the target to provide covering fire while a boarding party of forty marines approached in two CH-46 Sea Knight helicopters. The marines fast-roped down onto the platform, did a thorough search, removed everything of intelligence value, and planted thirteen hundred pounds of explosives. Seven minutes after their departure *Sassan* blew up in an explosion that could be seen for miles. Later in the day a Sea Cobra was lost with its two crew members dead, but probably not from hostile fire.

In June 1988, Contingency MAGTF 3-88, commanded by Col. John H. Admire, came out to relieve Rakow's marines. Tension heightened after the unfortunate downing of an Iranian commercial Airbus by the guided missile cruiser *Vincennes*. A fourth contingency MAGTF was formed and trained, but it would not be needed. On 20 August Iran agreed to a cease-fire and U.S. forces gradually withdrew. The last marines left in September 1989.

# 20

# *1990‒1991*
## Breaching the So-Called
## Impenetrable Barrier

## Desert Shield

Few Americans could have identified Saddam Hussein on Wednesday, 1 August 1990, the day before the Iraqi invasion of Kuwait. In the Marine Corps, the most interesting things that were happening were taking place in the Philippines and off the coast of Liberia.

Afloat in Philippine waters was the 13th Marine Expeditionary Unit (Special Operations Capable) under Col. John E. Rhodes. Originally scheduled for a port visit to Subic Bay and training ashore, the 13th MEU was conveniently at hand to assist in earthquake relief. Already ashore at Subic was a contingency Marine air-ground force of about two thousand marines, ostensibly for training, but also with the unstated, but obvious, purpose of deterring guerrilla or terrorist activity by increasingly restive anti-American Filipino elements.

In the South Atlantic, standing off Monrovia, Liberia, was the 22d MEU(SOC) under Col. Granville Amos, who had commanded the helicopters at Grenada. It was obvious that the government of President Samuel K. Doe was about to fall. The 22d MEU was present to evacuate American citizens if that became necessary.

In opening moves sharply similar to North Korea's invasion of South Korea forty years earlier, three Iraqi Republican Guard divisions crossed the Kuwaiti border at about 0100 local time, 2 August, and converged on Kuwait City from the north and west, coordinating their move with the landing by helicopter of a special-operations division in the city itself. The forces had linked up by 0530 and by nightfall Kuwait City was in Iraqi hands. By noon of the next day Iraqi forces had reached Kuwait's border with Saudi Arabia.

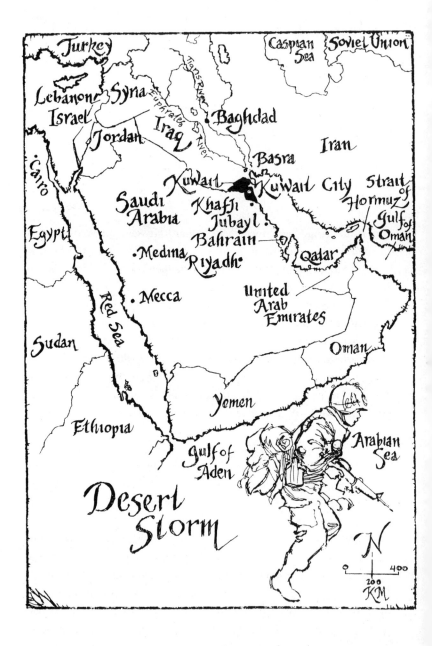

Turkey
Caspian Sea
Soviet Union
Lebanon
Syria
Israel
Euphrates River
Trans River
Baghdad
Jordan
Iraq
Iran
Basra
Kuwait
Kuwait City
Strait of Hormuz
Cairo
Saudi Arabia
Khafji
Jubayl
Bahrain
Gulf of Oman
Egypt
Medina
Riyadh
Qatar
Mecca
United Arab Emirates
Red Sea
Sudan
Oman
Ethiopia
Yemen
Arabian Sea
Gulf of Aden

Desert Storm

N

0    200    400
KM

On Saturday, 4 August, the Joint Chiefs of Staff chairman, Gen. Colin L. Powell, and Commander in Chief, Central Command, Gen. H. Norman ("the Bear") Schwarzkopf met with President George Bush at Camp David, Maryland. General Powell would be the first JCS chairman to make full use of the new powers conveyed by the Goldwater-Nichols Act. In the Persian Gulf War he would function clearly as the single chief of staff, with its implications of the German General Staff system, a centralization of power the Marine Corps had feared and fought for so many years. Wheels were set in motion for U.S. intervention.

On Monday, 6 August, the 26th MEU(SOC), headed by Col. William C. Fite III, began loading out at Morehead City, North Carolina, in Amphibious Squadron Two. It was a scheduled deployment that had nothing to do with Iraq. The 26th MEU was to relieve the 22d MEU on station off Liberia. Meanwhile, the 22d MEU had put a rifle company ashore at Monrovia to protect the American Embassy and had begun evacuation operations.

On Tuesday, 7 August, General Powell, as directed by Secretary of Defense Dick Cheney, ordered the first actual deployments of forces for Operation Desert Shield, as the positioning of U.S. forces in the Persian Gulf would be called.

Three Marine expeditionary brigades, the 7th MEB in California, the 1st MEB in Hawaii, and the 4th MEB in North Carolina, had been alerted for possible deployment. The gears of command meshed as follows: Schwarzkopf, as CinCCent, was the designated theater commander and the supported unified commander. CinCPac, as one of the supporting unified commanders, tasked his component commanders, CinCPacFlt among them, to provide designated forces. CG FMFPac, subordinate to CinCPacFlt, in turn ordered CG I MEF to ready the 1st and 7th MEBs for deployment. Similarly, 4th MEB received its tasking from FMFLant, which in turn had been tasked by CinCLant through CinCLantFlt. Much to Gen. Al Gray's frustration, the service chiefs, although members of the Joint Chiefs of Staff, had little or no say in these operational matters.

On Wednesday, 8 August, MPS Squadron 2 began steaming from Diego Garcia, that speck of an island in the middle of the Indian Ocean, and MPS Squadron 3 sailed from Guam. They were to marry up with the 7th and 1st MEBs, if and when those two brigades deployed. The marriage of men and materiel on a probable battlefield was problematic. Desert Shield would provide an acid test for the maritime prepositioning concept.

## CALL FOR MARINES

On Friday, 10 August, General Schwarzkopf called for not only the airlifted 7th and 1st MEBs, but also the seaborne 4th MEB. Schwarzkopf had succeeded Marine Gen. George B. Crist in November 1988 as commander of Central Command. In June 1990, Marine Maj. Gen. Robert B. Johnston joined his command as chief of staff. Johnston, born in Scotland in 1937, emigrated to the United States in 1955 and was commissioned in the Marine Corps after graduating from San Diego State College. He had two tours in Viet Nam, including command of a rifle company, and subsequently would have command of a battalion in Lebanon and the peacetime command of a regiment and the 9th Marine Amphibious Brigade.

On Sunday, 12 August, the 7th Marine Expeditionary Brigade under Maj. Gen. John I. Hopkins began moving out from its desert base at Twentynine Palms, the marines equipped with little more than their packs and rifles. Hopkins, a tough marine who looked the part, had a Silver Star from Viet Nam. The 7th MEB, as with the other Marine air-ground task forces, had a standing command element or headquarters. Other elements of the brigade were not permanently assigned, but all were designated and all had recently exercised with the brigade. Behind them was a long series of annual Gallant Eagle exercises, played to a scenario that almost exactly matched the present deployment.

The 7th MEB's ground combat element (GCE) was Regimental Landing Team 7 (RLT-7), under Col. Carlton W. Fulford Jr., with four infantry battalions and a light armored infantry battalion. The 3d Battalion, 9th Marines, one of the four infantry battalions, was embarked in the amphibious assault ship *Belleau Wood*, taking part in the annual Sea Fair at Seattle. The Marines asked for its immediate return. The *Belleau Wood* steamed back to San Diego. The battalion disembarked and readied itself for air embarkation. Some sixteen thousand marines entered the air flow for Saudi Arabia.

Marine Aircraft Group 70 (MAG-70), the aviation element (ACE), under Col. Manfred A. Rietsch, had both fixed-wing aircraft, which could flight-ferry themselves to Saudi Arabia, and helicopters, which would require air transport. The combat service support element was Brigade Service Support Group 7, commanded by Col. Alexander W. Powell.

On Tuesday, 14 August, 7th MEB began arriving, first at Dhahran, but then, with their destination quickly shifted, to the port city of Al Jubayl. Hopkins came in the next day as did the first ships of Maritime Prepositioning Squadron 2. The "benign" port required for unloading was provided by the superbly modern port facilities bought by oil dollars in Saudi Arabia. Rolling out of the MPS ships came the tanks, howitzers, amphibious assault vehicles (as LVTs were now called), the light armored vehicles (the LAVs of which so much was expected), and the other weapons, supplies, and equipment that would give the 7th MEB its combat punch.

There were some rough spots. To perhaps a majority of the conservative and deeply religious Saudis, the arrival of a large body of nonbelieving and armed foreigners (many of them bare-faced women who did such unseemly things as drive trucks) was cause for resentful apprehension. Central Command leaned over backwards to accommodate to local sensitivity. American flags were not to be flown officially at any Marine installation. General Schwarzkopf's General Order No. 1 was a complete ban of alcohol within the theater.

CentCom assigned 7th MEB the mission of protecting critical oil and port facilities at Jubayl, Ju'aymah, and Ras Tannurah and the island emirate Bahrain, by defending as far forward as possible, and to be prepared for several possible contingencies, including being prepared to reembark for amphibious operations—a large order for what was initially a small force.

The arriving troops were housed in four huge, un-airconditioned warehouses, where they sweltered in temperatures that went up to 120 degrees while they awaited their disposition. There wasn't much usable intelligence and there wasn't much in the way of defense, except distance, between Hopkins's brigade and the Kuwaiti border. He flew reconnaissance in helicopters and talked with the local Saudi commanders. By 20 August he had met Saudi concerns and his brigade began to move out of the port area. (Hopkins: "The decision-making system in Saudi Arabia took a long time to get moving.")

On 25 August, Hopkins reported to General Schwarzkopf that he was ready to assume responsibility for the defense of the approaches to Jubayl, confident that he could counter an Iraqi offensive in his zone of action. On that date his brigade numbered 15,248 marines and sailors with 123 tanks, 425 heavy weapons including artillery pieces, and 124 aircraft, both fixed-wing and helicopters. The twelve-thousand-mile air movement of the brigade had required 259 Military Airlift Command sorties, mostly Air Force C-141s.

Hopkins, after declaring his brigade combat-ready, sent RCT 7 northward as a covering force. Out in front, as a long-range screen, he deployed the 1st

Light Armored Infantry Battalion, designated as Task Force Shepherd, with their light armored vehicles (LAVs). Working with them was the reinforced 3d Battalion, 9th Marines (the battalion that had hurried home from Seattle), which now morosely called itself "the speed bump," meaning that they could do little more than slow down an Iraqi attack in force. Hopkins decided the most defensible ground was "by the cement factory" about forty miles north of Jubayl. He put the better part of the 7th Marines there.

Maj. Gen. Royal N. Moore Jr., commanding general of the 3d Marine Aircraft Wing, arrived in Saudi Arabia on 16 August, one day after General Hopkins. Moore himself had flown 287 combat missions and earned a Distinguished Flying Cross in Viet Nam. Shortly after his arrival he predicted a short, violent air war against the Iraqis. Central Command assigned the Marines two small airfields: one at Jubayl and one at King Abdul Aziz Naval Base. Both were inadequate for fighter and attack operations. More or less on its own, the Marine Corps negotiated for use of the roomier Shaikh Isa Air Base on neighboring Bahrain. Marine air required the support of two specialized aviation logistics support ships—*Curtiss* and *Wright*—which were slow in arriving. The 3d Naval Construction Regiment with four battalions of hard-working SeaBees was provided by U.S. Pacific Fleet; their first task was to enlarge the ramp space at the three fields.

## BOOMER TAKES COMMAND

Lt. Gen. Walter E. Boomer, with the I Marine Expeditionary Force command element, arrived at Riyadh on 17 August. Boomer was "double-hatted" as both CG I MEF and as commander of CentCom's Marine service component, U.S. Marine Force, Central Command (USMarCent). The Marines were on the same command level as the Air Force (USAFCent), Navy (USNavCent), Army (USArCent), and, something new, a Special Operations Command (SOCCent). Boomer had dispatched Brig. Gen. James A. Brabham, who had been to Saudi Arabia before and knew the ground and who would be his logistics chief, to Riyadh on 10 August to set up MarCent (Forward) and to otherwise assist the arriving marines.

Boomer had just taken command of I MEF on 8 August at Camp Pendleton as part of a command change planned months before Desert Shield. General Gray officiated. Brig. Gen. James M. ("Mike") Myatt (soon to be selected for promotion to major general) received command of the 1st

Marine Division at the same ceremony. For fifty-two-year-old Boomer, who was coming from the command of the Reserve 4th Marine Division at New Orleans, it meant a promotion to lieutenant general. As a captain, Boomer had two tours in Viet Nam, the first as a rifle company commander, the second as an advisor to the Vietnamese Marines. He had a chest full of ribbons, as do most general officers, but no decoration was more significant than the two Silver Stars from Viet Nam. Silver Stars require gallantry in action and were not given lightly in the Marine Corps.

On 25 August, the air movement of the 1st Marine Expeditionary Brigade from Hawaii began. The core of 1st MEB was the 3d Marines with two infantry battalions. Next day, Maritime Prepositioning Squadron 3 arrived at Al Jubayl from Guam and the marriage of 1st MEB and MPSRon-3 proceeded.

The flow of marines to the Gulf continued, smaller units being combined into larger units as each arrived in a process called "compositing." The uniform for the desert was camouflage utilities, tan with rather whimsical darker spots, worn with a floppy desert hat and inevitably called "chocolate chips." All services wore it (once initial shortages were overcome) and the marines distinguished themselves by ironing the decal of their eagle, globe, and anchor insignia on their breast pocket.

The operational life of Hopkins's 7th MEB was short. Both the 1st and 7th MEBs were dissolved and absorbed into the I Marine Expeditionary Force, which officially "stood up" on 2 September. Boomer established his command post in Jubayl on 3 September in an unused commercial building. Hopkins became the deputy commander, I MEF.

Also on 3 September, Royal Moore opened the headquarters of the 3d Marine Aircraft Wing on Bahrain. MAG 70 split apart its fixed-wing and helo squadrons. Fixed-wing went to Marine Aircraft Group 11 and helicopters to Marine Aircraft Group 16, as they had in Viet Nam a quarter century earlier.

The new commanding general of the 1st Marine Division, Mike Myatt, like Boomer, had served two tours in Viet Nam, the first as a platoon and company commander and the second as an advisor to the Vietnamese marines. He, too, had a Silver Star. On 5 September, Myatt "stood up" the 1st Marine Division, signifying that his headquarters was in place and that he was ready to assume control of the ground combat element of I MEF. Ground elements of 7th and 1st MEBs were "composited" into the 1st Marine Division on the following day. Fully formed, the 1st Marine Division would have four infantry regiments, the 1st, 3d, 4th, and 7th Marines; an artillery regiment, the

11th Marines reinforced with two battalions from the 12th Marines; and six separate battalions: the 1st Light Armored Infantry, 1st Combat Engineers, 1st Reconnaissance, 3d Assault Amphibian, and the 1st and 3d Tanks. Myatt, a close student of desert tactics, would progressively refine his regimental combat teams into specific-mission task forces. (By late October he would have his entire division north of the cement factory.)

Enough combat service support personnel were in country by 6 September to stand up the 1st Force Service Support Group at Jubayl. Jim Brabham came east from Riyadh to resume command and reorganize BSSGs 1 and 7 into General and Direct Support Groups. During his two tours in Viet Nam, he had commanded a shore party company and had been an engineer advisor to the Vietnamese Marines. In recent years he had been Deputy J-4 at USCentCom, ideal preparation for his present assignment as I MEF's logistics chief.

First FSSG took over responsibility for port operations. Al Jubayl was a sixteen-berth port with full facilities and an indigenous work force in place. The Saudis had an abundant supply of fuel and some water. In Brabham's mind, water supply and distribution, not ammunition, would be the primary drivers of the logistical effort. He soon found himself faced with an acute shortage of "line haul" transportation. Marine Corps organic motor transport was geared to an amphibious objective area not more than fifty miles deep. Brabham was dealing with twice or triple, and eventually four or five times this distance. Eventually he would augment his organic transportation with some two thousand "line haulers," big trucks of all types, from the Army, from the Saudis, and leased from commercial firms, and about two hundred Saudi buses and six hundred or so four-wheel civilian-type passenger vehicles of various types and origins.

His Royal Highness Lt. Gen. Khalid bin Sultan bin Abdul Aziz (more simply, "Prince Khalid") commanded the theater of operations and coordinated all Arab coalition force operations. Boomer would place a high priority on effective relations with the Saudis.

Predictably, the most contentious issue at the joint and combined level was the control of tactical air power. With a melange of air forces, large and small, either present or coming, some form of overall control was obviously necessary. With the Air Force doctrinally insistent on the indivisibility of air power and the requirement for centralized operational control, and the U.S. Marine Corps equally insistent on the integrated nature of its Marine air-ground teams, friction between the two services was inevitable, but, after years of consultation and compromise, it would be less than in either Korea or Viet Nam. Lt. Gen. Charles A. Horner, Commander, U.S. Air Forces Central Command, argued for a single manager for air, the Viet Nam War formula. The Marines' major concern was that their air-ground team not be broken up. Horner and Boomer worked hard at arriving at an agreement and became close friends in the process. Roughly, the final arrangement was that Marine air would continue to support Marine forces but would also provide a percentage of fixed-wing sorties to Central Command for theater missions. Primary airborne defense of the adjacent skies over the Persian Gulf was by combat air patrols flown by the Marines' F/A 18s. For close-in and medium-range air defense Moore's 3d Wing would eventually have two low-altitude air defense battalions with shoulder-fired heat-seeking Stingers and two light antiaircraft missile battalions with semi-active homing Improved Hawks.

## FORCES AFLOAT

As ComUSMarCent, Boomer would have operational control of all Marine forces ashore, but not of those still afloat. Command lines at sea would run from USCinCCent (Schwarzkopf) to ComUSNavCent (also Commander, Seventh Fleet; initially Vice Adm. Henry H. Mauz and, after December, Vice Adm. Stanley R. Arthur) to CATF (Commander, Amphibious Task Force) to CLF (Commander, Landing Force). Commander, Landing Force, would be Maj. Gen. Harry W. Jenkins Jr., the commanding general of the 4th Marine Expeditionary Brigade, which was wending its seaward way to the Gulf. He, too, had commanded a rifle company with distinction in Viet Nam.

With a strength of about eight thousand, his brigade, essentially Regimental Landing Team 2 and Marine Aircraft Group 40, was half the size of 7th MEB. Movement had been in the Atlantic-based Amphibious Group Two. First ships sailed from Morehead City, North Carolina, on 17 August. It was a long voyage, across the Atlantic, past Gibraltar into the Mediterranean, through the Suez Canal, down the Red Sea, around the Arabian peninsula (a land mass as large as the United States east of the Mississippi and most of it sand), to the Gulf of Oman. Jenkins's first echelon arrived off Masirah Island on 11 September. The 13th MEU was already in the Persian Gulf, having arrived on 7 September, but would not initially come under Jenkins's command.

Schwarzkopf, appreciative of the flexibility in having an amphibious force offshore (and perhaps with a bit of naval pressure), decided to keep both the 4th MEB and 13 MEU afloat. Jenkins and his Navy bosses began a series of landing exercises to publicize the presence of the amphibious forces and to rehearse their probable employment. The first of four "Sea Soldier" exercises was a night raid by 13th MEU (now under 4th MEB tactical control) followed by a 4th MEB landing, by both surface craft and helicopters, across the beaches of Oman near Ras Al Madrakah.

Workhorses for the surface landing were the Marine Corps' amphibian tractors. In 1985 the Marine Corps changed the designation of the LVTP7A1 to AAV7A1—Amphibious Assault Vehicle—representing a shift in emphasis away from the long-time "LVT" designation, meaning "landing vehicle, tracked." Without a change of a bolt or plate, the AAV7A1 was to be more of an armored personnel carrier and less of an amphibian landing vehicle. The LVTP7, which had come into the Marine Corps inventory in the early 1970s, was the last of a long line of LVTs stretching back to Guadalcanal.

## THE "DESERT RATS"

About this time, I MEF learned that the 7th Armoured Brigade ("Desert Rats") of the British Army of the Rhine was to come under I MEF's tactical control (something slightly less than operational control), to be followed later by all of the British 1st Armoured Division. The Desert Rats, numbering some fourteen thousand, had earned their name fighting with the British Eighth Army in North Africa in World War II, but it had been a long time since they had served in the desert. Their fighting vehicles, however, had names that seemed well-suited to the task at hand—Challengers, Warriors, Scimitars, and Scorpions. The Desert Rats, under command of Brig. Patrick Cordingley, brought with them 170 Challenger tanks and seventy-two self-propelled 155-mm guns. Anticipating the arrival of the remainder of the 1st Armoured Division, Boomer began to plan for the employment of three powerful divisions.

## LIBERIAN EVACUATION

In the South Atlantic, the 26th MEU had arrived on schedule off Monrovia, on 20 August, and had begun the relief of 22d MEU. By that time 683 persons had been evacuated and the Marine presence ashore had been reduced to half a company. Next day, 26th MEU received a change of mission. It was to proceed to the Mediterranean, leaving behind the amphibious transport *Whidbey Island* and the tank landing ship *Barnstable County* and a heavily reinforced rifle company, along with helicopters and a combat service support detachment to continue evacuation operations and protection of the embassy. (The Monrovia evacuation operation ended on 30 November after 185 continuous days of Navy and Marine Corps presence. A total of 2,439 persons, of whom 226 were American citizens, were evacuated.)

## THE THREAT

Years earlier the Saudis had delineated the border with a fifteen-foot-high earth barrier, known to the Americans as "the Berm," punctuated by police posts at about ten-mile intervals, brown stone towers or "castles" which now served as Saudi forward observation posts. The Iraqis, who enjoyed a formidable reputation (exaggerated, as it turned out) for combat engineering and field fortifications, were digging in deeply on the southern Kuwaiti border. The fortifications took the form of multiple minefield and obstacle belts defended, in the zone of greatest concern to I MEF, by five infantry divisions on line backed by two tank divisions in operational reserve. Along the coast, the Iraqis had extended their defenses southward for the length of Kuwait's shoreline. In addition to their enormous number of tanks and guns, Boomer firmly believed that the Iraqis would use chemical weapons and that biological weapons were a serious possibility.

General Schwarzkopf's initial concept of operations, developed by a cell of Army planners, treated I Marine Expeditionary Force as the equivalent of an Army corps. A considerable educational effort was needed to convince Schwarzkopf's planners that I MEF as an air-ground team was something different.

## PHASE II, DESERT SHIELD

By the first week of November, Phase I of the Desert Shield deployment was complete. Nearly forty-two thousand marines, close to one-quarter of the Marine Corps' total active-duty strength and a fifth of the total U.S. force in the Persian Gulf, had been deployed. But there was much more to come.

During an 8 November press conference, President Bush announced that U.S. forces in the Persian Gulf area would be increased by an additional two hundred thousand troops. The JCS deployment order of 9 November 1990 specified the II Marine Expeditionary Force and the 5th Marine Expeditionary Brigade. The number of marines committed to the theater of operations would double.

It was a point of pride with General Gray that the Marine Corps had completed Phase I deployments without a call-up of the Marine Corps Reserve except for a few individuals. (One exception to the "no Reserve" rule was the early arrival of the 3d Civil Affairs Group, a small number of specialists, whose members volunteered to help handle relations with the civilian community. Before the jump-off, 3d CAG would be reinforced by the Army Reserve's 403d Civil Affairs Battalion from Syracuse, New York.)

On 13 November the involuntary call-up of Selected Marine Corps Reserve units began. For the first time since the Korean War the readiness of the Reserve for combat would be tested. Eighty Marine Reserve units were activated, coming from all over the country from the widely dispersed Reserve 4th Marine Division and 4th Marine Aircraft Wing along with about seventy-five hundred individual reservists. Within two months thirty-one thousand Marine Corps reservists were on active duty.

## "IMMINENT THUNDER"

In early November Schwarzkopf directed his component commanders to develop an offensive scenario reflecting their expanded forces. The Marines were short on mine-clearing equipment and that would be a problem. Boomer still expected the use of the entire British 1st Armoured Division. At the moment he was compressed into a zone of operations just thirty kilometers wide. He thought this much too narrow for a three-division attack.

Central Command ran "Imminent Thunder," a five-phase combined exercise, from 15 to 21 November. For I MEF the play of the problem called for a link-up with the Saudi's National Guard 2d Brigade and a landing by 4th MEB. Chancy landing conditions, created by rough sea states whipped up by shallow water and high winds, caused the amphibious task force commander to cancel the surface assault. The media got on to this, pontificating on the fragility of amphibious landings. Jenkins countered with the obvious explanation that a prudent commander did not risk the unnecessary break-up of landing craft and vehicles in an exercise. The helicopter-borne part of the assault, launched from over the horizon, went well. A Marine battalion landing team coming from the sea linked up with I MEF forces ashore.

President and Mrs. George Bush visited 4th MEB at sea and I MEF on shore Thanksgiving Day, 22 November, charming the marines of the 1st Marine Division by eating their dinner with them seated on a pile of sandbags. Force headquarters was at Camp Gray, named for the commandant, outside of Jubayl. General Boomer shifted his command post to an empty police station within walking distance of Camp Gray late in November.

## 5TH MEB DEPLOYS

The 5th Marine Expeditionary Brigade, numbering about seventy-five hundred (one-third of them Reservists), sailed from San Diego on 1 December in the thirteen ships of Amphibious Group Three led by the amphibious assault ship *Tarawa*. The ground element of 5th MEB was the reinforced 5th Marine regiment from Camp Pendleton; the aviation element, MAG-50; and the combat service support element, BSSG-5. Brig. Gen. Peter J. Rowe was in command. In Viet Nam, after completing Vietnamese language training, he had headed an interrogation-translation team in the battles for Hue City and Khe Sanh.

## II MEF DEPLOYS

On the East Coast, the II Marine Expeditionary Force consisted essentially of the 2d Marine Division and 2d Force Service Support Group, based mainly at Camp Lejeune, and the 2d Marine Aircraft Wing, from Marine Corps Air Stations at Cherry Point, Beaufort, and Camp Lejeune. The current FMFLant commander was Lt. Gen. Carl E. Mundy Jr. He had served as an operations officer and executive officer of an infantry battalion in Viet Nam and his string of operational commands later included the 36th and 38th MAUs and the 4th MAB, but he was not destined to go to the Persian Gulf.

Nearly thirty thousand marines and sailors from II MEF were scheduled for the Gulf. Movement of the fly-in echelon began on 9 December and was to continue, at the rate of about a thousand a day, until 15 January. The departure of the major part for the Gulf was marked by an elaborate farewell ceremony at Camp Lejeune on Monday, 10 December, that saw some twenty-four thousand departing troops drawn up in massive squares on the parade ground. Most impressive of all was the massing of the scarlet-and-gold colors of II MEF and its subordinate units.

But of the major elements, only the colors of the 2d Division and 2d Force Service Support Group would be going to the Gulf, it having been decided that there was not yet a requirement for the command elements of II Marine Expeditionary Force and the 2d Marine Aircraft Wing. The deploying aviation units would be joining the already deployed 3d Marine Aircraft Wing.

On arrival the 2d Marine Division moved first into positions south and to the right of 1st Division. By the end of December the division was encamped in "the Triangle," an area north of Abu Hadriyah and An Nuayrihah. Commanding the 2d Division was big, burly Maj. Gen. William M. ("Bill") Keys. He, too, had commanded a rifle company during his first tour in Viet Nam and had advised the Vietnamese Marines during his second, earning both a Navy Cross and a Silver Star. His division included two infantry regiments—the 6th and 8th Marines; an artillery regiment—the 10th Marines; and six separate fighting battalions: the 2d Light Armored Infantry, 2d and 8th Tanks, 2d Assault Amphibians, 2d Combat Engineers, and 2d Reconnaissance. Three of his battalions were from the Marine Corps Reserve: the 8th Tanks; the 3d Battalion, 23d Marines, which joined the 8th Marines; and the 1st Battalion, 25th Marines (later assigned to the 1st Division). Walt Boomer and Bill Keys had been advisors together in Viet Nam and there was a bond of great trust and confidence between the two.

Jim Brabham's 1st Force Service Group, reinforced, was now divided into a General Support Command with two general support groups and a Direct Support Command (essentially the 2d Force Service Command), under Brig. Gen. Charles C. ("Chuck") Krulak. Brabham remained in overall command and Krulak would run the forward logistics battle. Chuck Krulak was the youngest of three sons of Lt. Gen. Victor H. Krulak. His Viet Nam service was in the same mold as the other generals: two tours, command of a rifle platoon and two companies, a Silver Star, and two Purple Hearts.

Just before Christmas, General Boomer directed Krulak to find a place farther north for a logistic support area big enough to support a division-size breach of the Iraqi defenses. Krulak located an abandoned airstrip near a cluster of huts called Kibrit about thirty miles inland from the minor port of Al Mishab. A well there promised a water supply.

I MEF's area of operations was expanded to include Mishab, thirty miles southeast of the Kuwaiti border. Cargo ships, if they didn't mind finding their way through a naval minefield, could unload through Mishab, shortening I MEF's supply lines considerably. (Two battalions of Saudi marines were training at a naval base near Mishab with the help of a U.S. Marine training team.) Kibrit was far out in front of the 1st and 2d Division camps and nothing stood between it and the Kuwaiti border but light Saudi and Qatari screening forces and the 1st Light Armored Infantry Battalion.

## PLANNING FOR "DESERT STORM"

Code name for the offensive would be "Desert Storm." Schwarzkopf wanted to deceive the Iraqis into thinking that the main effort would be the frontal attack into Kuwait with a supporting attack on the western flank and an amphibious assault on the Kuwaiti coast. Boomer's planners actually worked on the premise that I MEF would conduct a supporting attack in coordination with U.S Army Forces, Central Command, and Arab Joint Forces/Theater of Operations Forces.

Numerically, all the advantages seemed to be with the Iraqis: twice as many troops, four times as many tanks and nearly five times the artillery. Boomer's overriding concern was the liberation of Kuwait at a minimum cost in Marine casualties. The think-tank Center for Naval Analyses came up with the dismaying projection of over ten thousand Marine casualties in a seven-day campaign. A large question was whether there would be an amphibious assault against the Kuwaiti coast.

After going through several iterations and variations, Boomer's plan was to have the 1st Division break through the Iraqi defenses between the Al Wafrah oilfield and the coast, then hold open the breach, while the 2d Division passed through to link up with the two afloat brigades which would be landing near Ras Al Qualayah.

On 17 December, Boomer received a rude shock. Schwarzkopf informed him that not only was he not going to get the British 1st Armoured Division, but also the Desert Rats were going to be withdrawn. For reasons that seem to have been more political than military, the British wanted their forces deployed in the "main effort" to the west rather than in the "holding action" contemplated for the Marines.

Boomer's staff had the completed I MEF plan for Desert Storm ready for his signature just before midnight on 31 December. I MEF's plan derived from CentCom's plan, which foresaw four overlapping phases: (1) a strategic air campaign to attain air supremacy; (2) tactical air supremacy in the Kuwaiti theater; (3) preparation of the battlefield to reduce the combat effectiveness of the enemy; and (4) the ground offensive which, in turn, would incorporate the four classic stages of penetration, exploitation, pursuit, and consolidation.

Boomer signed the plan the next day. It called for the 1st Marine Division to breach the Iraqi defensive lines in the vicinity of Al Wafrah. After the breach, the 2d Division was to execute a passage of the lines, becoming the main effort. A link-up with an amphibious landing near the Kuwaiti port of Ash Shuaybah was still a possibility.

## THE MOGADISHU DIGRESSION

The New Year brought an unexpected diversion of forces from the Persian Gulf. On Thursday, 3 January, a cable arrived in Washington from the U.S. Embassy in Mogadishu, Somalia, requesting immediate evacuation. A two-week urban battle had reached its climax and the government of the octogenarian president, Mohamed Siad Barre, was collapsing. Armed looters had entered the embassy compound. Orders went out to the Seventh Fleet. The amphibious transport *Trenton*, operating in the Indian Ocean, launched two CH-53Es loaded with a rescue force of fifty-one marines and nine Navy SEALS. The distance was 460 miles; nighttime aerial refueling was done twice from Marine KC-130s flying from Bahrain. The helicopters arrived over Mogadishu early Friday morning, 4 January, and sat down just inside the embassy gate. Part of the Marine detachment secured the perimeter of the luxurious ($35 million) compound, big enough to include a nine-hole golf course. The rest of the marines sallied forth into the corpse-littered streets to bring in stranded Americans and assorted foreign nationals, including the ambassador and staff of thirty-five from the Soviet Embassy a mile away. Hired security guards held off the looters with small arms fire. An hour after landing the two CH-53Es lifted out sixty-two evacuees. Next day, Saturday, 5 January, ten CH-46 helicopters from the amphibious assault ship *Guam*, which had closed the distance to Mogadishu, continued the evacuation. Altogether more than 260 persons were taken out, including thirty nationalities and senior diplomats from ten countries. As it would turn out, the Marines were not yet finished with Somalia.

## FRUSTRATION IN WASHINGTON

In Washington, General Gray, having sent a superbly trained and equipped force to the Gulf, fumed and fretted and met with his generals every day. His logisticians, at his instigation, were searching the world for the best equipment with which to breach Saddam Hussein's ominous fortified line.

Going into Desert Shield, the Marines' main battle tank was the M60A1, an improvement, several generations removed, of the M48 tank of the Korean and Viet Nam wars. The M60A1 had as its main armament a 105-mm gun and some questioned if it were equal to the best tank in the Iraqi inventory, the much-vaunted Soviet T-72, with its long-barreled 125-mm gun. The M1A1 Abrams, the U.S. Army's premier battle tank, with its smooth-bore 120-mm gun, was regarded as more than a match for the T-72, but the Marine Corps was not scheduled to get any significant number of M1A1s until late in 1991. General Gray met with Gen. Carl E. Vuono, the Army's chief of staff, and successfully negotiated the loan of enough Army M1A1s to equip one battalion.

In a reprise of expeditionary practices before World War I, Gray had a rifle company stripped out of the ceremonial guard at Marine Barracks, Washington, and sent to Saudi Arabia, where it would perform command post security.

Gray's greatest frustration was that he had no operational role to play in the war. He charged Maj. Gen. Matthew P. Caulfield at Quantico to develop a plan for an amphibious assault. The target would be Basra in an Inchon-like deep turning movement. Gray pondered the advisability of deploying the headquarters of the II Marine Expeditionary Force or, alternatively, of creating a IV MEF headquarters to bring together the three afloat MAGTFs under one command. He finally sent Maj. Gen. John J. Sheehan and an amphibious planning cell, later designated MarCent Forward, to assist Admiral Arthur. By the middle of January 1991, Gray had been to Saudi Arabia twice to visit "his" marines, visits not always completely welcomed by either Schwarzkopf or Boomer, who felt that Gray was interfering too much in operational matters.

## POISED FOR BATTLE

During the first week of January, Boomer moved his command post forward to an Aramco oil separation plant near Saffiniyah, about forty miles southeast of the Kuwaiti border. Maj. Gen. Richard D. Hearney, a top Marine aviator, arrived to be deputy I MEF commander. Hopkins remained at Jubayl as commander of the I MEF (Rear). By then the I Marine Expeditionary Force was very much like the III Marine Amphibious Force in Viet Nam in structure and size: two divisions, a very large wing, and a substantial service support command. In addition, under USNavCent, there were two Marine expeditionary brigades and a special operations-capable Marine expeditionary unit afloat, offering a very powerful landing force for any contemplated amphibious operations.

Royal Moore's 3d Marine Aircraft Wing now consisted of two fixed-wing aircraft groups, MAGs 11 and 13; two helicopter groups, MAGs 16 and 26; Marine Air Control Group 38; and Marine Wing Support Group 37. Mishab had an airfield, which, with SeaBee improvement, could handle the helicopters of MAG 26. The second helicopter group, MAG-16, moved north to the Aramco jet-capable airfield at Tanajib.

The largest Reserve unit deployed was the 24th Marines, headquartered in Kansas City with battalions and companies from throughout the Middle West. The regiment was activated on 13 November under Col. George E. Germann, a regular. The 1st Battalion, 24th Marines deployed to Okinawa, where it filled in behind a battalion that had gone to the Gulf. The regiment's headquarters and 2d and 3d Battalions arrived in Jubayl at the first of the new year and were assigned to rear area defense.

Chuck Krulak reported Kibrit ready on 2 February. In a hard month's hard work, seven days of ammunition and supplies had been piled up at Kibrit. Behind its earthen blast walls Kibrit had a 470-bed hospital, 2 million gallons of fuel storage, and 16,000 tons of ammunition. The faint trace of an unused 6,500-foot dirt strip had been improved enough to handle C-130s.

## DESERT STORM

By 10 January the transfer of British forces was complete. Schwarzkopf, overruling the dissent of Lt. Gen. John G. Yeosock, USA, Commander, U.S. Army Forces, Central Command, compensated for the loss of tank strength by assigning the 1st Brigade, U.S. 2d Armored Division, to I MEF operational control. The "Tiger Brigade" was a good one, desert-trained for two years. Commanded by Col. John B. Sylvester, USA, it would bring with it 116 Abrams tanks in exchange for 179 British Challengers, but only twenty-four 155-mm self-propelled guns in place of the seventy-two British guns. Boomer put the Tiger Brigade with Keys's 2d Marine Division. Keys was given full operational control of the brigade. The only limitation was that he fight them always as a unit.

D-day for Desert Storm was 16 January 1991. Before dawn on that day the air campaign began. Initially the targeting was strategic: gaining air superiority (which almost immediately became air supremacy), destroying Saddam Hussein's command and control mechanisms, disrupting communications and transportation systems, going after the Iraqi strategic reserve—the vaunted Republican Guard—and, as a political imperative, seeking out the SCUD ballistic-missile launching sites.

An air campaign within the air campaign was the "shaping," much of it by Marine aviation, of the Kuwaiti Theater of Operations ("KTO")—both the isolation of the KTO and the destruction or neutralization of the Iraqi forces within it. As G-day, the day when the ground campaign was to begin, approached, weight of the air offensive shifted from attacks against the Republican Guard strategic reserve divisions in southern Iraq to the armored divisions in tactical reserve in central Kuwait, finally culminating in the last fifteen days in intensified strikes against Iraqi forward positions. General Schwarzkopf would later estimate that Iraqi front-line divisions were reduced by 50 percent or more and the second line cut down to something between 50 and 75 percent.

Royal Moore's 3d Marine Aircraft Wing, with about one-quarter of the total U.S. fixed-wing aircraft in the theater, played a full role. Marine air's first offensive action came at 0400, 17 January, with the launching by MAG-11 of a night air strike by forty-eight aircraft (F/A 18 Hornets and A-6 Intruders) against targets in southern Iraq. MAG-13 joined in at dawn with strikes against targets in southern Kuwait by AV-8B Harriers and OV-10 Bronchos. The 3d Marine Aircraft Wing would fly over eighteen thousand missions and deliver 29.7 million pounds of ordnance before the air campaign was over.

## AL KHAFJI

On the night of 29 January, two Iraqi armored columns crossed the southern boundary of Kuwait and slammed into I MEF's general outpost line held by the 1st Force Reconnaissance Battalion, backed by Task Force Shepherd and the 2d LAI Battalion. Initially it wasn't clear if this was a raid or the vanguard of a major attack.

In front of the 1st Marine Division, the Iraqis first hit a recon platoon manning Observation Post 4, one of those old Saudi border police stations. Elements of Task Force Shepherd converged on OP-4 and a lively fire fight developed. Both Marine F/A-18 Hornets and Air Force A-10 Thunderbolts took station overhead to give close air support. Unhappily, a missile fired by an A-10 struck an LAV, killing seven of its eight crew members. A second Iraqi attack hit Observation Post 6 sometime after midnight but got nowhere. In a later action at OP-4 another LAV was lost at a cost of its four-man crew. When daylight came the advantage passed completely to the marines and the aircraft overhead. When the dust and smoke had cleared, seventeen prisoners of war had been taken and the destruction of twenty-two tanks could be claimed.

Something much the same, but of lesser intensity, happened in front of the 2d Marine Division. There the attack had come against Observation Post 2 and it was the 2d Light Armored Infantry Battalion that came to the rescue. There was concern that if the Iraqis broke through they might get to the supply point at Kibrit. Chuck Krulak was given the loan of a tank company from the Tiger Brigade against that eventuality. It wasn't needed.

I MEF could not have asked for a better exercise to test command and control and also to measure the mettle of the Iraqis. The marines began to suspect that the Iraqis were not going to live up to their fearsome reputation.

The two Iraqi probes, however, had served their purpose. They had held the marines' attention while, farther to the east, an armored Iraqi division had come south with ambitions of reaching Mishab. Two brigades were stopped by air action, but one brigade rolled on and was into Al Khafji (which gave its name to the battle), an evacuated coastal town in the Joint Forces Command–East sector, by early morning hours on 30 January. Two 1st Marine Division reconnaissance teams were trapped in the town. The Saudis and Qataris counterattacked to regain the town at dawn on 31 January. They reached the holed-up marines by noon, and by dusk the following day they had cleared the town and taken 642 prisoners in the process. After Khafji the 1st and 2d Divisions closed up closer to the border.

Concurrent with Khafji, 13th MEU conducted an amphibious raid against Maradim Island to distract Saddam's attention. The 13th MEU and 4th MEB would also play a role in the quarantine of Iraq. As part of the maritime interdiction force, Marine boarding parties boarded six ships, including the takedown of the "peace ship" *Ibn Khaldoon* loaded with women antiwar activists.

## The Ground War

In the third week of January, I MEF began a series of artillery raids which could have been better called "combined arms raids." The scheme was to move an artillery battery close to the Kuwaiti border at night with a light armored infantry escort. Overhead would be a Marine EA6B Prowler to jam the Iraqi ground surveillance radars. The Marine guns would fire away, mostly against suspected Iraqi gun and rocket positions, sucking the Iraqis into counterbattery fires and then hitting them heavily with waiting F/A18 Hornets and AV8B Harriers.

A few Iraqi soldiers came across the lines to surrender. The winter rains had begun. In the Arabian desert it doesn't rain much, but it rains all at once; the dust turned to mud and the dry lakes to marsh. It was now clear that there would be no amphibious assault, only a demonstration, so a link-up with the landing forces would not be necessary. More breaching equipment from Israel had arrived by the first of February. Keys, confident that his 2d Division was fully ready to execute its own breach and not happy with the prospect of executing a passage of lines through the 1st Division, proposed to Boomer two breaches, at widely separated sites. On 6 February Boomer agreed to Keys's proposal and decided that the 2d Division would make the main effort, but a two-division breach would require that a much larger supply of ammunition, rations, and fuel be positioned much closer to the border.

Krulak, who had just opened Kibrit, now found an unnamed spot twenty miles southwest of "the Heel" of Kuwait. He named his new logistic support area "Al Khanjar," meaning "the dagger." Construction began immediately and, in two weeks of incredible effort, was completed on 20 February. Khanjar covered 11,280 acres. The ammunition supply point alone was 780 acres. Brabham's "Baghdad Express" filled up Al Khanjar in ten days with 3,755 line-haul runs by his big trucks, which numbered something more than 1,200. Drivers were a collection of reservists, volunteers, and third world civilians; at one point 575 trucks had broken down on the road, mostly between Kibrit and Khanjar. Five million gallons of fuel and nearly a million gallons of water were in place. All of this was dug in; none of it was above ground. Two 5,700-foot airstrips capable of handling C-130 transports had been rolled out. The C-130s would land 540 loads of high-priority cargo, mostly breaching equipment. Most of the water—and a lot was required—

at Khanjar would have to come from desalination units at Mishab, a hundred miles away. Eventually a well was found near Khanjar that yielded 4,000 gallons an hour. MAG-26 moved its helicopters to "Lonesome Dove," a new airfield built by SeaBees and Marine engineers west of Khanjar. Expecting heavy casualties, a second hospital was made ready with fourteen operating rooms. Sixty buses were leased from the Saudis, their seats taken out, and replaced with litters.

The air campaign masked the forward movement of the Allied ground forces to their attack positions. The advance of the ground combat element of the I Marine Expeditionary Force was further screened by Task Force Shepherd. The 1st Marine Division moved forward and slightly to the west. On their immediate right flank, between the main road leading north and the Persian Gulf, was the Joint Forces Command East, comprised of five Saudi, Qatari, Kuwaiti, Omani, and United Arab Emirate mechanized brigades.

As the 2d Division moved west and north, the 1st Division covered its vacated positions with Task Force Troy, a hundred-man deception force under Brig. Gen. Thomas V. Draude, assistant commander of the 1st Marine Division. Draude (with two Silver Stars from Viet Nam), by making a lot of radio noise and calling in a great number of air strikes against Iraqi positions in the Al Wafrah area, successfully gave the impression that the decamped division was still in place. To the 2d Division's left was the Joint Forces Command North, an Egyptian-Syrian force.

Boomer moved his command post forward once again, this time to a site five miles south of Khanjar. The absence of the expected British 1st Armoured Division left him with two large divisions, but no reserve. To make up for that lack, he asked Schwarzkopf that the ground combat elements of Pete Rowe's 5th MEB—essentially the 5th Regimental Combat Team—be landed on G-day, when the ground attack began.

Further west the U.S. Army's heavy VII Corps, arriving from Germany, and including the United Kingdom's 1st Armoured Division, moved into position. On VII Corps' left flank was the lighter U.S. XVIII Airborne Corps and even further west was the desert-wise French 6th Light Armored Division. In the Persian Gulf itself there were well-publicized amphibious rehearsals by the 4th and 5th Marine Expeditionary Brigades and the 13th Marine Expeditionary Unit, now all under Harry Jenkins's tactical control.

## THE GROUND OFFENSIVE

Last changes in the I MEF plan of attack were approved on 14 February. I MEF was to penetrate the Iraqi defenses between Al Wafrah and Al Manaqish oil fields. NavCent was to conduct an amphibious feint to fix enemy forces north and east of Al Burqan oil field. As G-day approached Krulak's engineers scraped two four-lane "highways" into the desert, from Al Khanjar north to the breaching sites, and made cuts in the Berm. On G-day, 24 February, Boomer's strength was 79,751—11,703 of them Reservists and 1,335 of them females—more marines than had landed at Iwo Jima.

During the night of 23 February, assault units of the 1st and 2d Division started infiltrating into positions beyond the border. Iraqi prisoners began trickling in. At 0100, G-day, the 16-inch guns of battleships *Wisconsin* and *Missouri* began thundering against the Kuwaiti coast as though to signal the beginning of an amphibious assault. Three hours later the ground attack began. At 0400, Myatt's 1st Marine Division jumped off. Task Forces Grizzly (RCT 4) and Taro (RCT 3) went forward on foot, picking their way through the obstacle belts, to secure an approach for the two mechanized Task Forces, Ripper (RCT 7) and Papa Bear (RCT 1). With five battalions of artillery to help blast their way through, Ripper and Papa Bear then pushed forward toward Burqan oil field.

The 2d Division, including the Tiger Brigade, jumped off at 0430. Light rain was falling and dense smoke was blowing in from the burning Wafrah and Burqan oil fields. The smoke helped conceal the breaching. Keys ran it much like an amphibious landing, with six lanes marked out on a 12,000-meter front: Red 1, Red 2, Blue 3, Blue 4, Green 5, and Green 6. The 6th Marines punched a hole through the center using mine plows, mine rakes, and line charges to blow the obstacles, followed by the Tiger Brigade and the 8th Marines. After coming through the obstacles the 2d Division fanned out toward Al Jaber Air Base. Opposition was light, mostly intermittent shelling, and quickly killed Iraqi tanks.

All marines in the assault were wearing "MOPP" (Mission Oriented Protective Posture) chemical protective suits and boots that made the troops look like space-walkers. Masks and gloves were to go on at the first sign of gas. The temperature stayed relatively cool, making the suits and masks tolerable. Gas detection devices picked up vague indications of chemical activity, but there was no evidence of biological agents.

At sea, Jenkins's 4th MEB conducted a night amphibious demonstration in the vicinity of As Shuaybah with naval gunfire support from the *Missouri*. Rowe's 5th MEB came ashore. RLT-5 landed smoothly at Mishab by helicopter and air-cushioned landing vehicles (LCACs). MAG-50 went into Tanajib with its helicopters. With 5th MEB ashore, I MEF's strength peaked at 84,515.

In early afternoon, Schwarzkopf telephoned Boomer, concerned that the Marines' unanticipated rate of advance had exposed I MEF's left flank. Boomer recommended that the main attack commence as soon as possible. The Army's VII Corps began crossing the line of departure at 1500. By then Task Force Ripper was consolidating its position east of Al Jaber Air Base. By the first day's end, the 1st Marine Division was poised to take Al Jaber airfield, claiming twenty-one enemy tanks destroyed and over four thousand prisoners. The 2d Marine Division had engaged an Iraqi armored column coming out of Kuwait City, defeated it, and took five thousand prisoners. That made something like nine thousand Iraqi prisoners ("EPWs" or Enemy Prisoners of War in the new jargon) taken by the Marines that first day. Most got a bus ride back to the EPW compound at Kibrit. (A Iraqi brigadier general made it a point to surrender personally to General Keys.)

During the night the Iraqis made a three-pronged counterattack against the 1st Marine Division which was easily contained. At dawn on 25 February, Company B, 4th Tank Battalion (a Reserve outfit attached to the 2d Division's 8th Marines) turned in a virtuoso performance by destroying in minutes thirty-four out of thirty-five T-72 tanks advancing in a column against the 1st Division's left flank. The Iraqi attack had sputtered out by midday. On that second day, the 1st Marine Division began to clear Al Jaber airfield, destroying eighty more tanks and taking an additional two thousand prisoners.

A restless Boomer had left his command post at first light to join Keys and discuss the continuation of the attack. Out in front of the 2d Division was a grid of buildings, lying between Jaber and the western part of Kuwait, that seen on a map invited the name "Ice Tray." By early afternoon the 2d Division had begun the attack against the Ice Tray and by midafternoon had another eight thousand prisoners.

By the morning of the twenty-sixth, aerial reconnaissance had picked up hundreds, if not thousands, of vehicles fleeing north from Kuwait City. At 1300 Boomer ordered the 2d Division to seize blocking positions on Mutla Ridge overlooking the main road leading north from Kuwait City. Within half an hour Keys had the Tiger Brigade moving up on the left flank. The brigade's Abrams tanks and Bradley infantry fighting vehicles raced forward across the open desert and by evening had sealed off two major highway intersections north of Al Jahra.

To the southeast, the 1st Division was attacking north from Al Jaber headed for the Kuwait International Airport. The airport was being pounded by the *Missouri*'s 16-inch guns. In taking the airport the 1st Marine Division destroyed 320 tanks, settling once and for all the question whether the M60A1 was as good a tank as the T-72. The M60A1s got in close and took out the T-72s with sabot rounds.

RLT-5 from Rowe's 5th MEB moved up to Jaber to help with prisoner control. Some of the 5th Marines went by helo, but for most it was a night-long, bone-jarring, hundred-mile motor march. Krulak, impatient as always to move forward, began staking out a forward logistics transfer point at Al Jaber. Behind him the four-lane "highway" was being extended to Jaber. In the Gulf, Jenkins's 4th MEB carried out night heliborne demonstrations against Bubiyan and Faylaka islands, which controlled the seaward approaches to Kuwait City.

On the fourth day, 27 February, Myatt's 1st Marine Division completed the taking of Kuwait International Airport in the early morning and prepared for the passage of its lines by Joint Forces Command East, which was to have the honor of entering Kuwait City. Out in front, a platoon from the 2d Force Reconnaissance Company, under 1st Lt. Brian G. Knowles, slipped forward and was first to reach the U.S. Embassy. The recon marines found it apparently untouched, with the Stars and Stripes still flying. A composite Arab battalion passed through Task Force Shepherd's positions east of Kuwait International Airport to enter Kuwait City, where they joined early on the twenty-seventh with an Egyptian-Syrian force which had similarly come through the 2d Marine Division. Boomer and his command group rode into the Kuwaiti capital that afternoon and joined Knowles at the U.S. Embassy. Keys's 2d Marine Division stayed in the vicinity of Al Jahra, forming the bottom half of the box that caught the retreating Iraqi main force in what was publicized as the "Highway of Death."

Very early the next morning, 28 February, the Marines learned by short-wave radio that President Bush had called a halt to hostilities effective 0800. It had been a nightmarish battlefield, fought against a pall of black smoke from the burning Kuwaiti oil fields, but it was all over in 100 hours. In the four-day battle almost the entire Iraqi army in the Kuwaiti theater of operations (originally thought to be 500,000 strong, but more realistically about 300,000) had been encircled in a modern-day Cannae. Early estimates were four thousand tanks destroyed and forty-two divisions either destroyed or rendered ineffective. The Viet Nam War anathema of "body count" was avoided and no immediate estimate of enemy personnel casualties was forthcoming. Coalition killed-in-action were reported as 88 Americans; 41 Egyptians, Saudis, and Kuwaitis; 16 British; and 2 French. There were still some loose ends. Marine air continued to fly combat missions against Iraqi units in northern Kuwait. The 5th Marines began what was to be a five-day clearing operation southward toward Al Wafrah.

When the shooting stopped on 28 February, Marine strength in the theater, afloat and ashore, was 92,990, making Desert Storm by far the largest Marine Corps operation in history. A total of twenty-four Marine infantry battalions and forty Marine flying squadrons—nineteen fixed-wing and twenty-one helicopter—had been committed. The aircraft total at the beginning of the air campaign was 194 fixed wing and 178 helicopters. Losses were six fixed-wing and three helicopters. On G-day the Marines had 216 artillery pieces, 301 light armored vehicles (LAVs), 194 M60 tanks, and 74 M1A1s. The 532 AAVs *nee* LVTs did their job well of carrying troops and supplies across the sea of sand. The cost in human terms was twenty-four killed, ninety-two wounded.

As their share of the war, the Marines could claim 1,040 enemy tanks, 608 armored personnel carriers, and 432 artillery pieces destroyed or captured and, by best count, 22,308 prisoners. It was also learned that the amphibious demonstrations successfully held in place some six divisions or fifty thousand Iraqis along the Kuwait coast, prepared for the amphibious assault that never came. In a final seaborne flourish, after the "cease fire," 13th MEU went ashore on Faylaka Island to accept the surrender of an Iraqi marine brigade.

General Schwarzkopf in his fulsome "mother of all briefings" given on 27 February forgot to mention I MEF's defensive role in Desert Shield, but of Desert Storm he said, "I can't say enough about the two Marine divisions. If I used words like brilliant, it would really be an underdescription of an absolutely superb job that they did in breaching the so-called impenetrable barrier."

The retrograde movement home, informally named "Desert Calm," went smoothly. General Boomer and most of his staff left on 16 April. Marine Forces Southwest Asia under Maj. Gen. Norman E. Ehlert was established as the senior command. Heavy demands were put on the combat service troops; all departing equipment had to be environmentally purged. The last units of the 2d Division departed on 10 June.

# 21

## 1991-1998
## A Maritime Nation—Always Was, Always Will Be

### Provide Comfort

Within the borders of Iraq, Saddam Hussein, with much of his force battered but still intact, reacted savagely against dissident elements. The Kurds in the north, with their chronic dream of reestablishing "Kurdistan" from pieces, not only of Iraq, but also of Turkey, Iran, and Russia, had openly rebelled. Iraqi countermeasures were brutal; virtually all the Kurds were driven out of their homes. Torn by internal partisan dissension, hundreds of thousands of Kurds were milling about, hiding in the hills, seeking dubious sanctuary in Turkey, or gathering in squalid camps on Iran's borders. Five hundred or more a day were dying from disease, exposure, and malnutrition.

Coalition efforts, with the lukewarm support of the Turks and Arabs, to protect the Kurds from vengeful Iraqis without unduly encouraging their rebellion became a sequel to Desert Storm named Provide Comfort. The green-bereted U.S. 10th Special Forces Group came into northern Iraq at the end of March 1991 to give emergency help. A Combined Task Force (CTF Provide Comfort) was formed, soon to be commanded by Lt. Gen. John M. Shalikashvili, USA, with Marine Brig. Gen. Anthony C. Zinni as his deputy.

The 24th Marine Expeditionary Unit under Col. James L. Jones (nephew of Lt. Gen. William K. Jones) was on a landing exercise in Sardinia and halfway through its six-month deployment when orders arrived on 9 April to proceed to Iskenderun, Turkey. The 24th MEU(SOC) was to establish a forward support base at Silopi, Turkey. By 15 April 24th MEU had moved 450 miles inland and set up its base. During the next two weeks the MEU's helicopter squadron, HMM-264, under Lt. Col. Joseph A. Byrtus Jr., with twenty-three helicopters, would deliver a million pounds of relief supplies.

General Shalikashvili met with an Iraqi delegation on the Turkey-Iraqi border on 19 April; marines provided the security. The Iraqis were told that coalition forces would enter Iraq the next day; the mission would be humanitarian. The entering wedge was Lt. Col. Tony L. Corwin's BLT 2/8. The Iraqis were warned to stay out of the way. By nightfall on 20 April, BLT 2/8 had begun to build a resettlement camp east of Zakhu. Two days later the 45th Commando, Royal Marines, and the 1st Air Combat Group, Royal Netherlands Marines, began to arrive. Except for a party of fifty police, the Iraqis were ordered out of Zakhu, normally a city of 150,000, but now a ghost town. On 26 April coalition forces "liberated" Zakhu.

The 4th Brigade, 3d U.S. Infantry Division, reported for duty that day. On the twenty-seventh, the U.S. 3d Battalion, 325th Airborne Combat Team (3/325 ACT), arrived and was put under Colonel Jones's tactical control. The U.S. Engineer Brigade and Naval Mobile Construction Battalion 133 came in and soon had built a city of a thousand tents. A local hospital was put back into operation. Detachments of Italian and Spanish troops arrived. An airfield at Sirensk was repaired so that it could handle C-130s. Detachments arrived from the 3d Force Service Support Group on Okinawa. The 8th Regiment Parachutiste d'Infanterie de Marine came in and, in addition to other forms of humanitarian support, in best French style set up a bakery that could turn out twenty thousand loaves of bread a day. A growing trickle of refugees began coming down from the hills to return to Zakhu.

Farther east lay Dahuk, once a city of 350,000 but now deserted except for Iraqi soldiers. In mid-May 24th MEU, reinforced with Army paratroopers of the 3d Battalion, 325th Airborne Combat Team, received orders to clear Dahuk. The Iraqis wisely agreed to withdraw and on 20 May the coalition forces began to enter the city. On 25 May, the census of refugees in the three camps east of Zakhu stood at 55,200. By early June the camps had begun to empty out.

The coalition forces began to depart. Terms dictated to the Iraqis were that they were not to fly north of the 36th Parallel (thirty-five miles south of Dakhu), and Iraqi soldiers and secret police could not enter the security zone. The Iraqis would be watched from the sky for compliance. The last of the allied combatants to leave were the marines of BLT 2/8 and the paratroopers of 3/325 ACT. They withdrew on 15 July 1991.

## Angels from the Sea

Maj. Gen. Henry C. Stackpole III, CG of the Okinawa-based III Marine Expeditionary Force, was at a Seventh Fleet planning conference in Subic Bay in the Philippines when an alert reached him on 9 May 1991 that he might be tasked with a disaster-relief mission to Bangladesh. In Okinawa, III MEF formed a planning cell to follow the situation.

A cyclone had come roaring up the funnel of the Bay of Bengal the night of 29 April, with winds reaching 145 miles per hour and tidal waves cresting at twenty feet, crashing into the coastal areas of Bangladesh, the nation, once East Pakistan, that lies squeezed between India and Burma. In a country subject to natural and man-made catastrophes, this was one of the worst. Estimates were that from two and a half to five million persons were affected and more than one hundred thousand were probably dead.

Bangladesh's government, under Prime Minister Khaleda Zia, widow of dictator-president General Zia, was new and fragile and in the midst of swift political change. The prime minister's late husband, Maj. Gen. Ziaur ("Zia") Rahman, had fought for Bangladesh's independence in 1971, had come into power in a military coup in 1975, and was assassinated in a short-lived but violent rebellion in 1981. A succession of military regimes followed. Elections in September 1990 returned Bangladesh to a parliamentary system with his widow, a democratic moderate, as prime minister.

Food, shelter, clothing, medical supplies and services, and, most importantly, safe and potable water, were all desperately needed. Relief supplies were pouring in, eventually to be received from thirty-two countries and numerous humanitarian agencies such as CARE, Red Crescent, and others, but Bangladesh did not have the infrastructure to deliver the goods to the saturated, wind-whipped coastal flatlands and offshore islands. Shallow draft shipping was sunk or scattered. Bridges were down. The roads were washed away or under water. The railroad from Dhaka, the capital, to Chittatong, the major port, with a teeming population of over two million, was cut in a dozen or more places. At Chittagong, the airport was under three feet of water and most of the dock and wharf facilities had been carried away. Leasing by the government of commercial helicopters was out of the question because of exorbitant costs.

U.S. Ambassador William B. Milam, through his defense attaché, asked Adm. Charles R. Larson, Commander in Chief, Pacific, for Navy and Marine

Corps air and surface assistance in cutting the Gordian knot of paralyzed transportation. The wheels of the decision-making machinery in the State Department and Defense Department whirred and meshed and necessary approval from President Bush came on 11 May.

The operation was code-named Productive Effort. Admiral Larson designated General Stackpole as Joint Task Force commander. Amphibious Group Three, under Rear Adm. Stephen S. Clarey, with 5th Marine Expeditionary Brigade embarked, en route from the Persian Gulf to the West Coast, was diverted to the Bay of Bengal. Brig. Gen. Peter Rowe and his 5th Marine Expeditionary Brigade, retrograding from Desert Storm, had been on alert for a possible evacuation of American citizens from Ethiopia. The embedded 11th Marine Expeditionary Unit had sailed away, leaving the brigade at two-thirds strength and short of combat service support capability.

Gen. Hank Stackpole, determined that the American "footprint" ashore be as light as possible, and his advance party arrived in Dhaka early on the morning of 12 May. A platoon of U.S. Army engineers was already in country. A Special Forces detachment from Okinawa came in with two Air Force HC-130s; these would move bulk supplies from Dhaka to Chittagong. Next day, while Stackpole reconnoitered the distressed area, further augmentation for his JTF headquarters arrived from Hawaii, including Col. Edward G. Hoffman, USAF, who would be his deputy and Air Force component commander. Five U.S. Army UH-60 Blackhawk helicopters came in, as did a SeaBee detachment and an environmental medicine unit. The amphibious cargo ship *St. Louis* was ordered to proceed from the Philippines to Okinawa to pick up twenty-eight water purification units (ROWPUs or "Row-pews") and additional Marine support personnel organized into a 250-man Contingency Marine Air-Ground Task Force 2-91 (CMAGTF 2-91) under Lt. Col. Larry A. Johnson.

On 15 May, the eight ships of PhibGru 3 arrived off Bangladesh and Stackpole established a forward JTF headquarters at Chittagong. First relief supplies began reaching remote areas. Millions of water purification tablets would be distributed. Next day PhibGru 3 and 5th MEB began full-scale relief operations employing twenty-eight helicopters, four air-cushion landing craft (LCACs) and three utility landing craft (LCUs). Amphibious assault vehicles (AAVs, the erstwhile LVTPs), which in a less rough sea state could have functioned as amphibian trucks, could not prevail against a current running from eight to twelve knots. A fifty-man Japanese rescue team with two French-built "Dauphin" light helicopters supplemented the effort. Chinese and Indian relief forces stood aloof of the JTF command but cooperated informally.

Gen. Colin Powell, chairman of the JCS, moved by a news story that reported the Bangladeshi as calling the relief forces "angels from the sea," changed the name of the operation on 17 May. Operation Productive Effort became Operation Sea Angel.

In addition to the twenty-eight ROWPUs coming by way of the *St. Louis,* eight units arrived by air on the eighteenth with the advance echelon of CMAGTF 2-91 and went on to the offshore islands shortly thereafter. On the nineteenth, 5th MEB began deploying its six Medical Civic Action Program ("MedCAP") teams.

BLT 3/5 established a second control center at Cox's Bazar, a resort town and relic of British colonial times, some distance from Chittagong, in anticipation of the arrival on the twentieth of the *Fort Grange,* a British auxiliary replenishment ship, with four medium-lift "Sea King" helicopters and a complement of twenty Royal marines.

Mrs. Marilyn Quayle, wife of the U.S. vice president, arrived on 21 May for a three-day visit. She and her small official party toured the devastated area but overnighted on Admiral Clarey's flagship, the amphibious assault ship *Tarawa,* where proper facilities were available.

On 29 May, with the arrival of the *St. Louis* and its embarked MAGTF 2-91 and twenty-eight ROWPUs, PhibGru 3 and 5th MEB departed. Another tropical cyclone came through on 2 June and caused a pause in relief operations but no further loss of life. *St. Louis* pulled out on 7 June for Thailand. Roads, ferry boats, and local transportation were back to pre-cyclone conditions. On 15 June Operation Sea Angel officially ended.

General Powell awarded the Joint Task Force with a Joint Service Unit Award, citing the 194 missions flown by the Air Force moving 2,430 tons of supplies, the 805 sorties by the Army's "Blackhawks" distributing 886 tons, and the 969 Navy and Marine air sorties which delivered 700 tons. Navy and Marine surface lift delivered 1,487 tons. The ROWPU crews produced 266,000 gallons of potable water. The six Navy medical contact teams treated fifteen thousand patients and supervised delivery of thirty-eight tons of medical supplies. Estimates were that supplies had reached over a million persons. It was likely that one hundred thousand were saved from starvation or serious illness if not death. More than 7,500 American military had taken part.

## MUNDY BECOMES COMMANDANT

Al Gray stepped down as commandant on 1 July 1991, succeeded by Carl E. Mundy Jr., a very different personality, affable where Gray had been confrontational. Mundy, a graduate of Auburn University, was the son of a small-town shopkeeper and had grown up in a variety of southern towns, mostly in North Carolina. He had seen less combat than most twentieth-century commandants of the Marine Corps, but had served well in Viet Nam. With a smooth, consensual leadership style, he would be an anodyne for the bruises and abrasions left by the raw energies of Al Gray.

When Mundy took over, the Marine Corps had just come out of Desert Storm and was at an operational peak. Mundy recognized and applauded this, but he also wanted to re-instill some traditional values. He captured his ideas on leadership in a field manual, FMFM 1-0, *Leading Marines,* a follow-up to General Gray's FMFM 1, *War-Fighting.* The flavor of the Mundy manual is reflected in some of the chapter and section headings: "Our Ethos," "Every Marine a Rifleman," "Soldiers of the Sea," "Setting the Example," "Unit Esprit," "Being Ready," "Fighting Power and Winning."

Mundy, a masterful communicator orally, both on the platform and informally, and in writing, made more and better use of the professional journals, such as *Marine Corps Gazette* and the U.S. Naval Institute *Proceedings,* than probably any of his predecessors.

He consolidated the Marine Corps' gains in "componency" status, making it a full operational partner in the unified commands, and skillfully led the Navy into recognition of a shared partnership in the redrafting of naval strategy. The collapse of the Soviet empire vitiated the long-held naval strategy of a deep-sea fleet targeted to match and win against the Soviet navy. As the Navy strategists sought new roles in a changed world, Mundy helped them find them. In his mind, the Navy had to be reshaped into a power-projection, littoral-oriented organization. A landmark in this reshaping was the "white paper" *From the Sea: A New Direction for the Naval Services,* which emerged in 1992 over the signatures of the secretary of the Navy, then Sean O'Keefe; the chief of naval operations, Adm. Frank Kelso; and the commandant of the Marine Corps, Gen. Carl Mundy.

With force levels plummeting for all services, Mundy successfully stopped the plunge of Marine Corps' "end" strength at 174,000 active-service marines and justified holding at that level. His closest associates in reshaping naval strategy, determining roles and missions, and defending force structure were Lt. Gen. Charles C. Krulak and Maj. Gen. Thomas L. Wilkerson. Several times during his tenure Mundy came to the brink of dismissal by speaking out against the Clinton administration's liberal initiatives on homosexuals serving in the armed forces and combat assignments for women. His capacity for getting along and mending fences and his genuine endorsement of "jointness" saved him.

## SOMALIA

Largest of the operational deployments during the Mundy years would be to Somalia in 1992 and again in 1995. On 28 January 1991, three weeks after the digression from Desert Shield that evacuated more than 260 persons from the U.S. embassy in Mogadishu, President Siad Barre fled Somalia, ending twenty-two years of dictatorship. The fragile government disintegrated and the country sank into chaos and famine. Television increasingly treated American audiences to nightly scenes of starving women and children, street fighting, and a United Nations seemingly wringing its hands in futile despair. After a year of this, on 18 August 1992, President Bush announced to a demanding American public that the United States would take part in an international famine relief effort.

Joint Task Force "Provide Relief" was formed under Brig. Gen. Frank Libutti to fly relief supplies from Mombasa in Kenya to Somalia airfields. An emergency air-lift of nearly a quarter-million tons of food began, but conditions within the country made distribution by international relief organizations almost impossible. Ghastly pictures continued to fill American television. On 14 September, the first U.N. troops, the 7th Battalion, Pakistani Frontier Forces, arrived in Mogadishu by U.S. airlift while the 11th Marine Expeditionary Unit hovered protectively offshore.

In November serious fighting broke out between the two major rival political groups, one led by Mohammed Ali Mahdi and the other by Mohammed Farah Aideed. Somalia fell into Central Command's operational area of responsibility. Marine Gen. Joseph P. Hoar had succeeded General Schwarzkopf as CinC. Late in the month the I Marine Expeditionary Force, commanded now by Lt. Gen. Robert Johnston, who as a major general had been Schwarzkopf's chief of staff in the Persian Gulf, was alerted for deployment. What followed paralleled closely the scenario for Marine forces in

Desert Shield. The intervening force would be the I MEF, home headquarters in Camp Pendleton, and would include elements of the 1st Marine Division, the 3d Marine Aircraft Wing, and the 1st Force Service Support Group, much the same organizations as had formed the first half of the deployments in Desert Shield.

General Johnston would command Joint Task Force, Somalia. Maj. Gen. Charles E. Wilhelm, Commanding General, 1st Marine Division, once deployed, would be commander of Marine Forces, Somalia. The largest other U.S. element of the JTF would be the Army's 10th Mountain Division. The JTF, charged with creating a safe environment within which international relief organizations could operate, would have a huge area of responsibility that included the coastal cities of Mogadishu and Kismayo and the inland towns of Baidoa, Bale Dogle, and Bardera.

On 4 December 1992 President Bush announced that U.S. troops were being sent into Somalia to alleviate the famine and prepare the way for a United Nations peace-keeping force. He promised the American people that the deployment would be brief, a promise that would have to be made good by his successor, President Clinton.

Johnston received the go signal for what was now called Operation Restore Hope on 7 December. Mahdi and Aideed were assured that the Americans would be neutral. The Somalis agreed to pull their forces back from the port and airfield facilities at Mogadishu. Immediately at hand in the Indian Ocean was the 15th Marine Expeditionary Unit (Special Operations Capable) under Col. Gregory S. Newbold, with battalion landing team 2/9 and composite medium helicopter squadron HMM-164.

Although there was no expectation of resistance, the landing at Mogadishu was staged as a full-fledged amphibious assault. Shortly before midnight on 8 December, Navy SEALS and reconnaissance marines went ashore across a narrow Green Beach in what was meant to be covert beach reconnaissance and were met by blinding television lights and a mob of reporters. The landing, largely by armored amphibious vehicles or "AAVs," the renamed LVTS, rumbled on and at 0720 the airport was declared secure.

Daylight on the ninth showed the marines a scene of utter desolation. A company of French Foreign Legion parachutists arrived at the airport at about noon. That afternoon the abandoned U.S. embassy compound was reoccupied without incident. The flag that was run up was one that had once flown over the headquarters building in Beirut. Scattered sniper fire harassed the marines as they moved out into the city.

General Johnston and his command group came in at noon on 10 December and established their headquarters in the embassy compound. (Next day Johnston's Combined Joint Task Force Somalia was redesignated the United Task Force Somalia [UNITAF].)

Company F cleared the prison that overlooked the port area. That stopped the sniper fire. Earlier that day two Marine Super Cobras took out a "Mad Max" "technical" mounting a 106-mm recoilless rifle that had the temerity to fire at them. "Technicals" were war wagons improvised out of trucks, great at terrorizing an unarmed populace but not much against real troops. A more formidable M-113 armored personnel carrier got the same treatment from the Cobras. At dusk the French legionnaires and U.S. marines shot up a vehicle that ran through a road block at high speed. Two passengers were killed, seven wounded. The wounded were treated on the *Tripoli*. They had not been gunmen.

Movement of follow-on Marine forces to the objective area posed an enormous logistic challenge, comparable to the first months of Desert Shield. Again there would have to be a marriage of air-lifted troops with maritime prepositioned shipping. Mogadishu did not offer the good port facilities that had facilitated unloading in Saudi Arabia. MPS ship *Lummus* came gingerly into the harbor.

General Wilhelm and his command element arrived next day. Wilhelm's immediate mission, in addition to consolidating the Marine hold on Mogadishu, was to send forces to Baidoa, Kismayo, and Bardera, all three at a considerable distance from Mogadishu. Some twenty-six hundred foreign nationals were reported to be in Baidoa, eight hundred in Bardera. Two days after arrival, elements of 15th MEU heli-hopped to Bale Dogle to secure the airfield, an intermediate stop to Baidoa, 130 miles away and called by the media, "The City of Death." Colonel Newbold's Task Force Hope, mostly U.S. marines but including the French Foreign Legion company, left Mogadishu at noon on 15 December. The convoy, moving under heavy air cover by way of Bale Dogle and unopposed except for a trickle of random sniper fire, reached Baidoa at dawn on the sixteenth to a warm welcome by the populace. A token delivery of a truckload of food was made. Holding to the policy of a neutral stance toward the warring factions, Newbold nevertheless ruled that no technicals, no visible display of weapons, and no heavy weapons would be allowed. The marines fanned out in a pattern of checkpoints and patrols. Weapons were confiscated. Raids were mounted against compounds reported to be bases for the urban guerrillas. Newbold nurtured the creation of a Somali police force. Civic action programs blossomed. Marine veterans of Haiti, Santo Domingo, Nicaragua, even Viet Nam, would have found it all quite familiar.

Gradually the marines learned the mysteries of Somali's all-important clan system that functioned in the absence of a formal government. As a reverse to that coin, to help the Somalis understand the marines, Somali-American interpreters provided by the U.S. Army presented the Marine Corps to the populace as a "clan"!

On its way to Somalia was the 7th Marines. The regiment's commander, Col. Emil R. ("Buck") Bedard, arrived in country on 16 December. Brig. Gen. Marvin T. ("Ted") Hopgood Jr. had the 1st Force Service Support Group. Marine Force Somalia's air element was Marine Aircraft Group 16, under Col. John P. Kline Jr., with its squadrons—VMGR-352 with its C-130s, light attack helicopter squadron HMLA-369, and heavy helicopter squadron HMH-363, plus a detachment from HMH-466—echeloned into the country during December.

Meanwhile, serious fighting was reported going on at the southern port city of Kismayo. The Belgian 1st Parachute Battalion, under Lt. Col. Marc Jacqmin, was tasked to secure the airfield, but Jacqmin had only one company in Somalia. Rather than delay until the rest of his battalion arrived, he asked for Marine reinforcements and received the services of Company G, 2d Battalion, 9th Marines, from Newbold's command. What was to have been an airborne operation with two days of planning turned into an amphibious operation. Jacqmin, bolstered by a Marine staff, became the landing force commander. The Marines gave the Belgians a blitz course in amphibious operations. D-day was set for 20 December. Jacqmin's task force embarked in amphibious ships *Juneau* and *Rushmore* with reconnaissance elements going forward in the French destroyer *Dupleix*. Force recon units went ashore in rubber boats. Company G landed at dawn from AAVs on Purple Beach. The Belgians came in by helicopter. The airfield and port, both in shabby state, were quickly secured. Only a few shots were received and it was not clear against whom they were directed. On 21 December Army Forces, Somalia, assumed responsibility for Kismayo and on the following day the marines went back on board the *Juneau*.

On 23 December General Wilhelm moved his command post forward to Baidoa and the 1st Battalion, 7th Marines, moved on to Bardera, observing Christmas with the delivery of food, a Christmas also marked by the arrival of General Mundy in Somalia. A week later, President Bush visited American forces in Mogadishu on 31 December, including a stop on the *Tripoli*, and went forward next day, 1 January 1993, to Baidoa. That would be the high point of the intervention.

By then all of the 7th Regimental Combat Team, consisting of a mixture of battalions—1st Battalion, 7th Marines; 3d Battalion, 9th Marines; 3d Battalion, 11th Marines; 1st Light Armored Infantry Battalion; and 3d Assault Amphibian Battalion—was in place. The pull-back of Marine forces began. Colonel Bedard took over the ground combat element from Newbold on 2 January. The 15th MEU(SOC) moved to Mogadishu to reembark in its amphibious ships. General Wilhelm returned to Mogadishu on 4 January. On that day Marine Forces, Somalia, reached a peak strength of 11,419 marines, sailors, soldiers, and civilians and had operational control of 1,551 coalition troops. (At one time or another, Marine Forces, Somalia, had under its operational control troops from France, Belgium, Kuwait, Saudi Arabia, Morocco, Egypt, Botswana, Zimbabwe, Turkey, Nigeria, Pakistan, and United Arab Emirate!)

On 5 January a regimental-size Task Force Mogadishu was formed under Col. Jack W. Klimp. Minor skirmishing broke out in the city. One marine was wounded. Marine search teams swept through Mogadishu looking for arms caches. On 12 January, Somalis ambushed a patrol from 3d Battalion, 11th Marines, killing one marine. Next day a Navy corpsman was wounded. Army Forces, Somalia, drawn from the 10th Mountain Division, took over from the Marines in the Mogadishu port area the fifteenth of January.

On 16 January the Army assumed responsibility for Baidoa and in turn turned it over to the 1st Battalion, Royal Australian Regiment. The 7th Marines withdrew to Mogadishu. During the month of January the 134-mile road from Baidoa to Bardera was repaired and reopened to truck traffic.

The first echelon of 3d Battalion, 9th Marines, left by air for Camp Pendleton on 19 January. Task Force Mogadishu stood down on 22 January. But there would still be Marine casualties: one wounded on 19 January and another dead of wounds on 26 January.

The 15th MEU finished the wash-down of its vehicles, a ritual of reembarkation, and sailed for the Persian Gulf on 5 February. Two weeks later

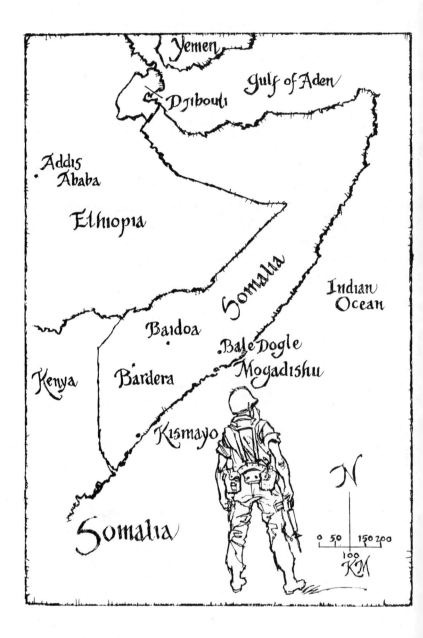

General Wilhelm received orders to reconfigure his remaining command into a "heavy brigade." Hopgood's 1st Force Service Group slimmed down to a brigade service support group.

Ramadan, Islam's most holy holiday, began on 23 February and also signaled a fresh outbreak of demonstrations. Veterans of Viet Nam were reminded of Tet. Three marines were wounded in street fighting on 24 February and three more the next day.

On 13 March, Marine forces started pulling out of Bardera. General Wilhelm began whittling his "heavy brigade" down to a "light brigade." Two more marines were wounded in the days that followed. Wilhelm turned command over to Colonel Klimp on 23 March and left for Camp Pendleton. By then Marine Forces, Somalia, numbers were down to 7,400, half of them U.S. and half coalition. Ramadan ended the next day. In turn, on 9 April, Jack Klimp relinquished command to Buck Bedard before departing. Marine air flew its last flight on 27 April and on 4 May the last marines left Somalia. General Johnston and his command element left the same day. In place behind them was a United Nations security force.

The Marines had left but troubles in Somalia continued. Most serious was a street battle that on the third and fourth of October cost the U.S. Army eighteen dead and seventy-five wounded. Days later President Clinton ordered fifteen thousand American troops into Somalia—including briefly the 13th and 22d MEUs—but with the promise that all would be out by the end of March 1994. The deadline was met. On 25 March 1994, the 24th MEU secured the withdrawal of the last U.S. combat troops. One platoon from the Marine Security Battalion in Norfolk was left behind to provide security for the U.S. diplomatic mission. Another year would pass. Then, on 3 March 1995, in a final repetition, the 13th MEU covered the evacuation of the last United Nations troops.

## Haiti Once Again

Special Purpose Marine Air-Ground Task Force Caribbean (SPMAGTF Carib) stood up at Camp Lejeune on 20 July 1994, tailored for the worsening crisis in Haiti. Similar, but smaller, special purpose MAGTFs had been dispatched to the Caribbean intermittently since the fall of 1993 as the U.S. moved to oust Lt. Gen. Raoul Cedras, commander of the Haitian army, from his position as de facto dictator.

Throughout the year the United States had been putting pressure on Haiti's military junta to resign and allow the return of Jean-Bertrand Aristide, a lapsed Roman Catholic priest, who had been elected president in December 1990 and deposed by military coup in September 1991. Thousands of Haitians were leaving Haiti in anything that could float and were being rescued at sea or were washing up, dead or half-alive, on the shores of Florida. The refugee camp at Guantánamo Bay was filled to overflowing with Haitian (and Cuban) "boat people." On 31 July, the U.N. Security Council authorized the United States to invade Haiti. In turn, Haiti's puppet president, Emile Jonassaint, declared a "state of siege."

Operation "Uphold/Support Democracy" was launched with everything but trumpets on the White House balcony. The Marine Corps' portion, SPMAGTF Carib, numbering some nineteen hundred sailors and marines, sailed from Morehead City on 13 August and embarked in the *Wasp* and *Nashville* with Rear Adm. William H. Wright IV as Commander Amphibious Task Force (CATF). On arrival in the Caribbean the task force relieved 24th MEU(SOC), which was on station.

Command of SPMAGTF Carib rested with Col. Thomas S. Jones, Viet Nam veteran and a battalion commander during the Persian Gulf War and now commanding officer of the 2d Marines. The MAGTF's battalion landing team was formed around the 2d Battalion, 2d Marines, which had just returned from a six-month deployment to the Western Pacific. Its commander, Lt. Col. George S. ("Steve") Hartley, had commanded Contingency MAGTF 3-90, which had been involved in the Liberian evacuation. The aviation element, commanded by Lt. Col. Anthony J. Zell, was the reinforced Marine Medium Helicopter Squadron 264, its organic CH-46E Sea Knights augmented with detachments of AH-1W Super Cobras, UH-1N Hueys, and CH-53E Super Stallions. A two-hundred-person Combat Service Support Detachment 29 under Maj. Lance R. McBride was formed for the occasion. Joining the marines would be a U.S. Army psychological operations detachment, liaison teams from the Army's XVIII Airborne Corps, and some three dozen Creole-speaking interpreters.

The Marine landing in the north was to be a sideshow to the main event: a landing at Port-au-Prince by the Army's XVIII Airborne Corps under Lt. Gen. Hugh Shelton, USA. The Marines' amphibious objective area (AOA) took in most of Haiti's Military Department of the North and its seaward approaches. Jones and Wright named the AOA for Capt. Herman H. Hanneken, slayer of Caco chieftain Charlemagne and recipient of the Medal of Honor. During the Marine Corps' 1915–34 occupation of Haiti, the forerunner of Jones's present 2d Marines had served in Cap-Haitien. With roads poor or nonexistent, Cap-Haitien was still geographically remote from Port-au-Prince. Both landings were scheduled for 19 September. Haitian National Army dispositions were known; no one expected them to fight. After sunset on 18 September, Navy SEALs went in to mark the Cap-Haitien beaches.

With naval forces standing offshore in full sight, a peace commission, headed by former president Jimmy Carter and including now-retired former JCS chairman Colin Powell and Senator Sam Nunn, had arrived in Port-au-Prince to meet with Cedras and Jonassaint, the elderly president. Carter laid out terms for stopping the invasion. Nunn expressed the support of Congress for President Clinton's position. Powell played on Cedras's honor as a military man. Cedras reluctantly agreed not to oppose the landing of American troops and promised to leave the country by October if he could take with him most of his possessions. Carter and Jonassaint signed the accord at H-Hour minus six.

While the Marines in the north waited impatiently on the sidelines, U.S. Army and Special Operations Command forces went peaceably ashore in Port-au-Prince on the morning of 19 September. The landing of the Marines, who were to hold northern Haiti until relieved by U.S. Army forces, would come one day later, on 20 September 1994. Jones hastily reoriented his command for this less violent mission and issued a gentler set of rules of engagement.

For the landing, Jones had task-organized BLT 2/2 into three elements. Task Force Irish, under Hartley, with the mission of securing the port, landed across a small beach just north of the town, touching down at 0700. Concurrently, HMM 264 heli-lifted Task Force Hawg, under Maj. Herman C. Broadstone, to the Cap-Haitien airport, some two miles south of the port. The third element, one rifle company, was held in reserve on the *Wasp*. By late morning Jones committed it to augment Task Force Irish. Jones and his headquarters, along with CSSG 29, went ashore that evening. The local populace seemed overjoyed at the Marines' arrival.

Jones located the commander of the Military Department of the North, a lieutenant colonel named Josephat, and informed him of the strength of his force and his objectives ashore. Having encountered no overt resistance, Jones's immediate mission now became that of helping the townspeople meet basic civic needs: medical supplies, emergency food stocks, fuel for the electric power plant, and restoration of some semblance of sanitation in the town. Task Force Hawg had the airport operational by 22 September. On that same day, in response to tales of continued abuse by remnants of the old regime, Hartley began a sweep of the town, his Company D broken down into squad-size foot patrols, backed by motorized patrols mounted in light armored vehicles and "Hum-vees." One violent episode occurred: Early on the evening of 24 September, a squad from Company E, accompanied by its platoon leader, 1st Lt. Virgil A. Palumbo, approached a group of Haitian military policemen outside their headquarters. One agitated Haitian drew down on the squad with his submachine gun. Palumbo shot the military policeman with his M16A2. The other Haitians scrambled for their weapons. In the melee that followed, one sailor, accompanying the squad as an interpreter, was slightly wounded. Ten Haitian solders were killed and one seriously wounded (he was taken to the *Wasp* for treatment).

Cedras arrived the next morning, irate over the shooting and demanding a court-martial for the marines. His local commander, Josephat, could not be found and Cedras placed a captain in command of the northern department. The fire fight, however, in Jones's words, "hastened the collapse of an organization already doomed to extinction." Haitian soldiers and policemen were shedding their uniforms and abandoning their posts. An ebullient populace (some of them "cockroaches" who had made a quick change of sides) began ransacking the police posts and army barracks. Company G was deployed to help restore order and to pick up the weapons that were surfacing, most of them eagerly offered.

On 25 September the first elements of the 2d Brigade, 10th Mountain Division, began to arrive. By the afternoon of the twenty-sixth an Army battalion was in place on the airport. Another battalion landed from Air Force C-130s by way of Homestead Air Force Base in Florida. Major Army equipment was coming in by sea lift. From then until 1 October Jones conducted a series of helicopter raids to outlying towns, including Grand Rivière du Nord (where Captain Hanneken had served) to pick up caches of arms. The electric plant patched up, power was turned on for a few hours after sunset beginning on 29 September. A third Army battalion arrived from Port-au-Prince on 1 October and SPMAGTF Carib began backloading on the *Wasp* and *Nashville*. Amphibious Objective Area Hanneken was turned over to the 2d Brigade, 10th Mountain Division, the next day. After a week-long environmental wash-down at

Roosevelt Roads, Puerto Rico, SPMAGTF Carib took station once again off the north coast of Haiti, where it remained in floating reserve until President Aristide was triumphantly re-ensconced in Port-au-Prince on 15 October.

## A Vision for the Twenty-First Century

Downsizing incident to President Clinton's "bottom-up" review of the armed services took the Corps from an active strength of 193,735 in 1991 to 174,000 in 1995. Throughout the last half of the 1990s the Corps strained to maintain an unprecedented level of peacetime readiness. Even with reduced numbers the Corps could argue persuasively that it was the armed force that could best project American power onto hostile shores.

Charles C. ("Chuck") Krulak, who had done so well in the Persian Gulf, replaced Mundy as commandant on 1 July 1995. After leaving the Gulf as a brigadier general, Krulak had shot up to lieutenant general, serving as the commanding general, of the Marine Corps Combat Development Command at Quantico and then as Commanding General, Marine Forces Pacific, the latter the same command held by his father a generation earlier.

The new commandant, short in stature, exuberant, and peripatetic, brought to his first day in office a detailed vision for the Marine Corps of the approaching twenty-first century, which he saw as bringing with it a wide variety of new threats: "The game is changing—and so are the rules." Predicting a "century of chaos," he foresaw ethnic conflict, religious strife, and clan warfare showing no respect for national boundaries. Weapons of mass destruction, specifically chemical and biological agents, would no longer be confined to the superpowers.

To fight in this environment of chaos the primacy of the individual Marine, in Krulak's mind, would take on even greater importance. He granted that technology held many promises, but he was even more convinced that he needed "not to man the equipment, but equip the man." Part of this "equipping the man" was to seek to inculcate in each Marine, male and female, the core values of honor, courage, and commitment. He divided the making of a Marine into a four-step "transformation" process: recruiting, recruit training, cohesion, and sustainment.

"The most exciting part occurs at recruit training," said Krulak. "It is a defining moment in the lives of the young people who experience it—it is the rite of passage to becoming a U.S. Marine."

He was referring to an event he named the "Crucible." Under conditions of sleep and food deprivation, the recruits underwent a fifty-four-hour ordeal in which they hiked over forty miles, used live ammunition, overcame numerous physical obstacles, and took part in exercises designed to teach trust, teamwork, and the strength to be found in the Marine Corps' core values.

"It is the toughest thing ever to hit boot camp," said Krulak. "When they are finished they receive the coveted Eagle, Globe and Anchor from their D.I. and for the first time are called *Marine*.

"But fighting the asymmetric threat on the chaotic battlefields of the twenty-first century will take more than the best Marines we can possibly make," Krulak added. "New concepts, new organizations and new equipment will be needed to keep ahead of our opponents."

In October 1995, General Krulak "stood up" a Warfighting Laboratory at Quantico and assigned it the task of investigating new and potential technologies and evaluating their impact on how the Corps was to organize, equip, educate, and train marines to fight in the future. Krulak, and many others, were convinced that the majority of combat in the next century would take place in cities.

The lab began a systematic process of experimentation it called Sea Dragon. Advance Warfighting Experiments (AWE) were designed to find out how the Marine Corps should be structured, how marines could best fight in the cities and in the distributed, noncontiguous battlefield, and how to best integrate Marine Corps capabilities with those of the other services.

From these experiments the Marine Corps found new capabilities for its infantry battalions such as the Dragon Drone Unmanned Aerial Vehicle (UAV). Uses of nonlethal weapons were explored and some of these weapons were deployed with Marine expeditionary units.

Firm in his conviction that "the United States is a maritime nation. Always was, always will be," Krulak moved forward into the operational art from the "From the Sea" strategy espoused by Mundy and his Navy counterparts. Krulak called for a blending of high technology and maneuver warfare with the advantages of sea-basing, which he called Operational Maneuver From The Sea (OMFTS).

New high-speed ship-to-shore vehicles were coming into the inventory— namely the tilt-wing V-22 Osprey, which would replace the medium helicopter; the LCAC, an air-cushioned landing craft; and the AAAV, an advanced assault amphibian vehicle replacing the amphibian tractor, which had not changed much since World War II. New doctrine, predicted on these vehicles, held the promise of moving Marines in the attack directly from ship to objective.

"No longer will Marines wade the bloody surf," said Krulak. "No longer will slow and vulnerable lodgments be formed at the water's edge, ripe for the asymmetric attack. Sea basing gives the force an unprecedented level of protection by keeping all but those forces necessary for a given action safely out at sea."

When President Clinton took the oath of office for his second term on 20 January 1997, the Marine Band performed for its fiftieth presidential inaugural. Sousa's "Semper Fidelis" and "The Thunderer" were played along the parade route, and, as the band passed the reviewing stand, it sounded off with "Four Ruffles and Flourishes" followed by "The Marines' Hymn."

Elsewhere in the world, the 26th Marine Expeditionary Unit was landing across Spanish beaches in an exercise that involved climbing sheer rock-face cliffs and live fire in Sierra de Retin. Embarked marines, whiling away time at sea, were more apt to be found playing computer-based war games than the acey-deucey, cribbage, poker, and crap shoots of previous generations of marines. During a typical period during that spring of 1997, the 26th MEU, standing by in the Adriatic for less humanitarian missions, delivered relief supplies to a camp of Bosnian refugees in Slovenia and spent a day sprucing up a school for underprivileged children in Trieste; the 11th MEU in the Persian Gulf exercised urban warfare techniques with Kuwaiti National Guardsmen and Special Forces; and close by in Kuwait a battery from the 11th Marines fired its M198 155-mm howitzers in a salute to St. Barbara, the patron saint of artillerymen. In the kind of rescue mission that was becoming increasingly frequent, marines from the 22d Marine Expeditionary Unit, launching from the Ionian Sea in March 1997, evacuated by helicopter 830 persons, 530 of them Americans, from troubled Albania. Covering Cobra gunships took sporadic fire and silenced its sources with return fire.

In Bosnia, the long, protracted stand-off dragged on. The Marine Corps role was relatively minor but continuing. Marine squadrons flew reconnaissance and support missions from bases in Italy and from the decks of carriers. Marine expeditionary units stood in the Adriatic Sea offering a spectrum of special operations capabilities. Most dramatic use occurred after the shoot-down on 2 June 1995 of the F-16C fighter being flown by Air Force Capt. Scott O'Grady near the Bosnian town of Banja Luka. Six days later, on

8 June, a Marine Corps TRAP ("Tactical Recovery of Aircraft and Personnel") team from the Special Operations Capable 24th Marine Expeditionary Unit, embarked in the helicopter carrier *Kearsarge,* made a daring and successful rescue that thrilled the nation.

As the new century approached, it did not appear that the United States Marine Corps would be underemployed.

## *Appendix* 1

# THE MARINES' HYMN

*From the halls of Montezuma*
    *To the shores of Tripoli,*
*We fight our country's battles*
    *In the air, on land, and sea.*
*First to fight for right and freedom,*
    *And to keep our honor clean,*
*We are proud to claim the title*
    *Of United States Marines.*

*Our flag's unfurl'd to every breeze*
    *From dawn to setting sun;*
*We have fought in every clime and place*
    *Where we could take a gun.*
*In the snow of far-off northern lands*
    *And in sunny tropic scenes,*
*You will find us always on the job—*
    *The United States Marines.*

*Here's health to you and to our Corps*
    *Which we are proud to serve;*
*In many a strife we've fought for life*
    *And never lost our nerve.*
*If the Army and the Navy*
    *Ever gaze on Heaven's scenes,*
*They will find the streets are guarded*
    *By United States Marines.*

# *Appendix 2*

## BATTLE HONORS

The official Battle Color of the Marine Corps is held by the Marine Barracks, Washington, D.C.; a duplicate is maintained in the office of the commandant of the Marine Corps; and a third Battle Color is displayed at the Marine Corps Museum, Washington Navy Yard. These colors bear streamers representing U.S. and foreign unit awards as well as those periods of service, expeditions, and campaigns in which the U.S. Marine Corps has participated since the American Revolution. The list that follows shows the honors, as of the close of 1997, commemorated by attachments to the Battle Color either by an unadorned streamer, as in the case of early wars, or by added stars or other devices for more recent actions. In general, a bronze star or oak leaf cluster indicates an additional award and a silver star five such awards. The Navy Unit Commendation, the Meritorious Unit Commendation, and the Joint Meritorious Unit Award streamers are now displayed as unadorned streamers. Combined, these three awards have been made to Marine units on more than five hundred occasions.

1. Presidential Unit Citation (Navy) (1941–1968)
   Streamer with six silver and two bronze stars (thirty-three awards).
2. Presidential Unit Citation (Army) (1942–1969)
   Streamer with one silver oak leaf cluster (six awards).
3. Joint Meritorious Unit Award (1986–1997)
4. Navy Unit Commendation (1942–1997)
5. Valorous Unit Award (Army) (1968)
6. Meritorious Unit Commendation (Navy–Marine Corps) (1965–1997)
7. Meritorious Unit Commendation (Army) (1967–1968)
8. Revolutionary War (1775–1783)
9. Quasi-War with France (1798–1801)
10. Barbary Wars (1801–1815)
11. War of 1812 (1812–1815)
12. African Slave Trade Patrol (1820–1861)

13. Indian Wars (1811–1812; 1836–1842)
14. Operations Against West Indian Pirates (1822–1830s)
15. Mexican War (1846–1848)
16. Civil War (1861–1865)
17. Marine Corps Expeditionary (1874–1994)
    Streamer with twelve silver stars, two bronze stars, and one silver "W" (sixty-three expeditions). The silver "W" is for the defense of Wake Island, 7–22 December 1941.
18. Spanish Campaign (1898)
19. Philippine Campaign (1899–1904)
20. China Relief Expedition (1900–1901)
21. Cuban Pacification (1906–1909)
22. Nicaraguan Campaign (1912)
23. Mexican Service (1914)
24. Haitian Campaign (1915; 1919–1920)
    Streamer with one bronze star.
25. Dominican Campaign (1916)
    Marine occupation 1916–1924 is commemorated on the Marine Corps Expeditionary Streamer.
26. World War I Victory (1917–1918; 1918–1920)
    Streamer with one silver and one bronze star for combat operations in France, 1918; one Maltese cross for service in France, 1918–1919; West Indies clasp, 1917–1918; and Siberia clasp, 1918–1920.
27. Army of Occupation of Germany (1918–1923)
28. Second Nicaraguan Campaign (1926–1933)
29. Yangtze Service (1926–1927; 1930–1932)
30. China Service (1937–1939; 1945–1957)
    Streamer with one bronze star.
31. American Defense Service (1939–1941)
    With bronze star indicating service outside continental limits of the United States.
32. American Campaign (1941–1946)
33. European–African–Middle Eastern Campaign (1941–1945)
    Streamer with one silver star and four bronze stars (nine actions).
34. Asiatic–Pacific Campaign (1941–1946)
    Streamer with eight silver stars and two bronze stars (forty-two operations and actions).

35. World War II Victory (1941–1946)
36. Navy Occupation Service (1945–1955)
    With Europe and Asia clasps.
37. National Defense Service (1950–1954; 1961–1974; 1990–1995)
38. Korean Service (1950–1954)
    Streamer with two silver stars (ten campaigns).
39. Armed Forces Expeditionary (1958–1992)
    Streamer with four silver and four bronze stars (twenty-four expeditions).
40. Vietnam Service (1962–1973)
    Streamer with three silver and two bronze stars (seventeen campaigns).
41. Southwest Asia Service (1990–1995)
    Streamer with three bronze stars (three campaigns).
42. French Croix de Guerre (1918)
    Streamer with two palms and one gilt star (three awards).
43. Philippine Defense (1941–1942)
    With bronze star indicating participation in engagements against the enemy.
44. Philippine Liberation (1944–1945)
    Streamer with two bronze stars representing three campaigns.
45. Philippine Independence (1941–1945)
46. Philippine Presidential Unit Citation (1941–1942; 1944–1945; 1970; 1972)
    Four citations.
47. Korean Presidential Unit Citation (1950–1954)
    Six citations.
48. Republic of Vietnam Meritorious Unit Citation of the Gallantry Cross with Palm (1965–1969)
49. Republic of Vietnam Meritorious Unit Citation, Civil Actions (1969–1970)

# Appendix 3

## Lejeune's 1921 Birthday Message

John A. Lejeune, the thirteenth commandant, who understood such things so well, in 1921 had published the following order which is still read to all marines on the Marine Corps Birthday:

1. On November 10, 1775, a Corps of Marines was created by a resolution of Continental Congress. Since that date many thousand men have borne the name "Marine." In memory of them it is fitting that we who are Marines should commemorate the birthday of our corps by calling to mind the glories of its long and illustrious history.

2. The record of our corps is one which will bear comparison with that of the most famous military organizations in the world's history. During 90 of the 146 years of its existence the Marine Corps has been in action against the Nation's foes. From the Battle of Trenton to the Argonne, Marines have won foremost honors in war, and in the long eras of tranquillity at home, generation after generation of Marines have grown gray in war in both hemispheres and in every corner of the seven seas, that our country and its citizens might enjoy peace and security.

3. In every battle and skirmish since the birth of our corps, Marines have acquitted themselves with the greatest distinction, winning new honors on each occasion until the term "Marine" has come to signify all that is highest in military efficiency and soldierly virtue.

4. This high name of distinction and soldierly repute we who are Marines today have received from those who preceded us in the corps. With it we have also received from them the eternal spirit which has animated our corps from generation to generation and has been the distinguishing mark of the Marines in every age. So long as that spirit continues to flourish, Marines will be found equal to every emergency in the future as they have been in the past, and the men of our Nation will regard us as worthy successors to the long line of illustrious men who have served as "Soldiers of the Sea" since the founding of the corps.

# Acknowledgments and Bibliography

This book began in 1969 when Leo Cooper of London asked Henry I. Shaw Jr., then the civilian chief historian of the Marine Corps, to suggest someone who might write a short history of the U. S. Marines for Mr. Cooper's Famous Regiments series. I was then between Viet Nam tours. Neither Mr. Cooper nor I realized the problems we would encounter in trying to fit two hundred years of history of a United States Marine Corps that had grown larger than the British army into a format originally designed for individual British regiments. *The United States Marines,* as published by Leo Cooper, Ltd., in 1974, was about twice the length of the other books in the Famous Regiments series. Still, it was shorter than I would have liked it to have been, as was the similar edition serialized in the *Marine Corps Gazette* in monthly installments from November 1973 until December 1974.

The Viking edition, published in 1976, was half again as long as the earlier versions. I was able to finish out the first two hundred years of Marine Corps history, making it *The United States Marines: The First Two Hundred Years, 1775–1975.* The Marine Corps Association kept this edition, which was also a Military History Book Club selection, in print, with two successive paperback printings.

The years since 1975 have been busy ones for the Marine Corps. There has also been a great deal of new scholarship in Marine Corps history. In this new edition the first eighteen chapters have been considerably revised; the last three chapters are completely new.

The Leo Cooper edition had photographs. The Viking edition had maps. This edition happily has both. The maps for the earlier edition were drawn by then-Maj. Charles H. Waterhouse, USMCR, from my sketches. This edition continues that practice with new maps by Waterhouse, now colonel, USMCR (Ret.).

The expansion of the Corps in successive wars, particularly during and since World War II, necessarily has forced me into a shift of perspective to successively higher echelons. Thus the narration as it moves to Marine Corps expeditionary brigade and Marine expeditionary force levels gets further and further away from the individual marine who makes up the heart and soul of the Corps. Realizing that some readers will want to make up for this deficiency, I have been concerned less in the bibliography that follows with documentation than with pointing the reader in the direction of amplifying sources. Most of the books I cite should be either found in any well-stocked public, scholastic, or post library, or, available, with the assistance of a friendly librarian, through interlibrary loan.

First off, I must mention the work of my close colleagues for the last quarter century: Col. Allan R. Millett and J. Robert Moskin, authors respectively of *Semper Fidelis* (1980, 1991) and *The Marine Corps Story* (1982, 1987, 1992). A more recent addition to the general histories of the Marine Corps is Col. Joseph H. Alexander's *A Fellowship of Valor* (1997).

Any historian of the U. S. Marines owes a great debt to the early work of Brig. Gen. Richard S. Collum, including his *The History of the United States Marine Corps* (1903), and Maj. Edwin N. McClellan, whose mimeographed history, compiled during the 1920s and 1930s, regrettably exists only in a very few copies. The standard history until World War II was Col. Clyde H. Metcalf's *A History of the United States Marine Corps* (1939), somewhat dry and patchwork, but nevertheless full of substance. Its place was later taken largely by Col. Robert D. Heinl's superb *Soldiers of the Sea* (1962).

The evolution of U. S. amphibious doctrine and practice is brilliantly developed in *The U. S. Marines and Amphibious War* (1951) by Jeter A. Isely and Phillip A. Crowl. The two best aviation histories are Robert Sherrod's *History of Marine Corps Aviation in World War II* (1952) and the more recent *U.S. Marine Corps Aviation, 1912–Present* (1983) by Cdr. Peter B. Mersky. For information on uniforms, Col. Robert H. Rankin's *Uniforms of the Marines* (1970) is outdated but still very useful.

The official *Marines in the Revolution* (1975) by Charles R. ("Rich") Smith continues to be the definitive history of the Continental marines. Heavily illustrated, including a great many works by Charles Waterhouse, *Marines in the Revolution* may be supplemented but is not likely to be supplanted. There is some Marine content in the standard naval histories of the Revolution, most notably Gardner W. Allen's *A Naval History of the American Revolution* (1913) and Charles O. Paullin's *The Navy of the American Revolution* (1906). Similarly, Allen should be consulted for *Our Navy and the Barbary Corsairs* (1905) and *Our Naval War with France* (1909).

The role of Marines in the War of 1812 can be found chiefly in more general naval histories and biographies such as Theodore Roosevelt's *The Naval War of 1812* (1882). For these early years, James Fenimore Cooper's *Naval History of the United States* (1839) has some interesting material. *Surf Boats and Horse Marines* (1969) by K. Jack Bauer deals with the Marines in the Mexican War. The exploits of Archibald Gillespie in the conquest of California are well covered in *Messenger of Destiny* (1955) by Werner H. Marti.

David M. Sullivan's exhaustive five-volume work on marines in the Civil War is just beginning to appear in print but not in time to be reflected in my history. For the Confederate marine corps there is no substitute for Ralph W. Donnelly's *Rebel Leathernecks* (1989). Dr. Jack Shulimson has covered the post–Civil War "Gilded Age" very well in his *The Marine Corps' Search for a Mission* (1993).

Pieces of the history of the Corps in the first half of the twentieth century, including the First World War, can be found in many places. The official *The United States Marine Corps in the World War* by Major McClellan has recently been reprinted by Battery Press. Ivan Musicant collects the Caribbean adventures in *The Banana Wars* (1990). Some of the most colorful reading can be found in the biographies, sometimes overblown, of various Marine leaders, including Lowell Thomas's *Old Gimlet Eye: The Adventures of Smedley D. Butler* (1933), Col. Frederic W. Wise's *A Marine Tells It to You* (1929), Maj. Gen. Comdt. John A. Lejeune's *The Reminiscences of a Marine* (1930), Gen. Holland M. Smith's *Coral and Brass* (1949), Burke Davis's *Marine! The Life of Lt. Gen. Lewis B. ("Chesty") Puller* (1962), and Gen. Alexander A. Vandegrift's *Once a Marine* (1964). Recent impressive additions to these biographies are Colonel Millett's *In Many a Strife: General Gerald C. Thomas and the U.S. Marine Corps, 1917–1956* (1993) and Lt. Col. Jon T. Hoffman's *Once a Legend: "Red Mike" Edson of the Marine Raiders* (1994). No one, of course, captures the color and flavor of the Marine Corps in this period better than Col. John W. Thomason Jr., in *Fix Bayonets!* (1926) and . . . *and a Few Marines* (1945).

First place on the list for Marines in World War II must go to the five-volume official *History of Marine Corps Operations in World War II.* This series has been brought back into print by Battery Press of Nashville, Tennessee. Good one-volume histories include Frank O. Hough's *The Island War* (1947), Fletcher Pratt's *The Marines' War* (1948), and Robert Leckie's *Strong Men Armed* (1962). Richard B. Frank's more recent *Guadalcanal* (1990) established—incontrovertibly, in my mind—that the Guadalcanal campaign, in all its land, sea, and air aspects, was the turning point of the Pacific War.

The Korean War also has its five-volume official history, *U. S. Marine Operations in Korea.* Robert J. Speights of Austin, Texas, has reprinted this series. No history of the Inchon landing surpasses Colonel Heinl's *Victory at High Tide* (1968). There are several good histories of the Chosin (the Koreans now prefer that it be called "Changjin") Reservoir campaign, including Eric Hammel's *Chosin: Heroic Ordeal of the Korean War* (1981).

For the Viet Nam conflict I originally drew largely from my own *Marine Corps Operations in Vietnam, 1965– 1972* (1968, 1969, 1973), which was published sequentially by the *Naval Review.* In revising chapters 17 and 18, which cover Viet Nam and its aftermath, I used for the most part the detailed and straightforward eight-volume official U.S. *Marines in Vietnam.* There are now many books on Marines in Viet Nam, some hand-wringing and anguished. One of the best is Lt. Col. Ronald H. Spector's *After Tet: The Bloodiest Year in Vietnam.* Others are Robert Pisor's *The End of the Line: The Siege of Khe Sanh* (1982), Col. Gerald H. Turley's *The Easter Offensive: Vietnam* (1972), and Frank Snepp's *Decent Interval: An Insider's Account of Saigon's Indecent End* (1977).

In chapter 19, the first of the entirely new chapters, my account of the Corps' brief adventure in Grenada draws from the official *U.S. Marines in Grenada, 1983* (1987) by Lieutenant Colonel Spector. The tragedy of the Beirut bombing is to be found in painful detail in the official *U.S. Marines in Lebanon, 1982–1984* (1987) by Ben Frank, who went there to see for himself. There is also Eric Hammel's *The Root: The Marines in Beirut* (1985). More on the intervention in Panama can be found in the official *Just Cause: Marine Operations in Panama, 1988–1990* (1996) by Lt. Col. Nicholas E. Reynolds. I owe Dr. V. Keith Fleming and Ms. Kerry Strong of the Marine Corps University my appreciation for the materials they provided on General Gray's reforms at Quantico. In the same chapter my thanks are due David B. Crist for his help with the Tanker War.

Chapter 20, which covers the Persian Gulf, began with my two articles, "Getting Marines to the Gulf" and "Getting the Job Done," in the May 1991 U.S. Naval Institute *Proceedings.* These articles were written contemporaneously with ongoing events from news reports, message traffic, and the daily briefings given the commandant of the Marine Corps, briefings at which I was a fly on the wall. Revision has been essentially a reconciliation of these early accounts with the monographs written by Marine Corps Reserve historians dispatched to the Gulf. In this same *U.S. Marines in the Persian Gulf, 1990–1991* series is a very useful *Anthology and Bibliography* (1992). My chapter has benefited enormously from a review by a good number of the principal Marine commanders deployed to the Gulf. For widely different perspectives on leadership, including Marine leadership, in Desert Shield/Desert Storm, see Gen. H. Norman Schwarzkopf, *The Autobiography: It Doesn't Take a Hero* (1982), HRH Gen. Khaled bin Sultan's *Desert Warrior* (1995), Sir Peter de la Billiere's *Storm Command: A Personal Account of the Gulf War* (1992), *The Generals' War* by Michael R. Gordon and Lt. Gen. Bernard E. Trainor, and Molly Moore's *A Woman at War: Storming Kuwait with the U.S. Marines* (1995).

Chapter 21 deals with events too recent to offer much in the way of book-length works. There are exceptions. The humanitarian operation to protect the Kurds in northern Iraq from the vengeance of Saddam Hussein has its comprehensive official monograph, *With Marines in Operation Provide Comfort* (1995) by Lt. Col. Ronald J. Brown, one of the Marine Corps Reserve's peripatetic combat historians. *Angels from the Sea: Relief Operations in Bangladesh, 1991* (1995) by Charles R. Smith, is also published. Two monographs on Operation Restore Hope, the large-scale humanitarian intervention in Somalia, are works-in-progress at the Marine Corps Historical Center, one at the Joint Task Force level and the other at the Marine Forces Somalia level.

The Marine Corps History and Museums Division has been particularly prolific through the years in producing historical reference pamphlets, monographs, unit histories, bibliographies, and chronologies. Official histories, widely varying in detail and completeness, have been published on all the regiments in the present Marine Corps force structure. A good number (but far from complete list) of squadron histories have also been published.

Among the official pamphlet histories I found most useful in my earlier editions were *United States Marines at Harpers Ferry* (1966), *The United States Marines in the War with Spain* (1967), *The United States Marines in Nicaragua* (1968), *The United States Marine Corps in the World War* (1968 reprint of 1920 edition), *The United States Marines on Iwo Jima* (1967), *The United States Marines in North China, 1945–1949* (1968), *The United States Marines in the Occupation of Japan* (1969), *Marine Corps Women's Reserve in World War II* (1968), and *The Eagle, Globe and Anchor, 1868–1968* (1971).

More recent official Marine Corps histories, which have been of considerable help in this revised edition, include *Marine Corps Aviation: The Early*

*Years, 1912–1940* (1977); *Marines and Helicopters, 1946–1962* (1976); *Marines and Helicopters, 1962–1973* (1978); *Quantico: Crossroads of the Marine Corps* (1978); *U.S. Marines at Twentynine Palms, California* (1989), *Blacks in the Marine Corps* (1975); *U.S. Marine Corps Operations in the Dominican Republic, April–June 1965* (1992); and *Marines in the Mexican War* (1991).

Readers looking for more on Marines in the Second World War should find of special interest the twenty-five pamphlets of the highly popular Marines in World War II Commemorative Series (1991–1998), ranging in time and titles from *Outpost in the North Atlantic: Marines in the Defense of Iceland* to *The Final Campaign: Marines in the Victory on Okinawa*. A similar series is planned for the fiftieth anniversary of the Korean War.

(A complete listing of official Marine Corps histories and how to obtain those in print can be obtained by writing the Director, History and Museums Division; Headquarters, U. S. Marine Corps; Washington, D.C. 20374-5040.)

I have made large use of a personality file of official biographies and clippings I have collected over the years. Such a file has to be accumulated, but for more accessible biographies there are Karl Schuon's *U. S. Marine Corps Biographical Dictionary* (1963), Jane Blakeney's *Heroes, U. S. Marine Corps, 1861–1955* (1957), and Charles L. Lewis's *Famous American Marines* (1950). There are also good biographical sketches of the commandants in the successive editions of the Marine Corps Association's *Home of the Commandants* (1956, 1966, 1974, and 1995).

The three periodicals I found most useful, not surprisingly, are the U. S. Naval Institute *Proceedings,* the *Marine Corps Gazette,* and *Fortitudine,* the last being the quarterly bulletin of the Marine Corps historical program.

I have gone to the Navy's peerless series *Dictionary of American Naval Fighting Ships* an untold number of times for a detail on a ship and almost as frequently to the various editions of *Jane's Fighting Ships* and related volumes such as *Jane's Infantry Weapons, Jane's All the World's Aircraft,* and *Brassey's Artillery of the World.*

Many persons have contributed in many ways to the putting together of the several editions. To cite only a few is to slight the many; however, I would be completely ungrateful if I failed to again thank the late Col. John H. Magruder III, USMCR, for his trenchant and useful criticism of early drafts, and Ben Frank, who succeeded Bud Shaw as chief historian, for his thoughtful comments and, with his wife Marylou, for the indexing of both this and earlier editions.

Many others in the Marine Corps Historical Center have been generous in their help. Miss Evelyn Englander, the Center's librarian, over the past quarter century has found for me literally thousands of books and journals, some very obscure. Those stalwarts in the Reference Section—most particularly Danny J. Crawford, Robert V. Aquilina, Ann A. Ferrante, Lena Kaljot, and, in years past, Gabrielle M. Neufeld Santelli, Ralph W. Donnelly, and Regina Strother—have made their indispensable files available and answered hundreds of questions for me. The Archives Section, gateway to official records and personal papers, has helped me immeasurably, as has the Oral History Unit. My chapters 19 and 21 benefited particularly from the extensive oral history interviews I conducted with three commandants: Gens. Louis H. Wilson Jr., Robert H. Barrow, and Carl E. Mundy Jr. The Museums Branch, at a distance in Quantico, has answered many "hardware" and aviation questions.

In addition to all the names mentioned above, there are hundreds of others, including the many authors and editors of the official histories who did not get individual mention, who need to be thanked. Some of the names—not all of whom are still with us, and this list is far from complete—are:

Lt. Col. Curtis G. ("Gene") Arnold, Capt. Robin L. Austin, Cathy Bakkela, Lt. Col. Merrill L. ("Skip") Bartlett, Lt. Col. Leonard A. Blaisol, Joyce E. Bonnett, Gen. Walter E. Boomer, Lt. Gen. James A. Brabham, Capt. Charles A. Braley, Lt. Col. Ronald J. Brown, Amy J. Cantin-Cohen, Col. Nicholas A. Canzona, Maj. Gen. Matthew P. Caulfield, Capt. John C. Chapin, Graham A. Cosmas, Robert J. Cressman, W. R. ("Billy Bob") Crim, Lt. Col. Charles H. Cureton, Capt. David A. Dawson, Col. James A. Donovan, Col. John A. Driscoll, Dr. William S. Dudley, Maj. George R. ("Ross") Dunham, Maj. John T. Dyer, Lt. Col. Harry W. Edwards, Lt. Col. William R. Fails, Lt. Col. Charles A. Fleming, George W. Garand, Brig. Gen. Gordon D. Gayle, Frederick J. Graboske, Col. John E. Greenwood, Col. Herbert M. Hart, Richard Harwood, Lt. Col. Norman W. Hicks, W. Stephen Hill, Joyce C. Hudson, Maj. Gen. Harry W. Jenkins Jr., Maj. Charles M. Johnson, Lt. Col. Edward C. Johnson, Col. Douglas T. Kane, Catherine A. Kerns, Lt. Gen. William M. Keys, Lt. Col. Hubard D. Kuokka, Brig. Gen. James F. Lawrence, Col. James Leon, Richard A. Long, Col. Verle E. Ludwig, Lt. Gen. Anthony Lukeman, George C. MacGillivray, M. Sgt. Philip R. Mackinnon, Lt. Col. Pat Meid, Maj. Charles D. Melson, Herbert C. Merillat, Col. John G. Miller, J. Michael Miller, Col. Michael F. Monigan, Lynn Montross, Maj. Gen. Royal N. Moore Jr., Patricia E. Morgan, Col. Dennis P. Mroczkowski, Maj. Gen. James M. Myatt, Bernard C. Nalty, Col. Brooke

Nihart, Cyril J. O'Brien, Col. Charles J. Quilter II, Col. David A. Quinlan, Maj. John T. Quinn II, Lt. Col. Eugene W. Rawlins, M.Gy. Sgt. Michael Ressler, Maj. Jack K. Ringler, Lt. Col. Lane Rogers, Maj. William J. Sambito, Capt. Clarke V. Simmons, USAR, Kenneth L. Smith-Christmas, Col. Mary V. Stremlow, Truman R. Strobridge, Robert E. Struder, Maj. Gary L. Telfer, Edwin T. Turnbladh, Frank Uhlig Jr., Capt. Robert H. Whitlow, Sgt. Maj. Ethyl M. Wilcox, Col. Roger Willock, Charles A. ("Tim") Wood, Maj. James M. Yingling, and Maj. Steven M. Zimmeck.

I must thank the staff of the Naval Institute Press for their care and professionalism in putting together this book, and, especially, Ronald D. Chambers, Scott E. Belliveau, J. Randall Baldini, Mary C. Hack, Tom Harnish, Susan Artigiani, Susan Todd Brook, Maureen Peterson, and Karen White for their patience with my sometimes quixotic ideas on book production and marketing. I would also like to thank my copy editor, Patricia J. Kennedy, and my proofreader, Judith Loeven.

And finally, unless otherwise specifically attributed, all opinions expressed are my own and are certainly not to be construed as official.

# Index

# ABOUT THE AUTHOR

Born at Billingsport, New Jersey, in 1921, almost on an American Revolution battle site, Brig. Gen. Edwin H. Simmons claims to have done his first bit of historical research and writing at the age of fourteen. Since then he has been published widely, mostly on military subjects. He came into the United States Marine Corps in 1942 and is now the Director Emeritus of Marine Corps History and Museums. He has a B.A. in journalism from Lehigh University (1942) and an M.A. in journalism from Ohio State (1955) and is a graduate of the National War College (1967). His numerous personal decorations from World War II, Korea, and Viet Nam include the Distinguished Service Medal, the Silver Star, three Legions of Merit, two Bronze Stars, a Meritorious Service Medal, and an unavoidable Purple Heart.

**The Naval Institute Press** is the book-publishing arm of the U.S. Naval Institute, a private, nonprofit, membership society for sea service professionals and others who share an interest in naval and maritime affairs. Established in 1873 at the U.S. Naval Academy in Annapolis, Maryland, where its offices remain today, the Naval Institute has members worldwide.

Members of the Naval Institute support the education programs of the society and receive the influential monthly magazine *Proceedings* and discounts on fine nautical prints and on ship and aircraft photos. They also have access to the transcripts of the Institute's Oral History Program and get discounted admission to any of the Institute-sponsored seminars offered around the country.

The Naval Institute also publishes *Naval History* magazine. This colorful bimonthly is filled with entertaining and thought-provoking articles, first-person reminiscences, and dramatic art and photography. Members receive a discount on *Naval History* subscriptions.

The Naval Institute's book-publishing program, begun in 1898 with basic guides to naval practices, has broadened its scope in recent years to include books of more general interest. Now the Naval Institute Press publishes about 100 titles each year, ranging from how-to books on boating and navigation to battle histories, biographies, ship and aircraft guides, and novels. Institute members receive discounts of 20 to 50 percent on the Press's nearly 600 books in print.

Full-time students are eligible for special half-price membership rates. Life memberships are also available.

For a free catalog describing Naval Institute Press books currently available, and for further information about subscribing to *Naval History* magazine or about joining the U.S. Naval Institute, please write to:

Membership Department
**U.S. Naval Institute**
118 Maryland Avenue
Annapolis, MD 21402-5035
Telephone: (800) 233-8764
Fax: (410) 269-7940
Web address: www.usni.org